Case Studies in Contemporary Criticism

HENRY JAMES

The Turn of the Screw

Case Studies in Contemporary Criticism

SERIES EDITOR: Ross C Murfin

Case Studies in Contemporary Criticism

SERIES EDITOR: Ross C Murfin, *University of Miami*

HENRY JAMES
The Turn of the Screw

Complete, Authoritative Text with Biographical and Historical Contexts, Critical History, and Essays from Five Contemporary Critical Perspectives

EDITED BY

Peter G. Beidler
Lehigh University

Bedford Books *of* **St. Martin's Press**
BOSTON • NEW YORK

Dedicated to James R. Frakes

For Bedford Books
President and Publisher: Charles H. Christensen
Associate Publisher/General Manager: Joan E. Feinberg
Managing Editor: Elizabeth M. Schaaf
Developmental Editor: Stephen A. Scipione
Production Editor: Jonathan R. Burns
Copyeditor: Cynthia Benn
Text Design: Sandra Rigney, The Book Department
Cover Design: Richard Emery Design, Inc.
Cover Photograph: Detail from a photograph of Crossways Farm by
Andrew Butler. Copyright © 1992.

Library of Congress Catalog Card Number: 94–65160
Copyright © 1995 by Bedford Books *of* St. Martin's Press

Manufactured in the United States of America.

9   8   7   6   5
f   e   d   c   b   a

For information, write: St. Martin's Press, Inc.
175 Fifth Avenue, New York, NY 10010
Editorial Offices: Bedford Books *of* St. Martin's Press
29 Winchester Street, Boston, MA 02116

ISBN: 0–312–08083–2 (paperback)
ISBN: 0–312–12260–8 (hardcover)

Published and distributed outside North America by:

MACMILLAN PRESS LTD.
Houndmills, Basingstoke, Hampshire RG21 2XS and London
Companies and representatives throughout the world.

ISBN: 0–333–63437–3

Acknowledgments

"'The grasp with which I recovered him': A Child Is Killed in *The Turn of the Screw*"
by Shoshana Felman was originally published as "The Death of a Child," part VII of her
"Turning the Screw of Interpretation," *Yale French Studies* 55/56 (1977) and her
Writing and Madness, Cornell University Press, 1985. Reprinted, with certain small
changes, with the permission of Yale French Studies.

*Acknowledgments and copyrights are continued at the back of the book on page 313,
which constitutes an extension of the copyright page.*

About the Series

Volumes in the *Case Studies in Contemporary Criticism* series provide college students with an entrée into the current critical and theoretical ferment in literary studies. Each volume reprints the complete text of a classic literary work and presents critical essays that approach the work from different theoretical perspectives, together with the editors' introductions to both the literary work and the critics' theoretical perspectives.

The volume editor of each *Case Study* has selected and prepared an authoritative text of the classic work, written an introduction to the work's biographical and historical contexts, and surveyed the critical responses to the work since its initial publication. Thus situated biographically, historically, and critically, the work is examined in five critical essays, each representing a theoretical perspective of importance to contemporary literary studies. These essays, prepared especially for undergraduates, show theory in praxis; whether written by established scholars or exceptional young critics, they demonstrate how current theoretical approaches can generate compelling readings of great literature.

As series editor, I have prepared introductions, with bibliographies, to the theoretical perspectives represented in the five critical essays. Each introduction presents the principal concepts of a particular theory in their historical context and discusses the major figures and key works that have influenced their formulation. It is my hope that these introductions will reveal to students that good criticism is informed by a set of coherent assumptions, and will encourage them to recognize and examine their own assumptions about literature. Finally, I have compiled a glossary of key terms that recur in these volumes and in the discourse of contemporary theory and criticism. We hope that the *Case Studies in Contemporary Criticism* series will reaffirm the richness of its literary works, even as it introduces invigorating new ways to mine their apparently inexhaustible wealth.

Ross C Murfin
Series Editor
University of Miami

About This Volume

In Part One of this volume we present the complete text of the New York Edition of Henry James's *The Turn of the Screw* as well as relevant portions of James's Preface to that edition.

Henry James wrote *The Turn of the Screw* at the invitation of Robert J. Collier. Collier had just taken over his father's magazine and hoped to improve the quality and sales of *Collier's Weekly* by publishing a serial story by Henry James, who was already making a name for himself as a writer of serious fiction. James worked on the story in the fall of 1897, finishing it by the end of November. The serialized version was published in twelve weekly installments in *Collier's Weekly* between January 27 and April 16, 1898.

From the start Henry James intended to bring out *The Turn of the Screw* in book form, and by October of 1898 it was printed in two separate editions, one by Heinemann in England and one by Macmillan in the United States. The title of both the English and the American books was *The Two Magics;* it contained both *The Turn of the Screw* and another long story by James, *Covering End.*

Ten years later Henry James supervised the publication of what has come to be called "The New York Edition" of his works. In volume 12 of that edition, published by Charles Scribner's Sons in 1908, were included four of James's tales: two long stories or "novellas," *The Aspern Papers* and *The Turn of the Screw*, and two short stories, "The Liar" and "The Two Faces."

James made some changes for the New York Edition, but that edition is not really much different from the earlier versions. To give just one example, at the end of chapter V the governess discovers that the man she has just described to Mrs. Grose was named Peter Quint and that Peter Quint had died. In an intense moment the puzzled and frightened governess asks, "'Died?'" James wrote for the *Collier's* version that Mrs. Grose planted her feet firmly to "articulate" her answer to the governess, "'Yes. Yes. Quint is dead.'" In the book version that year he changed "articulate" to "utter" and changed Mrs. Grose's speech to "'Yes. Mr. Quint is dead.'" In the New York Edition ten years later he changed "utter" to "express" and changed Mrs. Grose's speech to "'Yes. Mr. Quint's dead.'" The changes, in other words, were minor.

At no point did James undertake a rewriting of any portion of the story, and the few changes he did make were generally "tinkering" ones of punctuation, diction, and style. The only change that might be considered major was that after the *Collier's* edition James raised the age of Flora from six to eight years. Even though most of James's changes were minor, we follow here his final wishes — even his now obsolete practice of separating the elements of two-syllable contractions of negatives: "did n't," "has n't," and "is n't" rather than the more modern "didn't," "hasn't," and "isn't."

The most important feature of the New York Edition is Henry James's Preface to it — his retrospective account of the writing of and the reaction to *The Turn of the Screw*. We are pleased to reprint the relevant parts of the Preface after the text of the story itself.

The Turn of the Screw has been to critics a chameleon text, taking on a coloring that lets it blend in with almost any way of reading it. Depending on who is reading it, the story can be a gothic tale in the tradition of Poe, a romantic tale in the tradition of Hawthorne, or a realistic tale in the tradition of Howells. It can be a Freudian tale of sexual repression, an allegory of good and evil, a detective story about murder and deception, a call for better treatment of children, or a reflection of hidden truths about its author. It can demonstrate its author's knowledge of scientific research on ghosts, his rejection of that knowledge, his accord with the social structures of his time or his rejection of those structures. It can be read as a Marxist statement, a feminist statement, or a homosexual statement. So frequent and wide-ranging have been the published interpretations of *The Turn of the Screw* that critics do not even feel the need to identify either the author or the name of the story in the title of essays. A title like "The Mysteries at Bly" is sufficient to reveal to most readers that that article is about Henry James's *The Turn of the Screw.*

In Part Two of this volume we present, in addition to my essay summarizing the critical history of *The Turn of the Screw* and Ross Murfin's five introductory essays laying the groundwork for contemporary critical approaches, five essays by eminent critics. Wayne Booth has written an essay discussing "reader-response" criticism and how something he calls "ethical criticism" works in this story. Shoshana Felman shows us how a deconstructionist critic, one influenced by the French psychoanalyst Jacques Lacan, approaches the all-important death scene in the final chapter of the story. Stanley Renner has written a paper with a psychoanalytic slant, defending and extending the work of earlier Freudian critics. Priscilla Walton gives us a feminist reading of the story and particularly of the governess whose narration is all we *really* know about the strange happenings at Bly. Finally, Bruce Robbins shows us what a Marxist reading makes of the story by having us pay attention to the various classes represented at Bly. All five of these fine scholars resist being labeled as a certain type of critic, but they have agreed for purposes of this volume to emphasize a certain aspect of their complex critical demeanor. Taken together, these five essays, following my summary of the critical history of *The Turn of the Screw,* show the richness and the complexity of one of the most widely discussed pieces of fiction ever written.

Readers of these essays will not finish them knowing *the* answer to the questions about the governess, the ghosts, or the children, or *the* answer to the question of what this story means, but they will know something about the amazing variety of questions that a literary work can inspire and about the amazing variety of answers that readers can find to those questions. Armed with such knowledge, they will be better prepared to frame their own questions and answers and to understand what literary criticism is all about.

Acknowledgments

I offer thanks, first of all, to the five critics who agreed to write new essays or let me reprint essays already published. Their patience with editorial promptings and their speed and cooperation in meeting deadlines have been most gratifying. I offer thanks also to several people who were of particular help to me in my part of the project: my son Paul for helping to collect the many essays I read for the critical history essay; my colleague Jim Frakes, who knows Henry James's fiction better than I ever will; Suzi Naiburg of Harvard University and Cheryl Torsney of West Virgina University for reviewing parts of the manuscript; and two former students, Sandra Guy and Jian "Stan" Shi, for checking quotations for me. At Bedford Books Stephen Scipione has been an encouraging and efficient contact, and Jonathan Burns saw the volume through production with great patience and attention to detail. I also thank Charles Christensen, Joan Feinberg, Elizabeth Schaaf, and Laura Arcari. As for series editor Ross Murfin—well, who can help being grateful for his good humor, his grace, and his toughness in all matters relating to a project like this? Finally, I thank Anne for understanding why at certain times in the past year or so I have had to close the door of my study and crouch low over my desk.

Peter G. Beidler
Lehigh University

Contents

Case Studies in Contemporary Criticism

HENRY JAMES

The Turn of the Screw

PART ONE

The Turn of the Screw:
The Complete Text

Introduction:
Biographical and
Historical Contexts

On April 15, 1843, Henry James was born into what was to be one of the most intellectually powerful families in the United States. The original James emigrated from Ireland shortly after the American Revolution. He married three times (his first two wives died relatively young) and fathered thirteen children, among them a son named Henry, born and reared in Albany, New York. That Henry, usually referred to now as Henry Sr. because of his more famous son of the same name, eventually settled in New York City with his wife, Mary. There they had five children: William (1842–1910), Henry Jr. (1843–1916), Garth Wilkinson (1845–1883), Robertson (1846–1910), and Alice (1848–1892). Henry Jr., the author of *The Turn of the Screw*, is the subject of this sketch, but to understand his life we need to know something about the siblings with whom he grew up and with whom he corresponded for most of their lives.[1]

William James was to become one of the most famous Americans of his day. An ambitious youth, he did well in school and showed early promise in both science and the arts. William was also the pupil of the well-known painter William Morris Hunt in Newport, Rhode Island, but in the end he turned away from art, perhaps because of the difficulty

---

[1]For more information about the James family than I can include here, see R. W. B. Lewis, *The Jameses: A Family Narrative* (New York: Farrar, 1991).

he foresaw in trying to make a living as a painter. He studied science next and finally enrolled in Harvard Medical School. When, some years later, he was offered the chance to teach physiology at Harvard, he accepted the post. He was to spend the rest of his professional life at Harvard, eventually shifting from physiology to the new science of psychology. Before long his name and ideas were known on both sides of the Atlantic. His two-volume *Principles of Psychology* (1890) was *the* standard book on the subject, and the shorter, onevolume *Psychology*, published in 1892, remained for years the standard college textbook. By this time William had long since married and had fathered five children. Public lectures made him even more famous. His *Varieties of Religious Experience* (1902) won him both respect and admiration. William died of heart failure in August 1910 at age sixty-eight.

The younger brothers, Garth and Robertson, fought bravely in losing battles but on the winning side in the Civil War. Both were assigned to help lead the first black regiments, and both were wounded in battle. After the war they tried to make a go of agricultural enterprises in Florida by buying cheap land and by hiring the newly freed black laborers, but the farms failed and the two lived and died in the shadow of their older brothers. "Wilky" died in his late thirties, of various physical afflictions stemming from war wounds, kidney disease, a weak heart, and distress at his financial insolvency. His younger brother, "Bob," struggled with alcoholism most of his life. He had some small success as a writer, but his alcoholism and the financial security that came with marriage into a wealthy family kept him from serious work. He died in his early sixties of heart failure. His obituary in the Boston *Evening Transcript* for July 9, 1910 — just weeks before his brother William died — referred to him as the "youngest brother of Henry and William James, with talents as brilliant as theirs, had they been as steadily exercised" (Lewis 582).

Alice, the youngest James and only daughter, lived in precarious psychological and physical health, and she often contemplated suicide. She never married or had children. She spent the last decade of her life in Europe, never very far from her favorite brother Henry and her best friend, Katharine Peabody Loring. There has been some speculation, based in part on the brilliant journal she kept, that her fondness for Katharine had lesbian overtones. Alice died of cancer in 1892 in her mid-forties, leaving behind the journal, which her more literary brothers later had published.

This was a remarkable family indeed. The two younger brothers, while never famous, served heroically in America's most important war.

The two older brothers became, in turn, America's foremost psychologist and America's foremost man of letters. The sister, though afflicted with bad health, kept a journal that has given her a prominent place in the study of the history of women and the psychology of depression and mental distress. If the family was remarkable, so was their father. The senior Henry James came to reject the Presbyterian faith of his own father and to espouse instead the ideas of Emanuel Swedenborg, the Swedish Christian mystic (1688–1772) who was to have so large an influence on Ralph Waldo Emerson and other nineteenth-century thinkers. Because of an inheritance from his father, he was able to live comfortably and, with his wife, Mary Walsh James (the daughter of a well-to-do Irish-American manufacturer), to provide his family with unusual educational experiences. Henry Sr. made friends with many famous intellectuals and writers, and entertained several of them in his home: Emerson, Henry David Thoreau, Margaret Fuller, Washington Irving, and William Makepeace Thackeray. He and his wife reared their children in no particular religion or set of beliefs but gave them books to read, introduced them to interesting people, enrolled them in many different schools, and traveled with them to fascinating places — particularly Europe in 1855.

Henry Jr. was twelve at the time of that journey. The trip was to last three years — with long stays in Geneva, London, and Paris, where young Henry became fluent in French. Although he returned home to New York and later moved with his family to Cambridge, Massachusetts, that long trip to the Old World was young Henry's introduction to the Europe that was to be his home for most of his life and the place where he did most of his writing.

Henry James, Jr. — hereafter to be called simply "Henry James" or "James" — appears to have wanted, almost from the beginning, to be a writer of fiction. Certainly he got an early start and early encouragement in writing. In the February 1864 issue of the *Continental Monthly*, when he was not yet twenty-one, James published his first story, "A Tragedy of Error," about a woman who tries to have her husband murdered but, through a misunderstanding, has her lover murdered instead. Another story, published four years later, showed James's early interest in ghostly materials. "The Romance of Certain Old Clothes" ends with the ghost of a former wife murdering her husband's second wife. Melodramatic as these early stories were, they showed that James was serious, inventive, and motivated and that he had a sense of what would please the reading public. Because of the confidence of his early start and the steady conviction with which he pursued his art, he achieved an output exceeding that of any other great American writer: twenty novels and well over a hundred novellas and stories — not to mention criticism, plays, travel pieces, journals, sketches, reviews, and letters. Before he died he had met or corresponded with the most important literary artists of England and America: Ralph Waldo Emerson, Ivan Turgenev, Gustave Flaubert, Robert Browning, Rudyard Kipling, Guy de Maupassant, Walter Pater, Matthew Arnold, Lord Tennyson, William Dean Howells, Oscar Wilde, Robert Louis Stevenson, Henry Adams, Edith Wharton, James Russell Lowell, George Eliot, George Meredith, Constance Fenimore Woolson, Anthony Trollope, Sarah Orne Jewett, H. G. Wells. Few scholars will deny that James was at least the equal of any of them.

Both England and America claim Henry James as their own. We cannot know exactly why someone from so profoundly an American family came to feel more at home in Europe. Perhaps he wanted to assert his independence from his father and older brother. Perhaps in America, where other young men tended to be hustling — building and buying and selling things — he was made to feel ineffectual or lazy, or as if writing were an unmanly profession. Perhaps America had for him little culture, little literary history, little history at all in comparison with Europe. Europe had the "Eternal City" of Rome and a rich Renaissance heritage still visible in the houses and churches of almost every major city; what did America have except new towns and new wealth? Whatever the reasons, James became an artistic expatriate, living in France, Switzerland, Italy, and, especially, England for most of his adult life. He wrote home frequently, sailed home occasionally, and received many visits from American friends and family members, but he was in fact a citizen of Europe. Not long before his death at age seventy-three on February 28, 1916, James became a British subject. He changed citizenship in part to show his support for the British in what came to be called World War I, in part to make official what must have been as obvious to him as to others: that after living most of his life in England, he had become in most ways an Englishman.

FRATERNAL RIVALRY

Between Henry James and his brother William there was always a cautious friendship. Reared almost as twins, the two could scarcely help competing with one another. William showed earlier promise and seemed destined to make a more lasting intellectual contribution. He taught at Harvard, married and fathered four children, and was soon on his way to a reputation as a psychologist, researcher, writer, and lecturer. Henry, on the other hand, was a quiet and sensitive young man and was aware that as a bachelor he had chosen a more questionable — certainly a less conventional — lifeway.

To judge by the caustic tone of some of his letters, however, William felt he had reason to be jealous. His younger brother chose his profession and left home first (William was still single and living at home until he was thirty-seven), wrote and published much earlier than William did, and achieved fame first. To William, Henry's life must have looked enviably free, independent, creative, and exciting. William's writing was interrupted by the obligations of teaching and family. When he traveled, he did so encumbered by children. William never quite understood why his sister, Alice, seemed to prefer Henry's company to his own, or why their father named faraway Henry executor of his will rather than the nearby William.

For his part, Henry seemed always to stand in awe of his brother's accomplishments. He traveled in some circles where his brother came to be widely respected, and he must have been somewhat envious of William's scientific fame, occupational stability, and domestic normalcy. Although Henry became one of the most celebrated men of his day, he struggled to earn a living by his pen, knew many low periods and disappointments, and never married. To Henry, William must have looked enviably steady and respectable. Even their writing was so different that the two brothers must have felt at times like rival authors. William wrote psychology so clearly that it reads almost like fiction, whereas Henry wrote fiction so complexly that it reads almost like psychology.

Rather than emphasize the jealousies between the two brothers, however, let us remind ourselves that these two men remained friends and supportive correspondents all their lives and that their friendship far outweighed any small rivalries they may have felt. Both men had a large and warm circle of friends, and both were at the very top of their professions. If one brother can be said to have established the science of psychology as a legitimate subject of study, the other can be said to have altered the direction of fiction and literary criticism in ways that we are still learning to appreciate.

Although Henry James appeared to lead a private and sedentary life, the standard biography of his life runs to five volumes and kept its author, Leon Edel, busy for more than twenty years. A short biographical sketch like this cannot do justice to such a deep and subtly layered existence, but in what follows I will introduce a few of the issues most helpful to an understanding of the circumstances leading to James's writing of *The Turn of the Screw*.[2]

JAMES'S SEXUALITY

No one who comes to know Henry James through his writings can avoid seeking in those writings an answer to the question of why he never married. It used to be assumed that James was "married to his art" and did not want to take time away from his writing for domestic concerns. James lived in a time when men were the wage-earners, and if he had had the expense and time commitments of courting a wife and then rearing a family, he might not have been able to be a writer at all.

That early hypothesis about James's reason for not marrying, however, has been replaced with an alternative one: that James was homosexual. There is little that can be called proof, but there is some circumstantial evidence. Henry James's sensibility has struck more than a few readers as "feminine." A friend of James's, an American diplomat named Ehrman Nadal, described James in these words: "He seemed to look at women rather as women looked at them. Women looked at women as persons; men look at them as women. The quality of sex in women, which is their first and chief attraction to most men, was not their chief attraction to James" (Edel 234). Nadal's assessment may tell us less about James's sexuality than about his ability to write empathetic, perceptive fiction, but it is difficult *not* to see hints of homoerotic attraction in some of James's fiction — between Pemberton and Morgan Moreen in James's story "The Pupil," for example.

And James's letters suggest that he was attracted, on some level, to a series of men, most of them younger than he. In 1890, for example, he met in Europe a young American journalist named Morton Fullerton and began a long friendship with him. In letters he refers to him as "my dear boy" and "my dearest boy" (Kaplan 407), and in 1900 he used these words to invite Fullerton for a visit: "You are beautiful; you are more than tactful, you are tenderly, magically *tactile*. . . . I'm alone & think of you. . . . I'd meet you at Dover — I'd do anything for you" (Kaplan 409). Is this innocent friendship or homoerotic love? Certainly James knew about homosexuality, but he also knew the dangers of revealing it. In the mid-1890s, after the playwright Oscar Wilde was sen-

---

[2]For readers who want to know more about Henry James but are not ready to tackle five heavy volumes, I recommend Leon Edel's one-volume condensation, *Henry James: A Life* (New York: Harper, 1985). My quotations from Edel are from this shorter version.

tenced to prison for two years at hard labor for homosexual offenses, James wrote to a friend about the case. He found it "hideously, atrociously dramatic and really interesting" but also characterized by a "sickening horribility" (Edel 437). He wrote to his brother William that Wilde's "fall is hideously tragic — and the squalid violence of it gives him an interest (of misery) that he never had for me — in any degree — before" (Edel 439).

The most recent critical opinion is that while there is evidence that Henry James was probably homosexual by inclination, there is little evidence that he had an active physical or sexual relationship with any man — or, for that matter, any woman. In fact, however, we know very little about Henry James's sexuality, and perhaps it is wisest to focus more on his texts than on his closets. James had many close men and women friends. He refrained from writing much about the physical aspects of any human passion, and he was either puzzled or annoyed when others wrote about such subjects. In 1888 James read *Mensonges* by his friend the novelist Paul Bourget. He did not much like the novel and wrote Bourget to tell him why:

> Your out-and-out eroticism displeases me as well as this exposition of dirty linens and dirty towels. In a word, all this is far from being life as I feel it, as I see it, as I know it, as I wish to know it. . . . It would never occur to me to want to know what goes on in their bedroom, in their bed, between a man and a woman. (Edel 378–79)

It may, of course, be the explicit discussion of man-woman sex that James found so offensive, but it is just as likely that James shared the Victorian view that such matters were out of place in serious fiction.

The issue is of little interest for a reading of *The Turn of the Screw* except insofar as there has been speculation about a possible homosexual relationship between Peter Quint and Miles and related speculation that if Miles did have homosexual tendencies, his expression of them at school may have been what caused the headmaster to expel him.

FIVE TROUBLED YEARS

The Turn of the Screw is somewhat atypical of the work James was doing at the turn of the century. It is about ghosts — or what the governess thinks are ghosts; it shows the darker side of human nature; it is full of danger and melodrama. To understand what may have prompted Henry James to write this story at the end of 1897, we need to understand something about his life in the earlier part of that decade. His sister, Alice, died after a lingering illness in March 1892. James was with her in London during most of the long hours of her dying and wrote for her a final telegram to their brother William in Cambridge: "Tenderest love to all. Farewell. Am going soon. Alice" (Edel 370). A year later, Henry James turned fifty and was struck with a painful and temporarily crippling gout. Mortality and aging seemed suddenly closer. He wrote to a friend that he was "moody, misanthropic, melancholy, morbid, morose" (Edel 430).

An event that caused Henry James particular distress was the 1894 suicide of a writer named Constance Fenimore Woolson. A grandniece of James Fenimore Cooper, Woolson had come to Europe in 1880 to write. Unmarried and alone, Woolson had read about Europe in Henry James's writings, and she had hoped to meet him. Meet him she did in Florence. She wrote to a friend that Florence had "taken me pretty well off my feet! Perhaps I ought to add Henry James. He has been perfectly charming to me for the last three weeks" (Edel 256). The encounter was apparently charming for James as well. James was one of many who admired Woolson's work, and he later wrote a section on her in his *Partial Portraits* (1888). We gather that James enjoyed his new friend's company. James wrote to his aunt that his new friend was "old-maidish, deaf and 'intense,' but a good little woman, and a perfect lady" (Edel 256).

James and Woolson seem never to have had a full-blown romance, but they stayed friends for many years. One recent commentator puts it this way: "She was a woman he could admire without feeling threatened, a woman he could love without loving her as a woman" (Kaplan 313). In any case, they lived in different European cities for most of their friendship. They saw each other from time to time, but they kept their friendship alive mostly through letters and more letters. In January of 1894 Woolson fell or leaped from the window of her apartment in Venice. When James, then in London, learned of the circumstances of her death, he could not bring himself to go to Italy for the funeral. He put it this way to a friend: "I have utterly collapsed. I have let everything go. . . . Miss Woolson was so valued and close a friend of mine and had been for so many years that I feel an intense nearness of participation in every circumstance of her tragic end" (Edel 391). Despite his grief and possible sense of guilt, James later helped Woolson's relatives sort out her things in Venice, and it seems likely that at that time he recovered — and destroyed — all of his letters to her.[3]

<hr />

[3]For more on Woolson, see Cheryl B. Torsney, *Constance Fenimore Woolson: The Grief of Artistry* (Athens: U of Georgia P, 1989).

In addition to physical and emotional pain, the 1890s brought professional pain as well. James's books were not selling well, and he entered the 1890s with a sense of financial failure. Aware that writers were making a lot of money writing for the stage, he determined to try his hand as a playwright. He wrote to Robert Louis Stevenson in 1891 that "Chastening necessity has laid its brutal hand on me and I have had to try to make somehow or other the money I don't make by literature. My books don't sell, and it looks as if my plays might. Therefore I am going with a brazen front to write half a dozen" (Edel 364). As it turned out, the plays did not do well either. Companies were reluctant to produce his "talky" plays, and when they did, audiences found them too "refined" — that is, too cerebral.

As he continued to work on his own fledgling plays, James glanced nervously over his shoulder at the successful dramatic productions of Oscar Wilde and Henrik Ibsen. Only a few of James's plays were produced, and they played only short runs to unenthusiastic audiences. After several years, sensing that he might not be destined to succeed as a playwright, James decided to give the theater one more chance. He wrote to his brother William on December 29, 1893:

> I mean to wage this war ferociously for one year more — 1894 — and then (unless the victory and the spoils have by that become more proportionate than hitherto to the humiliations and vulgarities and disgusts, all the dishonor and chronic insult incurred) to "chuck" the whole intolerable experiment and return to more elevated and more independent courses. (Edel 389)

That year he put his efforts and his hopes into a promising new play, *Guy Domville*, which would star a then-famous actor named George Alexander. The play was about a young man who wants to become a Benedictine monk but is forced, by the death of his only brother, to marry so that he can produce children to carry on the family name.

Opening night for *Guy Domville* was January 5, 1895. The audience was strangely mixed. On the one hand were sophisticated intellectuals who liked James's work and wanted to see his play (among them three reviewers who were to make names for themselves in the literary world: George Bernard Shaw, H. G. Wells, and Arnold Bennett). On the other hand were unsophisticated Londoners who did not know James's other work but wanted to be entertained by George Alexander. The first group liked the play; the second hated it. After the final curtain there was applause, mostly for Alexander's performance. James's friends called for the author to come out for applause, and Henry obligingly joined Alexander in front of the curtain. When the gallery folk saw him, they jeered and hissed, while those downstairs, in the more expensive seats, applauded. James was later to put it this way in a letter to William: "All the forces of civilization in the house waged a battle of the most gallant, prolonged and sustained applause with the hoots and jeers and catcalls of the roughs, whose roars (like those of a cage of beasts at some infernal zoo) were only exacerbated by the conflict" (Edel 420). James quickly retreated backstage, and George Alexander stayed in front to apologize and to say that they would try to do better in the future. A voice from the gallery said, "T'aint your fault, guv'nor, it's a rotten play."

Guy Domville went on to a month of respectable performances, but James had gotten the message. Seeing that he could not be true to his art *and* please the "cage of beasts," he made his choice: he would be true to his art and leave the beasts to their own theatricals. Two weeks later, on January 23, 1895, James wrote in his notebook: "I take up my *own* pen again — the pen of all my old unforgettable efforts and sacred struggles. To myself — today — I need say no more. Large and full and high the future still opens. It is now indeed that I may do the work of my life. And I will" (*Notebooks* 179).

One of the first fruits of his *own* pen was *The Turn of the Screw*, which shows the effects of the difficult years he had recently endured. It is about unreturned love, death, neglect, virtue unappreciated, innocence corrupted, the evil forces in human existence. The story is also one of James's most theatrical: it has a single setting in a mysterious mansion, pale faces at windows, strange figures appearing and disappearing, dramatic scenes and dialogue, a melodramatic interplay of innocence with the haunting forces of darkness. James mined his past five years of death, sickness, and failure to produce one of his most popular and successful works.

THE GERM OF THE STORY

Five days after the humiliating opening night of *Guy Domville*, James was invited to tea at the home of his friend Edward White Benson, Archbishop of Canterbury, at Addington, just outside London. He and Benson started talking about ghosts. Soon after that visit, in a January 12, 1895, entry in his journal, James described in some detail the outlines of a ghost narrative told him by Benson:

> Note here the ghost-story told me at Addington (evening of Thursday 10th), by the Archbishop of Canterbury: the mere

vague, undetailed, faint sketch of it — being all he had been told (very badly and imperfectly), by a lady who had no art of relation, and no clearness: the story of the young children (indefinite number and age) left to the care of servants in an old country-house, through the death, presumably, of parents. The servants, wicked and depraved, corrupt and deprave the children; the children are bad, full of evil, to a sinister degree. The servants *die* (the story vague about the way of it) and their apparitions, figures, return to haunt the house *and* children, to whom they seem to beckon, whom they invite and solicit, from across dangerous places, the deep ditch of a sunk fence, etc. — so that the children may destroy themselves, lose themselves, by responding, by getting into their power. So long as the children are kept from them, they are not lost; but they try and try and try, these evil presences, to get hold of them. It is a question of the children "coming over to where they are." It is all obscure and imperfect, the picture, the story, but there is a suggestion of strangely gruesome effect in it. The story to be told — tolerably obviously — by an outside spectator, observer. (*Notebooks* 178–79)

That notebook entry, of course, was the germ of *The Turn of the Screw*, though James did not get around to expanding it into a full narrative until almost three years later.

The Turn of the Screw was James's response to an invitation from the editor of *Collier's Weekly*, the illustrated magazine published in New York, to write a twelve-part ghost story by the end of 1897. James was pleased to supply the request. He had just signed a twenty-one-year lease on Lamb House, in Rye, Sussex, and he was concerned about the upheaval that the permanent move from London would entail. The offer from *Collier's* would give him added money for the move and, moreover, would guarantee him a wider and more popular readership than most of his fiction had earned. Besides, still conveniently at hand was that old sketch of a ghost story, based on the experiences of a woman E. W. Benson had known.

MODERN SPIRITUALISM
AND THE GHOST STORY

Why would James contract to write a ghost story? That question has bothered many readers, some of whom conclude that *The Turn of the Screw* must be something *other* than a ghost story. Other readers say, well, why *wouldn't* James write a ghost story? Writers as great as Shakespeare had created literary ghosts, and James himself had written other stories in which the spirits of the dead appeared as characters. Having ghosts in *The Turn of the Screw* would be no real departure, except insofar as *these* ghosts would be more evil than others he had described.

Actually, Henry James can scarcely have avoided being interested in ghosts. His father had been fascinated by the various forms of spiritualism and possession by spirits. His brother William was an active researcher of spiritual phenomena. Indeed, in the last quarter of the nineteenth century, spirits of the dead were taken seriously as subjects for both scientific discussion and literary portrayal. Modern spiritualism can be said to have begun in 1848, when, not far from Henry James's birthplace in New York, the two daughters of a man named Fox, one aged twelve and the other fifteen, heard strange rappings in their bedroom. They began to ask the mysterious rapper questions and heard measured raps in reply. Investigators found the Fox sisters to be reliable witnesses who appeared really to have been in communication with the spirit of a dead person. The case attracted a lot of publicity, and overnight the Fox sisters became notorious.[4]

That same year Catherine Crowe published a book titled *The Night Side of Nature; or, Ghosts and Ghost Seers*, a serious report of what was then known about the science of ghosts. The book was a sensation and went through several editions and many printings. It even helped to inspire the Cambridge Ghost Club in 1851 at Trinity College, at Cambridge University in England. The purpose of the group was to conduct scientific investigations of reported cases of ghostly appearances and other supernatural phenomena. In 1882 the group was transmuted into the Society for Psychical Research under the leadership of Henry Sidgwick, a Cambridge professor of moral philosophy. Other founding members of the Society for Psychical Research were Frederic W. H. Myers and Edmund Gurney. Gurney was soon to publish (with help from Myers and Frank Podmore, another psychical researcher) a book called *Phantasms of the Living* (1886), important for its detailed discussion of some 700 reported ghost cases.

What does all this information about psychical research have to do with Henry James and *The Turn of the Screw*? The early founders of the Society for Psychical Research had praised Henry James's father as an early and reliable observer of spiritual phenomena. Henry James's brother William had a lifelong interest in spiritual phenomena, was a

---

[4]For further information about these matters, see Alan Gauld's *The Founders of Psychical Research* (London: Routledge, 1968).

guiding light of the American branch of the Society for Psychical Research, was a member of the British parent society almost since its inception, and was its president from 1894 to 1896 — the period just before Henry James wrote *The Turn of the Screw*. Henry James was personally acquainted with Sidgwick, Myers, and Gurney. He also, as we have seen, talked about ghosts with Archbishop Benson, a Trinity man deeply interested in ghostly phenomena. Although he was never himself a member of the Society for Psychical Research, Henry James attended at least one meeting of the Society in London, the minutes of which show that he read aloud, on behalf of his absent brother William, a scientific report about a woman named Mrs. Piper, a spirit medium whose body and voice seemed at times to be used by the spirit of a man long dead. We also know from his correspondence that Henry James purchased a copy of Gurney's *Phantasms of the Living* in 1886. James unquestionably knew about ghosts and spirit possession, and he was aware that some of the best scientists of his time took such phenomena seriously.

As an example of the ghost cases investigated and reported by James's friend Edmund Gurney, here are some passages from the published account of a woman identified only as "Mrs. G." or "Birdie." After her husband's death Mrs. G. rented a lovely village house for herself, her daughters Edith, age nine, and Florence, age ten, and a maid named Anne. Gurney, who visited Mrs. G. several times as part of his investigation of this case, tells us that in his opinion she was "an excellent witness. I have never received an account in which the words and manner of telling were less suggestive of exaggeration or superstition." The excerpts below are from Mrs. G.'s narrative as published in the 1889 *Proceedings of the Society for Psychical Research*:[5]

> I was in the drawing-room deeply thinking about business matters, when I was startled by Edith giving such a scream. I ran to the door, and found her running up, followed by Florence and the servant, the child so scared and deadly white, and could hardly breathe. "Oh, Birdie dear, I have seen such a dreadful white face peeping round the door! I saw only the head. I was playing with Floss (dog), and looking up, I saw this dreadful thing." Florence and Anne rushed in at once, but saw nothing.

Mrs. G. later finds out from some neighbors that an earlier tenant in the house had had "a wicked servant . . . a very wicked servant." Mrs. G. can

---

[5]For the full account, see my *Ghosts, Demons, and Henry James* (Columbia: U of Missouri P, 1989) 67–74.

get them to tell her nothing more of the servant, "but of course I imagined this very wicked servant had done something, and felt very uneasy." Later the skeptical Florence sees the face also:

> The next morning, as Florence was passing the room on the stairs, she saw a man standing by the window staring fixedly; blue eyes, dark brown hair, and freckles. She rushed up to me, looking very white and frightened; the house was searched at once, and nothing seen.

There is also a female ghost, dressed in black:

> One day, when I was out, the children were playing with Anne in the room downstairs; they all distinctly heard a very heavy footfall walk across the drawing-room, play two notes on the piano, and walk out. I came in shortly after, astonished to see them, candle in hand, looking under the beds. It was a dreadful time. . . . I then had an interview with Miss M., the former tenant, who told me she had gone through precisely what I had, but had said very little about it, for fear of being laughed at. I was far too angry to take notice whether any one laughed or not. Miss M. said one afternoon between four and five she was in very good spirits, and was playing the piano, and as she crossed the room a figure enveloped in black, with a very white face, and such a forlorn look, stood before her, and then it faded away.

After five months of these strange experiences, which terrify and sicken her children, Mrs. G. breaks the lease and leaves: "All is quite true that I have stated, whether mortal or immortal I know not. I am glad to say my children are recovering, though Edith is still very weak." A later investigation revealed that ten years earlier a forty-two-year-old woman had committed suicide by hanging herself by a skip rope from a peg in one of the bedrooms in the house.

Thousands of such narrative reports were published in the quarter-century before James wrote *The Turn of the Screw*. The characters Peter Quint and Miss Jessel are both described to be in appearance like many of the ghosts reported in these scientific investigations, and it is interesting to note that James describes Douglas, in the prologue of *The Turn of the Screw*, as a *Trinity* College student when he first meets the governess and learns of her experiences at Bly. As James well knew, Trinity College was the center of psychical research in his time, and it is significant that the man who vouches for the governess and who has her manuscript is associated with that college.

It is important to remember, then, that James launched *The Turn of the Screw* into a world that seriously investigated ghostly phenomena. We don't know whether Henry James personally believed in ghosts, but he was undoubtedly interested in them, knew about scientific research into reports about them, and was acquainted with the men most directly involved in such research. And there is no question that when James was invited to write a "ghost story" for *Collier's*, he had a wealth of information about "real" ghost cases to draw on.

THE COMPOSITION OF THE STORY

Modern readers might want to remember two facts about the composition of *The Turn of the Screw*. First, James wrote this story for publication in installments in a popular weekly magazine, *Collier's*. The first publication had, to be sure, the prologue and the twenty-four continuously numbered chapters of the current edition, but it also had the twelve groups of chapters and five larger parts. These are all indicated in the notes to the edition in this volume. The point here is that many people who read that first serialized version might have been barely able to remember the main events from previous installments, let alone the details. Unless they saved the earlier installments and read the twelve issues all at once, their reading would have been a more discontinuous experience than it is for us who read the story as James later presented it in the 1908 New York edition — the edition used for this Bedford volume.

And, second, strictly speaking, James did not "write" *The Turn of the Screw* at all. By his mid-fifties James's lifetime of writing with a pen had all but ruined his wrist. We would now call this painful phenomenon carpal tunnel syndrome. To continue to ply his trade James had to buy a typewriter — a recent invention in the 1890s. He never learned to type, but he hired others to type for him. As you read *The Turn of the Screw*, do not imagine Henry James writing the story longhand but imagine him, rather, dictating to his secretary, William MacAlpine, who typed as James spoke. Initially, then, the story of the governess and Miles and Flora was an oral tale told very much in the tradition of the ghost story recounted in front of the fire of a Christmas evening.

James made his deadline. In December of 1897 he wrote to his sister-in-law: "I *have*, at last, finished my little book" (Edel 462–63). The little book he spoke of was *The Turn of the Screw*. It appeared in *Collier's* from January to April 1898. Thus was launched the work that was to become Henry James's most widely read — and most controversial — piece of fiction. In a reminiscence written just after James's

death, Yale professor William Lyon Phelps called James "the best example of the psychological realist that we have in American literature"
(788) and *The Turn of the Screw* "the most powerful, the most nerve-
shattering ghost story I have ever read. . . . This story made my blood
chill, my spine curl, and every individual hair to stand on end." When
Phelps described his reaction to Henry James, his friend replied, "I
meant to scare the whole world with that story; and you had precisely
the emotion that I hoped to arouse in everybody" (Phelps 794).

But not everybody, particularly in the last fifty years, has had the
reaction Phelps described. Indeed, so divergent have been the reactions
to James's "little book" that *The Turn of the Screw* has become as famous for the critical controversies as for the emotions it has aroused.
These controversies are the subject of my essay "A Critical History of
The Turn of the Screw," which opens Part Two of this book, following
the story itself.

Peter G. Beidler

WORKS CITED

Beidler, Peter G. *Ghosts, Demons, and Henry James: "The Turn of the
    Screw" at the Turn of the Century.* Columbia: U of Missouri P,
    1989.

Crowe, Catherine Stevens. *The Night Side of Nature; or, Ghosts and
    Ghost Seers.* London: T. C. Newby, 1848.

Edel, Leon. *Henry James: A Life.* New York: Harper, 1985.

Gauld, Alan. *The Founders of Psychical Research.* London: Routledge,
    1968.

Gurney, Edmund, Frederic W. H. Myers, and Frank Podmore. *Phan-
    tasms of the Living.* 2 vols. London: Trubner, 1886.

James, Alice. *The Diary of Alice James.* Ed. Leon Edel. New York:
    Dodd, Mead, 1964.

James, William. *The Principles of Psychology.* 2 vols. New York: Holt,
    1890.

———. *Psychology.* New York: Holt, 1892.

Kaplan, Fred. *Henry James: The Imagination of Genius.* New York:
    Morrow, 1992.

Lewis, R. W. B. *The Jameses: A Family Narrative.* New York: Farrar,
    1991.

Matthiessen, F. O., and Kenneth B. Murdock, eds. *The Notebooks of Henry James.* New York: Braziller, 1955.

Phelps, William Lyon. "Henry James." *Yale Review* 5 (1916): 783–97.

Torsney, Cheryl B. *Constance Fenimore Woolson: The Grief of Artistry.* Athens: U of Georgia P, 1989.

The Turn of the Screw°

The story° had held us, round the fire, sufficiently breathless, but except the obvious remark that it was gruesome, as on Christmas Eve in an old house a strange tale should essentially be, I remember no comment uttered till somebody happened to note it as the only case he had met in which such a visitation had fallen on a child. The case, I may mention, was that of an apparition in just such an old house as had gathered us for the occasion — an appearance, of a dreadful kind, to a little boy sleeping in the room with his mother and waking her up in the terror of it; waking her not to dissipate his dread and soothe him to sleep again, but to encounter also herself, before she had succeeded in doing so, the same sight that had shocked him. It was this observation that drew from Douglas — not immediately, but later in the evening — a reply that had the interesting consequence to which I call attention. Some one else told a story not particularly effective, which I saw he was

The Turn of the Screw: In the original *Collier's Weekly* publication, *The Turn of the Screw* was divided into five "parts" and twelve installments in addition to the prologue and twenty-four roman-numeraled chapters of the New York edition. *Part First* and the first weekly installment started here. The various parts and installments were deleted in the book edition, but for readers who want some sense of the pace of the periodical version, these notes indicate where the five parts and twelve installments began. **story:** This term refers to the tale told by Griffin, one of the men gathered around the fire. It was traditional in James's time to tell ghost stories on Christmas Eve. Griffin's story had been about the appearance of a ghost to a little boy and his mother.

not following. This I took for a sign that he had himself something to produce and that we should only have to wait. We waited in fact till two nights later; but that same evening, before we scattered, he brought out what was in his mind.

"I quite agree — in regard to Griffin's ghost, or whatever it was — that its appearing first to the little boy, at so tender an age, adds a particular touch. But it's not the first occurrence of its charming kind that I know to have been concerned with a child. If the child gives the effect another turn of the screw, what do you say to *two* children — ?"

"We say of course," somebody exclaimed, "that two children give two turns! Also that we want to hear about them."

I can see Douglas there before the fire, to which he had got up to present his back, looking down at this converser with his hands in his pockets. "Nobody but me, till now, has ever heard. It's quite too horrible." This was naturally declared by several voices to give the thing the utmost price, and our friend, with quiet art, prepared his triumph by turning his eyes over the rest of us and going on: "It's beyond everything. Nothing at all that I know touches it."

"For sheer terror?" I remember asking.

He seemed to say it was n't so simple as that; to be really at a loss how to qualify it. He passed his hand over his eyes, made a little wincing grimace. "For dreadful — dreadfulness!"

"Oh how delicious!" cried one of the women.

He took no notice of her; he looked at me, but as if, instead of me, he saw what he spoke of. "For general uncanny ugliness and horror and pain."

"Well then," I said, "just sit right down and begin."

He turned round to the fire, gave a kick to a log, watched it an instant. Then as he faced us again: "I can't begin. I shall have to send to town°." There was a unanimous groan at this, and much reproach; after which, in his preoccupied way, he explained. "The story's written. It's in a locked drawer — it has not been out for years. I could write to my man and enclose the key; he could send down the packet as he finds it." It was to me in particular that he appeared to propound this — appeared almost to appeal for aid not to hesitate. He had broken a thickness of ice, the formation of many a winter; had had his reasons for a long silence. The others resented postponement, but it was just his scruples that charmed me. I adjured him to write by the first post and to

---

town: London. The guests are visitors at a country estate not far from London, which would have been accessible by coach.

agree with us for an early hearing; then I asked him if the experience in question had been his own. To this his answer was prompt. "Oh thank God, no!"

"And is the record yours? You took the thing down?"

"Nothing but the impression. I took that *here*" — he tapped his heart. "I've never lost it."

"Then your manuscript — ?"

"Is in old faded ink and in the most beautiful hand." He hung fire° again. "A woman's. She has been dead these twenty years. She sent me the pages in question before she died." They were all listening now, and of course there was somebody to be arch, or at any rate to draw the inference. But if he put the inference by without a smile it was also without irritation. "She was a most charming person, but she was ten years older than I. She was my sister's governess," he quietly said. "She was the most agreeable woman I've ever known in her position; she'd have been worthy of any whatever. It was long ago, and this episode was long before. I was at Trinity,° and I found her at home on my coming down the second summer. I was much there that year — it was a beautiful one; and we had, in her off-hours, some strolls and talks in the garden — talks in which she struck me as awfully clever and nice. Oh yes; don't grin: I liked her extremely and am glad to this day to think she liked me too. If she had n't she would n't have told me. She had never told any one. It was n't simply that she said so, but that I knew she had n't. I was sure; I could see. You'll easily judge why when you hear."

"Because the thing had been such a scare?"

He continued to fix° me. "You'll easily judge," he repeated: "*you* will."

I fixed him too. "I see. She was in love."

He laughed for the first time. "You *are* acute. Yes, she was in love. That is she *had* been. That came out — she could n't tell her story without its coming out. I saw it, and she saw I saw it; but neither of us spoke of it. I remember the time and the place — the corner of the lawn, the shade of the great beeches and the long hot summer afternoon. It was n't a scene for a shudder; but oh — !" He quitted the fire and dropped back into his chair.

"You'll receive the packet Thursday morning?" I said.

"Probably not till the second post."

"Well then; after dinner — "

---

hung fire: Paused.   **Trinity:** Trinity College, Cambridge. Several of the faculty and students at Trinity were among the earliest serious scientific researchers into ghostly and other psychical or paranormal phenomena.   **fix:** Stare at, gaze "fixedly" at.

"You'll all meet me here?" He looked us round again. "Is n't any-
body going?" It was almost the tone of hope.

"Everybody will stay!"

"*I* will — and *I* will!" cried the ladies whose departure had been
fixed.° Mrs. Griffin, however, expressed the need for a little more light.
"Who was it she was in love with?"

"The story will tell," I took upon myself to reply.

"Oh I can't wait for the story!"

"The story *won't* tell," said Douglas; "not in any literal vulgar way."

"More's the pity then. That's the only way I ever understand."

"Won't *you* tell, Douglas?" somebody else enquired.

He sprang to his feet again. "Yes — to-morrow. Now I must go to
bed. Good-night." And, quickly catching up a candlestick, he left us
slightly bewildered. From our end of the great brown hall we heard his
step on the stair; whereupon Mrs. Griffin spoke. "Well, if I don't know
who she was in love with I know who *he* was."

"She was ten years older," said her husband.

"*Raison de plus*° — at that age! But it's rather nice, his long reticence."

"Forty years!" Griffin put in.

"With this outbreak at last."

"The outbreak," I returned, "will make a tremendous occasion of
Thursday night"; and every one so agreed with me that in the light of it
we lost all attention for everything else. The last story, however incomplete and like the mere opening of a serial, had been told; we handshook
and "candlestuck,"° as somebody said, and went to bed.

I knew the next day that a letter containing the key had, by the first
post, gone off to his London apartments; but in spite of — or perhaps
just on account of — the eventual diffusion of this knowledge we quite
let him alone till after dinner, till such an hour of the evening in fact as
might best accord with the kind of emotion on which our hopes were
fixed. Then he became as communicative as we could desire, and indeed
gave us his best reason for being so. We had it from him again before
the fire in the hall, as we had had our mild wonders of the previous
night. It appeared that the narrative he had promised to read us really
required for a proper intelligence a few words of prologue. Let me say
here distinctly, to have done with it, that this narrative, from an exact

---

fixed: Settled, agreed upon.   ***Raison de plus:*** French for "all the more reason."   **"candlestuck":** Lit their candles by touching them to one another so they could find their way
to their chambers for the night.

transcript of my own made much later, is what I shall presently give. Poor Douglas, before his death — when it was in sight — committed to me the manuscript that reached him on the third of these days and that, on the same spot, with immense effect, he began to read to our hushed little circle on the night of the fourth. The departing ladies who had said they would stay did n't, of course, thank heaven, stay: they departed, in consequence of arrangements made, in a rage of curiosity, as they professed, produced by the touches with which he had already worked us up. But that only made his little final auditory° more compact and select, kept it, round the hearth, subject to a common thrill.

The first of these touches conveyed that the written statement took up the tale at a point after it had, in a manner, begun. The fact to be in possession of was therefore that his old friend, the youngest of several daughters of a poor country parson, had at the age of twenty, on taking service for the first time in the schoolroom, come up to London, in trepidation, to answer in person an advertisement that had already placed her in brief correspondence with the advertiser. This person proved, on her presenting herself for judgement at a house in Harley Street° that impressed her as vast and imposing — this prospective patron proved a gentleman, a bachelor in the prime of life, such a figure as had never risen, save in a dream or an old novel, before a fluttered anxious girl out of a Hampshire° vicarage. One could easily fix his type; it never, happily, dies out. He was handsome and bold and pleasant, offhand and gay and kind. He struck her, inevitably, as gallant and splendid, but what took her most of all and gave her the courage she afterwards showed was that he put the whole thing to her as a favour, an obligation he should gratefully incur. She figured him as rich, but as fearfully extravagant — saw him all in a glow of high fashion, of good looks, of expensive habits, of charming ways with women. He had for his town residence a big house filled with the spoils of travel and the trophies of the chase; but it was to his country home, an old family place in Essex,° that he wished her immediately to proceed.

He had been left, by the death of his parents in India, guardian to a small nephew and a small niece, children of a younger, a military brother whom he had lost two years before. These children were, by the strangest of chances for a man in his position — a lone man without the right sort of experience or a grain of patience — very heavy on his

---

auditory: Group of listeners.   **Harley Street:** A fashionable street in London, not yet associated with the medical profession.   **Hampshire:** A county southwest of London. **Essex:** A county northeast of London.

hands. It had all been a great worry and, on his own part doubtless, a series of blunders, but he immensely pitied the poor chicks and had done all he could; had in particular sent them down to his other house, the proper place for them being of course the country, and kept them there from the first with the best people he could find to look after them, parting even with his own servants to wait on them and going down himself, whenever he might, to see how they were doing. The awkward thing was that they had practically no other relations and that his own affairs took up all his time. He had put them in possession of Bly,° which was healthy and secure, and had placed at the head of their little establishment — but belowstairs only — an excellent woman, Mrs. Grose,° whom he was sure his visitor would like and who had formerly been maid to his mother. She was now housekeeper and was also acting for the time as superintendent to the little girl, of whom, without children of her own, she was by good luck extremely fond. There were plenty of people to help, but of course the young lady who should go down as governess would be in supreme authority. She would also have, in holidays, to look after the small boy, who had been for a term at school — young as he was to be sent, but what else could be done? — and who, as the holidays were about to begin, would be back from one day to the other. There had been for the two children at first a young lady whom they had had the misfortune to lose. She had done for them quite beautifully — she was a most respectable person — till her death, the great awkwardness of which had, precisely, left no alternative but the school for little Miles. Mrs. Grose, since then, in the way of manners and things, had done as she could for Flora; and there were, further, a cook, a housemaid, a dairywoman, an old pony, an old groom and an old gardener, all likewise thoroughly respectable.

So far had Douglas presented his picture when some one put a question. "And what did the former governess die of? Of so much respectability?"

Our friend's answer was prompt. "That will come out. I don't anticipate."

"Pardon me — I thought that was just what you *are* doing."

"In her successor's place," I suggested, "I should have wished to learn if the office brought with it — "

Bly: The name of the uncle's country estate in Essex, possibly an allusion to the Bly family in Cotton Mather's account of the witchcraft trial of Bridget Bishop.   **Grose:** Possibly an allusion to the antiquarian Francis Grose (d. 1791), who wrote about ghosts and was commemorated in some of Robert Burns's poems.

"Necessary danger to life?" Douglas completed my thought. "She did wish to learn, and she did learn. You shall hear to-morrow what she learnt. Meanwhile of course the prospect struck her as slightly grim. She was young, untried, nervous: it was a vision of serious duties and little company, of really great loneliness. She hesitated — took a couple of days to consult and consider. But the salary offered much exceeded her modest measure, and on a second interview she faced the music, she engaged." And Douglas, with this, made a pause that, for the benefit of the company, moved me to throw in —

"The moral of which was of course the seduction exercised by the splendid young man. She succumbed to it."

He got up and, as he had done the night before, went to the fire, gave a stir to a log with his foot, then stood a moment with his back to us. "She saw him only twice."

"Yes, but that's just the beauty of her passion."

A little to my surprise, on this, Douglas turned round to me. "It *was* the beauty of it. There were others," he went on, "who had n't succumbed. He told her frankly all his difficulty — that for several applicants the conditions had been prohibitive. They were somehow simply afraid. It sounded dull — it sounded strange; and all the more so because of his main condition."

"Which was — ?"

"That she should never trouble him — but never, never: neither appeal nor complain nor write about anything; only meet all questions herself, receive all moneys from his solicitor, take the whole thing over and let him alone. She promised to do this, and she mentioned to me that when, for a moment, disburdened, delighted, he held her hand, thanking her for the sacrifice, she already felt rewarded."

"But was that all her reward?" one of the ladies asked.

"She never saw him again."

"Oh!" said the lady; which, as our friend immediately again left us, was the only other word of importance contributed to the subject till, the next night, by the corner of the hearth, in the best chair, he opened the faded red cover of a thin old-fashioned gilt-edged album. The whole thing took indeed more nights than one, but on the first occasion the same lady put another question. "What's your title?"

"I have n't one."

"Oh *I* have!" I said. But Douglas, without heeding me, had begun to read with a fine clearness that was like a rendering to the ear of the beauty of his author's hand.

I°

I remember the whole beginning as a succession of flights and drops, a little see-saw of the right throbs and the wrong. After rising, in town, to meet his appeal I had at all events a couple of very bad days — found all my doubts bristle again, felt indeed sure I had made a mistake. In this state of mind I spent the long hours of bumping swinging coach that carried me to the stopping-place at which I was to be met by a vehicle from the house. This convenience, I was told, had been ordered, and I found, toward the close of the June afternoon, a commodious fly° in waiting for me. Driving at that hour, on a lovely day, through a country the summer sweetness of which served as a friendly welcome, my fortitude revived and, as we turned into the avenue, took a flight that was probably but a proof of the point to which it had sunk. I suppose I had expected, or had dreaded, something so dreary that what greeted me was a good surprise. I remember as a thoroughly pleasant impression the broad clear front, its open windows and fresh curtains and the pair of maids looking out; I remember the lawn and the bright flowers and the crunch of my wheels on the gravel and the clustered tree-tops over which the rooks° circled and cawed in the golden sky. The scene had a greatness that made it a different affair from my own scant home, and there immediately appeared at the door, with a little girl in her hand, a civil person who dropped me as decent a curtsey as if I had been the mistress or a distinguished visitor. I had received in Harley Street a narrower notion of the place, and that, as I recalled it, made me think the proprietor still more of a gentleman, suggested that what I was to enjoy might be a matter beyond his promise.

I had no drop again till the next day, for I was carried triumphantly through the following hours by my introduction to the younger of my pupils. The little girl who accompanied Mrs. Grose affected me on the spot as a creature too charming not to make it a great fortune to have to do with her. She was the most beautiful child I had ever seen, and I afterwards wondered why my employer had n't made more of a point to me of this. I slept little that night — I was too much excited; and this astonished me too, I recollect, remained with me, adding to my sense of the liberality with which I was treated. The large impressive room, one of the best in the house, the great state bed, as I almost felt it, the figured full draperies, the long glasses° in which, for the first time, I could see myself from head to foot, all struck me — like the wonderful appeal

I: The second weekly *Collier's* installment began here.   **commodious fly:** Large horse-drawn carriage.   **rooks:** Black crows.   **glasses:** Mirrors.

of my small charge — as so many things thrown in. It was thrown in as well, from the first moment, that I should get on with Mrs. Grose in a relation over which, on my way, in the coach, I fear I had rather brooded. The one appearance indeed that in this early outlook might have made me shrink again was that of her being so inordinately glad to see me. I felt within half an hour that she was so glad — stout simple plain clean wholesome woman — as to be positively on her guard against showing it too much. I wondered even then a little why she should wish *not* to show it, and that, with reflexion, with suspicion, might of course have made me uneasy.

But it was a comfort that there could be no uneasiness in a connexion with anything so beatific as the radiant image of my little girl, the vision of whose angelic beauty had probably more than anything else to do with the restlessness that, before morning, made me several times rise and wander about my room to take in the whole picture and prospect; to watch from my open window the faint summer dawn, to look at such stretches of the rest of the house as I could catch, and to listen, while in the fading dusk the first birds began to twitter, for the possible recurrence of a sound or two, less natural and not without but within, that I had fancied I heard. There had been a moment when I believed I recognised, faint and far, the cry of a child; there had been another when I found myself just consciously starting as at the passage, before my door, of a light footstep. But these fancies were not marked enough not to be thrown off, and it is only in the light, or the gloom, I should rather say, of other and subsequent matters that they now come back to me. To watch, teach, "form" little Flora would too evidently be the making of a happy and useful life. It had been agreed between us downstairs that after this first occasion I should have her as a matter of course at night, her small white bed being already arranged, to that end, in my room. What I had undertaken was the whole care of her, and she had remained just this last time with Mrs. Grose only as an effect of our consideration for my inevitable strangeness and her natural timidity. In spite of this timidity — which the child herself, in the oddest way in the world, had been perfectly frank and brave about, allowing it, without a sign of uncomfortable consciousness, with the deep sweet serenity indeed of one of Raphael's holy infants,° to be discussed, to be imputed to her, and to determine us — I felt quite sure she would presently like me. It was part of what I already liked Mrs. Grose herself for, the

Raphael's holy infants: Angelic children in paintings by the Italian artist Raphael (1483–1520).

pleasure I could see her feel in my admiration and wonder as I sat at supper with four tall candles and with my pupil, in a high chair and a bib, brightly facing me between them over bread and milk. There were naturally things that in Flora's presence could pass between us only as prodigious and gratified looks, obscure and roundabout allusions.

"And the little boy — does he look like her? Is he too so very remarkable?"

One would n't, it was already conveyed between us, too grossly flatter a child. "Oh Miss, *most* remarkable. If you think well of this one!" — and she stood there with a plate in her hand, beaming at our companion, who looked from one of us to the other with placid heavenly eyes that contained nothing to check us.

"Yes; if I do — ?"

"You *will* be carried away by the little gentleman!"

"Well, that, I think, is what I came for — to be carried away. I'm afraid, however," I remember feeling the impulse to add, "I'm rather easily carried away. I was carried away in London!"

I can still see Mrs. Grose's broad face as she took this in. "In Harley Street?"

"In Harley Street."

"Well, Miss, you 're not the first — and you won't be the last."

"Oh I've no pretensions," I could laugh, "to being the only one. My other pupil, at any rate, as I understand, comes back to-morrow?"

"Not to-morrow — Friday, Miss. He arrives, as you did, by the coach, under care of the guard,° and is to be met by the same carriage."

I forthwith wanted to know if the proper as well as the pleasant and friendly thing would n't therefore be that on the arrival of the public conveyance I should await him with his little sister; a proposition to which Mrs. Grose assented so heartily that I somehow took her manner as a kind of comforting pledge — never falsified, thank heaven! — that we should on every question be quite at one. Oh she was glad I was there!

What I felt the next day was, I suppose, nothing that could be fairly called a reaction from the cheer of my arrival; it was probably at the most only a slight oppression produced by a fuller measure of the scale, as I walked round them, gazed up at them, took them in, of my new circumstances. They had, as it were, an extent and mass for which I had not been prepared and in the presence of which I found myself, freshly, a little scared not less than a little proud. Regular lessons, in this agita-

guard: Man who rides with the coach to protect mail and passengers.

tion, certainly suffered some wrong; I reflected that my first duty was, by the gentlest arts I could contrive, to win the child into the sense of knowing me. I spent the day with her out of doors; I arranged with her, to her great satisfaction, that it should be she, she only, who might show me the place. She showed it step by step and room by room and secret by secret, with droll delightful childish talk about it and with the result, in half an hour, of our becoming tremendous friends. Young as she was I was struck, throughout our little tour, with her confidence and courage, with the way, in empty chambers and dull corridors, on crooked staircases that made me pause and even on the summit of an old machicolated° square tower that made me dizzy, her morning music, her disposition to tell me so many more things than she asked, rang out and led me on. I have not seen Bly since the day I left it, and I dare say that to my present older and more informed eyes it would show a very reduced importance. But as my little conductress, with her hair of gold and her frock of blue, danced before me round corners and pattered down passages, I had the view of a castle of romance inhabited by a rosy sprite, such a place as would somehow, for diversion of the young idea, take all colour out of story-books and fairy-tales. Was n't it just a story-book over which I had fallen a-doze and a-dream? No; it was a big ugly antique but convenient house, embodying a few features of a building still older, half-displaced and half-utilised, in which I had the fancy of our being almost as lost as a handful of passengers in a great drifting ship. Well, I was strangely at the helm!

II

This came home to me when, two days later, I drove over with Flora to meet, as Mrs. Grose said, the little gentleman; and all the more for an incident that, presenting itself the second evening, had deeply disconcerted me. The first day had been, on the whole, as I have expressed, reassuring; but I was to see it wind up to a change of note. The postbag that evening — it came late — contained a letter for me which, however, in the hand of my employer, I found to be composed but of a few words enclosing another, addressed to himself, with a seal still unbroken. "This, I recognise, is from the head-master, and the head-master's an awful bore. Read him, please; deal with him; but mind you don't report. Not a word. I'm off!" I broke the seal with a great effort — so

machicolated: Provided with holes through which the defenders of a castle might drop rocks, coals, or hot liquids on attackers below.

great a one that I was a long time coming to it; took the unopened missive at last up to my room and only attacked it just before going to bed. I had better have let it wait till morning, for it gave me a second sleepless night. With no counsel to take, the next day, I was full of distress; and it finally got so the better of me that I determined to open myself at least to Mrs. Grose.

"What does it mean? The child's dismissed his school."°

She gave me a look that I remarked at the moment; then, visibly, with a quick blankness, seemed to try to take it back. "But are n't they all — ?"

"Sent home — yes. But only for the holidays. Miles may never go back at all."

Consciously, under my attention, she reddened. "They won't take him?"

"They absolutely decline."

At this she raised her eyes, which she had turned from me; I saw them fill with good tears. "What has he done?"

I cast about; then I judged best simply to hand her my document — which, however, had the effect of making her, without taking it, simply put her hands behind her. She shook her head sadly. "Such things are not for me, Miss."

My counsellor could n't read! I winced at my mistake, which I attenuated as I could, and opened the letter again to repeat it to her; then, faltering in the act and folding it up once more, I put it back in my pocket. "Is he really *bad*?"

The tears were still in her eyes. "Do the gentlemen say so?"

"They go into no particulars. They simply express their regret that it should be impossible to keep him. That can have but one meaning." Mrs. Grose listened with dumb emotion; she forbore to ask me what this meaning might be; so that, presently, to put the thing with some coherence and with the mere aid of her presence to my own mind, I went on: "That he's an injury to the others."

At this, with one of the quick turns of simple folk, she suddenly flamed up. "Master Miles! — *him* an injury?"

There was such a flood of good faith in it that, though I had not yet seen the child, my very fears made me jump to the absurdity of the idea. I found myself, to meet my friend the better, offering it, on the spot, sarcastically. "To his poor little innocent mates!"

---

dismissed his school: Been expelled from the boarding school he has been attending.

"It's too dreadful," cried Mrs. Grose, "to say such cruel things! Why he's scarce ten years old."

"Yes, yes; it would be incredible."

She was evidently grateful for such a profession. "See him, Miss, first. *Then* believe it!" I felt forthwith a new impatience to see him; it was the beginning of a curiosity that, all the next hours, was to deepen almost to pain. Mrs. Grose was aware, I could judge, of what she had produced in me, and she followed it up with assurance. "You might as well believe it of the little lady. Bless her," she added the next moment — "*look* at her!"

I turned and saw that Flora, whom, ten minutes before, I had established in the schoolroom with a sheet of white paper, a pencil and a copy of nice "round O's,"° now presented herself to view at the open door. She expressed in her little way an extraordinary detachment from disagreeable duties, looking at me, however, with a great childish light that seemed to offer it as a mere result of the affection she had conceived for my person, which had rendered necessary that she should follow me. I needed nothing more than this to feel the full force of Mrs. Grose's comparison, and, catching my pupil in my arms, covered her with kisses in which there was a sob of atonement.

None the less, the rest of the day, I watched for further occasion to approach my colleague, especially as, toward evening, I began to fancy she rather sought to avoid me. I overtook her, I remember, on the staircase; we went down together and at the bottom I detained her, holding her there with a hand on her arm. "I take what you said to me at noon as a declaration that *you've* never known him to be bad."

She threw back her head; she had clearly by this time, and very honestly, adopted an attitude. "Oh never known him — I don't pretend *that!*"

I was upset again. "Then you *have* known him — ?"

"Yes indeed, Miss, thank God!"

On reflexion I accepted this. "You mean that a boy who never is — ?"

"Is no boy for *me!*"

I held her tighter. "You like them with the spirit to be naughty?" Then, keeping pace with her answer, "So do I!" I eagerly brought out. "But not to the degree to contaminate — "

"To contaminate?" — my big word left her at a loss.

I explained it. "To corrupt."

"round O's": The governess had set Flora the task of practicing her penmanship in anticipation of learning to read and write.

She stared, taking my meaning in; but it produced in her an odd laugh. "Are you afraid he'll corrupt *you?*" She put the question with such a fine bold humour that with a laugh, a little silly doubtless, to match her own, I gave way for the time to the apprehension of ridicule.

But the next day, as the hour for my drive approached, I cropped up in another place. "What was the lady who was here before?"

"The last governess? She was also young and pretty — almost as young and almost as pretty, Miss, even as you."

"Ah then I hope her youth and her beauty helped her!" I recollect throwing off. "He seems to like us young and pretty!"

"Oh he *did,*" Mrs. Grose assented: "it was the way he liked every one!" She had no sooner spoken indeed than she caught herself up. "I mean that's *his* way — the master's."

I was struck. "But of whom did you speak first?"

She looked blank, but she coloured. "Why of *him.*"

"Of the master?"

"Of who else?"

There was so obviously no one else that the next moment I had lost my impression of her having accidentally said more than she meant; and I merely asked what I wanted to know. "Did *she* see anything in the boy — ?"

"That was n't right? She never told me."

I had a scruple, but I overcame it. "Was she careful — particular?"

Mrs. Grose appeared to try to be conscientious. "About some things — yes."

"But not about all?"

Again she considered. "Well, Miss — she's gone. I won't tell tales."

"I quite understand your feeling," I hastened to reply; but I thought it after an instant not opposed to this concession to pursue: "Did she die here?"

"No — she went off."

I don't know what there was in this brevity of Mrs. Grose's that struck me as ambiguous. "Went off to die?" Mrs. Grose looked straight out of the window, but I felt that, hypothetically, I had a right to know what young persons engaged for Bly were expected to do. "She was taken ill, you mean, and went home?"

"She was not taken ill, so far as appeared, in this house. She left it, at the end of the year, to go home, as she said, for a short holiday, to which the time she had put in had certainly given her a right. We had then a young woman — a nursemaid who had stayed on and who was a good girl and clever; and *she* took the children altogether for the interval. But our young lady never came back, and at the very moment I was expecting her I heard from the master that she was dead."

I turned this over. "But of what?"

"He never told me! But please, Miss," said Mrs. Grose, "I must get to my work."

III°

Her thus turning her back on me was fortunately not, for my just preoccupations, a snub that could check the growth of our mutual esteem. We met, after I had brought home little Miles, more intimately than ever on the ground of my stupefaction, my general emotion: so monstrous was I then ready to pronounce it that such a child as had now been revealed to me should be under an interdict.° I was a little late on the scene of his arrival, and I felt, as he stood wistfully looking out for me before the door of the inn at which the coach had put him down, that I had seen him on the instant, without and within, in the great glow of freshness, the same positive fragrance of purity, in which I had from the first moment seen his little sister. He was incredibly beautiful, and Mrs. Grose had put her finger on it: everything but a sort of passion of tenderness for him was swept away by his presence. What I then and there took him to my heart for was something divine that I have never found to the same degree in any child — his indescribable little air of knowing nothing in the world but love. It would have been impossible to carry a bad name with a greater sweetness of innocence, and by the time I had got back to Bly with him I remained merely bewildered — so far, that is, as I was not outraged — by the sense of the horrible letter locked up in one of the drawers of my room. As soon as I could compass a private word with Mrs. Grose I declared to her that it was grotesque.

She promptly understood me. "You mean the cruel charge — ?"

"It does n't live an instant. My dear woman, *look* at him!"

She smiled at my pretension to have discovered his charm. "I assure you, Miss, I do nothing else! What will you say then?" she immediately added.

"In answer to the letter?" I had made up my mind. "Nothing at all."

"And to his uncle?"

I was incisive. "Nothing at all."

"And to the boy himself?"

III: The third weekly *Collier's* installment began here.   **interdict:** Excommunication or expulsion from school.

I was wonderful. "Nothing at all."

She gave with her apron a great wipe to her mouth. "Then I'll stand by you. We'll see it out."

"We'll see it out!" I ardently echoed, giving her my hand to make it a vow.

She held me there a moment, then whisked up her apron again with her detached hand. "Would you mind, Miss, if I used the freedom — "

"To kiss me? No!" I took the good creature in my arms and after we had embraced like sisters felt still more fortified and indignant.

This at all events was for the time: a time so full that as I recall the way it went it reminds me of all the art I now need to make it a little distinct. What I look back at with amazement is the situation I accepted. I had undertaken, with my companion, to see it out, and I was under a charm apparently that could smooth away the extent and the far and difficult connexions of such an effort. I was lifted aloft on a great wave of infatuation and pity. I found it simple, in my ignorance, my confusion, and perhaps my conceit, to assume that I could deal with a boy whose education for the world was all on the point of beginning. I am unable even to remember at this day what proposal I framed for the end of his holidays and the resumption of his studies. Lessons with me indeed, that charming summer, we all had a theory that he was to have; but I now feel that for weeks the lessons must have been rather my own. I learnt something — at first certainly — that had not been one of the teachings of my small smothered life; learnt to be amused, and even amusing, and not to think for the morrow. It was the first time, in a manner, that I had known space and air and freedom, all the music of summer and all the mystery of nature. And then there was consideration — and consideration was sweet. Oh it was a trap — not designed but deep — to my imagination, to my delicacy, perhaps to my vanity; to whatever in me was most excitable. The best way to picture it all is to say that I was off my guard. They gave me so little trouble — they were of a gentleness so extraordinary. I used to speculate — but even this with a dim disconnectedness — as to how the rough future (for all futures are rough!) would handle them and might bruise them. They had the bloom of health and happiness; and yet, as if I had been in charge of a pair of little grandees,° of princes of the blood, for whom everything, to be right, would have to be fenced about and ordered and arranged, the only form that in my fancy the after-years could take for them was that of a romantic, a really royal extension of the garden and the park. It may

grandees: Persons of high nobility or importance.

be of course above all that what suddenly broke into this gives the previous time a charm of stillness — that hush in which something gathers
or crouches. The change was actually like the spring of a beast.

In the first weeks the days were long; they often, at their finest, gave
me what I used to call my own hour, the hour when, for my pupils,
tea-time and bed-time having come and gone, I had before my final
retirement a small interval alone. Much as I liked my companions this
hour was the thing in the day I liked most; and I liked it best of all when,
as the light faded — or rather, I should say, the day lingered and the last
calls of the last birds sounded, in a flushed sky, from the old trees — I
could take a turn into the grounds and enjoy, almost with a sense of
property that amused and flattered me, the beauty and dignity of the
place. It was a pleasure at these moments to feel myself tranquil and
justified; doubtless perhaps also to reflect that by my discretion, my
quiet good sense and general high propriety, I was giving pleasure — if
he ever thought of it! — to the person to whose pressure I had yielded.
What I was doing was what he had earnestly hoped and directly asked of
me, and that I *could*, after all, do it proved even a greater joy than I had
expected. I dare say I fancied myself in short a remarkable young
woman and took comfort in the faith that this would more publicly
appear. Well, I needed to be remarkable to offer a front to the remarkable things that presently gave their first sign.

It was plump, one afternoon, in the middle of my very hour: the
children were tucked away and I had come out for my stroll. One of the
thoughts that, as I don't in the least shrink now from noting, used to be
with me in these wanderings was that it would be as charming as a
charming story suddenly to meet some one. Some one would appear
there at the turn of a path and would stand before me and smile and
approve. I did n't ask more than that — I only asked that he should
know; and the only way to be sure he knew would be to see it, and the
kind light of it, in his handsome face. That was exactly present to me —
by which I mean the face was — when, on the first of these occasions,
at the end of a long June day, I stopped short on emerging from one of
the plantations° and coming into view of the house. What arrested me
on the spot — and with a shock much greater than any vision had allowed for — was the sense that my imagination had, in a flash, turned
real. He did stand there! — but high up, beyond the lawn and at the
very top of the tower to which, on that first morning, little Flora had
conducted me. This tower was one of a pair — square incongruous

---

plantations: Groves or gardens.

crenellated° structures — that were distinguished, for some reason, though I could see little difference, as the new and the old. They flanked opposite ends of the house and were probably architectural absurdities, redeemed in a measure indeed by not being wholly disengaged nor of a height too pretentious, dating, in their gingerbread antiquity, from a romantic revival that was already a respectable past. I admired them, had fancies about them, for we could all profit in a degree, especially when they loomed through the dusk, by the grandeur of their actual battlements°; yet it was not at such an elevation that the figure I had so often invoked seemed most in place.

It produced in me, this figure, in the clear twilight, I remember, two distinct gasps of emotion, which were, sharply, the shock of my first and that of my second surprise. My second was a violent perception of the mistake of my first: the man who met my eyes was not the person I had precipitately supposed. There came to me thus a bewilderment of vision of which, after these years, there is no living view that I can hope to give. An unknown man in a lonely place is a permitted object of fear to a young woman privately bred; and the figure that faced me was — a few more seconds assured me — as little any one else I knew as it was the image that had been in my mind. I had not seen it in Harley Street — I had not seen it anywhere. The place moreover, in the strangest way in the world, had on the instant and by the very fact of its appearance become a solitude. To me at least, making my statement here with a deliberation with which I have never made it, the whole feeling of the moment returns. It was as if, while I took in, what I did take in, all the rest of the scene had been stricken with death. I can hear again, as I write, the intense hush in which the sounds of evening dropped. The rooks stopped cawing in the golden sky and the friendly hour lost for the unspeakable minute all its voice. But there was no other change in nature, unless indeed it were a change that I saw with a stranger sharpness. The gold was still in the sky, the clearness in the air, and the man who looked at me over the battlements was as definite as a picture in a frame. That's how I thought, with extraordinary quickness, of each person he might have been and that he was n't. We were confronted across our distance quite long enough for me to ask myself with intensity who then he was and to feel, as an effect of my inability to say, a wonder that in a few seconds more became intense.

crenellated: Notched as on an old castle wall to provide protection for archers and other defenders.   **battlements:** Fortifications atop a tower wall, usually with open spaces for shooting.

The great question,° or one of these, is afterwards, I know, with regard to certain matters, the question of how long they have lasted. Well, this matter of mine, think what you will of it, lasted while I caught at a dozen possibilities, none of which made a difference for the better, that I could see, in there having been in the house — and for how long, above all? — a person of whom I was in ignorance. It lasted while I just bridled a little with the sense of how my office seemed to require that there should be no such ignorance and no such person. It lasted while this visitant, at all events — and there was a touch of the strange freedom, as I remember, in the sign of familiarity of his wearing no hat — seemed to fix me, from his position, with just the question, just the scrutiny through the fading light, that his own presence provoked. We were too far apart to call to each other, but there was a moment at which, at shorter range, some challenge between us, breaking the hush, would have been the right result of our straight mutual stare. He was in one of the angles, the one away from the house, very erect, as it struck me, and with both hands on the ledge. So I saw him as I see the letters I form on this page; then, exactly, after a minute, as if to add to the spectacle, he slowly changed his place — passed, looking at me hard all the while, to the opposite corner of the platform. Yes, it was intense to me that during this transit he never took his eyes from me, and I can see at this moment the way his hand, as he went, moved from one of the crenellations to the next. He stopped at the other corner, but less long, and even as he turned away still markedly fixed me. He turned away; that was all I knew.

IV°

It was not that I did n't wait, on this occasion, for more, since I was as deeply rooted as shaken. Was there a "secret" at Bly — a mystery of Udolpho° or an insane, an unmentionable relative° kept in unsuspected confinement? I can't say how long I turned it over, or how long, in a confusion of curiosity and dread, I remained where I had had my collision; I only recall that when I re-entered the house darkness had quite

---

The great question: Probably a reference to one of the standard questions asked by psychical researchers of people who claimed to have seen a ghost: "How long did the apparition remain there?" **IV:** The fourth weekly *Collier's* installment and *Part Second* began here. **mystery of Udolpho:** An allusion to Ann Radcliffe's famous gothic novel *The Mysteries of Udolpho* (1794), in which the heroine is carried away to a gloomy castle. **an unmentionable relative:** Almost certainly an allusion to Bertha, Rochester's insane wife, hidden upstairs in Charlotte Brontë's *Jane Eyre* (1847).

closed in. Agitation, in the interval, certainly had held me and driven me, for I must, in circling about the place, have walked three miles; but I was to be later on so much more overwhelmed that this mere dawn of alarm was a comparatively human chill. The most singular part of it in fact — singular as the rest had been — was the part I became, in the hall, aware of in meeting Mrs. Grose. This picture comes back to me in the general train — the impression, as I received it on my return, of the wide white panelled space, bright in the lamplight and with its portraits and red carpet, and of the good surprised look of my friend, which immediately told me she had missed me. It came to me straightway, under her contact, that, with plain heartiness, mere relieved anxiety at my appearance, she knew nothing whatever that could bear upon the incident I had there ready for her. I had not suspected in advance that her comfortable face would pull me up, and I somehow measured the importance of what I had seen by my thus finding myself hesitate to mention it. Scarce anything in the whole history seems to me so odd as this fact that my real beginning of fear was one, as I may say, with the instinct of sparing my companion. On the spot, accordingly, in the pleasant hall and with her eyes on me, I, for a reason that I could n't then have phrased, achieved an inward revolution — offered a vague pretext for my lateness and, with the plea of the beauty of the night and of the heavy dew and wet feet, went as soon as possible to my room.

Here it was another affair; here, for many days after, it was a queer affair enough. There were hours, from day to day — or at least there were moments, snatched even from clear duties — when I had to shut myself up to think. It was n't so much yet that I was more nervous than I could bear to be as that I was remarkably afraid of becoming so; for the truth I had now to turn over was simply and clearly the truth that I could arrive at no account whatever of the visitor with whom I had been so inexplicably and yet, as it seemed to me, so intimately concerned. It took me little time to see that I might easily sound, without forms of enquiry and without exciting remark, any domestic complication. The shock I had suffered must have sharpened all my senses; I felt sure, at the end of three days and as the result of mere closer attention, that I had not been practised upon by the servants nor made the object of any "game." Of whatever it was that I knew nothing was known around me. There was but one sane inference: some one had taken a liberty rather monstrous. That was what, repeatedly, I dipped into my room and locked the door to say to myself. We had been, collectively, subject to an intrusion; some unscrupulous traveller, curious in old houses, had made his way in unobserved, enjoyed the prospect from the best point of view and then stolen out as he came. If he had given me such a bold hard stare, that was but a part of his indiscretion. The good thing, after all, was that we should surely see no more of him.

This was not so good a thing, I admit, as not to leave me to judge that what, essentially, made nothing else much signify was simply my charming work. My charming work was just my life with Miles and Flora, and through nothing could I so like it as through feeling that to throw myself into it was to throw myself out of my trouble. The attraction of my small charges was a constant joy, leading me to wonder afresh at the vanity of my original fears, the distaste I had begun by entertaining for the probable grey prose of my office. There was to be no grey prose, it appeared, and no long grind; so how could work not be charming that presented itself as daily beauty? It was all the romance of the nursery and the poetry of the schoolroom. I don't mean by this of course that we studied only fiction and verse; I mean that I can express no otherwise the sort of interest my companions inspired. How can I describe that except by saying that instead of growing deadly used to them — and it's a marvel for a governess: I call the sisterhood to witness! — I made constant fresh discoveries. There was one direction, assuredly, in which these discoveries stopped: deep obscurity continued to cover the region of the boy's conduct at school. It had been promptly given me, I have noted, to face that mystery without a pang. Perhaps even it would be nearer the truth to say that — without a word — he himself had cleared it up. He had made the whole charge absurd. My conclusion bloomed there with the real rose-flush of his innocence: he was only too fine and fair for the little horrid unclean school-world, and he had paid a price for it. I reflected acutely that the sense of such individual differences, such superiorities of quality, always, on the part of the majority — which could include even stupid sordid head-masters — turns infallibly to the vindictive.

Both the children had a gentleness — it was their only fault, and it never made Miles a muff° — that kept them (how shall I express it?) almost impersonal and certainly quite unpunishable. They were like those cherubs of the anecdote who had — morally at any rate — nothing to whack!° I remember feeling with Miles in especial as if he had

---

muff: A sissy; an unmanly boy.   **nothing to whack:** A humorous reference to angels so immaterial that they have no bottoms to spank and so good that there could be nothing to spank them for.

had, as it were, nothing to call even an infinitesimal history. We expect of a small child scant enough "antecedents," but there was in this beautiful little boy something extraordinarily sensitive, yet extraordinarily happy, that, more than in any creature of his age I have seen, struck me as beginning anew each day. He had never for a second suffered. I took this as a direct disproof of his having really been chastised. If he had been wicked he would have "caught" it, and I should have caught it by the rebound — I should have found the trace, should have felt the wound and the dishonour. I could reconstitute nothing at all, and he was therefore an angel. He never spoke of his school, never mentioned a comrade or a master; and I, for my part, was quite too much disgusted to allude to them. Of course I was under the spell, and the wonderful part is that, even at the time, I perfectly knew I was. But I gave myself up to it; it was an antidote to any pain, and I had more pains than one. I was in receipt in these days of disturbing letters from home, where things were not going well. But with this joy of my children what things in the world mattered? That was the question I used to put to my scrappy retirements. I was dazzled by their loveliness.

There was a Sunday — to get on — when it rained with such force and for so many hours that there could be no procession to church; in consequence of which, as the day declined, I had arranged with Mrs. Grose that, should the evening show improvement, we would attend together the late service. The rain happily stopped, and I prepared for our walk, which, through the park and by the good road to the village, would be a matter of twenty minutes. Coming downstairs to meet my colleague in the hall, I remembered a pair of gloves that had required three stitches and that had received them — with a publicity perhaps not edifying — while I sat with the children at their tea, served on Sundays, by exception, in that cold clean temple of mahogany and brass, the "grown-up" dining-room. The gloves had been dropped there, and I turned in to recover them. The day was grey enough, but the afternoon light still lingered, and it enabled me, on crossing the threshold, not only to recognise, on a chair near the wide window, then closed, the articles I wanted, but to become aware of a person on the other side of the window and looking straight in. One step into the room had sufficed; my vision was instantaneous; it was all there. The person looking straight in was the person who had already appeared to me. He appeared thus again with I won't say greater distinctness, for that was impossible, but with a nearness that represented a forward stride in our intercourse° and made me, as I met him, catch my breath and turn cold. He was the same — he was the same, and seen, this time, as he had been seen before, from the waist up, the window, though the dining-room was on the ground floor, not going down to the terrace on which he stood. His face was close to the glass, yet the effect of this better view was, strangely, just to show me how intense the former had been. He remained but a few seconds — long enough to convince me he also saw and recognised; but it was as if I had been looking at him for years and had known him always. Something, however, happened this time that had not happened before; his stare into my face, through the glass and across the room, was as deep and hard as then, but it quitted me for a moment during which I could still watch it, see it fix successively several other things. On the spot there came to me the added shock of a certitude that it was not for me he had come. He had come for some one else.

The flash of this knowledge — for it was knowledge in the midst of dread — produced in me the most extraordinary effect, starting, as I stood there, a sudden vibration of duty and courage. I say courage because I was beyond all doubt already far gone. I bounded straight out of the door again, reached that of the house, got in an instant upon the drive and, passing along the terrace as fast as I could rush, turned a corner and came full in sight. But it was in sight of nothing now — my visitor had vanished. I stopped, almost dropped, with the real relief of this; but I took in the whole scene — I gave him time to reappear. I call it time, but how long was it? I can't speak to the purpose to-day of the duration of these things. That kind of measure must have left me: they could n't have lasted as they actually appeared to me to last. The terrace and the whole place, the lawn and the garden beyond it, all I could see of the park, were empty with a great emptiness. There were shrubberies and big trees, but I remember the clear assurance I felt that none of them concealed him. He was there or was not there: not there if I did n't see him. I got hold of this; then, instinctively, instead of returning as I had come, went to the window. It was confusedly present to me that I ought to place myself where he had stood. I did so; I applied my face to the pane and looked, as he had looked, into the room. As if, at this moment, to show me exactly what his range had been, Mrs. Grose,

---

intercourse: Dealings or communications between persons or groups; interchange of thoughts and feelings. The word had not yet come to carry overtones of "sexual intercourse."

as I had done for himself just before, came in from the hall. With this I
had the full image of a repetition of what had already occurred. She saw
me as I had seen my own visitant; she pulled up short as I had done; I
gave her something of the shock that I had received. She turned white,
and this made me ask myself if I had blanched as much. She stared, in
short, and retreated just on *my* lines, and I knew she had then passed
out and come round to me and that I should presently meet her. I remained where I was, and while I waited I thought of more things than
one. But there's only one I take space to mention. I wondered why *she*
should be scared.

V

Oh she let me know as soon as, round the corner of the house,
she loomed again into view. "What in the name of goodness is the matter — ?" She was now flushed and out of breath.

I said nothing till she came quite near. "With me?" I must have
made a wonderful face. "Do I show it?"

"You're as white as a sheet. You look awful."

I considered; I could meet on this, without scruple, any degree of
innocence. My need to respect the bloom of Mrs. Grose's had dropped,
without a rustle, from my shoulders, and if I wavered for the instant it
was not with what I kept back. I put out my hand to her and she took
it; I held her hard a little, liking to feel her close to me. There was a kind
of support in the shy heave of her surprise. "You came for me for
church, of course, but I can't go."

"Has anything happened?"

"Yes. You must know now. Did I look very queer?"

"Through this window? Dreadful!"

"Well," I said, "I've been frightened." Mrs. Grose's eyes expressed
plainly that *she* had no wish to be, yet also that she knew too well her
place not to be ready to share with me any marked inconvenience. Oh it
was quite settled that she *must* share! "Just what you saw from the
dining-room a minute ago was the effect of that. What *I* saw — just
before — was much worse."

Her hand tightened. "What was it?"

"An extraordinary man. Looking in."

"What extraordinary man?"

"I have n't the least idea."

Mrs. Grose gazed round us in vain. "Then where is he gone?"

"I know still less."

"Have you seen him before?"

"Yes — once. On the old tower."

She could only look at me harder. "Do you mean he's a stranger?"

"Oh very much!"

"Yet you did n't tell me?"

"No — for reasons. But now that you've guessed — "

Mrs. Grose's round eyes encountered this charge. "Ah I have n't guessed!" she said very simply. "How can I if *you* don't imagine?"

"I don't in the very least."

"You've seen him nowhere but on the tower?"

"And on this spot just now."

Mrs. Grose looked round again. "What was he doing on the tower?"

"Only standing there and looking down at me."

She thought a minute. "Was he a gentleman?"

I found I had no need to think. "No." She gazed in deeper wonder. "No."

"Then nobody about the place? Nobody from the village?"

"Nobody — nobody. I did n't tell you, but I made sure."

She breathed a vague relief: this was, oddly, so much to the good. It only went indeed a little way. "But if he is n't a gentleman — "

"What *is* he? He's a horror."

"A horror?"

"He's — God help me if I know *what* he is!"

Mrs. Grose looked round once more; she fixed her eyes on the duskier distance and then, pulling herself together, turned to me with full inconsequence. "It's time we should be at church."

"Oh I'm not fit for church!"

"Won't it do you good?"

"It won't do *them* — !" I nodded at the house.

"The children?"

"I can't leave them now."

"You're afraid — ?"

I spoke boldly. "I'm afraid of *him*."

Mrs. Grose's large face showed me, at this, for the first time, the far-away faint glimmer of a consciousness more acute: I somehow made out in it the delayed dawn of an idea I myself had not given her and that was as yet quite obscure to me. It comes back to me that I thought instantly of this as something I could get from her; and I felt it to be connected with the desire she presently showed to know more. "When was it — on the tower?"

"About the middle of the month. At this same hour."

"Almost at dark," said Mrs. Grose.

"Oh no, not nearly. I saw him as I see you."

"Then how did he get in?"

"And how did he get out?"° I laughed. "I had no opportunity to ask him! This evening, you see," I pursued, "he has not been able to get in."

"He only peeps?"

"I hope it will be confined to that!" She had now let go my hand; she turned away a little. I waited an instant; then I brought out: "Go to church. Good-bye. I must watch."

Slowly she faced me again. "Do you fear for them?"

We met in another long look. "Don't *you?*" Instead of answering she came nearer to the window and, for a minute, applied her face to the glass. "You see how he could see," I meanwhile went on.

She did n't move. "How long was he here?"

"Till I came out. I came to meet him."

Mrs. Grose at last turned round, and there was still more in her face. "*I* could n't have come out."

"Neither could I!" I laughed again. "But I did come. I've my duty."

"So have I mine," she replied; after which she added: "What's he like?"

"I've been dying to tell you. But he's like nobody."

"Nobody?" she echoed.

"He has no hat." Then seeing in her face that she already, in this, with a deeper dismay, found a touch of picture, I quickly added stroke to stroke. "He has red hair, very red, close-curling, and a pale face, long in shape, with straight good features and little rather queer whiskers that are as red as his hair. His eyebrows are somehow darker; they look particularly arched and as if they might move a good deal. His eyes are sharp, strange — awfully; but I only know clearly that they're rather small and very fixed. His mouth's wide, and his lips are thin, and except

---

Then how . . . did he get out? This exchange echoes a line in a ghost narrative reported in the 1885 *Proceedings of the Society for Psychical Research* 3 (1885): 126–32. Mrs. Vatas-Simpson's narrative shows a number of parallels that suggest that it might have served as a source for some features of James's story: It is about a woman left in a house with two small children; she hears the unexplained cry of an infant; she has a female cohort; she reports seeing two ghosts, one male figure and one female; and so on. More specifically, she writes of being frightened by a strange figure in her house and wonders, "Now, then, how did that man get in? — or rather, how did he get *out?*"

for his little whiskers he's quite clean-shaven. He gives me a sort of sense of looking like an actor."

"An actor!" It was impossible to resemble one less, at least, than Mrs. Grose at that moment.

"I've never seen one, but so I suppose them. He's tall, active, erect," I continued, "but never — no, never! — a gentleman."

My companion's face had blanched as I went on; her round eyes started and her mild mouth gaped. "A gentleman?" she gasped, confounded, stupefied: "a gentleman *he?*"

"You know him then?"

She visibly tried to hold herself. "But he *is* handsome?"

I saw the way to help her. "Remarkably!"

"And dressed — ?"

"In somebody's clothes. They're smart, but they're not his own."

She broke into a breathless affirmative groan. "They're the master's!"

I caught it up. "You *do* know him?"

She faltered but a second. "Quint!" she cried.

"Quint?"

"Peter Quint° — his own man,° his valet, when he was here!"

"When the master was?"

Gaping still, but meeting me, she pieced it all together. "He never wore his hat, but he did wear — well, there were waistcoats missed! They were both here — last year. Then the master went, and Quint was alone."

I followed, but halting a little. "Alone?"

"Alone with *us*." Then as from a deeper depth, "In charge," she added.

"And what became of him?"

She hung fire so long that I was still more mystified. "He went too," she brought out at last.

"Went where?"

Peter Quint: Perhaps an allusion to Peter Quince in Shakespeare's *A Midsummer Night's Dream?*   **his own man:** This scene is one of those most discussed by scholars trying to explain *The Turn of the Screw*. For scholars who read it as a ghost story this scene is proof that the governess really did see a ghost; after all, she has never heard of Peter Quint, has not known of the existence at Bly of the uncle's valet, yet is able to give to Mrs. Grose the very detailed description by which she identifies him. For scholars who read the story as a case study of a neurotic governess who merely imagines that she sees ghosts, the scene is proof that she had earlier learned from someone else about Quint and his appearance, and so is able to convince the gullible Mrs. Grose that he still hovers about.

Her expression, at this, became extraordinary. "God knows where! He died."

"Died?" I almost shrieked.

She seemed fairly to square herself, plant herself more firmly to express the wonder of it. "Yes. Mr. Quint's dead."

VI°

It took of course more than that particular passage to place us together in presence of what we had now to live with as we could, my dreadful liability° to impressions of the order so vividly exemplified, and my companion's knowledge henceforth — a knowledge half consternation and half compassion — of that liability. There had been this evening, after the revelation that left me for an hour so prostrate — there had been for either of us no attendance on any service but a little service of tears and vows, of prayers and promises, a climax to the series of mutual challenges and pledges that had straightway ensued on our retreating together to the schoolroom and shutting ourselves up there to have everything out. The result of our having everything out was simply to reduce our situation to the last rigour of its elements. She herself had seen nothing, not the shadow of a shadow, and nobody in the house but the governess was in the governess's plight; yet she accepted without directly impugning my sanity the truth as I gave it to her, and ended by showing me on this ground an awestricken tenderness, a deference to my more than questionable privilege, of which the very breath has remained with me as that of the sweetest of human charities.

What was settled between us accordingly that night was that we thought we might bear things together; and I was not even sure that in spite of her exemption° it was she who had the best of the burden. I knew at this hour, I think, as well as I knew later, what I was capable of meeting to shelter my pupils; but it took me some time to be wholly sure of what my honest comrade was prepared for to keep terms with so stiff an agreement. I was queer company enough — quite as queer as the company I received; but as I trace over what we went through I see how much common ground we must have found in the one idea that, by good fortune, *could* steady us. It was the idea, the second movement, that led me straight out, as I may say, of the inner chamber of my dread.

VI: The fifth weekly *Collier's* installment began here.   **dreadful liability:** Unwanted ability to see the visible presence of a spirit.   **exemption:** Inability to see the ghost.

I could take the air in the court, at least, and there Mrs. Grose could join me. Perfectly can I recall now the particular way strength came to me before we separated for the night. We had gone over and over every feature of what I had seen.

"He was looking for some one else, you say — some one who was not you?"

"He was looking for little Miles." A portentous clearness now possessed me. "*That's* whom he was looking for."

"But how do you know?"

"I know, I know, I know!" My exaltation grew. "And *you* know, my dear!"

She did n't deny this, but I required, I felt, not even so much telling as that. She took it up again in a moment. "What if *he* should see him?"

"Little Miles? That's what he wants!"

She looked immensely scared again. "The child?"

"Heaven forbid! The man. He wants to appear to *them*." That he might was an awful conception, and yet somehow I could keep it at bay; which moreover, as we lingered there, was what I succeeded in practically proving. I had an absolute certainty that I should see again what I had already seen, but something within me said that by offering myself bravely as the sole subject of such experience, by accepting, by inviting, by surmounting it all, I should serve as an expiatory victim and guard the tranquillity of the rest of the household. The children in especial I should thus fence about and absolutely save. I recall one of the last things I said that night to Mrs. Grose.

"It does strike me that my pupils have never mentioned — !"

She looked at me hard as I musingly pulled up. "His having been here and the time they were with him?"

"The time they were with him, and his name, his presence, his history, in any way. They've never alluded to it."

"Oh the little lady does n't remember. She never heard or knew."

"The circumstances of his death?" I thought with some intensity. "Perhaps not. But Miles would remember — Miles would know."

"Ah don't try him!" broke from Mrs. Grose.

I returned her the look she had given me. "Don't be afraid." I continued to think. "It *is* rather odd."

"That he has never spoken of him?"

"Never by the least reference. And you tell me they were 'great friends.'"

"Oh it was n't *him!*" Mrs. Grose with emphasis declared. "It was

Quint's own fancy. To play with him, I mean — to spoil him." She paused a moment; then she added: "Quint was much too free."

This gave me, straight from my vision of his face — *such* a face! — a sudden sickness of disgust. "Too free with *my* boy?"

"Too free with every one!"

I forbore for the moment to analyse this description further than by the reflexion that a part of it applied to several of the members of the household, of the half-dozen maids and men who were still of our small colony. But there was everything, for our apprehension, in the lucky fact that no discomfortable legend, no perturbation of scullions,° had ever, within any one's memory, attached to the kind old place. It had neither bad name nor ill fame, and Mrs. Grose, most apparently, only desired to cling to me and to quake in silence. I even put her, the very last thing of all, to the test. It was when, at midnight, she had her hand on the school-room door to take leave. "I *have* it from you then — for it's of great importance — that he was definitely and admittedly bad?"

"Oh not admittedly. *I* knew it — but the master did n't."

"And you never told him?"

"Well, he did n't like tale-bearing — he hated complaints. He was terribly short with anything of that kind, and if people were all right to *him* — "

"He would n't be bothered with more?" This squared well enough with my impression of him: he was not a trouble-loving gentleman, nor so very particular perhaps about some of the company he himself kept. All the same, I pressed my informant. "I promise you *I* would have told!"

She felt my discrimination. "I dare say I was wrong. But really I was afraid."

"Afraid of what?"

"Of things that man could do. Quint was so clever — he was so deep."

I took this in still more than I probably showed. "You were n't afraid of anything else? Not of his effect — ?"

"His effect?" she repeated with a face of anguish and waiting while I faltered.

"On innocent little precious lives. They were in your charge."

"No, they were n't in mine!" she roundly and distressfully returned. "The master believed in him and placed him here because he was supposed not to be quite in health and the country air so good for him. So

scullions: Unskilled kitchen workers.

he had everything to say. Yes" — she let me have it — "even about
them."

"Them — that creature?" I had to smother a kind of howl. "And
you could bear it?"

"No. I could n't — and I can't now!" And the poor woman burst
into tears.

A rigid control, from the next day, was, as I have said, to follow
them; yet how often and how passionately, for a week, we came back
together to the subject! Much as we had discussed it that Sunday night,
I was, in the immediate later hours in especial — for it may be imagined
whether I slept — still haunted with the shadow of something she had
not told me. I myself had kept back nothing, but there was a word Mrs.
Grose had kept back. I was sure moreover by morning that this was not
from a failure of frankness, but because on every side there were fears. It
seems to me indeed, in raking it all over, that by the time the morrow's
sun was high I had restlessly read into the facts before us almost all the
meaning they were to receive from subsequent and more cruel occurrences. What they gave me above all was just the sinister figure of the
living man — the dead one would keep a while! — and of the months
he had continuously passed at Bly, which, added up, made a formidable
stretch. The limit of this evil time had arrived only when, on the dawn
of a winter's morning, Peter Quint was found, by a labourer going to
early work, stone dead on the road from the village: a catastrophe explained — superficially at least — by a visible wound to his head; such a
wound as might have been produced (and as, on the final evidence, *had*
been) by a fatal slip, in the dark and after leaving the public-house, on
the steepish icy slope, a wrong path altogether, at the bottom of which
he lay. The icy slope, the turn mistaken at night and in liquor, accounted for much — practically, in the end and after the inquest and
boundless chatter, for everything; but there had been matters in his life,
strange passages and perils, secret disorders, vices more than suspected,
that would have accounted for a good deal more.

I scarce know how to put my story into words that shall be a credible picture of my state of mind; but I was in these days literally able to
find a joy in the extraordinary flight of heroism the occasion demanded
of me. I now saw that I had been asked for a service admirable and
difficult; and there would be a greatness in letting it be seen — oh in the
right quarter! — that I could succeed where many another girl might
have failed. It was an immense help to me — I confess I rather applaud
myself as I look back! — that I saw my response so strongly and so simply. I was there to protect and defend the little creatures in the world

the most bereaved and the most loveable, the appeal of whose helpless-
ness had suddenly become only too explicit, a deep constant ache of
one's own engaged affection. We were cut off, really, together; we were
united in our danger. They had nothing but me, and I — well, I had
them. It was in short a magnificent chance. This chance presented itself
to me in an image richly material. I was a screen — I was to stand before
them. The more I saw the less they would. I began to watch them in a
stifled suspense, a disguised tension, that might well, had it continued
too long, have turned to something like madness. What saved me, as I
now see, was that it turned to another matter altogether. It did n't last
as suspense — it was superseded by horrible proofs. Proofs, I say, yes —
from the moment I really took hold.

This moment dated from an afternoon hour that I happened to
spend in the grounds with the younger of my pupils alone. We had left
Miles indoors, on the red cushion of a deep window-seat; he had wished
to finish a book, and I had been glad to encourage a purpose so laudable
in a young man whose only defect was a certain ingenuity of restlessness. His sister, on the contrary, had been alert to come out, and I
strolled with her half an hour, seeking the shade, for the sun was still
high and the day exceptionally warm. I was aware afresh with her, as we
went, of how, like her brother, she contrived — it was the charming
thing in both children — to let me alone without appearing to drop me
and to accompany me without appearing to oppress. They were never
importunate and yet never listless. My attention to them all really went
to seeing them amuse themselves immensely without me: this was a
spectacle they seemed actively to prepare and that employed me as an
active admirer. I walked in a world of their invention — they had no
occasion whatever to draw upon mine; so that my time was taken only
with being for them some remarkable person or thing that the game of
the moment required and that was merely, thanks to my superior, my
exalted stamp, a happy and highly distinguished sinecure. I forget what
I was on the present occasion; I only remember that I was something
very important and very quiet and that Flora was playing very hard. We
were on the edge of the lake, and, as we had lately begun geography, the
lake was the Sea of Azof.°

Suddenly, amid these elements, I became aware that on the other
side of the Sea of Azof we had an interested spectator. The way this

---

Sea of Azof: An inland sea (now often spelled Azov) on the north or Russian side of the
Black Sea. The governess is having Flora learn a bit of geography by having her imagine
that the pond at Bly is this sea.

knowledge gathered in me was the strangest thing in the world — the strangest, that is, except the very much stranger in which it quickly merged itself. I had sat down with a piece of work° — for I was something or other that could sit — on the old stone bench which overlooked the pond; and in this position I began to take in with certitude and yet without direct vision the presence, a good way off, of a third person. The old trees, the thick shrubbery, made a great and pleasant shade, but it was all suffused with the brightness of the hot still hour. There was no ambiguity in anything; none whatever at least in the conviction I from one moment to another found myself forming as to what I should see straight before me and across the lake as a consequence of raising my eyes. They were attached at this juncture to the stitching in which I was engaged, and I can feel once more the spasm of my effort not to move them till I should so have steadied myself as to be able to make up my mind what to do. There was an alien object in view — a figure whose right of presence I instantly and passionately questioned. I recollect counting over perfectly the possibilities, reminding myself that nothing was more natural for instance than the appearance of one of the men about the place, or even of a messenger, a postman or a tradesman's boy, from the village. That reminder had as little effect on my practical certitude as I was conscious — still even without looking — of its having upon the character and attitude of our visitor. Nothing was more natural than that these things should be the other things they absolutely were not.

Of the positive identity of the apparition I would assure myself as soon as the small clock of my courage should have ticked out the right second; meanwhile, with an effort that was already sharp enough, I transferred my eyes straight to little Flora, who, at the moment, was about ten yards away. My heart had stood still for an instant with the wonder and terror of the question whether she too would see; and I held my breath while I waited for what a cry from her, what some sudden innocent sign either of interest or of alarm, would tell me. I waited, but nothing came; then in the first place — and there is something more dire in this, I feel, than in anything I have to relate — I was determined by a sense that within a minute all spontaneous sounds from her had dropped; and in the second by the circumstance that also within the minute she had, in her play, turned her back to the water. This was her attitude when I at last looked at her — looked with the confirmed conviction that we were still, together, under direct personal notice. She

°**a piece of work:** A bit of knitting or mending.

had picked up a small flat piece of wood which happened to have in it a little hole that had evidently suggested to her the idea of sticking in another fragment that might figure as a mast and make the thing a boat. This second morsel, as I watched her, she was very markedly and intently attempting to tighten in its place. My apprehension of what she was doing sustained me so that after some seconds I felt I was ready for more. Then I again shifted my eyes — I faced what I had to face.

VII

I got hold of Mrs. Grose as soon after this as I could; and I can give no intelligible account of how I fought out the interval. Yet I still hear myself cry as I fairly threw myself into her arms: "They *know* — it's too monstrous: they know, they know!"

"And what on earth — ?" I felt her incredulity as she held me.

"Why all that *we* know — and heaven knows what more besides!" Then as she released me I made it out to her, made it out perhaps only now with full coherency even to myself. "Two hours ago, in the garden" — I could scarce articulate — "Flora *saw!*"

Mrs. Grose took it as she might have taken a blow in the stomach. "She has told you?" she panted.

"Not a word — that's the horror. She kept it to herself! The child of eight,° *that* child!" Unutterable still for me was the stupefaction of it.

Mrs. Grose of course could only gape the wider. "Then how do you know?"

"I was there — I saw with my eyes: saw she was perfectly aware."

"Do you mean aware of *him*?"

"No — of *her*." I was conscious as I spoke that I looked prodigious things, for I got the slow reflexion of them in my companion's face. "Another person — this time; but a figure of quite as unmistakeable horror and evil: a woman in black, pale and dreadful — with such an air also, and such a face! — on the other side of the lake. I was there with the child — quiet for the hour; and in the midst of it she came."

---

child of eight: In the original version published in *Collier's* James had written "child of six." In the first chapter she is said to sit in a high chair and to wear a bib and she is referred to elsewhere as both an "infant" and a "baby." Perhaps because a reader had suggested that at times Flora acts and talks like an older girl, James changed her age to eight in the book version.

"Came how — from where?"

"From where they come from! She just appeared and stood there — but not so near."

"And without coming nearer?"

"Oh for the effect and the feeling she might have been as close as you!"

My friend, with an odd impulse, fell back a step. "Was she some one you've never seen?"

"Never. But some one the child has. Some one *you* have." Then to show how I had thought it all out: "My predecessor — the one who died."

"Miss Jessel?"

"Miss Jessel. You don't believe me?" I pressed.

She turned right and left in her distress. "How can you be sure?"

This drew from me, in the state of my nerves, a flash of impatience. "Then ask Flora — *she's* sure!" But I had no sooner spoken than I caught myself up. "No, for God's sake *don't!* She'll say she is n't — she'll lie!"

Mrs. Grose was not too bewildered instinctively to protest. "Ah how *can* you?"

"Because I'm clear. Flora does n't want me to know."

"It's only then to spare you."

"No, no — there are depths, depths! The more I go over it the more I see in it, and the more I see in it the more I fear. I don't know what I *don't* see, what I *don't* fear!"

Mrs. Grose tried to keep up with me. "You mean you're afraid of seeing her again?"

"Oh no; that's nothing — now!" Then I explained. "It's of *not* seeing her."

But my companion only looked wan. "I don't understand."

"Why, it's that the child may keep it up — and that the child assuredly *will* — without my knowing it."

At the image of this possibility Mrs. Grose for a moment collapsed, yet presently to pull herself together again as from the positive force of the sense of what, should we yield an inch, there would really be to give way to. "Dear, dear — we must keep our heads! And after all, if she does n't mind it — !" She even tried a grim joke. "Perhaps she likes it!"

"Like *such* things — a scrap of an infant!"

"Isn't it just a proof of her blest innocence?" my friend bravely enquired.

She brought me, for the instant, almost round. "Oh we must clutch at *that* — we must cling to it! If it is n't a proof of what you say, it's a proof of — God knows what! For the woman's a horror of horrors."

Mrs. Grose, at this, fixed her eyes a minute on the ground; then at last raising them, "Tell me how you know," she said.

"Then you admit it's what she was?" I cried.

"Tell me how you know," my friend simply repeated.

"Know? By seeing her! By the way she looked."

"At you, do you mean — so wickedly?"

"Dear me, no — I could have borne that. She gave me never a glance. She only fixed the child."

Mrs. Grose tried to see it. "Fixed her?"

"Ah with such awful eyes!"

She stared at mine as if they might really have resembled them. "Do you mean of dislike?"

"God help us, no. Of something much worse."

"Worse than dislike?" — this left her indeed at a loss.

"With a determination — indescribable. With a kind of fury of intention."

I made her turn pale. "Intention?"

"To get hold of her." Mrs. Grose — her eyes just lingering on mine — gave a shudder and walked to the window; and while she stood there looking out I completed my statement. "*That's* what Flora knows."

After a little she turned round. "The person was in black, you say?"

"In mourning — rather poor, almost shabby. But — yes — with extraordinary beauty." I now recognised to what I had at last, stroke by stroke, brought the victim of my confidence, for she quite visibly weighed this. "Oh handsome — very, very," I insisted; "wonderfully handsome. But infamous."

She slowly came back to me. "Miss Jessel — *was* infamous." She once more took my hand in both her own, holding it as tight as if to fortify me against the increase of alarm I might draw from this disclosure. "They were both infamous," she finally said.

So for a little we faced it once more together; and I found absolutely a degree of help in seeing it now so straight. "I appreciate," I said, "the great decency of your not having hitherto spoken; but the time has certainly come to give me the whole thing." She appeared to assent to this, but still only in silence; seeing which I went on: "I must have it now. Of what did she die? Come, there was something between them."

"There was everything."

"In spite of the difference — ?"

"Oh of their rank, their condition" — she brought it woefully out. "*She* was a lady."

I turned it over; I again saw. "Yes — she was a lady."

"And he so dreadfully below," said Mrs. Grose.

I felt that I doubtless need n't press too hard, in such company, on the place of a servant in the scale; but there was nothing to prevent an acceptance of my companion's own measure of my predecessor's abasement. There was a way to deal with that, and I dealt; the more readily for my full vision — on the evidence — of our employer's late clever good-looking "own" man; impudent, assured, spoiled, depraved. "The fellow was a hound."°

Mrs. Grose considered as if it were perhaps a little a case for a sense of shades. "I've never seen one like him. He did what he wished."

"With *her?*"

"With them all."

It was as if now in my friend's own eyes Miss Jessel had again appeared. I seemed at any rate for an instant to trace their evocation of her as distinctly as I had seen her by the pond; and I brought out with decision: "It must have been also what *she* wished!"

Mrs. Grose's face signified that it had been indeed, but she said at the same time: "Poor woman — she paid for it!"

"Then you do know what she died of?" I asked.

"No — I know nothing. I wanted not to know; I was glad enough I did n't; and I thanked heaven she was well out of this!"

"Yet you had then your idea — "

"Of her real reason for leaving?° Oh yes — as to that. She could n't have stayed. Fancy it here — for a governess! And afterwards I imagined — and I still imagine. And what I imagine is dreadful."

"Not so dreadful as what *I* do," I replied; on which I must have shown her — as I was indeed but too conscious — a front of miserable defeat. It brought out again all her compassion for me, and at the renewed touch of her kindness my power to resist broke down. I burst, as I had the other time made her burst, into tears; she took me to her motherly breast, where my lamentation overflowed. "I don't do it!" I sobbed in despair; "I don't save or shield them! It's far worse than I dreamed. They're lost!"°

---

a hound: Sexually indiscriminate man.   **her real reason for leaving:** The implication is that Miss Jessel left because she was pregnant. Her appearance beside the pond may be a hint that she drowned herself.   **lost:** Damned, given over to the devil.

VIII°

What I had said to Mrs. Grose was true enough: there were in the matter I had put before her depths and possibilities that I lacked resolution to sound; so that when we met once more in the wonder of it we were of a common mind about the duty of resistance to extravagant fancies. We were to keep our heads if we should keep nothing else — difficult indeed as that might be in the face of all that, in our prodigious experience, seemed least to be questioned. Late that night, while the house slept, we had another talk in my room; when she went all the way with me as to its being beyond doubt that I had seen exactly what I had seen. I found that to keep her thoroughly in the grip of this I had only to ask her how, if I had "made it up," I came to be able to give, of each of the persons appearing to me, a picture disclosing, to the last detail, their special marks — a portrait on the exhibition of which she had instantly recognised and named them. She wished, of course — small blame to her! — to sink the whole subject; and I was quick to assure her that my own interest in it had now violently taken the form of a search for the way to escape from it. I closed with her cordially on the article of the likelihood that with recurrence — for recurrence we took for granted — I should get used to my danger; distinctly professing that my personal exposure had suddenly become the least of my discomforts. It was my new suspicion that was intolerable; and yet even to this complication the later hours of the day had brought a little ease.

On leaving her, after my first outbreak, I had of course returned to my pupils, associating the right remedy for my dismay with that sense of their charm which I had already recognised as a resource I could positively cultivate and which had never failed me yet. I had simply, in other words, plunged afresh into Flora's special society and there become aware — it was almost a luxury! — that she could put her little conscious hand straight upon the spot that ached. She had looked at me in sweet speculation and then had accused me to my face of having "cried." I had supposed the ugly signs of it brushed away; but I could literally — for the time at all events — rejoice, under this fathomless charity, that they had not entirely disappeared. To gaze into the depths of blue of the child's eyes and pronounce their loveliness a trick of premature cunning was to be guilty of a cynicism in preference to which I naturally preferred to abjure° my judgement and, so far as might be, my

---

VIII: The sixth weekly *Collier's* installment and *Part Third* began here. **abjure:** Give up, retract. She would rather recant her suspicions of Flora than imagine evil in one whose blue eyes seem to signal such innocence.

agitation. I could n't abjure for merely wanting to, but I could repeat to Mrs. Grose — as I did there, over and over, in the small hours — that with our small friends' voices in the air, their pressure on one's heart and their fragrant faces against one's cheek, everything fell to the ground but their incapacity and their beauty. It was a pity that, somehow, to settle this once for all, I had equally to re-enumerate the signs of subtlety that, in the afternoon, by the lake, had made a miracle of my show of self-possession. It was a pity to be obliged to re-investigate the certitude of the moment itself and repeat how it had come to me as a revelation that the inconceivable communion I then surprised must have been for both parties a matter of habit. It was a pity I should have had to quaver out again the reasons for my not having, in my delusion, so much as questioned that the little girl saw our visitant even as I actually saw Mrs. Grose herself, and that she wanted, by just so much as she did thus see, to make me suppose she did n't, and at the same time, without showing anything, arrive at a guess as to whether I myself did! It was a pity I needed to recapitulate the portentous little activities by which she sought to divert my attention — the perceptible increase of movement, the greater intensity of play, the singing, the gabbling of nonsense and the invitation to romp.

Yet if I had not indulged, to prove there was nothing in it, in this review, I should have missed the two or three dim elements of comfort that still remained to me. I should n't for instance have been able to asseverate° to my friend that I was certain — which was so much to the good — that *I* at least had not betrayed myself. I should n't have been prompted, by stress of need, by desperation of mind — I scarce know what to call it — to invoke such further aid to intelligence as might spring from pushing my colleague fairly to the wall. She had told me, bit by bit, under pressure, a great deal; but a small shifty spot on the wrong side of it all still sometimes brushed my brow like the wing of a bat; and I remember how on this occasion — for the sleeping house and the concentration alike of our danger and our watch seemed to help — I felt the importance of giving the last jerk to the curtain. "I don't believe anything so horrible," I recollect saying; "no, let us put it definitely, my dear, that I don't. But if I did, you know, there's a thing I should require now, just without sparing you the least bit more — oh not a scrap, come! — to get out of you. What was it you had in mind when, in our distress, before Miles came back, over the letter from his school, you said, under my insistence, that you did n't pretend for him he had n't

---

asseverate: Assert, proclaim.

literally *ever* been 'bad'? He has *not*, truly, 'ever,' in these weeks that I myself have lived with him and so closely watched him; he has been an imperturbable little prodigy of delightful loveable goodness. Therefore you might perfectly have made the claim for him if you had not, as it happened, seen an exception to take. What was your exception, and to what passage in your personal observation of him did you refer?"

It was a straight question enough, but levity was not our note, and in any case I had before the grey dawn admonished us to separate got my answer. What my friend had had in mind proved immensely to the purpose. It was neither more nor less than the particular fact that for a period of several months Quint and the boy had been perpetually to-gether. It was indeed the very appropriate item of evidence of her hav-ing ventured to criticise the propriety, to hint at the incongruity, of so close an alliance, and even to go so far on the subject as a frank overture to Miss Jessel would take her. Miss Jessel had, with a very high manner about it, requested her to mind her business, and the good woman had on this directly approached little Miles. What she had said to him, since I pressed, was that *she* liked to see young gentlemen not forget their station.

I pressed again, of course, the closer for that. "You reminded him that Quint was only a base menial?"

"As you might say! And it was his answer, for one thing, that was bad."

"And for another thing?" I waited. "He repeated your words to Quint?"

"No, not that. It's just what he *would n't!*" she could still impress on me. "I was sure, at any rate," she added, "that he did n't. But he denied certain occasions."

"What occasions?"

"When they had been about together quite as if Quint were his tutor — and a very grand one — and Miss Jessel only for the little lady. When he had gone off with the fellow, I mean, and spent hours with him."

"He then prevaricated about it — he said he had n't?" Her assent was clear enough to cause me to add in a moment: "I see. He lied."

"Oh!" Mrs. Grose mumbled. This was a suggestion that it did n't matter; which indeed she backed up by a further remark. "You see, after all, Miss Jessel did n't mind. She did n't forbid him."

I considered. "Did he put that to you as a justification?"

At this she dropped again. "No, he never spoke of it."

"Never mentioned her in connexion with Quint?"

She saw, visibly flushing, where I was coming out. "Well, he did n't show anything. He denied," she repeated; "he denied."

Lord, how I pressed her now! "So that you could see he knew what was between the two wretches?"

"I don't know — I don't know!" the poor woman wailed.

"You do know, you dear thing," I replied; "only you have n't my dreadful boldness of mind, and you keep back, out of timidity and modesty and delicacy, even the impression that in the past, when you had, without my aid, to flounder about in silence, most of all made you miserable. But I shall get it out of you yet! There was something in the boy that suggested to you," I continued, "his covering and concealing their relation."

"Oh he could n't prevent — "

"Your learning the truth? I dare say! But, heavens," I fell, with vehemence, a-thinking, "what it shows that they must, to that extent, have succeeded in making of him!"

"Ah nothing that's not nice *now!*" Mrs. Grose lugubriously° pleaded.

"I don't wonder you looked queer," I persisted, "when I mentioned to you the letter from his school!"

"I doubt if I looked as queer as you!" she retorted with homely force. "And if he was so bad then as that comes to, how is he such an angel now?"

"Yes indeed — and if he was a fiend at school! How, how, how? Well," I said in my torment, "you must put it to me again, though I shall not be able to tell you for some days. Only put it to me again!" I cried in a way that made my friend stare. "There are directions in which I must n't for the present let myself go." Meanwhile I returned to her first example — the one to which she had just previously referred — of the boy's happy capacity for an occasional slip. "If Quint — on your remonstrance at the time you speak of — was a base menial, one of the things Miles said to you, I find myself guessing, was that you were another." Again her admission was so adequate that I continued: "And you forgave him that?"

"Wouldn't *you?*"

"Oh yes!" And we exchanged there, in the stillness, a sound of the oddest amusement. Then I went on: "At all events, while he was with the man — "

"Miss Flora was with the woman. It suited them all!"

---

lugubriously: Mournfully.

It suited me too, I felt, only too well; by which I mean that it suited exactly the particular deadly view I was in the very act of forbidding myself to entertain. But I so far succeeded in checking the expression of this view that I will throw, just here, no further light on it than may be offered by the mention of my final observation to Mrs. Grose. "His having lied and been impudent are, I confess, less engaging specimens than I had hoped to have from you of the outbreak in him of the little natural man.° Still," I mused, "they must do, for they make me feel more than ever that I must watch."

It made me blush, the next minute, to see in my friend's face how much more unreservedly she had forgiven him than her anecdote struck me as pointing out to my own tenderness any way to do. This was marked when, at the schoolroom door, she quitted me. "Surely you don't accuse *him* — "

"Of carrying on an intercourse that he conceals from me? Ah remember that, until further evidence, I now accuse nobody." Then before shutting her out to go by another passage to her own place, "I must just wait," I wound up.

IX

I waited and waited, and the days took as they elapsed something from my consternation. A very few of them, in fact, passing, in constant sight of my pupils, without a fresh incident, sufficed to give to grievous fancies and even to odious memories a kind of brush of the sponge. I have spoken of the surrender to their extraordinary childish grace as a thing I could actively promote in myself, and it may be imagined if I neglected now to apply at this source for whatever balm it would yield. Stranger than I can express, certainly, was the effort to struggle against my new lights. It would doubtless have been a greater tension still, however, had it not been so frequently successful. I used to wonder how my little charges could help guessing that I thought strange things about them; and the circumstance that these things only made them more interesting was not by itself a direct aid to keeping them in the dark. I trembled lest they should see that they *were* so immensely more interesting. Putting things at the worst, at all events, as in meditation I so often did, any clouding of their innocence could only be — blameless

---

natural man: The part that is bad or even merely human. None of what Mrs. Grose has told her about Miles makes him sound particularly evil.

and foredoomed as they were — a reason the more for taking risks. There were moments when I knew myself to catch them up by an irresistible impulse and press them to my heart. As soon as I had done so I used to wonder — "What will they think of that? Doesn't it betray too much?" It would have been easy to get into a sad wild tangle about how much I might betray; but the real account, I feel, of the hours of peace I could still enjoy was that the immediate charm of my companions was a beguilement still effective even under the shadow of the possibility that it was studied. For if it occurred to me that I might occasionally excite suspicion by the little outbreaks of my sharper passion for them, so too I remember asking if I might n't see a queerness in the traceable increase of their own demonstrations.

They were at this period extravagantly and preternaturally fond of me; which, after all, I could reflect, was no more than a graceful response in children perpetually bowed down over and hugged. The homage of which they were so lavish succeeded in truth for my nerves quite as well as if I never appeared to myself, as I may say, literally to catch them at a purpose in it. They had never, I think, wanted to do so many things for their poor protectress; I mean — though they got their lessons better and better, which was naturally what would please her most — in the way of diverting, entertaining, surprising her; reading her passages, telling her stories, acting her charades, pouncing out at her, in disguises, as animals and historical characters, and above all astonishing her by the "pieces" they had secretly got by heart and could interminably recite. I should never get to the bottom — were I to let myself go even now — of the prodigious private commentary, all under still more private correction, with which I in these days overscored their full hours. They had shown me from the first a facility for everything, a general faculty which, taking a fresh start, achieved remarkable flights. They got their little tasks as if they loved them; they indulged, from the mere exuberance of the gift, in the most unimposed little miracles of memory. They not only popped out at me as tigers and as Romans, but as Shakespeareans, astronomers, and navigators. This was so singularly the case that it had presumably much to do with the fact as to which, at the present day, I am at a loss for a different explanation: I allude to my unnatural composure on the subject of another school for Miles. What I remember is that I was content for the time not to open the question, and that contentment must have sprung from the sense of his perpetually striking show of cleverness. He was too clever for a bad governess, for a parson's daughter, to spoil; and the strangest if not the brightest thread in the pensive embroidery I just spoke of was the impression I

might have got, if I had dared to work it out, that he was under some
influence operating in his small intellectual life as a tremendous incite-
ment.

If it was easy to reflect, however, that such a boy could postpone
school, it was at least as marked that for such a boy to have been "kicked
out" by a schoolmaster was a mystification without end. Let me add
that in their company now — and I was careful almost never to be out
of it — I could follow no scent very far. We lived in a cloud of music and
affection and success and private theatricals. The musical sense in each
of the children was of the quickest, but the elder in especial had a mar-
vellous knack of catching and repeating. The schoolroom piano broke
into all gruesome fancies; and when that failed there were confabula-
tions in corners, with a sequel of one of them going out in the highest
spirits in order to "come in" as something new. I had had brothers myself, and it was no revelation to me that little girls could be slavish idol-
aters of little boys. What surpassed everything was that there was a little
boy in the world who could have for the inferior age, sex, and intelligence so fine a consideration. They were extraordinarily at one, and to
say that they never either quarrelled or complained is to make the note
of praise coarse for their quality of sweetness. Sometimes perhaps indeed (when I dropped into coarseness) I came across traces of little un-
derstandings between them by which one of them should keep me occupied while the other slipped away. There is a naïf side, I suppose, in
all diplomacy; but if my pupils practised upon me it was surely with the
minimum of grossness. It was all in the other quarter that, after a lull,
the grossness broke out.

I find that I really hang back; but I must take my horrid plunge. In
going on with the record of what was hideous at Bly I not only challenge the most liberal faith — for which I little care; but (and this is
another matter) I renew what I myself suffered, I again push my dreadful way through it to the end. There came suddenly an hour after which,
as I look back, the business seems to me to have been all pure suffering;
but I have at least reached the heart of it, and the straightest road out is
doubtless to advance. One evening — with nothing to lead up or prepare it — I felt the cold touch of the impression that had breathed on
me the night of my arrival and which, much lighter then as I have mentioned, I should probably have made little of in memory had my subsequent sojourn been less agitated. I had not gone to bed; I sat reading by
a couple of candles. There was a roomful of old books at Bly — last-
century fiction some of it, which, to the extent of a distinctly deprecated
renown, but never to so much as that of a stray specimen, had reached

the sequestered home and appealed to the unavowed curiosity of my youth. I remember that the book I had in my hand was Fielding's "Amelia";° also that I was wholly awake. I recall further both a general conviction that it was horribly late and a particular objection to looking at my watch. I figure finally that the white curtain draping, in the fashion of those days, the head of Flora's little bed, shrouded, as I had assured myself long before, the perfection of childish rest. I recollect in short that though I was deeply interested in my author I found myself, at the turn of a page and with his spell all scattered, looking straight up from him and hard at the door of my room. There was a moment during which I listened, reminded of the faint sense I had had, the first night, of there being something undefinably astir in the house, and noted the soft breath of the open casement just move the half-drawn blind. Then, with all the marks of a deliberation that must have seemed magnificent had there been any one to admire it, I laid down my book, rose to my feet and, taking a candle, went straight out of the room and, from the passage, on which my light made little impression, noiselessly closed and locked the door.

I can say now neither what determined nor what guided me, but I went straight along the lobby, holding my candle high, till I came within sight of the tall window that presided over the great turn of the staircase. At this point I precipitately found myself aware of three things. They were practically simultaneous, yet they had flashes of succession. My candle, under a bold flourish, went out, and I perceived, by the uncovered window, that the yielding dusk of earliest morning rendered it unnecessary. Without it, the next instant, I knew that there was a figure on the stair. I speak of sequences, but I required no lapse of seconds to stiffen myself for a third encounter with Quint. The apparition had reached the landing half-way up and was therefore on the spot nearest the window, where, at sight of me, it stopped short and fixed me exactly as it had fixed me from the tower and from the garden. He knew me as well as I knew him; and so, in the cold faint twilight, with a glimmer in the high glass and another on the polish of the oak stair below, we faced each other in our common intensity. He was absolutely, on this occasion, a living detestable dangerous presence. But that was not the wonder of wonders; I reserve this distinction for quite another circumstance: the circumstance that dread had unmistakeably quitted me and that there was nothing in me unable to meet and measure him.

Fielding's "Amelia": A novel by Henry Fielding (1707–1754) published in 1751. *Amelia* is about an unfailingly good and faithful heroine pursued by an assortment of men.

I had plenty of anguish after that extraordinary moment, but I had, thank God, no terror. And he knew I had n't — I found myself at the end of an instant magnificently aware of this. I felt, in a fierce rigour of confidence, that if I stood my ground a minute I should cease — for the time at least — to have him to reckon with; and during the minute, accordingly, the thing was as human and hideous as a real interview: hideous just because it *was* human, as human as to have met alone, in the small hours, in a sleeping house, some enemy, some adventurer, some criminal. It was the dead silence of our long gaze at such close quarters that gave the whole horror, huge as it was, its only note of the unnatural. If I had met a murderer in such a place and at such an hour we still at least would have spoken. Something would have passed, in life, between us; if nothing had passed one of us would have moved. The moment was so prolonged that it would have taken but little more to make me doubt if even *I* were in life. I can't express what followed it save by saying that the silence itself — which was indeed in a manner an attestation of my strength — became the element into which I saw the figure disappear; in which I definitely saw it turn, as I might have seen the low wretch to which it had once belonged turn on receipt of an order, and pass, with my eyes on the villainous back that no hunch could have more disfigured, straight down the staircase and into the darkness in which the next bend was lost.

X°

I remained a while at the top of the stair, but with the effect presently of understanding that when my visitor had gone, he had gone; then I returned to my room. The foremost thing I saw there by the light of the candle I had left burning was that Flora's little bed was empty; and on this I caught my breath with all the terror that, five minutes before, I had been able to resist. I dashed at the place in which I had left her lying and over which — for the small silk counterpane and the sheets were disarranged — the white curtains had been deceivingly pulled forward; then my step, to my unutterable relief, produced an answering sound: I noticed an agitation of the window-blind, and the child, ducking down, emerged rosily from the other side of it. She stood there in so much of her candour and so little of her night-gown, with her pink bare feet and the golden glow of her curls. She looked intensely

X: The seventh weekly *Collier's* installment began here.

grave, and I had never had such a sense of losing an advantage acquired (the thrill of which had just been so prodigious) as on my consciousness that she addressed me with a reproach — "You naughty: where *have* you been?" Instead of challenging her own irregularity I found myself arraigned and explaining. She herself explained, for that matter, with the loveliest eagerest simplicity. She had known suddenly, as she lay there, that I was out of the room, and had jumped up to see what had become of me. I had dropped, with the joy of her reappearance, back into my chair — feeling then, and then only, a little faint; and she had pattered straight over to me, thrown herself upon my knee, given herself to be held with the flame of the candle full in the wonderful little face that was still flushed with sleep. I remember closing my eyes an instant, yieldingly, consciously, as before the excess of something beautiful that shone out of the blue of her own. "You were looking for me out of the window?" I said. "You thought I might be walking in the grounds?"

"Well, you know, I thought some one was" — she never blanched as she smiled out that at me.

Oh how I looked at her now! "And did you see any one?"

"Ah *no!*" she returned almost (with the full privilege of childish inconsequence) resentfully, though with a long sweetness in her little drawl of the negative.

At that moment, in the state of my nerves, I absolutely believed she lied; and if I once more closed my eyes it was before the dazzle of the three or four possible ways in which I might take this up. One of these for a moment tempted me with such singular force that, to resist it, I must have gripped my little girl with a spasm that, wonderfully, she submitted to without a cry or a sign of fright. Why not break out at her on the spot and have it all over? — give it to her straight in her lovely little lighted face? "You see, you see, you *know* that you do and that you already quite suspect I believe it; therefore why not frankly confess it to me, so that we may at least live with it together and learn perhaps, in the strangeness of our fate, where we are and what it means?" This solicitation dropped, alas, as it came: if I could immediately have succumbed to it I might have spared myself — well, you'll see what. Instead of succumbing I sprang again to my feet, looked at her bed and took a helpless middle way. "Why did you pull the curtain over the place to make me think you were still there?"

Flora luminously considered; after which, with her little divine smile: "Because I don't like to frighten you!"

"But if I had, by your idea, gone out — ?"

She absolutely declined to be puzzled; she turned her eyes to the flame of the candle as if the question were as irrelevant, or at any rate as impersonal, as Mrs. Marcet° or nine-times-nine. "Oh but you know," she quite adequately answered, "that you might come back, you dear, and that you *have!*" And after a little, when she had got into bed, I had, a long time, by almost sitting on her for the retention of her hand, to show how I recognised the pertinence of my return.

You may imagine the general complexion, from that moment, of my nights. I repeatedly sat up till I did n't know when; I selected moments when my room-mate unmistakeably slept, and, stealing out, took noise-less turns in the passage. I even pushed as far as to where I had last met Quint. But I never met him there again, and I may as well say at once that I on no other occasion saw him in the house. I just missed, on the staircase, nevertheless, a different adventure. Looking down it from the top I once recognised the presence of a woman seated on one of the lower steps with her back presented to me, her body half-bowed and her head, in an attitude of woe, in her hands. I had been there but an in-stant, however, when she vanished without looking round at me. I knew, for all that, exactly what dreadful face she had to show; and I wondered whether, if instead of being above I had been below, I should have had the same nerve for going up that I had lately shown Quint. Well, there continued to be plenty of call for nerve. On the eleventh night after my latest encounter with that gentleman — they were all numbered now — I had an alarm that perilously skirted it and that in-deed, from the particular quality of its unexpectedness, proved quite my sharpest shock. It was precisely the first night during this series that, weary with vigils, I had conceived I might again without laxity lay my-self down at my old hour. I slept immediately and, as I afterwards knew, till about one o'clock; but when I woke it was to sit straight up, as com-pletely roused as if a hand had shaken me. I had left a light burning, but it was now out, and I felt an instant certainty that Flora had extin-guished it. This brought me to my feet and straight, in the darkness, to her bed, which I found she had left. A glance at the window enlightened me further, and the striking of a match completed the picture.

The child had again got up — this time blowing out the taper, and had again, for some purpose of observation or response, squeezed in behind the blind and was peering out into the night. That she now saw — as she had not, I had satisfied myself, the previous time — was proved to me by the fact that she was disturbed neither by my re-illumination nor by the haste I made to get into slippers and into a wrap.

Mrs. Marcet: Jane Marcet (1769–1858), a writer of children's books.

Hidden, protected, absorbed, she evidently rested on the sill — the casement opened forward — and gave herself up. There was a great still moon to help her, and this fact had counted in my quick decision. She was face to face with the apparition we had met at the lake, and could now communicate with it as she had not then been able to do. What I, on my side, had to care for was, without disturbing her, to reach, from the corridor, some other window turned to the same quarter. I got to the door without her hearing me; I got out of it, closed it and listened, from the other side, for some sound from her. While I stood in the passage I had my eyes on her brother's door, which was but ten steps off and which, indescribably, produced in me a renewal of the strange impulse that I lately spoke of as my temptation. What if I should go straight in and march to *his* window? — what if, by risking to his boyish bewilderment a revelation of my motive, I should throw across the rest of the mystery the long halter of my boldness?

This thought held me sufficiently to make me cross to his threshold and pause again. I preternaturally listened; I figured to myself what might portentously be; I wondered if his bed were also empty and he also secretly at watch. It was a deep soundless minute, at the end of which my impulse failed. He was quiet; he might be innocent; the risk was hideous; I turned away. There was a figure in the grounds — a figure prowling for a sight, the visitor with whom Flora was engaged; but it was n't the visitor most concerned with my boy. I hesitated afresh, but on other grounds and only a few seconds; then I had made my choice. There were empty rooms enough at Bly, and it was only a question of choosing the right one. The right one suddenly presented itself to me as the lower one — though high above the gardens — in the solid corner of the house that I have spoken of as the old tower. This was a large square chamber, arranged with some state as a bedroom, the extravagant size of which made it so inconvenient that it had not for years, though kept by Mrs. Grose in exemplary order, been occupied. I had often admired it and I knew my way about in it; I had only, after just faltering at the first chill gloom of its disuse, to pass across it and unbolt in all quietness one of the shutters. Achieving this transit I uncovered the glass without a sound and, applying my face to the pane, was able, the darkness without being much less than within, to see that I commanded the right direction. Then I saw something more. The moon made the night extraordinarily penetrable and showed me on the lawn a person, diminished by distance, who stood there motionless and as if fascinated, looking up to where I had appeared — looking, that is, not so much straight at me as at something that was apparently above me.

There was clearly another person above me — there was a person on the tower; but the presence on the lawn was not in the least what I had conceived and had confidently hurried to meet. The presence on the lawn — I felt sick as I made it out — was poor little Miles himself.

XI

It was not till late next day that I spoke to Mrs. Grose; the rigour with which I kept my pupils in sight making it often difficult to meet her privately: the more as we each felt the importance of not provoking — on the part of the servants quite as much as on that of the children — any suspicion of a secret flurry or of a discussion of mysteries. I drew a great security in this particular from her mere smooth aspect. There was nothing in her fresh face to pass on to others the least of my horrible confidences. She believed me, I was sure, absolutely: if she had n't I don't know what would have become of me, for I could n't have borne the strain alone. But she was a magnificent monument to the blessing of a want of imagination, and if she could see in our little charges nothing but their beauty and amiability, their happiness and cleverness, she had no direct communication with the sources of my trouble. If they had been at all visibly blighted or battered she would doubtless have grown, on tracing it back, haggard enough to match them; as matters stood, however, I could feel her, when she surveyed them with her large white arms folded and the habit of serenity in all her look, thank the Lord's mercy that if they were ruined the pieces would still serve. Flights of fancy gave place, in her mind, to a steady fireside glow, and I had already begun to perceive how, with the development of the conviction that — as time went on without a public accident — our young things could, after all, look out for themselves, she addressed her greatest solicitude to the sad case presented by their deputy-guardian. That, for myself, was a sound simplification: I could engage that, to the world, my face should tell no tales, but it would have been, in the conditions, an immense added worry to find myself anxious about hers.

At the hour I now speak of she had joined me, under pressure, on the terrace, where, with the lapse of the season, the afternoon sun was now agreeable; and we sat there together while before us and at a distance, yet within call if we wished, the children strolled to and fro in one of their most manageable moods. They moved slowly, in unison, below us, over the lawn, the boy, as they went, reading aloud from a story-book and passing his arm round his sister to keep her quite in touch.

Mrs. Grose watched them with positive placidity; then I caught the suppressed intellectual creak with which she conscientiously turned to take from me a view of the back of the tapestry. I had made her a receptacle of lurid things, but there was an odd recognition of my superiority — my accomplishments and my function — in her patience under my pain. She offered her mind to my disclosures as, had I wished to mix a witch's broth and proposed it with assurance, she would have held out a large clean saucepan. This had become thoroughly her attitude by the time that, in my recital of the events of the night, I reached the point of what Miles had said to me when, after seeing him, at such a monstrous hour, almost on the very spot where he happened now to be, I had gone down to bring him in; choosing then, at the window, with a concentrated need of not alarming the house, rather that method than any noisier process. I had left her meanwhile in little doubt of my small hope of representing with success even to her actual sympathy my sense of the real splendour of the little inspiration with which, after I had got him into the house, the boy met my final articulate challenge. As soon as I appeared in the moonlight on the terrace he had come to me as straight as possible; on which I had taken his hand without a word and led him, through the dark spaces, up the staircase where Quint had so hungrily hovered for him, along the lobby where I had listened and trembled, and so to his forsaken room.

Not a sound, on the way, had passed between us, and I had wondered — oh *how* I had wondered! — if he were groping about in his dreadful little mind for something plausible and not too grotesque. It would tax his invention certainly, and I felt, this time, over his real embarrassment, a curious thrill of triumph. It was a sharp trap for any game hitherto successful. He could play no longer at perfect propriety, nor could he pretend to it; so how the deuce would he get out of the scrape? There beat in me indeed, with the passionate throb of this question, an equal dumb appeal as to how the deuce *I* should. I was confronted at last, as never yet, with all the risk attached even now to sounding my own horrid note. I remember in fact that as we pushed into his little chamber, where the bed had not been slept in at all and the window, uncovered to the moonlight, made the place so clear that there was no need of striking a match — I remember how I suddenly dropped, sank upon the edge of the bed from the force of the idea that he must know how he really, as they say, "had" me. He could do what he liked, with all his cleverness to help him, so long as I should continue to defer to the old tradition of the criminality of those caretakers of the young who minister to superstitions and fears. He "had" me indeed, and in a cleft stick; for who would ever absolve me, who would consent that I should go unhung, if, by the faintest tremor of an overture, I were the first to introduce into our perfect intercourse an element so dire? No, no: it was useless to attempt to convey to Mrs. Grose, just as it is scarcely less so to attempt to suggest here, how, during our short stiff brush there in the dark, he fairly shook me with admiration. I was of course thoroughly kind and merciful; never, never yet had I placed on his small shoulders hands of such tenderness as those with which, while I rested against the bed, I held him there well under fire. I had no alternative but, in form at least, to put it to him.

"You must tell me now — and all the truth. What did you go out for? What were you doing there?"

I can still see his wonderful smile, the whites of his beautiful eyes and the uncovering of his clear teeth, shine to me in the dusk. "If I tell you why, will you understand?" My heart, at this, leaped into my mouth. *Would* he tell me why? I found no sound on my lips to press it, and I was aware of answering only with a vague repeated grimacing nod. He was gentleness itself, and while I wagged my head at him he stood there more than ever a little fairy prince. It was his brightness indeed that gave me a respite. Would it be so great if he were really going to tell me? "Well," he said at last, "just exactly in order that you should do this."

"Do what?"

"Think me — for a change — *bad!*" I shall never forget the sweetness and gaiety with which he brought out the word, nor how, on top of it, he bent forward and kissed me. It was practically the end of everything. I met his kiss and I had to make, while I folded him for a minute in my arms, the most stupendous effort not to cry. He had given exactly the account of himself that permitted least my going behind it, and it was only with the effect of confirming my acceptance of it that, as I presently glanced about the room, I could say —

"Then you did n't undress at all?"

He fairly glittered in the gloom. "Not at all. I sat up and read."

"And when did you go down?"

"At midnight. When I'm bad I *am* bad!"

"I see, I see — it's charming. But how could you be sure I should know it?"

"Oh I arranged that with Flora." His answers rang out with a readiness! "She was to get up and look out."

"Which is what she did do." It was I who fell into the trap!

"So she disturbed you, and, to see what she was looking at, you also looked — you saw."

"While you," I concurred, "caught your death in the night air!"

He literally bloomed so from this exploit that he could afford radiantly to assent. "How otherwise should I have been bad enough?" he asked. Then, after another embrace, the incident and our interview closed on my recognition of all the reserves of goodness that, for his joke, he had been able to draw upon.

XII

The particular impression I had received proved in the morning light, I repeat, not quite successfully presentable to Mrs. Grose, though I re-enforced it with the mention of still another remark that he had made before we separated. "It all lies in half a dozen words," I said to her, "words that really settle the matter. 'Think, you know, what I *might* do!' He threw that off to show me how good he is. He knows down to the ground what he 'might do.' That's what he gave them a taste of at school."

"Lord, you do change!" cried my friend.

"I don't change — I simply make it out. The four, depend upon it, perpetually meet. If on either of these last nights you had been with either child you'd clearly have understood. The more I've watched and waited the more I've felt that if there were nothing else to make it sure it would be made so by the systematic silence of each. *Never,* by a slip of the tongue, have they so much as alluded to either of their old friends, any more than Miles has alluded to his expulsion. Oh yes, we may sit here and look at them, and they may show off to us there to their fill; but even while they pretend to be lost in their fairy-tale they're steeped in their vision of the dead restored to them. He's not reading to her," I declared; "they're talking of *them* — they're talking horrors! I go on, I know, as if I were crazy; and it's a wonder I'm not. What I've seen would have made *you* so; but it has only made me more lucid, made me get hold of still other things."

My lucidity must have seemed awful, but the charming creatures who were victims of it, passing and repassing in their interlocked sweetness, gave my colleague something to hold on by; and I felt how tight she held as, without stirring in the breath of my passion, she covered them still with her eyes. "Of what other things have you got hold?"

"Why of the very things that have delighted, fascinated, and yet, at bottom, as I now so strangely see, mystified and troubled me. Their more than earthly beauty, their absolutely unnatural goodness. It's a game," I went on; "it's a policy and a fraud!"

"On the part of little darlings — ?"

"As yet mere lovely babies? Yes, mad as that seems!" The very act of bringing it out really helped me to trace it — follow it all up and piece it all together. "They have n't been good — they've only been absent. It has been easy to live with them because they're simply leading a life of their own. They're not mine — they're not ours. They're his and they're hers!"

"Quint's and that woman's?"

"Quint's and that woman's. They want to get to them."

Oh how, at this, poor Mrs. Grose appeared to study them! "But for what?"

"For the love of all the evil that, in those dreadful days, the pair put into them. And to ply them with that evil still, to keep up the work of demons, is what brings the others back."

"Laws!" said my friend under her breath. The exclamation was homely, but it revealed a real acceptance of my further proof of what, in the bad time — for there had been a worse even than this! — must have occurred. There could have been no such justification for me as the plain assent of her experience to whatever depth of depravity I found credible in our brace of scoundrels. It was in obvious submission of memory that she brought out after a moment: "They *were* rascals! But what can they now do?" she pursued.

"Do?" I echoed so loud that Miles and Flora, as they passed at their distance, paused an instant in their walk and looked at us. "Don't they do enough?" I demanded in a lower tone, while the children, having smiled and nodded and kissed hands to us, resumed their exhibition. We were held by it a minute; then I answered: "They can destroy them!" At this my companion did turn, but the appeal she launched was a silent one, the effect of which was to make me more explicit. "They don't know as yet quite how — but they're trying hard. They're seen only across, as it were, and beyond — in strange places and on high places, the top of towers, the roof of houses, the outside of windows, the further edge of pools; but there's a deep design, on either side, to shorten the distance and overcome the obstacle: so the success of the tempters is only a question of time. They've only to keep to their suggestions of danger."

"For the children to come?"

"And perish in the attempt!" Mrs. Grose slowly got up, and I scrupulously added: "Unless, of course, we can prevent!"

Standing there before me while I kept my seat she visibly turned things over. "Their uncle must do the preventing. He must take them away."

"And who's to make him?"

She had been scanning the distance, but she now dropped on me a foolish face. "You, Miss."

"By writing to him that his house is poisoned and his little nephew and niece mad?"

"But if they *are*, Miss?"

"And if I am myself, you mean? That's charming news to be sent him by a person enjoying his confidence and whose prime undertaking was to give him no worry."

Mrs. Grose considered, following the children again. "Yes, he do hate worry. That was the great reason — "

"Why those fiends took him in so long? No doubt, though his indifference must have been awful. As I'm not a fiend, at any rate, I should n't take him in."

My companion, after an instant and for all answer, sat down again and grasped my arm. "Make him at any rate come to you."

I stared. "To *me*?" I had a sudden fear of what she might do. "'Him'?"

"He ought to *be* here — he ought to help."

I quickly rose and I think I must have shown her a queerer face than ever yet. "You see me asking him for a visit?" No, with her eyes on my face she evidently could n't. Instead of it even — as a woman reads another — she could see what I myself saw: his derision, his amusement, his contempt for the breakdown of my resignation at being left alone and for the fine machinery I had set in motion to attract his attention to my slighted charms. She did n't know — no one knew — how proud I had been to serve him and to stick to our terms; yet she none the less took the measure, I think, of the warning I now gave her. "If you should so lose your head as to appeal to him for me — "

She was really frightened. "Yes, Miss?"

"I would leave, on the spot, both him and you."

XIII°

It was all very well to join them, but speaking to them proved quite as much as ever an effort beyond my strength — offered, in close quar-

---

XIII: The eighth weekly *Collier's* installment and *Part Fourth* began here.

ters, difficulties as insurmountable as before. This situation continued a
month, and with new aggravations and particular notes, the note above
all, sharper and sharper, of the small ironic consciousness on the part of
my pupils. It was not, I am as sure to-day as I was sure then, my mere
infernal imagination: it was absolutely traceable that they were aware of
my predicament and that this strange relation made, in a manner, for a
long time, the air in which we moved. I don't mean that they had their
tongues in their cheeks or did anything vulgar, for that was not one of
their dangers: I do mean, on the other hand, that the element of the
unnamed and untouched became, between us, greater than any other,
and that so much avoidance could n't have been made successful without a great deal of tacit arrangement. It was as if, at moments, we were
perpetually coming into sight of subjects before which we must stop
short, turning suddenly out of alleys that we perceived to be blind, closing with a little bang that made us look at each other — for, like all
bangs, it was something louder than we had intended — the doors we
had indiscreetly opened. All roads lead to Rome, and there were times
when it might have struck us that almost every branch of study or subject of conversation skirted forbidden ground. Forbidden ground was
the question of the return of the dead in general and of whatever, in
especial, might survive, for memory, of the friends little children had
lost. There were days when I could have sworn that one of them had,
with a small invisible nudge, said to the other: "She thinks she'll do it
this time — but she *won't!*" To "do it" would have been to indulge for
instance — and for once in a way — in some direct reference to the lady
who had prepared them for my discipline. They had a delightful endless
appetite for passages in my own history to which I had again and again
treated them; they were in possession of everything that had ever happened to me, had had, with every circumstance, the story of my smallest
adventures and of those of my brothers and sisters and of the cat and the
dog at home, as well as many particulars of the whimsical bent of my
father, of the furniture and arrangement of our house and of the conversation of the old women of our village. There were things enough, taking one with another, to chatter about, if one went very fast and knew
by instinct when to go round. They pulled with an art of their own the
strings of my invention and my memory; and nothing else perhaps,
when I thought of such occasions afterwards, gave me so the suspicion
of being watched from under cover. It was in any case over *my* life, *my*
past, and *my* friends alone that we could take anything like our ease; a
state of affairs that led them sometimes without the least pertinence to
break out into sociable reminders. I was invited — with no visible con-

nexion — to repeat afresh Goody Gosling's celebrated *mot*° or to confirm the details already supplied as to the cleverness of the vicarage pony.

It was partly at such junctures as these and partly at quite different ones that, with the turn my matters had now taken, my predicament, as I have called it, grew most sensible. The fact that the days passed for me without another encounter ought, it would have appeared, to have done something toward soothing my nerves. Since the light brush, that second night on the upper landing, of the presence of a woman at the foot of the stair, I had seen nothing, whether in or out of the house, that one had better not have seen. There was many a corner round which I expected to come upon Quint, and many a situation that, in a merely sinister way, would have favoured the appearance of Miss Jessel. The summer had turned, the summer had gone; the autumn had dropped upon Bly and had blown out half our lights. The place, with its grey sky and withered garlands, its bared spaces and scattered dead leaves, was like a theatre after the performance — all strewn with crumpled play-bills. There were exactly states of the air, conditions of sound and of stillness, unspeakable impressions of the *kind* of ministering moment, that brought back to me, long enough to catch it, the feeling of the medium in which, that June evening out of doors, I had had my first sight of Quint, and in which too, at those other instants, I had, after seeing him through the window, looked for him in vain in the circle of shrubbery. I recognised the signs, the portents — I recognised the moment, the spot. But they remained unaccompanied and empty, and I continued unmolested; if unmolested one could call a young woman whose sensibility had, in the most extraordinary fashion, not declined but deepened. I had said in my talk with Mrs. Grose on that horrid scene of Flora's by the lake — and had perplexed her by so saying — that it would from that moment distress me much more to lose my power than to keep it. I had then expressed what was vividly in my mind: the truth that, whether the children really saw or not — since, that is, it was not yet definitely proved — I greatly preferred, as a safeguard, the fulness of my own exposure. I was ready to know the very worst that was to be known. What I had then had an ugly glimpse of was that my eyes might be sealed just while theirs were most opened.

---

mot: French for "word." Goody (that is, Goodwife) Gosling is one of the "old women of our village" referred to earlier in this paragraph. She had apparently made some clever retort that Miles and Flora ask the governess to tell them about yet once again. The point is not what Goody Gosling said but that the children are keeping the governess occupied telling them stories about her home and family.

Well, my eyes *were* sealed,° it appeared, at present — a consummation for which it seemed blasphemous not to thank God. There was, alas, a difficulty about that: I would have thanked him with all my soul had I not had in a proportionate measure this conviction of the secret of my pupils.

How can I retrace to-day the strange steps of my obsession? There were times of our being together when I would have been ready to swear that, literally, in my presence, but with my direct sense of it closed, they had visitors who were known and were welcome. Then it was that, had I not been deterred by the very chance that such an injury might prove greater than the injury to be averted, my exaltation would have broken out. "They're here, they're here, you little wretches," I would have cried, "and you can't deny it now!" The little wretches denied it with all the added volume of their sociability and their tenderness, just in the crystal depths of which — like the flash of a fish in a stream — the mockery of their advantage peeped up. The shock had in truth sunk into me still deeper than I knew on the night when, looking out either for Quint or for Miss Jessel under the stars, I had seen there the boy over whose rest I watched and who had immediately brought in with him — had straightway there turned on me — the lovely upward look with which, from the battlements above us, the hideous apparition of Quint had played. If it was a question of a scare my discovery on this occasion had scared me more than any other, and it was essentially in the scared state that I drew my actual conclusions. They harassed me so that sometimes, at odd moments, I shut myself up audibly to rehearse — it was at once a fantastic relief and a renewed despair — the manner in which I might come to the point. I approached it from one side and the other while, in my room, I flung myself about, but I always broke down in the monstrous utterance of names. As they died away on my lips I said to myself that I should indeed help them to represent something infamous if by pronouncing them I should violate as rare a little case of instinctive delicacy as any schoolroom probably had ever known. When I said to myself: "*They* have the manners to be silent, and you, trusted as you are, the baseness to speak!" I felt myself crimson and covered my face with my hands. After these secret scenes I chattered more than ever, going on volubly enough till one of our prodigious palpable hushes occurred — I can call them nothing else — the strange dizzy lift or swim (I try for terms!) into a stillness, a pause of all life, that

my eyes *were* sealed: Because she has not seen either Peter Quint or Miss Jessel for some time, she wonders whether she has lost the ability she once had.

had nothing to do with the more or less noise we at the moment might be engaged in making and that I could hear through any intensified mirth or quickened recitation or louder strum of the piano. Then it was that the others, the outsiders, were there. Though they were not angels they "passed," as the French say, causing me, while they stayed, to tremble with the fear of their addressing to their younger victims some yet more infernal message or more vivid image than they had thought good enough for myself.

What it was least possible to get rid of was the cruel idea that, whatever I had seen, Miles and Flora saw *more* — things terrible and unguessable and that sprang from dreadful passages of intercourse in the past. Such things naturally left on the surface, for the time, a chill that we vociferously denied we felt; and we had all three, with repetition, got into such splendid training that we went, each time, to mark the close of the incident, almost automatically through the very same movements. It was striking of the children at all events to kiss me inveterately with a wild irrelevance and never to fail — one or the other — of the precious question that had helped us through many a peril. "When do you think he *will* come? Don't you think we *ought* to write?" — there was nothing like that enquiry, we found by experience, for carrying off an awkwardness. "He" of course was their uncle in Harley Street; and we lived in much profusion of theory that he might at any moment arrive to mingle in our circle. It was impossible to have given less encouragement than he had administered to such a doctrine, but if we had not had the doctrine to fall back upon we should have deprived each other of some of our finest exhibitions. He never wrote to them — that may have been selfish, but it was a part of the flattery of his trust of myself; for the way in which a man pays his highest tribute to a woman is apt to be but by the more festal celebration of one of the sacred laws of his comfort. So I held that I carried out the spirit of the pledge given not to appeal to him when I let our young friends understand that their own letters were but charming literary exercises. They were too beautiful to be posted; I kept them myself; I have them all to this hour. This was a rule indeed which only added to the satiric effect of my being plied with the supposition that he might at any moment be among us. It was exactly as if our young friends knew how almost more awkward than anything else that might be for me. There appears to me moreover as I look back no note in all this more extraordinary than the mere fact that, in spite of my tension and of their triumph, I never lost patience with them. Adorable they must in truth have been, I now feel, since I did n't in these days hate them! Would exasperation, however, if relief had longer been postponed, finally have betrayed me? It little matters, for relief arrived. I call it relief though it was only the relief that a snap brings to a strain or the burst of a thunderstorm to a day of suffocation. It was at least change, and it came with a rush.

XIV

Walking to church a certain Sunday morning, I had little Miles at my side and his sister, in advance of us and at Mrs. Grose's, well in sight. It was a crisp clear day, the first of its order for some time; the night had brought a touch of frost and the autumn air, bright and sharp, made the church-bells almost gay. It was an odd accident of thought that I should have happened at such a moment to be particularly and very gratefully struck with the obedience of my little charges. Why did they never resent my inexorable, my perpetual society? Something or other had brought nearer home to me that I had all but pinned the boy to my shawl, and that in the way our companions were marshalled before me I might have appeared to provide against some danger of rebellion. I was like a gaoler° with an eye to possible surprises and escapes. But all this belonged — I mean their magnificent little surrender — just to the special array of the facts that were most abysmal. Turned out for Sunday by his uncle's tailor, who had had a free hand and a notion of pretty waistcoats and of his grand little air, Miles's whole title to independence, the rights of his sex and situation, were so stamped upon him that if he had suddenly struck for freedom I should have had nothing to say. I was by the strangest of chances wondering how I should meet him when the revolution unmistakeably occurred. I call it a revolution because I now see how, with the word he spoke, the curtain rose on the last act of my dreadful drama and the catastrophe was precipitated. "Look here, my dear, you know," he charmingly said, "when in the world, please, am I going back to school?"

Transcribed here the speech sounds harmless enough, particularly as uttered in the sweet, high, casual pipe° with which, at all interlocutors, but above all at his eternal governess, he threw off intonations as if he were tossing roses. There was something in them that always made one "catch," and I caught at any rate now so effectually that I stopped as short as if one of the trees of the park had fallen across the road. There was something new, on the spot, between us, and he was perfectly

---

gaoler: British spelling for "jailer."   **pipe:** Singing voice.

aware I recognised it, though to enable me to do so he had no need to look a whit less candid and charming than usual. I could feel in him how he already, from my at first finding nothing to reply, perceived the advantage he had gained. I was so slow to find anything that he had plenty of time, after a minute, to continue with his suggestive but inconclusive smile: "You know, my dear, that for a fellow to be with a lady *always* — !" His "my dear" was constantly on his lips for me, and nothing could have expressed more the exact shade of the sentiment with which I desired to inspire my pupils than its fond familiarity. It was so respectfully easy.

But oh how I felt that at present I must pick my own phrases! I remember that, to gain time, I tried to laugh, and I seemed to see in the beautiful face with which he watched me how ugly and queer I looked. "And always with the same lady?" I returned.

He neither blenched nor winked.° The whole thing was virtually out between us. "Ah of course she's a jolly 'perfect' lady; but after all I'm a fellow, don't you see? who's — well, getting on."

I lingered there with him an instant ever so kindly. "Yes, you're getting on." Oh but I felt helpless!

I have kept to this day the heartbreaking little idea of how he seemed to know that and to play with it. "And you can't say I've not been awfully good, can you?"

I laid my hand on his shoulder, for though I felt how much better it would have been to walk on I was not yet quite able. "No, I can't say that, Miles."

"Except just that one night, you know — !"

"That one night?" I could n't look as straight as he.

"Why when I went down — went out of the house."

"Oh yes. But I forget what you did it for."

"You forget?" — he spoke with the sweet extravagance of childish reproach. "Why it was just to show you I could!"

"Oh yes — you could."

"And I can again."

I felt I might perhaps after all succeed in keeping my wits about me. "Certainly. But you won't."

"No, not *that* again. It was nothing."

"It was nothing," I said. "But we must go on."

He resumed our walk with me, passing his hand into my arm. "Then when *am* I going back?"

blenched nor winked: Blanched (grew pale) nor blinked.

I wore, in turning it over, my most responsible air. "Were you very happy at school?"

He just considered. "Oh I'm happy enough anywhere!"

"Well then," I quavered, "if you're just as happy here — !"

"Ah but that is n't everything! Of course *you* know a lot — "

"But you hint that you know almost as much?" I risked as he paused.

"Not half I want to!" Miles honestly professed. "But it is n't so much that."

"What is it then?"

"Well — I want to see more life."

"I see; I see." We had arrived within sight of the church and of various persons, including several of the household of Bly, on their way to it and clustered about the door to see us go in. I quickened our step; I wanted to get there before the question between us opened up much further; I reflected hungrily that he would have for more than an hour to be silent; and I thought with envy of the comparative dusk of the pew and of the almost spiritual help of the hassock on which I might bend my knees. I seemed literally to be running a race with some confusion to which he was about to reduce me, but I felt he had got in first when, before we had even entered the churchyard, he threw out —

"I want my own sort!"

It literally made me bound forward. "There are n't many of your own sort, Miles!" I laughed. "Unless perhaps dear little Flora!"

"You really compare me to a baby girl?"

This found me singularly weak. "Don't you then *love* our sweet Flora?"

"If I did n't — and you too; if I did n't — !" he repeated as if retreating for a jump, yet leaving his thought so unfinished that, after we had come into the gate, another stop, which he imposed on me by the pressure of his arm, had become inevitable. Mrs. Grose and Flora had passed into the church, the other worshippers had followed and we were, for the minute, alone among the old thick graves. We had paused, on the path from the gate, by a low oblong table-like tomb.

"Yes, if you did n't — ?"

He looked, while I waited, about at the graves. "Well, you know what!" But he did n't move, and he presently produced something that made me drop straight down on the stone slab as if suddenly to rest. "Does my uncle think what *you* think?"

I markedly rested. "How do you know what I think?"

"Ah well, of course I don't; for it strikes me you never tell me. But I mean does *he* know?"

"Know what, Miles?"

"Why,° the way I'm going on."

I recognised quickly enough that I could make, to this enquiry, no answer that would n't involve something of a sacrifice of my employer. Yet it struck me that we were all, at Bly, sufficiently sacrificed to make that venial. "I don't think your uncle much cares."

Miles, on this, stood looking at me. "Then don't you think he can be made to?"

"In what way?"

"Why, by his coming down."

"But who'll get him to come down?"

"*I* will!" the boy said with extraordinary brightness and emphasis. He gave me another look charged with that expression and then marched off alone into church.

XV

The business was practically settled from the moment I never followed him. It was a pitiful surrender to agitation, but my being aware of this had somehow no power to restore me. I only sat there on my tomb and read into what our young friend had said to me the fulness of its meaning; by the time I had grasped the whole of which I had also embraced, for absence, the pretext that I was ashamed to offer my pupils and the rest of the congregation such an example of delay. What I said to myself above all was that Miles had got something out of me and that the gage of it for him would be just this awkward collapse. He had got out of me that there was something I was much afraid of, and that he should probably be able to make use of my fear to gain, for his own purpose, more freedom. My fear was of having to deal with the intolerable question of the grounds of his dismissal from school, since that was really but the question of the horrors gathered behind. That his uncle should arrive to treat with me of these things was a solution that, strictly speaking, I ought now to have desired to bring on; but I could so little face the ugliness and the pain of it that I simply procrastinated and lived from hand to mouth. The boy, to my deep discomposure, was immensely in the right, was in a position to say to me: "Either you clear up with my guardian the mystery of this interruption of my studies, or you

---

Why: The commas after "Why" in this line, in the ninth line below, and in the next-to-last line in chapter XVII (p. 92) are not in the New York edition, but they were in the earlier *Collier's* edition. These three commas, reinserted to show that these are statements, not questions, are our only emendations to the New York edition.

cease to expect me to lead with you a life that's so unnatural for a boy."
What was so unnatural for the particular boy I was concerned with was
this sudden revelation of a consciousness and a plan.

That was what really overcame me, what prevented my going in. I
walked round the church, hesitating, hovering; I reflected that I had
already, with him, hurt myself beyond repair. Therefore I could patch
up nothing and it was too extreme an effort to squeeze beside him into
the pew: he would be so much more sure than ever to pass his arm into
mine and make me sit there for an hour in close mute contact with his
commentary on our talk. For the first minute since his arrival I wanted
to get away from him. As I paused beneath the high east window and
listened to the sounds of worship I was taken with an impulse that
might master me, I felt, and completely, should I give it the least encouragement. I might easily put an end to my ordeal by getting away
altogether. Here was my chance; there was no one to stop me; I could
give the whole thing up — turn my back and bolt. It was only a question of hurrying again, for a few preparations, to the house which the
attendance at church of so many of the servants would practically have
left unoccupied. No one, in short, could blame me if I should just drive
desperately off. What was it to get away if I should get away only till
dinner? That would be in a couple of hours, at the end of which — I
had the acute prevision — my little pupils would play at innocent wonder about my non-appearance in their train.

"What *did* you do, you naughty bad thing? Why in the world, to
worry us so — and take our thoughts off too, don't you know? — did
you desert us at the very door?" I could n't meet such questions nor, as
they asked them, their false little lovely eyes; yet it was all so exactly what
I should have to meet that, as the prospect grew sharp to me, I at last let
myself go.

I got, so far as the immediate moment was concerned, away; I came
straight out of the churchyard and, thinking hard, retraced my steps
through the park. It seemed to me that by the time I reached the house
I had made up my mind to cynical flight. The Sunday stillness both of
the approaches and of the interior, in which I met no one, fairly stirred
me with a sense of opportunity. Were I to get off quickly this way I
should get off without a scene, without a word. My quickness would
have to be remarkable, however, and the question of a conveyance was
the great one to settle. Tormented, in the hall, with difficulties and obstacles, I remember sinking down at the foot of the staircase — suddenly collapsing there on the lowest step and then, with a revulsion,
recalling that it was exactly where, more than a month before, in the

darkness of night and just so bowed with evil things, I had seen the spectre of the most horrible of women. At this I was able to straighten myself; I went the rest of the way up; I made, in my turmoil, for the schoolroom, where there were objects belonging to me that I should have to take. But I opened the door to find again, in a flash, my eyes unsealed. In the presence of what I saw I reeled straight back upon resistance.

Seated at my own table in the clear noonday light I saw a person whom, without my previous experience, I should have taken at the first blush for some housemaid who might have stayed at home to look after the place and who, availing herself of rare relief from observation and of the schoolroom table and my pens, ink, and paper, had applied herself to the considerable effort of a letter to her sweetheart. There was an effort in the way that, while her arms rested on the table, her hands, with evident weariness, supported her head; but at the moment I took this in I had already become aware that, in spite of my entrance, her attitude strangely persisted. Then it was — with the very act of its announcing itself — that her identity flared up in a change of posture. She rose, not as if she had heard me, but with an indescribable grand melancholy of indifference and detachment, and, within a dozen feet of me, stood there as my vile predecessor. Dishonoured and tragic, she was all before me; but even as I fixed and, for memory, secured it, the awful image passed away. Dark as midnight in her black dress, her haggard beauty and her unutterable woe, she had looked at me long enough to appear to say that her right to sit at my table was as good as mine to sit at hers. While these instants lasted indeed I had the extraordinary chill of a feeling that it was I who was the intruder. It was as a wild protest against it that, actually addressing her — "You terrible miserable woman!" — I heard myself break into a sound that, by the open door, rang through the long passage and the empty house. She looked at me as if she heard me, but I had recovered myself and cleared the air. There was nothing in the room the next minute but the sunshine and the sense that I must stay.

XVI°

I had so perfectly expected the return of the others to be marked by a demonstration that I was freshly upset at having to find them merely dumb and discreet about my desertion. Instead of gaily denouncing and

---

XVI: The ninth weekly *Collier's* installment began here.

caressing me they made no allusion to my having failed them, and I was left, for the time, on perceiving that she too said nothing, to study Mrs. Grose's odd face. I did this to such purpose that I made sure they had in some way bribed her to silence; a silence that, however, I would en-gage to break down on the first private opportunity. This opportunity came before tea: I secured five minutes with her in the housekeeper's room, where, in the twilight, amid a smell of lately-baked bread, but with the place all swept and garnished, I found her sitting in pained placidity before the fire. So I see her still, so I see her best: facing the flame from her straight chair in the dusky shining room, a large clean picture of the "put away" — of drawers closed and locked and rest without a remedy.

"Oh yes, they asked me to say nothing; and to please them — so long as they were there — of course I promised. But what had hap-pened to you?"

"I only went with you for the walk," I said. "I had then to come back to meet a friend."

She showed her surprise. "A friend — *you?*"

"Oh yes, I've a couple!" I laughed. "But did the children give you a reason?"

"For not alluding to your leaving us? Yes; they said you'd like it better. *Do* you like it better?"

My face had made her rueful. "No, I like it worse!" But after an instant I added: "Did they say why I should like it better?"

"No; Master Miles only said 'We must do nothing but what she likes!' "

"I wish indeed he would! And what did Flora say?"

"Miss Flora was too sweet. She said 'Oh of course, of course!' — and I said the same."

I thought a moment. "You were too sweet too — I can hear you all. But none the less, between Miles and me, it's now all out."

"All out?" My companion stared. "But what, Miss?"

"Everything. It does n't matter. I've made up my mind. I came home, my dear," I went on, "for a talk with Miss Jessel."°

---

a talk with Miss Jessel: This interchange between the governess and Mrs. Grose is pivotal for those who think the governess is either neurotic or generally untrustworthy as a narra-tor. For such readers, because Miss Jessel and the governess had clearly *not* talked in the schoolroom at Bly, the governess must here be either lying or deluded. Other readers, however, point out that the governess qualifies her statement that they had had a talk by telling Mrs. Grose a few lines later that "it came to that" (that is, "it amounted to that" or "we might just as well have"). Such readers find it acceptable that the governess imagina-tively recreates for the unimaginative Mrs. Grose the import of her own intuitional dis-course with Miss Jessel.

I had by this time formed the habit of having Mrs. Grose literally well in hand in advance of my sounding that note; so that even now, as she bravely blinked under the signal of my word, I could keep her comparatively firm. "A talk! Do you mean she spoke?"

"It came to that. I found her, on my return, in the schoolroom."

"And what did she say?" I can hear the good woman still, and the candour of her stupefaction.

"That she suffers the torments — !"

It was this, of a truth, that made her, as she filled out my picture, gape. "Do you mean," she faltered " — of the lost?"

"Of the lost. Of the damned. And that's why, to share them — " I faltered myself with the horror of it.

But my companion, with less imagination, kept me up. "To share them — ?"

"She wants Flora." Mrs. Grose might, as I gave it to her, fairly have fallen away from me had I not been prepared. I still held her there, to show I was. "As I've told you, however, it does n't matter."

"Because you've made up your mind? But to what?"

"To everything."

"And what do you call 'everything'?"

"Why to sending for their uncle."

"Oh Miss, in pity do," my friend broke out.

"Ah but I will, I *will!* I see it's the only way. What's 'out,' as I told you, with Miles is that if he thinks I'm afraid to — and has ideas of what he gains by that — he shall see he's mistaken. Yes, yes; his uncle shall have it here from me on the spot (and before the boy himself if necessary) that if I'm to be reproached with having done nothing again about more school — "

"Yes, Miss — " my companion pressed me.

"Well, there's that awful reason."

There were now clearly so many of these for my poor colleague that she was excusable for being vague. "But — a — which?"

"Why the letter from his old place."

"You'll show it to the master?"

"I ought to have done so on the instant."

"Oh no!" said Mrs. Grose with decision.

"I'll put it before him," I went on inexorably, "that I can't undertake to work the question on behalf of a child who has been expelled — "

"For we've never in the least known what!" Mrs. Grose declared.

"For wickedness. For what else — when he's so clever and beautiful and perfect? Is he stupid? Is he untidy? Is he infirm? Is he ill-natured? He's exquisite — so it can be only *that;* and that would open up the whole thing. After all," I said, "it's their uncle's fault. If he left here such people — !'"

"He did n't really in the least know them. The fault's mine." She had turned quite pale.

"Well, you shan't suffer," I answered.

"The children shan't!" she emphatically returned.

I was silent a while; we looked at each other. "Then what am I to tell him?"

"You need n't tell him anything. *I'll* tell him."

I measured this. "Do you mean you'll write — ?" Remembering she could n't, I caught myself up. "How do you communicate?"

"I tell the bailiff.° *He* writes."

"And should you like him to write our story?"

My question had a sarcastic force that I had not fully intended, and it made her after a moment inconsequently break down. The tears were again in her eyes. "Ah Miss, *you* write!"

"Well — to-night," I at last returned; and on this we separated.

XVII

I went so far, in the evening, as to make a beginning. The weather had changed back, a great wind was abroad, and beneath the lamp, in my room, with Flora at peace beside me, I sat for a long time before a blank sheet of paper and listened to the lash of the rain and the batter of the gusts. Finally I went out, taking a candle; I crossed the passage and listened a minute at Miles's door. What, under my endless obsession, I had been impelled to listen for was some betrayal of his not being at rest, and I presently caught one, but not in the form I had expected. His voice tinkled out. "I say, you there — come in." It was gaiety in the gloom!

I went in with my light and found him in bed, very wide awake but very much at his ease. "Well, what are *you* up to?" he asked with a grace of sociability in which it occurred to me that Mrs. Grose, had she been present, might have looked in vain for proof that anything was "out."

I stood over him with my candle. "How did you know I was there?"

---

bailiff: An administrative official or magistrate.

"Why of course I heard you. Did you fancy you made no noise? You're like a troop of cavalry!" he beautifully laughed.

"Then you were n't asleep?"

"Not much! I lie awake and think."

I had put my candle, designedly, a short way off, and then, as he held out his friendly old hand to me, had sat down on the edge of his bed. "What is it," I asked, "that you think of?"

"What in the world, my dear, but *you?*"

"Ah the pride I take in your appreciation does n't insist on that! I had so far rather you slept."

"Well, I think also, you know, of this queer business of ours."

I marked the coolness of his firm little hand. "Of what queer business, Miles?"

"Why the way you bring me up. And all the rest!"

I fairly held my breath a minute, and even from my glimmering taper there was light enough to show how he smiled up at me from his pillow. "What do you mean by all the rest?"

"Oh you know, you know!"

I could say nothing for a minute, though I felt as I held his hand and our eyes continued to meet that my silence had all the air of admitting his charge and that nothing in the whole world of reality was perhaps at that moment so fabulous° as our actual relation. "Certainly you shall go back to school," I said, "if it be that that troubles you. But not to the old place — we must find another, a better. How could I know it did trouble you, this question, when you never told me so, never spoke of it at all?" His clear listening face, framed in its smooth whiteness, made him for the minute as appealing as some wistful patient in a children's hospital; and I would have given, as the resemblance came to me, all I possessed on earth really to be the nurse or the sister of charity who might have helped to cure him. Well, even as it was I perhaps might help! "Do you know you've never said a word to me about your school — I mean the old one; never mentioned it in any way?"

He seemed to wonder; he smiled with the same loveliness. But he clearly gained time; he waited, he called for guidance. "Haven't I?" It was n't for *me* to help him — it was for the thing° I had met!

Something in his tone and the expression of his face, as I got this from him, set my heart aching with such a pang as it had never yet known; so unutterably touching was it to see his little brain puzzled and his little resources taxed to play, under the spell laid on him, a part of

fabulous: Strange, unreal, fable-like. **the thing:** The apparition of Peter Quint.

innocence and consistency. "No, never — from the hour you came back. You've never mentioned to me one of your masters, one of your comrades, nor the least little thing that ever happened to you at school. Never, little Miles — no never — have you given me an inkling of anything that *may* have happened there. Therefore you can fancy how much I'm in the dark. Until you came out, that way, this morning, you had since the first hour I saw you scarce even made a reference to anything in your previous life. You seemed so perfectly to accept the present." It was extraordinary how my absolute conviction of his secret precocity — or whatever I might call the poison of an influence that I dared but half-phrase — made him, in spite of the faint breath of his inward trouble, appear as accessible as an older person, forced me to treat him as an intelligent equal. "I thought you wanted to go on as you are."

It struck me that at this he just faintly coloured. He gave, at any rate, like a convalescent slightly fatigued, a languid shake of his head. "I don't — I don't. I want to get away."

"You're tired of Bly?"

"Oh no, I like Bly."

"Well then — ?"

"Oh *you* know what a boy wants!"

I felt I did n't know so well as Miles, and I took temporary refuge. "You want to go to your uncle?"

Again, at this, with his sweet ironic face, he made a movement on the pillow. "Ah you can't get off with that!"

I was silent a little, and it was I now, I think, who changed colour. "My dear, I don't want to get off!"

"You can't even if you do. You can't, you can't!" — he lay beautifully staring. "My uncle must come down and you must completely settle things."

"If we do," I returned with some spirit, "you may be sure it will be to take you quite away."

"Well, don't you understand that that's exactly what I 'm working for? You'll have to *tell* him — about the way you've let it all drop: you'll have to tell him a tremendous lot!"

The exultation with which he uttered this helped me somehow for the instant to meet him rather more. "And how much will *you*, Miles, have to tell him? There are things he'll ask you!"

He turned it over. "Very likely. But what things?"

"The things you've never told me. To make up his mind what to do with you. He can't send you back — "

"I don't want to go back!" he broke in. "I want a new field."

He said it with admirable serenity, with positive unimpeachable gaiety; and doubtless it was that very note that most evoked for me the poignancy, the unnatural childish tragedy, of his probable reappearance at the end of three months with all this bravado and still more dishonour. It overwhelmed me now that I should never be able to bear that, and it made me let myself go. I threw myself upon him and in the tenderness of my pity I embraced him. "Dear little Miles, dear little Miles — !"

My face was close to his, and he let me kiss him, simply taking it with indulgent good humour. "Well, old lady?"

"Is there nothing — nothing at all that you want to tell me?"

He turned off a little, facing round toward the wall and holding up his hand to look at as one had seen sick children look. "I've told you — I told you this morning."

Oh I was sorry for him! "That you just want me not to worry you?"

He looked round at me now as if in recognition of my understanding him; then ever so gently, "To let me alone," he replied.

There was even a strange little dignity in it, something that made me release him, yet, when I had slowly risen, linger beside him. God knows *I* never wished to harass him, but I felt that merely, at this, to turn my back on him was to abandon or, to put it more truly, lose him. "I've just begun a letter to your uncle," I said.

"Well then, finish it!"

I waited a minute. "What happened before?"

He gazed up at me again. "Before what?"

"Before you came back. And before you went away."

For some time he was silent, but he continued to meet my eyes. "What happened?"

It made me, the sound of the words, in which it seemed to me I caught for the very first time a small faint quaver of consenting consciousness — it made me drop on my knees beside the bed and seize once more the chance of possessing him. "Dear little Miles, dear little Miles, if you *knew* how I want to help you! It's only that, it's nothing but that, and I'd rather die than give you a pain or do you a wrong — I'd rather die than hurt a hair of you. Dear little Miles" — oh I brought it out now even if I *should* go too far — "I just want you to help me to save you!" But I knew in a moment after this that I had gone too far. The answer to my appeal was instantaneous, but it came in the form of an extraordinary blast and chill, a gust of frozen air and a shake of the room as great as if, in the wild wind, the casement had crashed in. The boy gave a loud high shriek which, lost in the rest of the shock of sound, might have seemed, indistinctly, though I was so close to him, a note either of jubilation or of terror. I jumped to my feet again and was conscious of darkness. So for a moment we remained, while I stared about me and saw the drawn curtains unstirred and the window still tight. "Why, the candle's out!" I then cried.

"It was I who blew it, dear!" said Miles.

XVIII

The next day, after lessons, Mrs. Grose found a moment to say to me quietly: "Have you written, Miss?"

"Yes — I've written." But I did n't add — for the hour — that my letter, sealed and directed, was still in my pocket. There would be time enough to send it before the messenger should go to the village. Meanwhile there had been on the part of my pupils no more brilliant, more exemplary morning. It was exactly as if they had both had at heart to gloss over any recent little friction. They performed the dizziest feats of arithmetic, soaring quite out of *my* feeble range, and perpetrated, in higher spirits than ever, geographical and historical jokes. It was conspicuous of course in Miles in particular that he appeared to wish to show how easily he could let me down. This child, to my memory, really lives in a setting of beauty and misery that no words can translate; there was a distinction all his own in every impulse he revealed; never was a small natural creature, to the uninformed eye all frankness and freedom, a more ingenious, a more extraordinary little gentleman. I had perpetually to guard against the wonder of contemplation into which my initiated view betrayed me; to check the irrelevant gaze and discouraged sigh in which I constantly both attacked and renounced the enigma of what such a little gentleman could have done that deserved a penalty. Say that, by the dark prodigy I knew, the imagination of all evil *had* been opened up to him: all the justice within me ached for the proof that it could ever have flowered into an act.

He had never at any rate been such a little gentleman as when, after our early dinner on this dreadful day, he came round to me and asked if I should n't like him for half an hour to play to me. David playing to Saul could never have shown a finer sense of the occasion. It was literally a charming exhibition of tact, of magnanimity, and quite tantamount to his saying outright: "The true knights we love to read about never push an advantage too far. I know what you mean now: you mean that — to be let alone yourself and not followed up — you'll cease to worry and spy upon me, won't keep me so close to you, will let me go and come. Well, I 'come,' you see — but I don't go! There'll be plenty of time for that. I do really delight in your society and I only want to show you that I contended for a principle." It may be imagined whether I resisted this appeal or failed to accompany him again, hand in hand, to the school-room. He sat down at the old piano and played as he had never played; and if there are those who think he had better have been kicking a foot-ball I can only say that I wholly agree with them. For at the end of a time that under his influence I had quite ceased to measure I started up with a strange sense of having literally slept at my post. It was after lun-cheon, and by the schoolroom fire, and yet I had n't really in the least slept; I had only done something much worse — I had forgotten. Where all this time was Flora? When I put the question to Miles he played on a minute before answering, and then could only say: "Why, my dear, how do *I* know?" — breaking moreover into a happy laugh which immediately after, as if it were a vocal accompaniment, he pro-longed into incoherent extravagant song.

I went straight to my room, but his sister was not there; then, before going downstairs, I looked into several others. As she was nowhere about she would surely be with Mrs. Grose, whom in the comfort of that theory I accordingly proceeded in quest of. I found her where I had found her the evening before, but she met my quick challenge with blank scared ignorance. She had only supposed that, after the repast, I had carried off both the children; as to which she was quite in her right, for it was the very first time I had allowed the little girl out of my sight without some special provision. Of course now indeed she might be with the maids, so that the immediate thing was to look for her without an air of alarm. This we promptly arranged between us; but when, ten minutes later and in pursuance of our arrangement, we met in the hall, it was only to report on either side that after guarded enquiries we had altogether failed to trace her. For a minute there, apart from observa-tion, we exchanged mute alarms, and I could feel with what high inter-est my friend returned me all those I had from the first given her.

"She'll be above," she presently said — "in one of the rooms you have n't searched."

"No; she's at a distance." I had made up my mind. "She has gone out."

Mrs. Grose stared. "Without a hat?"

I naturally also looked volumes. "Isn't that woman always without one?"

"She's with *her?*"

"She's with *her!*" I declared. "We must find them."

My hand was on my friend's arm, but she failed for the moment, confronted with such an account of the matter, to respond to my pressure. She communed, on the contrary, where she stood, with her uneasiness. "And where's Master Miles?"

"Oh *he's* with Quint. They'll be in the schoolroom."

"Lord, Miss!" My view, I was myself aware — and therefore I suppose my tone — had never yet reached so calm an assurance.

"The trick's played," I went on; "they've successfully worked their plan. He found the most divine little way to keep me quiet while she went off."

" 'Divine'?" Mrs. Grose bewilderedly echoed.

"Infernal then!" I almost cheerfully rejoined. "He has provided for himself as well. But come!"

She had helplessly gloomed at the upper regions. "You leave him — ?"

"So long with Quint? Yes — I don't mind that now."

She always ended at these moments by getting possession of my hand, and in this manner she could at present still stay me. But after gasping an instant at my sudden resignation, "Because of your letter?" she eagerly brought out.

I quickly, by way of answer, felt for my letter, drew it forth, held it up, and then, freeing myself, went and laid it on the great hall-table. "Luke will take it," I said as I came back. I reached the house-door and opened it; I was already on the steps.

My companion still demurred: the storm of the night and the early morning had dropped, but the afternoon was damp and grey. I came down to the drive while she stood in the doorway. "You go with nothing on?"

"What do I care when the child has nothing? I can't wait to dress," I cried, "and if you must do so I leave you. Try meanwhile yourself upstairs."

"With *them?*" Oh on this the poor woman promptly joined me!

XIX°

We went straight to the lake, as it was called at Bly, and I dare say rightly called, though it may have been a sheet of water less remarkable than my untravelled eyes supposed it. My acquaintance with sheets of

XIX: The tenth weekly *Collier's* installment and *Part Fifth* began here.

water was small, and the pool of Bly, at all events on the few occasions
of my consenting, under the protection of my pupils, to affront its surface in the old flat-bottomed boat moored there for our use, had impressed me both with its extent and its agitation. The usual place of
embarkation was half a mile from the house, but I had an intimate conviction that, wherever Flora might be, she was not near home. She had
not given me the slip for any small adventure, and, since the day of the
very great one that I had shared with her by the pond, I had been aware,
in our walks, of the quarter to which she most inclined. This was why I
had now given to Mrs. Grose's steps so marked a direction — a direction making her, when she perceived it, oppose a resistance that showed
me she was freshly mystified. "You're going to the water, Miss? — you
think she's *in* — ?"

"She may be, though the depth is, I believe, nowhere very great.
But what I judge most likely is that she's on the spot from which, the
other day, we saw together what I told you."

"When she pretended not to see — ?"

"With that astounding self-possession! I've always been sure she
wanted to go back alone. And now her brother has managed it for her."

Mrs. Grose still stood where she had stopped. "You suppose they
really *talk* of them?"

I could meet this with an assurance! "They say things that, if we
heard them, would simply appal us."

"And if she *is* there — ?"

"Yes?"

"Then Miss Jessel is?"

"Beyond a doubt. You shall see."

"Oh thank you!" my friend cried, planted so firm that, taking it in,
I went straight on without her. By the time I reached the pool, however, she was close behind me, and I knew that, whatever, to her apprehension, might befall me, the exposure of sticking to me struck her as
her least danger. She exhaled a moan of relief as we at last came in sight
of the greater part of the water without a sight of the child. There was
no trace of Flora on that nearer side of the bank where my observation
of her had been most startling, and none on the opposite edge, where,
save for a margin of some twenty yards, a thick copse came down to the
pond. This expanse, oblong in shape, was so narrow compared to its
length that, with its ends out of view, it might have been taken for a
scant river. We looked at the empty stretch, and then I felt the suggestion in my friend's eyes. I knew what she meant and I replied with a
negative headshake.

"No, no; wait! She has taken the boat."

My companion stared at the vacant mooring-place and then again across the lake. "Then where is it?"

"Our not seeing it is the strongest of proofs. She has used it to go over, and then has managed to hide it."

"All alone — that child?"

"She's not alone, and at such times she's not a child: she's an old, old woman." I scanned all the visible shore while Mrs. Grose took again, into the queer element I offered her, one of her plunges of sub-mission; then I pointed out that the boat might perfectly be in a small refuge formed by one of the recesses of the pool, an indentation masked, for the hither side, by a projection of the bank and by a clump of trees growing close to the water.

"But if the boat's there, where on earth's *she?*" my colleague anx-iously asked.

"That's exactly what we must learn." And I started to walk further.

"By going all the way round?"

"Certainly, far as it is. It will take us but ten minutes, yet it's far enough to have made the child prefer not to walk. She went straight over."

"Laws!" cried my friend again: the chain of my logic was ever too strong for her. It dragged her at my heels even now, and when we had got halfway round — a devious tiresome process, on ground much bro-ken and by a path choked with overgrowth — I paused to give her breath. I sustained her with a grateful arm, assuring her that she might hugely help me; and this started us afresh, so that in the course of but few minutes more we reached a point from which we found the boat to be where I had supposed it. It had been intentionally left as much as possible out of sight and was tied to one of the stakes of a fence that came, just there, down to the brink and that had been an assistance to disembarking. I recognised, as I looked at the pair of short thick oars, quite safely drawn up, the prodigious character of the feat for a little girl; but I had by this time lived too long among wonders and had panted to too many livelier measures. There was a gate in the fence, through which we passed, and that brought us after a trifling in-terval more into the open. Then "There she is!" we both exclaimed at once.

Flora, a short way off, stood before us on the grass and smiled as if her performance had now become complete. The next thing she did, however, was to stoop straight down and pluck — quite as if it were all she was there for — a big ugly spray of withered fern. I at once felt sure she had just come out of the copse. She waited for us, not herself taking a step, and I was conscious of the rare solemnity with which we presently approached her. She smiled and smiled, and we met; but it was all done in a silence by this time flagrantly ominous. Mrs. Grose was the first to break the spell: she threw herself on her knees and, drawing the child to her breast, clasped in a long embrace the little tender yielding body. While this dumb convulsion lasted I could only watch it — which I did the more intently when I saw Flora's face peep at me over our companion's shoulder. It was serious now — the flicker had left it; but it strengthened the pang with which I at that moment envied Mrs. Grose the simplicity of *her* relation. Still, all this while, nothing more passed between us save that Flora had let her foolish fern again drop to the ground. What she and I had virtually said to each other was that pretexts were useless now. When Mrs. Grose finally got up she kept the child's hand, so that the two were still before me; and the singular reticence of our communion was even more marked in the frank look she addressed me. "I'll be hanged," it said, "if *I'll* speak!"

It was Flora who, gazing all over me in candid wonder, was the first. She was struck with our bare-headed aspect. "Why where are your things?"

"Where yours are, my dear!" I promptly returned.

She had already got back her gaiety and appeared to take this as an answer quite sufficient. "And where's Miles?" she went on.

There was something in the small valour of it that quite finished me: these three words from her were in a flash like the glitter of a drawn blade the jostle of the cup that my hand for weeks and weeks had held high and full to the brim and that now, even before speaking, I felt overflow in a deluge. "I'll tell you if you'll tell *me* — " I heard myself say, then heard the tremor in which it broke.

"Well, what?"

Mrs. Grose's suspense blazed at me, but it was too late now, and I brought the thing out handsomely. "Where, my pet, is Miss Jessel?"

XX

Just as in the churchyard with Miles, the whole thing was upon us. Much as I had made of the fact that this name had never once, between us, been sounded, the quick smitten glare with which the child's face now received it fairly likened my breach of the silence to the smash of a pane of glass. It added to the interposing cry, as if to stay the blow, that

Mrs. Grose at the same instant uttered over my violence — the shriek of a creature scared, or rather wounded, which, in turn, within a few seconds, was completed by a gasp of my own. I seized my colleague's arm. "She's there, she's there!"

Miss Jessel stood before us on the opposite bank exactly as she had stood the other time, and I remember, strangely, as the first feeling now produced in me, my thrill of joy at having brought on a proof. She was there, so I was justified; she was there, so I was neither cruel nor mad. She was there for poor scared Mrs. Grose, but she was there most for Flora; and no moment of my monstrous time was perhaps so extraordinary as that in which I consciously threw out to her — with the sense that, pale and ravenous demon as she was, she would catch and understand it — an inarticulate message of gratitude. She rose erect on the spot my friend and I had lately quitted, and there was n't in all the long reach of her desire an inch of her evil that fell short. This first vividness of vision and emotion were things of a few seconds, during which Mrs. Grose's dazed blink across to where I pointed struck me as showing that she too at last saw, just as it carried my own eyes precipitately to the child. The revelation then of the manner in which Flora was affected startled me in truth far more than it would have done to find her also merely agitated, for direct dismay was of course not what I had expected. Prepared and on her guard as our pursuit had actually made her, she would repress every betrayal; and I was therefore at once shaken by my first glimpse of the particular one for which I had not allowed. To see her, without a convulsion of her small pink face, not even feign to glance in the direction of the prodigy I announced, but only, instead of that, turn at *me* an expression of hard still gravity, an expression absolutely new and unprecedented and that appeared to read and accuse and judge me — this was a stroke that somehow converted the little girl herself into a figure portentous. I gaped at her coolness even though my certitude of her thoroughly seeing was never greater than at that instant, and then, in the immediate need to defend myself, I called her passionately to witness. "She's there, you little unhappy thing — there, there, *there,* and you know it as well as you know me!" I had said shortly before to Mrs. Grose that she was not at these times a child, but an old, old woman, and my description of her could n't have been more strikingly confirmed than in the way in which, for all notice of this, she simply showed me, without an expressional concession or admission, a countenance of deeper and deeper, of indeed suddenly quite fixed reprobation. I was by this time — if I can put the whole thing at all together — more appalled at what I may properly call her manner than at anything else, though it was quite simultaneously that I became aware of having Mrs. Grose also, and very formidably, to reckon with. My elder companion, the next moment, at any rate, blotted out everything but her own flushed face and her loud shocked protest, a burst of high disapproval. "What a dreadful turn, to be sure, Miss! Where on earth do you see anything?"

I could only grasp her more quickly yet, for even while she spoke the hideous plain presence stood undimmed and undaunted. It had already lasted a minute, and it lasted while I continued, seizing my colleague, quite thrusting her at it and presenting her to it, to insist with my pointing hand. "You don't see her exactly as *we* see? — you mean to say you don't now — *now*? She's as big as a blazing fire! Only look, dearest woman, *look* — !" She looked, just as I did, and gave me, with her deep groan of negation, repulsion, compassion — the mixture with her pity of her relief at her exemption — a sense, touching to me even then, that she would have backed me up if she had been able. I might well have needed that, for with this hard blow of the proof that her eyes were hopelessly sealed I felt my own situation horribly crumble, I felt — I *saw* — my livid predecessor press, from her position, on my defeat, and I took the measure, more than all, of what I should have from this instant to deal with in the astounding little attitude of Flora. Into this attitude Mrs. Grose immediately and violently entered, breaking, even while there pierced through my sense of ruin a prodigious private triumph, into breathless reassurance.

"She is n't there, little lady, and nobody's there — and you never see nothing, my sweet! How can poor Miss Jessel — when poor Miss Jessel's dead and buried? *We* know, don't we, love?" — and she appealed, blundering in, to the child. "It's all a mere mistake and a worry and a joke — and we'll go home as fast as we can!"

Our companion, on this, had responded with a strange quick primness of propriety, and they were again, with Mrs. Grose on her feet, united, as it were, in shocked opposition to me. Flora continued to fix me with her small mask of disaffection, and even at that minute I prayed God to forgive me for seeming to see that, as she stood there holding tight to our friend's dress, her incomparable childish beauty had suddenly failed, had quite vanished. I've said it already — she was literally, she was hideously hard; she had turned common and almost ugly. "I don't know what you mean. I see nobody. I see nothing. I never *have*. I think you're cruel. I don't like you!" Then, after this deliverance, which might have been that of a vulgarly pert little girl in the street, she hugged Mrs. Grose more closely and buried in her skirts the dreadful little face. In this position she launched an almost furious wail. "Take me away, take me away — oh take me away from *her!*"

"From *me?*" I panted.

"From you — from you!" she cried.

Even Mrs. Grose looked across at me dismayed; while I had nothing to do but communicate again with the figure that, on the opposite bank, without a movement, as rigidly still as if catching, beyond the interval, our voices, was as vividly there for my disaster as it was not there for my service. The wretched child had spoken exactly as if she had got from some outside source° each of her stabbing little words, and I could therefore, in the full despair of all I had to accept, but sadly shake my head at her. "If I had ever doubted all my doubt would at present have gone. I've been living with the miserable truth, and now it has only too much closed round me. Of course I've lost you: I've interfered, and you've seen, under *her* dictation" — with which I faced, over the pool again, our infernal witness — "the easy and perfect way to meet it. I've done my best, but I've lost you. Good-bye." For Mrs. Grose I had an imperative, an almost frantic "Go, go!" before which, in infinite distress, but mutely possessed of the little girl and clearly convinced, in spite of her blindness, that something awful had occurred and some collapse engulfed us, she retreated, by the way we had come, as fast as she could move.

Of what first happened when I was left alone I had no subsequent memory. I only knew that at the end of, I suppose, a quarter of an hour, an odorous dampness and roughness, chilling and piercing my trouble, had made me understand that I must have thrown myself, on my face, to the ground and given way to a wildness of grief. I must have lain there long and cried and wailed, for when I raised my head the day was almost done. I got up and looked a moment, through the twilight, at the grey pool and its blank haunted edge, and then I took, back to the house, my dreary and difficult course. When I reached the gate in the fence the boat, to my surprise, was gone, so that I had a fresh reflexion to make on Flora's extraordinary command of the situation. She passed that night, by the most tacit and, I should add, were not the word so grotesque a false note, the happiest of arrangements, with Mrs. Grose. I saw neither of them on my return, but on the other hand I saw, as by an ambiguous compensation, a great deal of Miles. I saw — I can use no

---

from some outside source: This phrase may be a clue that Flora is "possessed" — that is, that her body is temporarily occupied by the spirit of Miss Jessel. The concept of possession was well-known in James's time. Note the word "dispossessed" in the last line of the story.

other phrase — so much of him that it fairly measured more than it had ever measured. No evening I had passed at Bly was to have had the portentous quality of this one; in spite of which — and in spite also of the deeper depths of consternation that had opened beneath my feet — there was literally, in the ebbing actual, an extraordinarily sweet sadness. On reaching the house I had never so much as looked for the boy; I had simply gone straight to my room to change what I was wearing and to take in, at a glance, much material testimony to Flora's rupture. Her little belongings had all been removed. When later, by the schoolroom fire, I was served with tea by the usual maid, I indulged, on the article of my other pupil, in no enquiry whatever. He had his freedom now — he might have it to the end! Well, he did have it; and it consisted — in part at least — of his coming in at about eight o'clock and sitting down with me in silence. On the removal of the tea-things I had blown out the candles and drawn my chair closer: I was conscious of a mortal coldness and felt as if I should never again be warm. So when he appeared I was sitting in the glow with my thoughts. He paused a moment by the door as if to look at me; then — as if to share them — came to the other side of the hearth and sank into a chair. We sat there in absolute stillness; yet he wanted, I felt, to be with me.

XXI°

Before a new day, in my room, had fully broken, my eyes opened to Mrs. Grose, who had come to my bedside with worse news. Flora was so markedly feverish that an illness was perhaps at hand; she had passed a night of extreme unrest, a night agitated above all by fears that had for their subject not in the least her former but wholly her present governess. It was not against the possible re-entrance of Miss Jessel on the scene that she protested — it was conspicuously and passionately against mine. I was at once on my feet, and with an immense deal to ask; the more that my friend had discernibly now girded her loins to meet me afresh. This I felt as soon as I had put to her the question of her sense of the child's sincerity as against my own. "She persists in denying to you that she saw, or has ever seen, anything?"

My visitor's trouble truly was great. "Ah Miss, it is n't a matter on which I can push her! Yet it is n't either, I must say, as if I much needed to. It has made her, every inch of her, quite old."

XXI: The eleventh weekly *Collier's* installment began here.

"Oh I see her perfectly from here. She resents, for all the world like some high little personage, the imputation on her truthfulness and, as it were, her respectability. 'Miss Jessel indeed — *she!*' Ah she's 'respectable,' the chit! The impression she gave me there yesterday was, I assure you, the very strangest of all: it was quite beyond any of the others. I *did* put my foot in it! She'll never speak to me again."

Hideous and obscure as it all was, it held Mrs. Grose briefly silent; then she granted my point with a frankness which, I made sure, had more behind it. "I think indeed, Miss, she never will. She do have a grand manner about it!"

"And that manner" — I summed it up — "is practically what's the matter with her now."

Oh that manner, I could see in my visitor's face, and not a little else besides! "She asks me every three minutes if I think you're coming in."

"I see — I see." I too, on my side, had so much more than worked it out. "Has she said to you since yesterday — except to repudiate her familiarity with anything so dreadful — a single other word about Miss Jessel?"

"Not one, Miss. And of course, you know," my friend added, "I took it from her by the lake that just then and there at least there *was* nobody."

"Rather! And naturally you take it from her still."

"I don't contradict her. What else can I do?"

"Nothing in the world! You've the cleverest little person to deal with. They've made them — their two friends, I mean — still cleverer even than nature did; for it was wondrous material to play on! Flora has now her grievance, and she'll work it to the end."

"Yes, Miss; but to *what* end?"

"Why that of dealing with me to her uncle. She'll make me out to him the lowest creature — !"

I winced at the fair show of the scene in Mrs. Grose's face; she looked for a minute as if she sharply saw them together. "And him who thinks so well of you!"

"He has an odd way — it comes over me now," I laughed, " — of proving it! But that does n't matter. What Flora wants of course is to get rid of me."

My companion bravely concurred. "Never again to so much as look at you."

"So that what you've come to me now for," I asked, "is to speed me on my way?" Before she had time to reply, however, I had her in check. "I've a better idea — the result of my reflexions. My going *would* seem the right thing, and on Sunday I was terribly near it. Yet that won't do. It's *you* who must go. You must take Flora."

My visitor, at this, did speculate. "But where in the world — ?"

"Away from here. Away from *them*. Away, even most of all, now, from me. Straight to her uncle."

"Only to tell on you — ?"

"No, not 'only'! To leave me, in addition, with my remedy."

She was still vague. "And what *is* your remedy?"

"Your loyalty, to begin with. And then Miles's."

She looked at me hard. "Do you think he — ?"

"Won't, if he has the chance, turn on me? Yes, I venture still to think it. At all events I want to try. Get off with his sister as soon as possible and leave me with him alone." I was amazed, myself, at the spirit I had still in reserve, and therefore perhaps a trifle the more disconcerted at the way in which, in spite of this fine example of it, she hesitated. "There's one thing, of course," I went on: "they must n't, before she goes, see each other for three seconds." Then it came over me that, in spite of Flora's presumable sequestration° from the instant of her return from the pool, it might already be too late. "Do you mean," I anxiously asked, "that they *have* met?"

At this she quite flushed. "Ah, Miss, I 'm not such a fool as that! If I've been obliged to leave her three or four times, it has been each time with one of the maids, and at present, though she's alone, she's locked in safe. And yet — and yet!" There were too many things.

"And yet what?"

"Well, are you so sure of the little gentleman?"

"I'm not sure of anything but *you*. But I have, since last evening, a new hope. I think he wants to give me an opening. I do believe that — poor little exquisite wretch! — he wants to speak. Last evening, in the firelight and the silence, he sat with me for two hours as if it were just coming."

Mrs. Grose looked hard through the window at the grey gathering day. "And did it come?"

"No, though I waited and waited I confess it did n't, and it was without a breach of the silence, or so much as a faint allusion to his sister's condition and absence, that we at last kissed for good-night. All the same," I continued, "I can't, if her uncle sees her, consent to his seeing her brother without my having given the boy — and most of all because things have got so bad — a little more time."

---

sequestration: Seclusion, separation.

My friend appeared on this ground more reluctant than I could quite understand. "What do you mean by more time?"

"Well, a day or two — really to bring it out. He'll then be on *my* side — of which you see the importance. If nothing comes I shall only fail, and you at the worst have helped me by doing on your arrival in town whatever you may have found possible." So I put it before her, but she continued for a little so lost in other reasons that I came again to her aid. "Unless indeed," I wound up, "you really want *not* to go."

I could see it, in her face, at last clear itself: she put out her hand to me as a pledge. "I'll go — I'll go. I'll go this morning."

I wanted to be very just. "If you *should* wish still to wait I'd engage she should n't see me."

"No, no: it's the place itself. She must leave it." She held me a moment with heavy eyes, then brought out the rest. "Your idea's the right one. I myself, Miss — "

"Well?"

"I can't stay."

The look she gave me with it made me jump at possibilities. "You mean that, since yesterday, you *have* seen — ?"

She shook her head with dignity. "I've *heard* — !"

"Heard?"

"From that child — horrors! There!" she sighed with tragic relief. "On my honour, Miss, she says things — !" But at this evocation she broke down; she dropped with a sudden cry upon my sofa and, as I had seen her do before, gave way to all the anguish of it.

It was quite in another manner that I for my part let myself go. "Oh thank God!"

She sprang up again at this, drying her eyes with a groan. " 'Thank God'?"

"It so justifies me!"

"It does that, Miss!"

I could n't have desired more emphasis, but I just waited. "She's so horrible?"

I saw my colleague scarce knew how to put it. "Really shocking."

"And about me?"

"About you, Miss — since you must have it. It's beyond everything, for a young lady; and I can't think wherever she must have picked up — "

"The appalling language she applies to me? I can then!" I broke in with a laugh that was doubtless significant enough.

It only in truth left my friend still more grave. "Well, perhaps I ought to also — since I've heard some of it before!° Yet I can't bear it," the poor woman went on while with the same movement she glanced, on my dressing-table, at the face of my watch. "But I must go back."

I kept her, however. "Ah if you can't bear it — !"

"How can I stop with her, you mean? Why just *for* that: to get her away. Far from this," she pursued, "far from *them* — "

"She may be different? she may be free?" I seized her almost with joy. "Then in spite of yesterday you *believe* — "

"In such doings?" Her simple description of them required, in the light of her expression, to be carried no further, and she gave me the whole thing as she had never done. "I believe."

Yes, it was a joy, and we were still shoulder to shoulder: if I might continue sure of that I should care but little what else happened. My support in the presence of disaster would be the same as it had been in my early need of confidence, and if my friend would answer for my honesty I would answer for all the rest. On the point of taking leave of her, none the less, I was to some extent embarrassed. "There's one thing of course — it occurs to me — to remember. My letter giving the alarm will have reached town before you."

I now felt still more how she had been beating about the bush and how weary at last it had made her. "Your letter won't have got there. Your letter never went."

"What then became of it?"

"Goodness knows! Master Miles — "

"Do you mean *he* took it?" I gasped.

She hung fire, but she overcame her reluctance. "I mean that I saw yesterday, when I came back with Miss Flora, that it was n't where you had put it. Later in the evening I had the chance to question Luke, and he declared that he had neither noticed nor touched it." We could only exchange, on this, one of our deeper mutual soundings, and it was Mrs. Grose who first brought up the plumb with an almost elate "You see!"

"Yes, I see that if Miles took it instead he probably will have read it and destroyed it."

"And don't you see anything else?"

I faced her a moment with a sad smile. "It strikes me that by this time your eyes are open even wider than mine."

They proved to be so indeed, but she could still almost blush to show it. "I make out now what he must have done at school." And she

---

heard some of it before: She had heard some of it, that is, from Miss Jessel before she died.

gave, in her simple sharpness, an almost droll disillusioned nod. "He stole!"

I turned it over — I tried to be more judicial. "Well — perhaps."

She looked as if she found me unexpectedly calm. "He stole *letters!*"

She could n't know my reasons for a calmness after all pretty shallow; so I showed them off as I might. "I hope then it was to more purpose than in this case! The note, at all events, that I put on the table yesterday," I pursued, "will have given him so scant an advantage — for it contained only the bare demand for an interview — that he's already much ashamed of having gone so far for so little, and that what he had on his mind last evening was precisely the need of confession." I seemed to myself for the instant to have mastered it, to see it all. "Leave us, leave us" — I was already, at the door, hurrying her off. "I'll get it out of him. He'll meet me. He'll confess. If he confesses he's saved. And if he's saved — "

"Then *you* are?" The dear woman kissed me on this, and I took her farewell. "I'll save you without him!" she cried as she went.

XXII

Yet it was when she had got off — and I missed her on the spot — that the great pinch really came. If I had counted on what it would give me to find myself alone with Miles I quickly recognised that it would give me at least a measure. No hour of my stay in fact was so assailed with apprehensions as that of my coming down to learn that the carriage containing Mrs. Grose and my younger pupil had already rolled out of the gates. Now I *was,* I said to myself, face to face with the elements, and for much of the rest of the day, while I fought my weakness, I could consider that I had been supremely rash. It was a tighter place still than I had yet turned round in; all the more that, for the first time, I could see in the aspect of others a confused reflexion of the crisis. What had happened naturally caused them all to stare; there was too little of the explained, throw out whatever we might, in the suddenness of my colleague's act. The maids and the men looked blank; the effect of which on my nerves was an aggravation until I saw the necessity of making it a positive aid. It was in short by just clutching the helm that I avoided total wreck; and I dare say that, to bear up at all, I became that morning very grand and very dry. I welcomed the consciousness that I was charged with much to do, and I caused it to be known as well that, left thus to myself, I was quite remarkably firm. I wandered with that manner, for the next hour or two, all over the place and looked, I have no doubt, as if I were ready for any onset. So, for the benefit of whom it might concern, I paraded with a sick heart.

The person it appeared least to concern proved to be, till dinner, little Miles himself. My perambulations had given me meanwhile no glimpse of him, but they had tended to make more public the change taking place in our relation as a consequence of his having at the piano, the day before, kept me, in Flora's interest, so beguiled and befooled. The stamp of publicity had of course been fully given by her confinement and departure, and the change itself was now ushered in by our non-observance of the regular custom of the schoolroom. He had already disappeared when, on my way down, I pushed open his door, and I learned below that he had breakfasted — in the presence of a couple of the maids — with Mrs. Grose and his sister. He had then gone out, as he said, for a stroll; than which nothing, I reflected, could better have expressed his frank view of the abrupt transformation of my office. What he would now permit this office to consist of was yet to be settled: there was at the least a queer relief — I mean for myself in especial — in the renouncement of one pretension. If so much had sprung to the surface I scarce put it too strongly in saying that what had perhaps sprung highest was the absurdity of our prolonging the fiction that I had anything more to teach him. It sufficiently stuck out that, by tacit little tricks in which even more than myself he carried out the care for my dignity, I had had to appeal to him to let me off straining to meet him on the ground of his true capacity. He had at any rate his freedom now; I was never to touch it again: as I had amply shown, moreover, when, on his joining me in the schoolroom the previous night, I uttered, in reference to the interval just concluded, neither challenge nor hint. I had too much, from this moment, my other ideas. Yet when he at last arrived the difficulty of applying them, the accumulations of my problem, were brought straight home to me by the beautiful little presence on which what had occurred had as yet, for the eye, dropped neither stain nor shadow.

To mark, for the house, the high state I cultivated I decreed that my meals with the boy should be served, as we called it, downstairs; so that I had been awaiting him in the ponderous pomp of the room° outside the window of which I had had from Mrs. Grose, that first scared Sun-

---

the room: The "grown-up" dining room referred to in chapter IV, from which she had earlier seen Peter Quint outside the window.

day, my flash of something it would scarce have done to call light. Here
at present I felt afresh — for I had felt it again and again — how my
equilibrium depended on the success of my rigid will, the will to shut
my eyes as tight as possible to the truth that what I had to deal with was,
revoltingly, against nature. I could only get on at all by taking "nature"
into my confidence and my account, by treating my monstrous ordeal
as a push in a direction unusual, of course, and unpleasant, but demanding after all, for a fair front, only another turn of the screw of ordinary
human virtue. No attempt, none the less, could well require more tact
than just this attempt to supply, one's self, *all* the nature. How could I
put even a little of that article into a suppression of reference to what
had occurred? How on the other hand could I make a reference without
a new plunge into the hideous obscure? Well, a sort of answer, after a
time, had come to me, and it was so far confirmed as that I was met,
incontestably, by the quickened vision of what was rare in my little companion. It was indeed as if he had found even now — as he had so often
found at lessons — still some other delicate way to ease me off. Wasn't
there light in the fact which, as we shared our solitude, broke out with
a specious glitter it had never yet quite worn? — the fact that (opportunity aiding, precious opportunity which had now come) it would be
preposterous, with a child so endowed, to forego the help one might
wrest from absolute intelligence? What had his intelligence been given
him for but to save him? Might n't one, to reach his mind, risk the
stretch of a stiff arm across his character? It was as if, when we were face
to face in the dining-room, he had literally shown me the way. The roast
mutton was on the table and I had dispensed with attendance.° Miles,
before he sat down, stood a moment with his hands in his pockets and
looked at the joint,° on which he seemed on the point of passing some
humorous judgement. But what he presently produced was: "I say, my
dear, is she really very awfully ill?"

"Little Flora? Not so bad but that she'll presently be better. London
will set her up. Bly had ceased to agree with her. Come here and take
your mutton."

He alertly obeyed me, carried the plate carefully to his seat and,
when he was established, went on. "Did Bly disagree with her so terribly
all at once?"

"Not so suddenly as you might think. One had seen it coming on."

"Then why did n't you get her off before?"

"Before what?"

---

dispensed with attendance: Dismissed the servants.   **the joint:** The mutton roast.

"Before she became too ill to travel."

I found myself prompt. "She's *not* too ill to travel; she only might have become so if she had stayed. This was just the moment to seize. The journey will dissipate the influence" — oh I was grand! — "and carry it off."

"I see, I see" — Miles, for that matter, was grand too. He settled to his repast with the charming little "table manner" that, from the day of his arrival, had relieved me of all grossness of admonition. Whatever he had been expelled from school for, it was n't for ugly feeding. He was irreproachable, as always, today; but was unmistakeably more conscious. He was discernibly trying to take for granted more things than he found, without assistance, quite easy; and he dropped into peaceful silence while he felt his situation. Our meal was of the briefest — mine a vain pretence, and I had the things immediately removed. While this was done Miles stood again with his hands in his little pockets and his back to me — stood and looked out of the wide window through which, that other day, I had seen what pulled me up. We continued silent while the maid was with us — as silent, it whimsically occurred to me, as some young couple who, on their wedding-journey, at the inn, feel shy in the presence of the waiter. He turned round only when the waiter had left us. "Well — so we're alone!"

XXIII°

"Oh more or less." I imagine my smile was pale. "Not absolutely. We should n't like that!" I went on.

"No — I suppose we should n't. Of course we've the others."

"We've the others — we've indeed the others," I concurred.

"Yet even though we have them," he returned, still with his hands in his pockets and planted there in front of me, "they don't much count, do they?"

I made the best of it, but I felt wan. "It depends on what you call 'much'!"

"Yes" — with all accommodation — "everything depends!" On this, however, he faced to the window again and presently reached it with his vague restless cogitating step. He remained there a while with his forehead against the glass, in contemplation of the stupid shrubs I knew and the dull things of November. I had always my hypocrisy of

XXIII: The twelfth and last weekly *Collier's* installment began here.

"work,"° behind which I now gained° the sofa. Steadying myself with it there as I had repeatedly done at those moments of torment that I have described as the moments of my knowing the children to be given to something from which I was barred, I sufficiently obeyed my habit of being prepared for the worst. But an extraordinary impression dropped on me as I extracted a meaning from the boy's embarrassed back — none other than the impression that I was not barred now. This inference grew in a few minutes to sharp intensity and seemed bound up with the direct perception that it was positively *he* who was. The frames and squares of the great window were a kind of image, for him, of a kind of failure. I felt that I saw him, in any case, shut in or shut out. He was admirable but not comfortable: I took it in with a throb of hope. Wasn't he looking through the haunted pane for something he could n't see? — and was n't it the first time in the whole business that he had known such a lapse? The first, the very first: I found it a splendid portent. It made him anxious, though he watched himself; he had been anxious all day and, even while in his usual sweet little manner he sat at table, had needed all his small strange genius to give it a gloss. When he at last turned round to meet me it was almost as if this genius had succumbed. "Well, I think I'm glad Bly agrees with *me!*"

"You'd certainly seem to have seen, these twenty-four hours, a good deal more of it than for some time before. I hope," I went on bravely, "that you've been enjoying yourself."

"Oh yes, I've been ever so far; all round about — miles and miles away. I've never been so free."

He had really a manner of his own, and I could only try to keep up with him. "Well, do you like it?"

He stood there smiling; then at last he put into two words — "Do *you?*" — more discrimination° than I had ever heard two words contain. Before I had time to deal with that, however, he continued as if with the sense that this was an impertinence to be softened. "Nothing could be more charming than the way you take it, for of course if we're alone together now it's you that are alone most. But I hope," he threw in, "you don't particularly mind!"

"Having to do with you?" I asked. "My dear child, how can I help minding? Though I've renounced all claim to your company — you're so beyond me — I at least greatly enjoy it. What else should I stay on for?"

---

hypocrisy of "work": The pretense that she had mending or knitting to do.   **gained:** Moved to, sat down on.   **more discrimination:** More discernment of meaning.

He looked at me more directly, and the expression of his face, graver now, struck me as the most beautiful I had ever found in it. "You stay on just for *that?*"

"Certainly. I stay on as your friend and from the tremendous interest I take in you till something can be done for you that may be more worth your while. That need n't surprise you." My voice trembled so that I felt it impossible to suppress the shake. "Don't you remember how I told you, when I came and sat on your bed the night of the storm, that there was nothing in the world I would n't do for you?"

"Yes, yes!" He, on his side, more and more visibly nervous, had a tone to master; but he was so much more successful than I that, laughing out through his gravity, he could pretend we were pleasantly jesting. "Only that, I think, was to get me to do something for *you!*"

"It was partly to get you to do something," I conceded. "But, you know, you did n't do it."

"Oh yes," he said with the brightest superficial eagerness, "you wanted me to tell you something."

"That's it. Out, straight out. What you have on your mind, you know."

"Ah then is *that* what you've stayed over for?"

He spoke with a gaiety through which I could still catch the finest little quiver of resentful passion; but I can't begin to express the effect upon me of an implication of surrender even so faint. It was as if what I had yearned for had come at last only to astonish me. "Well, yes — I may as well make a clean breast of it. It was precisely for that."

He waited so long that I supposed it for the purpose of repudiating the assumption on which my action had been founded; but what he finally said was: "Do you mean now — here?"

"There could n't be a better place or time." He looked round him uneasily, and I had the rare — oh the queer! — impression of the very first symptom I had seen in him of the approach of immediate fear. It was as if he were suddenly afraid of me — which struck me indeed as perhaps the best thing to make him. Yet in the very pang of the effort I felt it vain to try sternness, and I heard myself the next instant so gentle as to be almost grotesque. "You want so to go out again?"

"Awfully!" He smiled at me heroically, and the touching little bravery of it was enhanced by his actually flushing with pain. He had picked up his hat, which he had brought in, and stood twirling it in a way that gave me, even as I was just nearly reaching port, a perverse horror of what I was doing. To do it in *any* way was an act of violence, for what did it consist of but the obtrusion of the idea of grossness and guilt on

a small helpless creature who had been for me a revelation of the possibilities of beautiful intercourse? Was n't it base to create for a being so
exquisite a mere alien awkwardness? I suppose I now read into our situation a clearness it could n't have had at the time, for I seem to see our
poor eyes already lighted with some spark of a prevision of the anguish
that was to come. So we circled about with terrors and scruples, fighters
not daring to close. But it was for each other we feared! That kept us a
little longer suspended and unbruised. "I'll tell you everything," Miles
said — "I mean I'll tell you anything you like. You'll stay on with me,
and we shall both be all right, and I *will* tell you — I *will*. But not now."

"Why not now?"

My insistence turned him from me and kept him once more at his
window in a silence during which, between us, you might have heard a
pin drop. Then he was before me again with the air of a person for
whom, outside, some one who had frankly to be reckoned with was
waiting. "I have to see Luke."

I had not yet reduced him to quite so vulgar a lie, and I felt propor-
tionately ashamed. But, horrible as it was, his lies made up my truth. I
achieved thoughtfully a few loops of my knitting. "Well then go to
Luke, and I'll wait for what you promise. Only in return for that satisfy,
before you leave me, one very much smaller request."

He looked as if he felt he had succeeded enough to be able still a
little to bargain. "Very much smaller — ?"

"Yes, a mere fraction of the whole. Tell me" — oh my work preoccupied me, and I was off-hand! — "if, yesterday afternoon, from the
table in the hall, you took, you know, my letter."

XXIV

My grasp of how he received this suffered for a minute from something that I can describe only as a fierce split of my attention — a stroke
that at first, as I sprang straight up, reduced me to the mere blind movement of getting hold of him, drawing him close and, while I just fell for
support against the nearest piece of furniture, instinctively keeping him
with his back to the window. The appearance was full upon us that I had
already had to deal with here: Peter Quint had come into view like a
sentinel before a prison. The next thing I saw was that, from outside, he
had reached the window, and then I knew that, close to the glass and
glaring in through it, he offered once more to the room his white face
of damnation. It represents but grossly what took place within me at the

sight to say that on the second my decision was made; yet I believe that no woman so overwhelmed ever in so short a time recovered her command of the *act*. It came to me in the very horror of the immediate presence that the act would be, seeing and facing what I saw and faced, to keep the boy himself unaware. The inspiration — I can call it by no other name — was that I felt how voluntarily, how transcendently,° I *might*. It was like fighting with a demon for a human soul, and when I had fairly so appraised it I saw how the human soul — held out, in the tremor of my hands, at arms' length — had a perfect dew of sweat on a lovely childish forehead. The face that was close to mine was as white as the face against the glass, and out of it presently came a sound, not low nor weak, but as if from much further away, that I drank like a waft of fragrance.

"Yes — I took it."

At this, with a moan of joy, I enfolded, I drew him close; and while I held him to my breast, where I could feel in the sudden fever of his little body the tremendous pulse of his little heart, I kept my eyes on the thing at the window and saw it move and shift its posture. I have likened it to a sentinel, but its slow wheel, for a moment, was rather the prowl of a baffled beast. My present quickened courage, however, was such that, not too much to let it through, I had to shade, as it were, my flame. Meanwhile the glare of the face was again at the window, the scoundrel fixed as if to watch and wait. It was the very confidence that I might now defy him, as well as the positive certitude, by this time, of the child's unconsciousness, that made me go on. "What did you take it for?"

"To see what you said about me."

"You opened the letter?"

"I opened it."

My eyes were now, as I held him off a little again, on Miles's own face, in which the collapse of mockery showed me how complete was the ravage of uneasiness. What was prodigious was that at last, by my success, his sense was sealed and his communication stopped: he knew that he was in presence, but knew not of what, and knew still less that I also was and that I did know. And what did this strain of trouble matter when my eyes went back to the window only to see that the air was clear again and — by my personal triumph — the influence quenched? There was nothing there. I felt that the cause was mine and that I should surely get *all*. "And you found nothing!" — I let my elation out.

transcendently: Intuitionally; utterly.

He gave the most mournful, thoughtful little headshake. "Nothing."

"Nothing, nothing!" I almost shouted in my joy.

"Nothing, nothing," he sadly repeated.

I kissed his forehead; it was drenched. "So what have you done with it?"

"I've burnt it."

"Burnt it?" It was now or never. "Is that what you did at school?"

Oh what this brought up! "At school?"

"Did you take letters? — or other things?"

"Other things?" He appeared now to be thinking of something far off and that reached him only through the pressure of his anxiety. Yet it did reach him. "Did I *steal*?"

I felt myself redden to the roots of my hair as well as wonder if it were more strange to put to a gentleman such a question or to see him take it with allowances that gave the very distance of his fall in the world. "Was it for that you might n't go back?"

The only thing he felt was rather a dreary little surprise. "Did you know I might n't go back?"

"I know everything."

He gave me at this the longest and strangest look. "Everything?"

"Everything. Therefore *did* you — ?" But I could n't say it again. Miles could, very simply. "No. I did n't steal."

My face must have shown him I believed him utterly; yet my hands — but it was for pure tenderness — shook him as if to ask him why, if it was all for nothing, he had condemned me to months of torment. "What then did you do?"

He looked in vague pain all round the top of the room and drew his breath, two or three times over, as if with difficulty. He might have been standing at the bottom of the sea and raising his eyes to some faint green twilight. "Well — I said things."

"Only that?"

"They thought it was enough!"

"To turn you out for?"

Never, truly, had a person "turned out" shown so little to explain it as this little person! He appeared to weigh my question, but in a manner quite detached and almost helpless. "Well, I suppose I ought n't."

"But to whom did you say them?"

He evidently tried to remember, but it dropped — he had lost it. "I don't know!"

He almost smiled at me in the desolation of his surrender, which was indeed practically, by this time, so complete that I ought to have left it there. But I was infatuated — I was blind with victory, though even then the very effect that was to have brought him so much nearer was already that of added separation. "Was it to every one?" I asked.

"No; it was only to — " But he gave a sick little headshake. "I don't remember their names."

"Were they then so many?"

"No — only a few. Those I liked."

Those he liked? I seemed to float not into clearness, but into a darker obscure, and within a minute there had come to me out of my very pity the appalling alarm of his being perhaps innocent. It was for the instant confounding and bottomless, for if he *were* innocent what then on earth was I? Paralysed, while it lasted, by the mere brush of the question, I let him go a little, so that, with a deep-drawn sigh, he turned away from me again; which, as he faced toward the clear window, I suffered, feeling that I had nothing now there to keep him from. "And did they repeat what you said?" I went on after a moment.

He was soon at some distance from me, still breathing hard and again with the air, though now without anger for it, of being confined against his will. Once more, as he had done before, he looked up at the dim day as if, of what had hitherto sustained him, nothing was left but an unspeakable anxiety. "Oh yes," he nevertheless replied — "they must have repeated them. To those *they* liked," he added.

There was somehow less of it than I had expected; but I turned it over. "And these things came round — ?"

"To the masters? Oh yes!" he answered very simply. "But I did n't know they'd tell."

"The masters? They did n't — they've never told. That's why I ask you."

He turned to me again his little beautiful fevered face. "Yes, it was too bad."

"Too bad?"

"What I suppose I sometimes said. To write home."

I can't name the exquisite pathos of the contradiction given to such a speech by such a speaker; I only know that the next instant I heard myself throw off with homely force: "Stuff and nonsense!" But the next after that I must have sounded stern enough. "What *were* these things?"

My sternness was all for his judge, his executioner; yet it made him avert himself again, and that movement made *me,* with a single bound and an irrepressible cry, spring straight upon him. For there again, against the glass, as if to blight his confession and stay his answer, was the hideous author of our woe — the white face of damnation. I felt a

sick swim at the drop of my victory and all the return of my battle, so
that the wildness of my veritable leap only served as a great betrayal. I
saw him, from the midst of my act, meet it with a divination, and on the
perception that even now he only guessed, and that the window was still
to his own eyes free, I let the impulse flame up to convert the climax of
his dismay into the very proof of his liberation. "No more, no more, no
more!" I shrieked to my visitant as I tried to press him against me.

"Is she *here?*" Miles panted as he caught with his sealed eyes° the
direction of my words. Then as his strange "she" staggered me and,
with a gasp, I echoed it, "Miss Jessel, Miss Jessel!" he with sudden fury
gave me back.

I seized, stupefied, his supposition — some sequel to what we had
done to Flora, but this made me only want to show him that it was
better still than that. "It's not Miss Jessel! But it's at the window —
straight before us. It's *there* — the coward horror, there for the last time!"

At this, after a second in which his head made the movement of a
baffled dog's on a scent and then gave a frantic little shake for air and
light, he was at me in a white rage, bewildered, glaring vainly over the
place and missing wholly, though it now, to my sense, filled the room
like the taste of poison, the wide overwhelming presence. "It's *he?*"

I was so determined to have all my proof that I flashed into ice to
challenge him. "Whom do you mean by 'he'?"

"Peter Quint — you devil!"° His face gave again, round the room,
its convulsed supplication. "*Where?*"

They are in my ears still, his supreme surrender of the name and his
tribute to my devotion. "What does he matter now, my own? — what
will he *ever* matter? *I* have you," I launched at the beast, "but he has lost
you for ever!" Then for the demonstration of my work, "There, *there!*"
I said to Miles.

But he had already jerked straight round, stared, glared again, and
seen but the quiet day. With the stroke of the loss I was so proud of he
uttered the cry of a creature hurled over an abyss, and the grasp with
which I recovered him might have been that of catching him in his fall.
I caught him, yes, I held him — it may be imagined with what a passion;
but at the end of a minute I began to feel what it truly was that I held.
We were alone with the quiet day, and his little heart, dispossessed, had
stopped.

---

sealed eyes: Eyes that, like Mrs. Grose's, cannot see apparitions.   **you devil:** One of the
critical questions in *The Turn of the Screw* is whether Miles refers here to the governess or
to Peter Quint as a "devil."

From the Preface
to Henry James's
1908 Edition of
The Turn of the Screw

This perfectly independent and irresponsible little fiction rejoices, beyond any rival on a like ground, in a conscious provision of prompt retort to the sharpest question that may be addressed to it. For it has the small strength — if I should n't say rather the unattackable ease — of a perfect homogeneity, of being, to the very last grain of its virtue, all of a kind; the very kind, as happens, least apt to be baited by earnest criticism, the only sort of criticism of which account need be taken. To have handled again this so full-blown flower of high fancy is to be led back by it to easy and happy recognitions. Let the first of these be that of the starting-point itself — the sense, all charming again, of the circle, one winter afternoon, round the hall-fire of a grave old country-house where (for all the world as if to resolve itself promptly and obligingly into convertible, into "literary" stuff) the talk turned, on I forget what homely pretext, to apparitions and night-fears, to the marked and sad drop in the general supply, and still more in the general quality, of such commodities. The good, the really effective and heart-shaking ghost-stories (roughly so to term them) appeared all to have been told, and neither new crop nor new type in any quarter awaited us. The new type indeed, the mere modern "psychical" case,° washed clean of all queer-

---

"psychical" case: Case reported by or commented on by a member of the Society for Psychical Research. Men and women who claimed to have seen ghosts were investigated and reported on by trained scientists in James's time.

ness as by exposure to a flowing laboratory tap, and equipped with credentials vouching for this — the new type clearly promised little, for the more it was respectably certified the less it seemed of a nature to rouse the dear old sacred terror. Thus it was, I remember, that amid our lament for a beautiful lost form, our distinguished host expressed the wish that he might but have recovered for us one of the scantest of fragments of this form at its best. He had never forgotten the impression made on him as a young man by the withheld glimpse, as it were, of a dreadful matter that had been reported years before, and with as few particulars, to a lady with whom he had youthfully talked. The story would have been thrilling could she but have found herself in better possession of it, dealing as it did with a couple of small children in an out-of-the way place, to whom the spirits of certain "bad" servants, dead in the employ of the house, were believed to have appeared with the design of "getting hold" of them. This was all, but there had been more, which my friend's old converser had lost the thread of: she could only assure him of the wonder of the allegations as she had anciently heard them made. He himself could give us but this shadow of a shadow — my own appreciation of which, I need scarcely say, was exactly wrapped up in that thinness. On the surface there was n't much, but another grain, none the less, would have spoiled the precious pinch addressed to its end as neatly as some modicum extracted from an old silver snuff-box and held between finger and thumb. I was to remember the haunted children and the prowling servile spirits as a "value," of the disquieting sort, in all conscience sufficient; so that when, after an interval, I was asked for something seasonable by the promoters of a periodical° dealing in the time-honoured Christmas-tide toy, I bethought myself at once of the vividest little note for sinister romance that I had ever jotted down.

Such was the private source of "The Turn of the Screw"; and I wondered, I confess, why so fine a germ, gleaming there in the wayside dust of life, had never been deftly picked up. The thing had for me the immense merit of allowing the imagination absolute freedom of hand, of inviting it to act on a perfectly clear field, with no "outside" control involved, no pattern of the usual or the true or the terrible "pleasant" (save always of course the high pleasantry of one's very form) to consort with. This makes in fact the charm of my second reference, that I find here a perfect example of an exercise of the imagination unassisted, un-

---

periodical: *Collier's Weekly.* In 1897 Robert Collier had invited James to submit a tale for its Christmas number.

associated — playing the game, making the score, in the phrase of our sporting day, off its own bat. To what degree the game was worth playing I need n't attempt to say: the exercise I have noted strikes me now, I confess, as the interesting thing, the imaginative faculty acting with the *whole* of the case on its hands. The exhibition involved is in other words a fairy-tale pure and simple — save indeed as to its springing not from an artless and measureless, but from a conscious and cultivated credulity. Yet the fairy-tale belongs mainly to either of two classes, the short and sharp and single, charged more or less with the compactness of anecdote (as to which let the familiars of our childhood, Cinderella and Blue-Beard and Hop o' my Thumb and Little Red Riding Hood and many of the gems of the Brothers Grimm directly testify), or else the long and loose, the copious, the various, the endless, where, dramatically speaking, roundness is quite sacrificed — sacrificed to fulness, sacrificed to exuberance, if one will: witness at hazard almost any one of the Arabian Nights. The charm of all these things for the distracted modern mind is in the clear field of experience, as I call it, over which we are thus led to roam; an annexed but independent world in which nothing is right save as we rightly imagine it. We have to do *that*, and we do it happily for the short spurt and in the smaller piece, achieving so perhaps beauty and lucidity; we flounder, we lose breath, on the other hand — that is we fail, not of continuity, but of an agreeable unity, of the "roundness" in which beauty and lucidity largely reside — when we go in, as they say, for great lengths and breadths. And this, oddly enough, not because "keeping it up" is n't abundantly within the compass of the imagination appealed to in certain conditions, but because the finer interest depends just on *how* it is kept up.

Nothing is so easy as improvisation, the running on and on of invention; it is sadly compromised, however, from the moment its stream breaks bounds and gets into flood. Then the waters may spread indeed, gathering houses and herds and crops and cities into their arms and wrenching off, for our amusement, the whole face of the land — only violating by the same stroke our sense of the course and the channel, which is our sense of the uses of a stream and the virtue of a story. Improvisation, as in the Arabian Nights, may keep on terms with encountered objects by sweeping them in and floating them on its breast; but the great effect it so loses — that of keeping on terms with itself. This is ever, I intimate, the hard thing for the fairy-tale; but by just so much as it struck me as hard did it in "The Turn of the Screw" affect me as irresistibly prescribed. To improvise with extreme freedom and yet at the same time without the possibility of ravage, without the hint of a flood; to keep the stream, in a word, on something like ideal terms with itself: that was here my definite business. The thing was to aim at absolute singleness, clearness, and roundness, and yet to depend on an imagination working freely, working (call it) with extravagance; by which law it would n't be thinkable except as free and would n't be amusing except as controlled. The merit of the tale, as it stands, is accordingly, I judge, that it has struggled successfully with its dangers. It is an excursion into chaos while remaining, like Blue-Beard and Cinderella, but an anecdote — though an anecdote amplified and highly emphasised and returning upon itself; as, for that matter, Cinderella and Blue-Beard return. I need scarcely add after this that it is a piece of ingenuity pure and simple, of cold artistic calculation, an *amusette* to catch those not easily caught (the "fun" of the capture of the merely witless being ever but small), the jaded, the disillusioned, the fastidious. Otherwise expressed, the study is of a conceived "tone," the tone of suspected and felt trouble, of an inordinate and incalculable sort — the tone of tragic, yet of exquisite, mystification. To knead the subject of my young friend's, the supposititious° narrator's, mystification thick, and yet strain the expression of it so clear and fine that beauty would result: no side of the matter so revives for me as that endeavour. Indeed if the artistic value of such an experiment be measured by the intellectual echoes it may again, long after, set in motion, the case would make in favour of this little firm fantasy — which I seem to see draw behind it to-day a train of associations. I ought doubtless to blush for thus confessing them so numerous that I can but pick among them for reference. I recall for instance a reproach made me by a reader° capable evidently, for the time, of some attention, but not quite capable of enough, who complained that I had n't sufficiently "characterised" my young woman engaged in her labyrinth; had n't endowed her with signs and marks, features and humours, had n't in a word invited her to deal with her own mystery as well as with that of Peter Quint, Miss Jessel, and the hapless children. I remember well, whatever the absurdity of its now coming back to me, my reply to that criticism — under which one's artistic, one's ironic heart shook for the instant almost to breaking. "You indulge in that stricture at your ease, and I don't mind confiding to you that — strange as it may ap-

---

supposititious: Imaginary, fictional.   **reader:** Probably H. G. Wells. We do not have a copy of Wells's letter, but we have James's response of December 9, 1898: "Of course I had, about my young woman, to take a very sharp line. . . . I had to rule out subjective complications of her own — play of tone etc.; and keep her impersonal save for the most obvious and indispensable little note of neatness, firmness, and courage — without which she wouldn't have had her data." The "young woman" is, of course, the governess.

pear! — one has to choose ever so delicately among one's difficulties, attaching one's self to the greatest, bearing hard on those and intelligently neglecting the others. If one attempts to tackle them all one is certain to deal completely with none; whereas the effectual dealing with a few casts a blest golden haze under cover of which, like wanton mocking goddesses in clouds, the others find prudent to retire. It was 'déjà très-joli,'° in 'The Turn of the Screw,' please believe, the general proposition of our young woman's keeping crystalline her record of so many intense anomalies and obscurities — by which I don't of course mean her explanation of them, a different matter; and I saw no way, I feebly grant (fighting, at the best too, periodically, for every grudged inch of my space) to exhibit her in relations other than those; one of which, precisely, would have been her relation to her own nature. We have surely as much of her own nature as we can swallow in watching it reflect her anxieties and inductions. It constitutes no little of a character indeed, in such conditions, for a young person, as she says, 'privately bred,' that she is able to make her particular credible statement of such strange matters. She has 'authority,' which is a good deal to have given her, and I could n't have arrived at so much had I clumsily tried for more."

For which truth I claim part of the charm latent on occasion in the extracted reasons of beautiful things — putting for the beautiful always, in a work of art, the close, the curious, the deep. Let me place above all, however, under the protection of that presence the side by which this fiction appeals most to consideration: its choice of its way of meeting its gravest difficulty. There were difficulties not so grave: I had for instance simply to renounce all attempt to keep the kind and degree of impression I wished to produce on terms with the to-day so copious psychical record° of cases of apparitions. Different signs and circumstances, in the reports, mark these cases; different things are done — though on the whole very little appears to be — by the persons appearing; the point is, however, that some things are never done at all: this negative quantity is large — certain reserves and proprieties and immobilities consistently impose themselves. Recorded and attested "ghosts" are in other words as little expressive, as little dramatic, above all as little continuous and conscious and responsive, as is consistent with their taking the

---

déjà très-joli: French for "already quite pretty enough."   psychical record: Published narratives and analyses of them by members of the Society for Psychical Research. Thousands of such reports about appearances of apparitions (ghosts) had been published in the quarter-century before James wrote *The Turn of the Screw*.

trouble — and an immense trouble they find it, we gather — to appear at all. Wonderful and interesting therefore at a given moment, they are inconceivable figures in an *action* — and "The Turn of the Screw" was an action, desperately, or it was nothing. I had to decide in fine between having my apparitions correct and having my story "good" — that is producing my impression of the dreadful, my designed horror. Good ghosts, speaking by book, make poor subjects, and it was clear that from the first my hovering prowling blighting presences, my pair of abnormal agents, would have to depart altogether from the rules. They would be agents in fact°; there would be laid on them the dire duty of causing the situation to reek with the air of Evil. Their desire and their ability to do so, visibly measuring meanwhile their effect, together with their ob-served and described success — this was exactly my central idea; so that, briefly, I cast my lot with pure romance, the appearances conforming to the true type being so little romantic.

This is to say, I recognise again, that Peter Quint and Miss Jessel are not "ghosts" at all, as we now know the ghost, but goblins, elves, imps, demons as loosely constructed as those of the old trials for witchcraft; if not, more pleasingly, fairies of the legendary order, wooing their victims forth to see them dance under the moon. Not indeed that I suggest their reducibility to any form of the pleasing pure and simple; they please at the best but through having helped me to express my subject all directly and intensely. Here it was — in the use made of them — that I felt a high degree of art really required; and here it is that, on reading the tale over, I find my precautions justified. The essence of the matter was the villainy of motive in the evoked predatory creatures; so that the result would be ignoble — by which I mean would be trivial — were this element of evil but feebly or inanely suggested. Thus arose on be-half of my idea the lively interest of a possible suggestion and process of adumbration°; the question of how best to convey that sense of the depths of the sinister without which my fable would so woefully limp. Portentous evil — how was I to save that, as an intention on the part of my demon-spirits, from the drop, the comparative vulgarity, inevitably attending, throughout the whole range of possible brief illustration, the offered example, the imputed vice, the cited act, the limited deplorable presentable instance? To bring the bad dead back to life for a second round of badness is to warrant them as indeed prodigious, and to be-come hence as shy of specifications as of a waiting anti-climax. One had

---

agents in fact: Spirits, evil "agents" from "the other side."   **adumbration:** Indication, signification, specification.

seen, in fiction, some grand form of wrong-doing, or better still of wrong-being, imputed, seen it promised and announced as by the hot breath of the Pit — and then, all lamentably, shrink to the compass of some particular brutality, some particular immorality, some particular infamy portrayed: with the result, alas, of the demonstration's falling sadly short. If *my* bad things, for "The Turn of the Screw," I felt, should succumb to this danger, if they should n't seem sufficiently bad, there would be nothing for me but to hang my artistic head lower than I had ever known occasion to do.

The view of that discomfort and the fear of that dishonour, it accordingly must have been, that struck the proper light for my right, though by no means easy, short cut. What, in the last analysis, had I to give the sense of? Of their being, the haunting pair, capable, as the phrase is, of everything — that is of exerting, in respect to the children, the very worst action small victims so conditioned might be conceived as subject to. What would *be* then, on reflexion, this utmost conceivability? — a question to which the answer all admirably came. There is for such a case no eligible *absolute* of the wrong; it remains relative to fifty other elements, a matter of appreciation, speculation, imagination — these things moreover quite exactly in the light of the spectator's, the critic's, the reader's experience. Only make the reader's general vision of evil intense enough, I said to myself — and that already is a charming job — and his own experience, his own imagination, his own sympathy (with the children) and horror (of their false friends) will supply him quite sufficiently with all the particulars. Make him *think* the evil, make him think it for himself, and you are released from weak specifications. This ingenuity I took pains — as indeed great pains were required — to apply; and with a success apparently beyond my liveliest hope. Droll enough at the same time, I must add, some of the evidence — even when most convincing — of this success. How can I feel my calculation to have failed, my wrought suggestion not to have worked, that is, on my being assailed, as has befallen me, with the charge of a monstrous emphasis, the charge of all indecently expatiating?° There is not only from beginning to end of the matter not an inch of expatiation, but my values are positively all blanks save so far as an excited horror, a promoted pity, a created expertness — on which punctual effects of strong causes no writer can ever fail to plume himself — proceed to read into them more or less fantastic figures. Of high interest to the author meanwhile — and by the same stroke a theme for the moralist — the artless

expatiating: Wandering on, writing or explaining at greater length than necessary.

resentful reaction of the entertained person who has abounded in the sense of the situation. He visits his abundance, morally, on the artist — who has but clung to an ideal of faultlessness. Such indeed, for this latter, are some of the observations by which the prolonged strain of that clinging may be enlivened!

PART TWO

The Turn of the Screw: A Case Study in Contemporary Criticism

A Critical History of
The Turn of the Screw

The fundamental question dealt with in the scholarship on *The Turn of the Screw* is how real the ghosts are. Are Peter Quint and Miss Jessel real in the sense that they are spirits of the dead come back to haunt the living? Or are they real only in the sense that the governess has hallucinations that make them *seem* real to her? Do they haunt the children or do they haunt only the governess's troubled imagination? Virtually every book and article on *The Turn of the Screw* — and there have been hundreds — deals at least indirectly with that question. It is almost impossible to read the story without taking sides and almost impossible to approach the story critically without knowing where one stands on it. Indeed, that question — and the fun that scholars and their students have had debating it — has elevated to star status what might otherwise have been seen as a rather ordinary James story. The two basic readings are so radically different and so apparently mutually exclusive that it is amazing that both sides have agreed on one essential fact: that *The Turn of the Screw* is a wonderfully successful story. It is an amazingly fine creepy, scary, soul-shuddering ghost story or, alternatively, it is an amazingly fine psychological case study of a neurotic young woman. The fact that the two readings seem mutually exclusive — how, after all, can a woman be both sane and insane, how can ghosts be both real and imaginary? — has not prevented a third position from emerging in recent years: that *The Turn of the Screw* is at once *both* a ghost story *and* a psychological study. Those who argue for this third or dualistic view also agree that it is an amazingly fine story — fine precisely because James has told it with such skillful ambiguity that readers can hold *both* views simultaneously.

Because of this rich disagreement about how to read it and because of the paradoxical agreement that whichever way we read it the story is brilliant, *The Turn of the Screw* is Henry James's most frequently read, taught, and discussed piece of fiction. The story compels us partly because we all want to discuss our own ways of answering its commanding question: Is this or is this not a story about ghosts? Related questions are sure to evoke spirited class discussions and interesting papers. Can we trust the governess's perceptions? Is she sane? What is the purpose of the "prologue"? Are the children innocent or corrupt? How does Mrs. Grose know from the governess's description that the ghost is that of Peter Quint? How does Miles die? Is this a story about sexual coercion or homosexuality? Is there a "best" way to read this story, or are all ways acceptable?

So fascinated have scholars been with *The Turn of the Screw*, and so insistent have they been about convincing other scholars that *their* view is right, that the published scholarship on this story has taken on a life of its own. This essay reviews that scholarship, but so much has been written on *The Turn of the Screw* that I cannot begin to report on all of it. This critical history paints the critical controversy with broad brushstrokes but with enough detail to suggest both the richness and the heat of that controversy. The full citations to the books and articles of the scholars I name appear in the list of Works Cited at the end of this essay.

ORIGINS OF THE STORY

In his notebooks for January 12, 1895, Henry James described in some detail an account he had heard two days earlier during a visit to Edward W. Benson, the Archbishop of Canterbury (quoted in full in my introduction, pp. 12–13). No one seriously doubts that the Archbishop's story *was* the central source for *The Turn of the Screw*. From the beginning, however, scholars have shown an eagerness to discover other literary and scientific influences that helped to shape *The Turn of the Screw*. Among the candidates for direct textual influence are these (in parentheses are the names of the critics who suggested them): a drawing entitled "The Haunted House" by T. Griffiths, showing two children looking across a lake at a mysterious house (Robert Lee Wolff); Mrs. Gaskell's "The Old Nurse's Story" (Miriam Alcott); Goethe's "Erlkönig" (Ignace Feuerlicht); Dickens's *Oliver Twist* (Jean Frantz Blackall); an anonymous serialized novel *Temptation* (Leon Edel and Adeline R. Tintner); Charlotte Brontë's *Jane Eyre* (Alice Hall Petry); a nineteenth-century medical book describing governesses (William J. Scheick); another medical text describing "temporal lobe epilepsy" (J. Purdon Martin); plays by Ibsen (E. A. Sheppard); Fielding's *Amelia* (May L. Ryburn); German literature (Ernst Braches); various fairy tales (Mary Y. Hallab).

Other scholars have suggested influences other than literary or scientific ones. They have suggested, for example, that some of the characters in *The Turn of the Screw* may be "drawn from life": the governess from "Miss Lucy R.," a patient of Sigmund Freud's, and from Henry James's sister, Alice, who had a history of mental illness (Oscar Cargill); Miles from an orphan James had known as a child (Vincent P. Pecora); Quint from the playwright George Bernard Shaw, and Douglas from Edward W. Benson (E. A. Sheppard). And a number of critics have tried to show that *The Turn of the Screw* grows more generally out of social attitudes prevalent at the end of the nineteenth century. Elliot Schrero reports, for example, that a study of late Victorian attitudes toward parents, servants, governesses, and children indicates that James was very much a part of his time in demonstrating that young children who are allowed to associate too freely with servants can be corrupted and that governesses can be successful in providing the loving care and protection that a child's own mother does not provide.

Although scholars have tried to connect *The Turn of the Screw* with other fictional "ghost stories" in the gothic tradition, a more persistent approach has been to connect it with "ghost cases" reported to and by practitioners of "psychical research." Henry James's brother William, the distinguished Harvard psychology professor, took active leadership in the Society for Psychical Research (established in 1882). Henry James never became a member of the society, but just seven years before he wrote *The Turn of the Screw* he attended one of its meetings, where he read one of his brother's professional papers about a spirit medium named Mrs. Piper.

Francis X. Roellinger was one of the first to write about the possible influence on *The Turn of the Screw* of the published reports and articles about people who had seen ghosts. He points out three or four of the cases that presented characters and situations similar to those in James's story, and he shows that James's Preface to the 1908 Edition of the story proves that he knew about psychical research. Ernest Tuveson sees the governess as a medium, a person who enables the spirits of the dead to manifest themselves. Martha Banta suggests that we not allow late-twentieth-century disbelief in ghosts to influence our reading of a story written when there was more widespread belief in them. E. A. Sheppard gives us a hundred-page chapter on the connection between James's story and psychical research, demonstrating parallels between the characters and events in *The Turn of the Screw* and those in the reports in the various publications of the Society for Psychical Research. David S. Miall connects *The Turn of the Screw* with one particular ghostly case history. A good discussion of the ghosts appears in an Italian book by Giovanna Mochi. For more on these matters, see also my own 1989 book, in which I review the evidence for James's knowledge of ghost cases and consider the evidence that James had knowledge of demonic possession and was influenced by that knowledge to hint that Miles and Flora are at times "possessed" by the spirits of Quint and Jessel.

All critics recognize that, despite the many influences that might have contributed to the story, *The Turn of the Screw* is very much its own thing: an amazingly original piece of fiction. And there is no question that for many critics a key feature of that originality is the character of the young woman whose first-person retrospective is *The Turn of the Screw*.

PSYCHOLOGICAL CASE STUDY

The possibility that the governess may be insane has never been far from the consciousness of readers of *The Turn of the Screw*. Although virtually all of James's contemporaries read it as a spine-chilling ghost story, as early as 1919 Henry A. Beers wrote, "I have sometimes thought . . . that the woman who saw the phantoms was mad" (44). At about that time Harold C. Goddard, a professor of English at Swarthmore, wrote an essay he never published. At his death his daughter found among his papers a manuscript, written apparently around 1920, arguing that by a close reading of the governess's language and of her notations about the reactions of others to her, sensitive readers can see that she is insane. By the time the essay was published in 1957, the view that the ghosts exist only in the mind of a deranged governess had already been popularized by others. Edna Kenton got the "mad governess" theory moving in 1924, when she published an article suggesting that the story is only on the surface about ghosts and children;

more fundamentally it is about the "little personal mystery" of the governess, for whom the ghosts and children are merely "figures for the ebb and flow of troubled thought within her mind" (255).

The landmark study of the governess's psychological makeup came in 1934 with Edmund Wilson's influential essay "The Ambiguity of Henry James." That essay, strongly influenced by Freud's ideas, has been so important that I must quote at some length from Wilson's 1948 revised and enlarged revision of it. Wilson's theory is that "the governess who is made to tell the story is a neurotic case of sex repression, and that the ghosts are not real ghosts but hallucinations of the governess" (88). Her infatuation with the uncle in Harley Street, combined with the sexual repression that would have been natural to the sheltered daughter of a country parson, makes her transfer her feelings for the uncle onto a self-generated vision of his former valet atop the tower at Bly. Later, by the lake, as she observes Flora trying to force a play-mast into a play-boat, the governess imagines that she sees the ghost of the dishonored Miss Jessel. "Observe," Wilson says, "from the Freudian point of view, the significance of the governess' interest in the little girl's pieces of wood and of the fact that the male apparition first takes shape on a tower and the female apparition on a lake" (90). These objects and settings become, then, literary representations of "Freudian symbols": the tower and mast as phallus, the boat hull and the lake as vagina. The governess's repression of her natural sexual drives, in Wilson's view, forces her into a neurotic pattern of visions and interpretations that are revealed to us through the story she tells. Indeed, according to Wilson, the story of the children and the ghosts at Bly is important not for its own sake, but as a kind of soliloquy "primarily intended as a characterization of the governess" (95). Quint and Jessel exist not to endanger or tempt the children but to prove to readers that the governess is insane.

Wilson's thesis has shaped subsequent criticism on *The Turn of the Screw*. That criticism culminated in a 1965 book-length study of *The Turn of the Screw* by Thomas M. Cranfill and Robert L. Clark, Jr. Building on the work of Wilson and Goddard, Cranfill and Clark show the governess growing more and more neurotic and dangerously insane as the story progresses. Their book is a relentless analysis, word by word, scene by scene, of the narrator's madness. But many others besides these two have built on the Freudian foundations laid by Wilson. John Lydenberg sees the governess as a "hysterical, compulsive, sado-masochistic" (57) woman who deprives Miles and Flora of the love that might have let them develop into adults. Mark Spilka finds that even the

Freudian critics have overlooked the evidence for precocious sexuality and infant repression in the story. The possibility of a psychoanalytic reading of the story is reinforced by Leon Edel, the most influential single interpreter of James's life and works, when he says in his biography of Henry James that the governess's "courage is a mask for a deep hysteria" and that Bly is filled "not so much with the evil of the ghosts, as the terror of the governess, her wild suppositions and soothing self-consoling explanations" (194). In Edel's reading it is not the ghosts but "the governess herself who haunts the children" (195). In an interesting variation on this reading, Elizabeth Schultz finds that the ghosts are kindly and "human" but that in misreading their characters and intentions as evil, the governess harms rather than helps the children.

A different kind of psychoanalytic reading examines *The Turn of the Screw* for what it may reveal about Henry James's own childhood. M. Katan, a practicing psychiatrist, finds in the story evidence that James had probably, at a very young age, seen his parents in a "primal scene" — that is, making love. C. Knight Aldrich, another practicing clinician, suggests that Mrs. Grose may be based, if only unconsciously, on James's mother, "a destructive woman" (173). Arno Bohlmeijer thinks that a Jungian analysis of the story is more promising than a Freudian one, while Karen Halttunen encourages us to seek in the works of Henry James's brother William for clues to the possible multiple personalities and spirit mediumship of the governess.

REACTIONS AGAINST THE PSYCHOANALYTIC READING

Almost immediately scholars began to argue against the Wilson theory. Nathan Bryllion Fagin, for example, finding it strange that Wilson focused on the influence of Freud, whom James could scarcely have read, takes *The Turn of the Screw* to be a Hawthornesque "allegory which dramatizes the conflict between Good and Evil" (200). Robert Heilman, by a different route, reads the story as a reflection of "the struggle of evil to possess the human soul" (278). For Heilman the children are symbolic representations of Adam and Eve, Bly is the Garden of Eden, Quint the devil. Similarly, Joseph J. Firebaugh finds the governess to be not sexually repressed but nonetheless dangerous to the two children, to whom she denies the knowledge that would allow them to grow and mature. Maxwell Geismar finds that denying the reality of the ghosts removes the emphasis from where it ought to be —

on the servile sexual experiences of the two children. Eli Siegel rejects both Wilson and Heilman and finds Miles and Flora not to be caught in a struggle between good and evil but to be just plain evil.

Several other scholars (Glenn A. Reed, Oliver Evans, Charles G. Hoffman, Alexander E. Jones, Dorothea Krook, John J. Allen, and Charles K. Wolfe) note problems with the psychoanalytic interpretation. Why, for example, if the governess is so neurotically unreliable and insane, does she go on to become the respected and much-loved governess of other small children? Why, if we are to see her as a danger to Miles and Flora, does Douglas give such a positive report of her character in the prologue? Why, since James wrote some half-dozen other stories about ghosts, must we read *this* one alone as a hallucination story? Why does the good Mrs. Grose, initially skeptical and unable to see the ghosts herself, admit by the end of the story that she believes that the spirits of Quint and Jessel have been visiting and corrupting the children? Why, if James wanted to write a psychological case study of a deranged governess, does he say in his 1908 Preface that *The Turn of the Screw* is a "fairy-tale pure and simple" (119) in which he means Peter Quint and Miss Jessel to be "fairies of the legendary order, wooing their victims" (122) into the moonlight? Why, if he wanted the story to focus on the governess, does James in that same Preface speak of "intelligently neglecting" the teller's "relation to her own nature," so that he could spend time on other subjects, such as making his "demon-spirits" seem "sufficiently bad" (121–23)? Why, if the ghosts are imaginary, does James in his letters to others who asked him about the story insist that he was much more interested in the ghosts and the children than in the governess who tells their story? And why, if the governess is really a pathological liar, should we believe *any*thing she says — that there is an uncle in Harley Street, that there is a place called Bly, that there are two children, that she is their governess?

One of the most telling pieces of evidence against Wilson's theory is the scene in which the governess describes Peter Quint in such detail that Mrs. Grose can positively identify him as the former valet. J. A. Waldock puts the case against Wilson this way: "How did the governess succeed in projecting on vacancy, out of her own subconscious mind, a perfectly precise, point-by-point image of a man, then dead, whom she had never seen in her life and never heard of? What psychology, normal or abnormal, will explain that? And what is the right word for such a vision but 'ghost'?" (333–34). So telling is this argument that Wilson retracted his thesis — for a time.

DEFENDING WILSON

Other scholars, distressed with Wilson's retraction, have come to Wilson's defense on this issue of the identification of Peter Quint by suggesting various "realistic" explanations for the governess's description of Quint and Mrs. Grose's identification of him. John Silver suggests that the governess had gone to town to make inquiries and had learned there about the details of Quint's appearance. John A. Clair thinks that Mrs. Grose is a liar who tries to deceive the governess about the real nature of the man she sees; the "ghost" of Peter Quint is no more than a living "prowler" whom Mrs. Grose falsely identifies as the spirit of a dead man. In a similar reading, C. Knight Aldrich believes that Mrs. Grose, quite possibly the mother of the two children by a former liaison with the "uncle" in Harley Street, is jealous of the younger, prettier governess and wants both to discredit the governess and drive her mad. She therefore identifies the man — and would have identified *any* man the governess described — as the dead former valet. (It is interesting that in this argument Aldrich was to some extent anticipated by a tongue-in-cheek article by Eric Solomon.) John Harmon McElroy questions the governess's details by asserting that the governess could scarcely have seen Quint clearly because of the hour of the day and the fact that the window would have been "blurred" by the recent rain. James B. Scott thinks that the governess's ghosts are hoaxes played on her by Miles: Miles dresses up in Quint's clothes and appears on the tower and at the window "to throw a little mystery" into the governess's life (115). Other scholars — C. B. Ives, A. W. Thompson, Sidney E. Lind, Fred L. Milne, Robert W. Hill, and Dennis Chase, for example — have risen to defend the Wilson–Goddard theory on other grounds. And Stanley Renner, in a psychoanalytic reading (223–41 in this book) tells us that the governess's fear of sexuality causes her to project onto the "man" on the tower certain sexual stereotypes embedded in the collective mind of her culture.

HAVING IT BOTH WAYS

Are the ghosts real? Is the governess mad? These two choices had long been considered mutually exclusive: if the ghosts are real, then the governess is sane; if she is mad, then the ghosts are mere figments of her imagination. One of the identifying features of contemporary criticism of *The Turn of the Screw* is that it has tended to move away from the "either-or" choices offered by earlier criticism. Instead of "X *or* Y," con-

temporary scholars tend to say "X *and* Y." Several earlier scholars —
John J. Enck, Paul N. Siegel, and Juliet McMaster, for example — had
suggested that the story permits both readings simultaneously, and in
the early 1970s Dorothea Krook tried to encompass both readings by
drawing a distinction between what James wrote *consciously* (a story of
children haunted by evil spirits) and what he wrote *unconsciously* (a story
about a young woman essentially good but whose moral nature is
"compounded by the . . . sexual complications of her maiden state"
[370]). The newer view, however, was not raised to prominence until
the late 1970s, when several scholars brought to bear the influence of
the structuralist Tzvetan Todorov and the psychoanalyst Jacques Lacan.
Todorov argues that the literature of the "fantastic" requires unresolved
possibilities and says specifically of *The Turn of the Screw* that it "does
not permit us to determine finally whether ghosts haunt the old estate,
or whether we are confronted by the hallucinations of a hysterical governess victimized by the disturbing atmosphere which surrounds her" (43).

Three studies form the foundation for the postmodern "we-can-
have-it-both-ways" view. In a three-part essay entitled "The Squirm of
the True," Christine Brooke-Rose dismisses most previous scholarship
on the tale as limiting or just plain wrong and tries to "preserve the total
ambiguity" of the story: "I shall not argue for the ghosts or for the
hallucinations, but take it as accepted there is no word or incident in the
story that cannot be interpreted both ways" (II, 513). In an essay published at about the same time, Shlomith Rimmon writes about the "im-
possibility of choice between mutually exclusive interpretations" (116)
of *The Turn of the Screw* and speaks of the "double-directedness" of
many of the linguistic and psychological "clues" James gives his readers.
The third study proclaiming the inconclusiveness of *The Turn of the
Screw* is Shoshana Felman's long article "Turning the Screw of Interpretation." Influenced by Lacan and Jacques Derrida, Felman "deconstructs" the story. Felman asserts that much of the governess's unconscious is inaccessible to readers — who are inevitably frustrated in their
attempts to understand fully either the governess or her story. Certainly
they are frustrated in their efforts to find the *one* right way to read the
story. Felman says, for example, that the question is not "simply to decide whether in effect the 'Freudian' reading is true or false, correct or
incorrect. It can be both at the same time" (117). She would have readers not try to solve the mysteries of *The Turn of the Screw* but "to follow,
rather, the significant path of its flight" (119). That portion of Felman's
influential study dealing with the death of Miles is reprinted in this book
(193–206) as a deconstructionist perspective on the story.

In the 1980s and 1990s critics have felt increasingly uncomfortable asking "either-or" questions about this story. The only "correct" answer is likely to be "both" or "we cannot decide." Ned Lukacher suggests that readers can never "be on the right track" when reading the story, and John Carlos Rowe backs away from some provocative suggestions he makes about Miles's uncle and concludes that the issue is "undecidable": "we cannot know . . . we are forever 'dupes' of the language that employs us" (144). In a study of James's revisions to two paragraphs in chapter IX of *The Turn of the Screw*, Norman Macleod supports the general indeterminacy of the author's intentions: "The evidence of punctuation and revisions reveals, not an author elucidating the particular meaning he strives for in his text, but an author intent on establishing a text that cannot be interpreted in a definite way" (134). And Richard Dilworth Rust speaks of many of the characters and events and settings in the story as "liminal": that is, as on the "threshold" between one condition and another and therefore inevitably ambiguous. In a book-length study Terry Heller resolves the "are-the-ghosts-real?" question by answering "yes, then no." Heller tells us that *The Turn of the Screw* demands two readings. On a first reading virtually all view it as a ghost story told by a sympathetic and reliable governess. The mysterious death of Miles at the end, however, pulls these readers back into a rereading of the story. The second time it is quite a different experience. The governess is now suspect, and readers focus more and more on her questionable motives, on possible inconsistencies in her narrative, and on her own psychology. They see her in this second reading as a love-starved woman for whom the various "characters" in the novel, such as Jessel and Quint, shadow forth repressed aspects of her own clouded personality.

Cook and Corrigan find the very point of *The Turn of the Screw* to be the "tension" between the two opposing but equally legitimate readings of the story: "The subject of *The Turn of the Screw* is the nature of narrative. . . . By constantly undermining and restoring his narrator's credibility, James transforms a narrative which is potentially either a ghost story or a mystery tale about a demented governess into a very subtle fiction about the process of fiction itself" (63, 65). William R. Goetz finds in the puzzlement of the governess and her being cut off from any recourse to truth or authority a reflection of the situation of all readers of the story: "If *The Turn of the Screw* is an exemplary fiction for hermeneutic problems, this is not because it will support radically divergent, even mutually exclusive, readings, but because it obliges the reader to choose one reading and at the same time to see the inadequacy of his choice" (74). Marcia M. Eaton applies "speech-act theory" to a reading of the story and finds that James "is doing at least two things at once: he provides us with utterances (in many-tiered narrative mouths) that at the same time tell *two* tales, one about ghosts, the other about a deranged governess" (336–37). Millicent Bell believes that the governess's problem — and by implication the problem of most scholars — is that she cannot accept ambiguity: she must have the children either all good or all bad; she must have Quint and Jessel either ghosts or nonghosts. According to Bell, the truth — for the governess and for critics — must remain uncertain and indeterminate: "The prolonged debate about the reality or irreality of the ghosts in the story, the principal pivot of controversy, seems finally to have come to a halt in the acceptance of the idleness of such a question" (228).

MARXIST AND GENDER-BASED READINGS

As the debate about the reality of the ghosts has subsided in recent years, a different kind of debate has replaced it — a debate about Marxist and gender-based interpretations of *The Turn of the Screw*. In a stimulating review of the scholarship on *The Turn of the Screw*, Brenda Murphy (1979) writes that "practically the only critical frameworks I don't remember having seen are the Marxist framework of class struggle . . . and the feminist approach" (198). The lack was not to last long. Edwin Fussell, in an early Marxist reading, reminds us that *The Turn of the Screw* is a story not by the educated and sophisticated Henry James but by the lower-class governess. Of particular interest in Fussell's reading is his suggestion that James has this oppressed governess rise above her station by proving that she can write a novel:

> The governess fits a pattern of economic and social exploitation all too well. She is a worker; she is poor; her security of employment is dubious; upward mobility is almost always denied her. . . . James's governess turns the screw on her own situation and on the people who grow sleek by her labor. . . . If a woman writes a novel as good as a man — the same novel as a man — why indeed should she be a governess? (128)

More squarely in the Marxist tradition is Heath Moon's assertion that in *The Turn of the Screw* James was showing the moral decline of the upper classes — "the fashionable leisured London 'society' preoccupied with self-gratification" (19). The uncle comes under particular attack in Moon's reading: "The master has abandoned his property, abdicated his responsibility over the most precious but inconvenient embodiment of his inheritance, the burdensome guardianship over his niece and nephew" (22). The governess does what she can to save them, but the outcome of the story suggests to Moon that James thought there was little hope for the upper classes.

Graham McMaster's Marxist reading makes much of the fact that Miles and Flora are "Indian orphans" — thus placing the events in the story squarely within what readers would have recognized as a particular social and political context. In this reading questions of imperialism, race, class, nationalism, and mobility come to the surface. McMaster believes, for example, that *The Turn of the Screw* "deals with a threat to the hegemony of the landed plutocracy" (32) and that "the ghosts at Bly represent an avenging, repressed class, taking advantage of moments of political crisis" (36). Bruce Robbins argues that the governess is both horrified at and fascinated by the prospect of "love between the classes" — a notion he develops further in an essay from a Marxist perspective on *The Turn of the Screw* (283–96 in this book).

One of the most interesting features of the criticism on *The Turn of the Screw* is the way it transforms the governess into whatever it wants. It makes her into anything from an innocent but responsible young woman resisting the forces of evil to a sexually obsessed neurotic who murders one of her pupils. One way of looking at the Wilson–Goddard critics is that they make the governess the victim of a subtle antifeminism that refuses to trust women to be what they say they are. One kind of feminist approach to the story would ask whether a *male* narrator of the story would have been so easily molded to fit into so many different critical interpretations, and whether he would have been considered be "hysterical" in so many of them. A study having a distinctly feminist cast is Paula Marantz Cohen's 1986 study comparing James's treatment of the governess with Freud's treatment (written three years later) of a neurotic young woman named Dora. Cohen finds that James, by allowing the governess to speak for herself, was much more sympathetic to the situation and oppression of women than was Freud. Indeed, Cohen classifies the two basic critical camps as "patriarchal" and "matriarchal":

> Those who, with Edmund Wilson, "diagnose" the governess simply as mad as a result of sexual repression would fall into the *patriarchal* camp. They read the governess as Freud reads Dora — as a collection of symptoms — and hence exclude her point of view.

> The *matriarchal* reading, in contrast, would posit the governess'
> point of view as a salutary reversal of patriarchal interpretation —
> as the rightful if violent return of the repressed in the assertion of
> the female perspective. (84)

Although Cohen is properly postmodern in her refusal to take sides ("It no longer," she says, "seems a matter of deciding whether she has *either* gone mad *or* has really encountered ghosts, but of accepting the possibility that *both* situations may be true" [79]), she clearly appreciates James's appearing to have taken a more matriarchal view of the governess. The focus of Patricia N. Klingenberg's essay is not directly on *The Turn of the Screw*, but she does call attention to the fact that James's story "expels the female," if only because her story is "framed and reframed in the introduction by two different male narrators, Douglas and the story's first 'I'" (493). For a somewhat different "feminist perspective" on the story, see the introduction to Priscilla Walton's book and, especially, her feminist interpretation written for this volume (253–67).

Other gender-related approaches to *The Turn of the Screw* focus on its homoerotic implications. The story has, from the very beginning, prompted some readers to wonder about the possibility of pederasty between Quint and Miles (see the F. W. H. Myers letter, published in Beidler, 106). Others have seen reflected in the story James's own possible homosexuality. Katan, a practicing psychiatrist, finds in the story evidence that James had certain homosexual tendencies. Richard Ellmann finds it notable that "James has Miles go off for hours with Peter Quint" (7). Anthony J. Mazzella tells us that the homoeroticism between Quint and Miles is "attributable to the relationship between Douglas and the narrator" (333). Michael J. H. Taylor seeks to avoid the suggestion that there may be a "homosexual union of some kind between Douglas and the narrator" (719) by arguing that the narrator of the frame may well be a woman. In an essay devoted mostly to a discussion of Whitman, Michael Moon talks about the homosexual implications of *The Turn of the Screw*: "Much in the tale turns on the mystery (or nonmystery) of little Miles's having been sent down from school for shocking misconduct toward some of his schoolmates — conduct into which he may have earlier been initiated by the literally haunting figure of Peter Quint" (256). In an interesting twist on gendered readings of the story, Helen Killoran thinks that the real secret of the story is that most of the characters — the governess, the uncle, Mrs. Grose, the children — are bisexual.

NOSTALGIA

As we have seen, it is fashionable in these postmodern times for scholars to reject all efforts to find "the" answer to the questions raised by the story. The ghosts are both real and imaginary, the governess is both sane and mad, the text both feminist and antifeminist, Quint both gay and straight. I begin to sense, however, a nostalgia for readings tending toward a more definite outcome, a growing annoyance with readings that refuse to decide. Readers may be starting to question the slippery conclusions of critics like Tobin Siebers, Darrel Mansell, Don Anderson, and Myler Wilkinson. Reading the story through the lenses provided by literary theorists like Tzvetan Todorov, Michel Foucault, and Claude Lévi-Strauss, Siebers reaches this conclusion: "The reader may choose to hesitate once more over the visitants, governess, or children; or he may choose to hesitate over hesitation" (571). In an analysis of the way words mean, Mansell finds in *The Turn of the Screw* only "a text describing merely itself. . . . The story begins as a mailable or sendable letter, and ends as an unsendable one" (60). Anderson tells us that reading James's story "is no longer possible" because "reading" suggests finding a meaning, attempting to answer the questions of the text, and such readings are sure to be "reductive, 'totalitarian,' 'terroristic'" (148). And Myler Wilkinson tells us that all is contradiction and indiscrimination: "good exists within evil, true becomes false, trust becomes fear, love doubles with hate, purity within corruption, the known within the unknowable — and James works very hard to eliminate all the markers that would help us discriminate between them" (164).

One senses, as I say, a growing dissatisfaction with such readings. Dieter Freundlieb, for example, thinks that the multiplicity of interpretations of *The Turn of the Screw*, many of them advanced with little more justification than that "no one thought of this one before" and with even less in the way of proof is "an intellectual scandal" (79); he suggests that literary "interpretation should never have been turned into an academic discipline" (94). And Vincent P. Pecora tells us that "the 'question' of the narrative has now become almost completely metacritical: one can hardly see the text except through the nearly opaque screen of more than half a century of professional critical argument" (176). Do readers long to read *The Turn of the Screw* as a story once again, quite ignoring the critical baggage it has acquired? Are they growing impatient with being told that *The Turn of the Screw* is ambiguous or indeterminate or undecidable or unreadable? Or do they merely yearn for the days when critics proposed definite readings and defended their readings with old-fashioned arguments and evidence drawn from a lovingly close reading of *The Turn of the Screw?*

To put the matter more specifically, are scholars beginning to insist that not all possible readings of Miles's death are equally valid, and that one of our jobs as readers is to *decide*, to argue on clear grounds and in clear language which is best?

THE DEATH OF MILES

In what remains of this essay I present a series of critical comments about Miles's death. I present them without comment of my own, thinking that perhaps students will want to test their own readings of the closing pages of the story against those of other readers. It is impossible, in any case, for readers *not* to pay some attention to Miles's death. Whether we see the ghosts as real or imaginary, whether we see the governess as insane or sane, whether we see the children as corrupt or innocent, whether we think the story resolves *any* questions, Miles's heart stops for us all — well almost all — in the last line of the story, and that stopping cries out to be explained. Explaining Miles's death has always been frustrating. Robert W. Hill puts it this way: "The narrative recording Miles's death is designed to be as uncooperative to a clear understanding as anything in literature can be" (69). In the following paragraphs I give a chronological medley of comments about Miles's death. To be fully understood, they should be read in the context of the books and articles from which they are taken. See the Works Cited for bibliographic details for each citation.

Wilson, 1934: "She has literally frightened him to death." (94)

Fagin, 1941: "Little Miles is dead . . . exhausted by the ordeal . . . too corrupted to live without evil." (201)

Liddell, 1947: "Miles's soul is purged by confession. . . . He dies, worn out by the struggle between good and evil, in the moment of triumph." (141)

Heilman, 1948: "His face gives a 'convulsive supplication' — that is, actually a prayer, for and to Quint, the demon who has become his total deity. But the god isn't there, and Miles despairs and dies." (285)

Hoffman, 1953: "Miles's death is caused by the governess's insistence on his confession; the confession is wrested from him, but he dies from the shock. . . . Miles is saved, Peter Quint has lost.

But the experience — the fright, the horror, the recognition of evil — is too much for Miles." (104–05)

Firebaugh, 1957: "Small wonder that Miles dies; he has been forced to see the only source of knowledge he has known in his brief life, Quint, as an embodiment of evil, and himself as a victim of Original Sin." (62)

Lydenberg, 1957: "Recall again the last long scene of Miles' death — or murder. She will make him confess, by whatever third-degree methods prove necessary; she will find a way to demonstrate that all actions, all explanations prove his guilt. He will not escape like Flora. She will hold him tight and keep him all for herself, even though she can possess him as she wishes only in death." (55)

Feuerlicht, 1959: "The death of a healthy child from mere mental shock seems . . . almost as unbelievable as the existence of evil ghosts. Miles's 'little heart,' as the governess says, — this, by the way, is the moving style of a loving and lovable person, not of a lunatic or a sadist — has stopped because it has been 'dispossessed' . . . exorcised." (74)

Katan, 1962: "The boy had a homosexual dependency upon Peter Quint. This power of Peter Quint's extends even after the valet's death. Yet this relation with Peter Quint protects him against the dangerous attachment to a mother figure. When the governess destroys Peter Quint's influence, she turns the clock back. The warded-off exciting oedipal relationship comes again to the fore. Out of necessity the boy has to die, for James had no other solution left. It was this dramatic ending through which James hoped to prevent the reader from having any discharge of the castration anxiety that James intended to arouse." (489)

Rubin, 1964: "What I am suggesting, of course, is . . . that Douglas *is* Miles, and that the story Douglas reads, supposedly about another little boy and the governess, is in fact about *him*. If this were so, then the scarcely-disguised erotic implications of the narrative are of direct importance. They would mean that . . . Miles [did] not die at all at the close." (318)

West, 1964: "The governess indulges in an exuberant debauch of violence that contributes to the sudden death of the little Miles — or she dreams that she did." (288)

Clair, 1965: "In a burst of fear and terror . . . he dies of shock." (54)

Cranfill and Clark, 1965: "The children suffer prolonged, helpless, lethally dangerous exposure to the mad governess. . . . Their
exposure ends only when Flora lies delirious and Miles lies dead in
the governess' arms, both victims of her endless harassment and of
mortal terror." (169)

Aldrich, 1967: "*The Turn of the Screw* is . . . a tragedy about an
evil older woman [Mrs. Grose] who drove an unstable younger
woman completely out of her mind, and whose jealousy was the
indirect cause of a little boy's death." (176–77)

Eli Siegel, 1968: "The reason Miles dies is because he can't decide. 'Extinction through indecision' would be the aesthetic
coroner's statement about him. . . . Because of this indecision,
Miles gets what can be called a quiet tantrum. It is a little bit like
what happens when babies turn blue with indecision: frantic indecision." (135, 148)

Sheppard, 1974: "She kills Miles on the spot, with mingled excite-
ment, fright, rage, and despair." (210)

Hill, 1981: "It is he, Miles, whom she has been intent upon de-
stroying all along. . . . Certainly 'his little heart, dispossessed, had
stopped' — dispossessed not of Quint's influence as the governess
had always supposed, but of a murderous plot against others
which had recoiled upon its maker." (70)

Milne, 1981: "The governess sees Quint again at the window and
desperately attempts to force Miles to enter her hallucination.
When the moment is over, Quint has vanished and Miles lies dead
in the governess' smothering grasp. Ironically, her attempt to
escape her 'small smothered life' has smothered the life out of
Miles." (298–99)

Schrero, 1981: "To deprive a person of sexuality is to deprive him
of life; for, on an unconscious level, it may well seem that the loss
of erotic freedom is what kills little Miles at the end of the tale."
(274)

Crowe, 1982: "She is the evil force, or at least its vehicle. Miles . . . is
dead, dispossessed, not of ghosts he never sees, but of the governess. For she, a bit like Hawthorne's Dr. Chillingworth, has presumed to invade the human heart; she has wanted to possess the
very soul of another." (42)

Matheson, 1982: "There are many indications throughout the
concluding scenes which point to Miles having been smothered by

the frantic, raving governess, that his death is the result of asphyxiation rather than strain, fright, or 'dispossession.'" (173)

Scott, 1983: "Miles collapses into the governess's arms, dead of a terror-induced heart-stoppage. . . . He has finally seen what he had caused the governess to see seven times . . . and since he is exhausted from a summer's sleeplessness, the shock of that single appearance proves fatal." (128)

Haggerty, 1989: "She seems to know that in liberating Miles from Quint she has lost him as well. She catches him and holds him for a minute before she realizes that Miles has succumbed to his own liberation. And his death leaves us ever to wander in the darkness of our own confusion." (157)

Heller, 1989: "Miles becomes angry in the end because he believes he has failed to expel Jessel; the governess possesses or is possessed by her, and he is helpless. His fear of the consequences, added to the other stresses of the situation, prove too much for his sensitive frame." (112)

Kaplan, 1992: "The insidious sexual element in the story — which combines Henry senior's fear of corruption and his role as a corrupting force, Miles's homoerotic sexual adventures, for which he has been expelled from school, and death by shock . . . — resonates as an artistic rendering of homosexual panic." (414)

Oates, 1994: "Miles gives an anguished cry. His face has gone dead-white, he appears on the verge of a collapse, yet, when [the governess] tries to secure him in her arms, he shoves her away. 'Don't touch me, leave me alone!' he shouts. '*I hate you.*' . . . Into the balmy-humid night the child Miles runs, runs for his life, damp hair sticking to his forehead, and his heart, that slithery fish, thumping against his ribs. Though guessing it is futile, for the madwoman was pointing at nothing, Miles cries, in a hopeful, dreading voice, 'Quint? — *Quint?*'" (282)

That last quotation, of course, is different from the rest. It was written by Joyce Carol Oates in a recent imaginative retelling of *The Turn of the Screw,* this time mostly from the points of view of the dead Jessel and Quint. In her story, entitled "Accursed Inhabitants of the House of Bly," Miles does not die at the end. Rather, as Oates herself put it in response to a reviewer's remarks on the story, he "escapes his oppressors, and lives" (31). Fiction, criticism, and now fiction once again continue to struggle with what *really* happened — or ought to have happened, or might have happened — at Bly.

What is the governess *really* like? Are the ghosts *really* real? Is Flora *really* corrupt? How does Miles *really* die? It is evident that there are almost as many readings of *The Turn of the Screw* as there are readers. What do we make of what Wayne Booth has called "the appalling chaos of critical opinions" (286)? Do we praise the readers for their marvelous ingenuity? Do we blame the readers for not reading more carefully? Do we praise James for the wonderful and all-encompassing ambiguity of his story? Do we blame James for this chaos, wishing that he had made his meaning clearer? Or do we dispense with all praise and blame and take on the stance of one kind of reader-response scholar and say that virtually any reading is legitimized by the very fact that some reader, somewhere, has offered it?

In the essays that follow we have five different ways of reading *The Turn of the Screw* — and its ending. In view of the multiplicity of readings possible, it makes most sense to begin with an account of what reader-response criticism is all about and with a reader-response interpretation written by Wayne Booth for this volume.

Peter G. Beidler

WORKS CITED

Alcott, Miriam. "Mrs. Gaskell's 'The Old Nurse's Story': A Link between *Wuthering Heights* and *The Turn of the Screw.*" *Notes and Queries* 8 (1961): 101–02.

Aldrich, C. Knight, M.D. "Another Twist to *The Turn of the Screw.*" *Modern Fiction Studies* 13 (1967): 167–78.

Allen, John J. "The Governess and the Ghosts in *The Turn of the Screw.*" *Henry James Review* 1 (1979): 73–80.

Anderson, Don. " 'A Fury of Intention': The Scandal of Henry James's *The Turn of the Screw.*" *Sydney Studies in English* 15 (1989–90): 140–52.

Banta, Martha. "The Berkelian Ghosts at Bly." *Henry James and the Occult.* Bloomington: Indiana UP, 1972. 114–29.

Beers, Henry A. *Four Americans.* New Haven: Yale UP, 1919.

Beidler, Peter G. *Ghosts, Demons, and Henry James: "The Turn of the Screw" at the Turn of the Century.* Columbia: U of Missouri P, 1989.

Bell, Millicent. "*The Turn of the Screw.*" In *Meaning in Henry James.* Cambridge: Harvard UP, 1991. 223–44.

Blackall, Jean Frantz. "Cruikshank's *Oliver* and *The Turn of the Screw.*" *American Literature* 51 (1979): 161–78.

Bohlmeijer, Arno. "Henry James and *The Turn of the Screw.*" *Encounter* 69 (1987): 41–50.

Booth, Wayne C. *Critical Understanding: The Powers and Limits of Pluralism.* Chicago: U of Chicago P, 1979. 284–301.

Braches, Ernst. *Engel en afrond over "The Turn of the Screw" van Henry James.* Amsterdam: Meulenhoff, 1983.

Brooke-Rose, Christine. "The Squirm of the True: I, An Essay in Non-Methodology; II, A Structural Analysis of Henry James's *The Turn of the Screw;* III, Surface Structure in Narrative." PTL: *A Journal for Descriptive Poetics and Theory of Literature* 1 (1976): 265–94 [Part I]; 1 (1976): 513–46 [Part II]; 2 (1977): 517–62 [Part III].

Cargill, Oscar. "*The Turn of the Screw* and Alice James." *PMLA* 78 (1963): 238–49.

Chase, Dennis. "The Ambiguity of Innocence: *The Turn of the Screw.*" *Extrapolation* 27 (1986): 197–202.

Clair, John A. "*The Turn of the Screw.*" In *The Ironic Dimension in the Fiction of Henry James.* Pittsburgh: Duquesne UP, 1965. 37–58.

Cohen, Paula Marantz. "Freud's *Dora* and James's *Turn of the Screw*: Two Treatments of the Female 'Case.'" *Criticism* 28 (1986): 73–87.

Cook, David A., and Timothy J. Corrigan. "Narrative Structure in *The Turn of the Screw*: A New Approach to Meaning." *Studies in Short Fiction* 17 (1980): 55–65.

Cranfill, Thomas Mabry, and Robert Lanier Clark, Jr. *An Anatomy of "The Turn of the Screw."* Austin: U of Texas P, 1965.

Crowe, M. Karen. "The Tapestry of Henry James's *The Turn of the Screw.*" *Nassau Review* 4 (1982): 37–48.

Eaton, Marcia M. "James's Turn of the Speech-Act." *British Journal of Aesthetics* 23 (1983): 333–45.

Edel, Leon. "The Little Boys." In *Henry James: The Treacherous Years, 1895–1901.* London: Hart-Davis, 1969. 191–203.

———, and Adeline R. Tintner. "The Private Life of Peter Quin[t]; Origins of *The Turn of the Screw.*" *Henry James Review* 7 (1985): 2–5.

Ellmann, Richard. "A Late Victorian Love Affair." *New York Review of Books*, August 4, 1977: 6–7.

Enck, John J. "*The Turn of the Screw* and the Turn of the Century." In the *Norton Critical Edition of "The Turn of the Screw,"* ed. Robert Kimbrough. New York: Norton, 1966. 259–69.

Evans, Oliver. "James's Air of Evil: *The Turn of the Screw*." *Partisan Review* 16 (1949): 175–87.

Fagin, Nathan Bryllion. "Another Reading of *The Turn of the Screw*." *Modern Language Notes* 56 (1941): 196–202.

Felman, Shoshana. "Turning the Screw of Interpretation." *Yale French Studies* 55/56 (1977): 94–207. Rpt. in *Writing and Madness: Literature/Philosophy/Psychoanalysis*. Ithaca: Cornell UP, 1985. 141–247.

Feuerlicht, Ignace. "'Erlkönig' and *The Turn of the Screw*." *Journal of English and German Philology* 58 (1959): 68–74.

Firebaugh, Joseph J. "Inadequacy in Eden: Knowledge and *The Turn of the Screw*." *Modern Fiction Studies* 3 (1957): 57–63.

Freundlieb, Dieter. "Explaining Interpretation: The Case of Henry James's *The Turn of the Screw*." *Poetics Today* 5 (1984): 79–95.

Fussell, Edwin. "The Ontology of *The Turn of the Screw*." *Journal of Modern Literature* 8 (1980): 118–28.

Geismar, Maxwell. *Henry James and the Jacobites*. Boston: Houghton Mifflin, 1963.

Goddard, Harold C. "A Pre-Freudian Reading of *The Turn of the Screw*." Prefatory note by Leon Edel. *Nineteenth-Century Fiction* 12 (1957): 1–36.

Goetz, William R. "The 'Frame' of *The Turn of the Screw*: Framing the Reader In." *Studies in Short Fiction* 18 (1981): 71–74.

Haggerty, George E. *Gothic Fiction/Gothic Form*. University Park: Pennsylvania State UP, 1989.

Hallab, Mary Y. "The Governess and the Demon Lover: The Return of a Fairy Tale." *Henry James Review* 8 (1987): 104–15.

Halttunen, Karen. "'Through the Cracked and Fragmented Self': William James and *The Turn of the Screw*." *American Quarterly* 40 (1988): 472–90.

Heilman, Robert. "*The Turn of the Screw* as Poem." *U of Kansas City Review* 14 (1948): 277–89.

Heller, Terry. *"The Turn of the Screw": Bewildered Vision*. Boston: Twayne, 1989.

Hill, Robert W., Jr. "A Counterclockwise Turn in James's *The Turn of the Screw*." *Twentieth-Century Literature* 27 (1981): 53–71.

Hoffman, Charles G. "Innocence and Evil in James's *The Turn of the Screw*." *U of Kansas City Review* 20 (1953): 97–105.

Ives, C. B. "James's Ghosts in *The Turn of the Screw*." *Nineteenth-Century Fiction* 18 (1963): 183–89.

Jones, Alexander E. "Point of View in *The Turn of the Screw*." *PMLA* 74 (1959): 112–22.

Kaplan, Fred. *Henry James: The Imagination of Genius*. New York: William Morrow, 1992.

Katan, M., M.D. "A Causerie on Henry James's *The Turn of the Screw*." *The Psychoanalytic Study of the Child* 17 (1962): 473–93.

Kenton, Edna. "Henry James to the Ruminant Reader: *The Turn of the Screw*." *The Arts* 4 (1924): 245–55.

Killoran, Helen. "The Governess, Mrs. Grose, and 'the Poison of an Influence' in *The Turn of the Screw*." *Modern Language Studies* 23 (1993): 13–24.

Kimbrough, Robert, ed. *"The Turn of the Screw": An Authoritative Text, Backgrounds, and Sources*. New York: Norton, 1966.

Klingenberg, Patricia N. "The Feminine 'I': Silvina Ocampo's Fantasies of the Subject." *Romance Language Annual* 6 (1989): 488–94.

Krook, Dorothea. "Intentions and Intentions: The Problem of Intention and Henry James's *The Turn of the Screw*" in *The Theory of the Novel: New Essays*, ed. John Halperin. New York: Oxford UP, 1974. 353–72.

Liddell, Robert. "The 'Hallucination' Theory of *The Turn of the Screw*." In *A Treatise on the Novel*. London: Jonathan Cape, 1947. 138–45.

Lind, Sidney E. "*The Turn of the Screw*: The Torment of Critics." *Centennial Review* 14 (1970): 225–40.

Lukacher, Ned. "'Hanging Fire': The Primal Scene of *The Turn of the Screw*." In *Primal Scenes: Literature, Philosophy, Psychoanalysis*. Ithaca: Cornell UP, 1986. 115–32.

Lydenberg, John. "The Governess Turns the Screws." *Nineteenth-Century Fiction* 12 (1957): 37–58.

Macleod, Norman. "Stylistics and the Ghost Story: Punctuation, Revisions, and Meaning in *The Turn of the Screw*." In *Edinburgh Studies in the English Language*, ed. John M. Anderson and Norman Macleod. Edinburgh: John Donald, 1988. 133–55.

Mansell, Darrel. "The Ghost of Language in *The Turn of the Screw*." *Modern Language Quarterly* 46 (1985): 48–63.

Martin, J. Purdon. "Neurology in Fiction: *The Turn of the Screw*." *British Medical Journal* 4 (1973): 717–21.

Matheson, Terence J. "Did the Governess Smother Miles?: A Note on

James's *The Turn of the Screw*." *Studies in Short Fiction* 19 (1982): 172–75.

Mazzella, Anthony J. "An Answer to the Mystery of *The Turn of the Screw*." *Studies in Short Fiction* 17 (1980): 327–33.

McElroy, John Harmon. "The Mysteries at Bly." *Arizona Quarterly* 37 (1981): 214–36.

McMaster, Graham. "Henry James and India: A Historical Reading of *The Turn of the Screw*." *Clio* 18 (1988): 23–40.

McMaster, Juliet. "'The Full Image of a Repetition' in *The Turn of the Screw*." *Studies in Short Fiction* 6 (1969), 377–82.

Miall, David S. "Designed Horror: James's Vision of Evil in *The Turn of the Screw*." *Nineteenth-Century Fiction* 39 (1984): 305–27.

Milne, Fred L. "Atmosphere as Triggering Device in *The Turn of the Screw*." *Studies in Short Fiction* 18 (1981): 293–99.

Mochi, Giovanna. *Le "cose cattive" di Henry James*. Parma: Pratiche Editrice Cooperativa, 1982.

Moon, Heath. "More Royalist Than the King: The Governess, the Telegraphist, and Mrs. Gracedew." *Criticism* 24 (1982): 16–35.

Moon, Michael. "Disseminating Whitman." *South Atlantic Quarterly* 88 (1989): 247–65.

Murphy, Brenda. "The Problem of Validity in the Critical Controversy over *The Turn of the Screw*." *Research Studies* 47 (1979): 191–201.

Oates, Joyce Carol. "Accursed Inhabitants of the House of Bly." In *Haunted: Tales of the Grotesque*. New York: Dutton, 1994. 254–83.

———. "To the Editor." *New York Times Book Review,* March 6, 1994, 31.

Pecora, Vincent P. "Reflection Rendered: James's *The Turn of the Screw*." In *Self and Form in Modern Narrative*. Baltimore: Johns Hopkins UP, 1989. 176–213.

Petry, Alice Hall. "Jamesian Parody, *Jane Eyre*, and *The Turn of the Screw*." *Modern Language Studies* 4 (1983): 61–78.

Reed, Glenn A. "Another Turn on James's *The Turn of the Screw*." *American Literature* 20 (1949): 413–23.

Rimmon, Shlomith. "*The Turn of the Screw*." In *The Concept of Ambiguity — the Example of James*. Chicago: U of Chicago P, 1977. 116–66.

Robbins, Bruce. "Shooting Off James's Blanks: Theory, Politics, and *The Turn of the Screw*." *Henry James Review* 5 (1984): 192–99.

Roellinger, Francis X. "Psychical Research and *The Turn of the Screw*." *American Literature* 20 (1949): 401–12.

Rowe, John Carlos. "Psychoanalytical Significances: The Use and Abuse of Uncertainty in *The Turn of the Screw*." In *The Theoretical Dimensions of Henry James*. Madison: U of Wisconsin P, 1984. 120–46.

Rubin, Louis D., Jr. "One More Turn of the Screw." *Modern Fiction Studies* 9 (1964): 314–28.

Rust, Richard Dilworth. "Liminality in *The Turn of the Screw*." *Studies in Short Fiction* 25 (1988): 441–46.

Ryburn, May L. "*The Turn of the Screw* and *Amelia*: A Source for Quint?" *Studies in Short Fiction* 16 (1979): 235–37.

Scheick, William J. "A Medical Source for *The Turn of the Screw*." *Studies in American Fiction* 19 (1991): 217–20.

Schrero, Elliot M. "Exposure in *The Turn of the Screw*." *Modern Philology* 78 (1981): 261–74.

Schultz, Elizabeth. "'The Pity and the Sanctity and the Terror': The Humanity of the Ghosts in *The Turn of the Screw*." *Markham Review* 9 (1980): 67–71.

Scott, James B. "How the Screw Is Turned: James's *Amusette*." *U of Mississippi Studies in English* 4 (1983): 112–31.

Sheppard, E[lizabeth]. A. *Henry James and "The Turn of the Screw."* Auckland: Auckland UP, 1974.

Siebers, Tobin. "Hesitation, History, and Reading: Henry James's *The Turn of the Screw*." *Texas Studies in Literature and Language* 25 (1983): 558–72.

Siegel, Eli. *James and the Children: A Consideration of Henry James's "The Turn of the Screw."* New York: Definition P, 1968.

Siegel, Paul N. "'Miss Jessel': Mirror Image of the Governess." *Literature and Psychology* 18 (1968): 30–38.

Silver, John. "A Note on the Freudian Reading of *The Turn of the Screw*." *American Literature* 29 (1957): 207–11.

Solomon, Eric. "The Return of the Screw." In the *Norton Critical Edition of "The Turn of the Screw,"* ed. Robert Kimbrough. New York: Norton, 1966. 237–45.

Spilka, Mark. "Turning the Freudian Screw: How Not to Do It." *Literature and Psychology* 13 (1963): 105–11.

Taylor, Michael J. H. "A Note on the First Narrator of *The Turn of the Screw*." *American Literature* 4 (1982): 717–22.

Thompson, A. W. "*The Turn of the Screw*: Some Points on the Hallucination Theory." *Review of English Literature* 6 (1965): 26–36.

Todorov, Tzvetan. *Introduction à la littérature fantastique.* Paris: Éditions du Seuil, 1970. Trans. Richard Howard as *The Fantastic: A Structural Approach to a Literary Genre.* Ithaca: Cornell UP, 1977.

Tuveson, Ernest. "*The Turn of the Screw*: A Palimpsest." *Studies in English Literature* 12 (1972): 783–800.

Waldock, J. A. "Mr. Edmund Wilson and *The Turn of the Screw.*" *Modern Language Notes* 62 (1947): 331–34.

Walton, Priscilla L. "Introduction: Releasing the Screw of Interpretation." In *The Disruption of the Feminine in Henry James.* Toronto: U of Toronto P, 1992. 3–12.

West, Muriel. "The Death of Miles in *The Turn of the Screw.*" *PMLA* 89 (1964): 283–88.

Wilkinson, Myler. "Henry James and the Ethical Moment." *Henry James Review* 11 (1990): 153–75.

Willen, Gerald, ed. *A Casebook on Henry James's "The Turn of the Screw."* 2nd ed. New York: Crowell, 1969.

Wilson, Edmund. "The Ambiguity of Henry James." *Hound and Horn* 7 (1934): 385–406. All quotations from *The Triple Thinkers*, rev. and enl. ed. New York: Oxford UP, 1948. 88–132.

Wolfe, Charles K. "Victorian Ghost Story Technique: The Case of Henry James." *Romantist* 3 (1979): 67–72.

Wolff, Robert Lee. "The Genesis of *The Turn of the Screw.*" *American Literature* 13 (1941): 1–8.

Reader-Response Criticism
and
The Turn of the Screw

WHAT IS READER-RESPONSE CRITICISM?

Students are routinely asked in English courses for their reactions to texts they are reading. Sometimes there are so many different reactions that we may wonder whether everyone has read the same text. And some students respond so idiosyncratically to what they read that we say their responses are "totally off the wall."

Reader-response critics are interested in the variety of our responses. Reader-response criticism raises theoretical questions about whether our responses to a work are the same as its meanings, whether a work can have as many meanings as we have responses to it, and whether some responses are more valid than, or superior to, others. It asks us to pose the following questions: What have we internalized that helps us determine what is and what isn't "off the wall"? In other words, what is the wall, and what standards help us to define it?

Reader-response criticism also provides models that are useful in answering such questions. Adena Rosmarin has suggested that a work can be likened to an incomplete work of sculpture: to see it fully, we *must* complete it imaginatively, taking care to do so in a way that responsibly takes into account what is there. An introduction to several other models of reader-response theory will allow you to understand better the reader-oriented essay that follows as well as to see a variety of ways in which, as a reader-response critic, you might respond to literary works.

Reader-response criticism, which emerged during the 1970s, focuses on what texts do to, or in, the mind of the reader, rather than regarding a text as something with properties exclusively its own. A poem, Louise M. Rosenblatt wrote as early as 1969, "is what the reader lives through under the guidance of the text and experiences as relevant to the text." Rosenblatt knew her definition would be difficult for many to accept: "The idea that a *poem* presupposes a *reader* actively involved with a *text*," she wrote, "is particularly shocking to those seeking to emphasize the objectivity of their interpretations" (127).

Rosenblatt is implicitly referring to the formalists, the old "New Critics," when she speaks of supposedly objective interpreters shocked by the notion that readers help make poems. Formalists preferred to discuss "the poem itself," the "concrete work of art," the "real poem." And they refused to describe what a work of literature makes a reader "live through." In fact, in *The Verbal Icon* (1954), William K. Wimsatt and Monroe C. Beardsley defined as fallacious the very notion that a reader's response is part of the meaning of a literary work:

> The Affective Fallacy is a confusion between the poem and its *results* (what it *is* and what it *does*). . . . It begins by trying to derive the standards of criticism from the psychological effects of a poem and ends in impressionism and relativism. The outcome . . . is that the poem itself, as an object of specifically critical judgment, tends to disappear. (21)

Reader-response critics take issue with their formalist predecessors. Stanley Fish, author of a highly influential article entitled "Literature in the Reader: Affective Stylistics" (1970), argues that any school of criticism that would see a work of literature as an object, that would claim to describe what it *is* and never what it *does*, is guilty of misconstruing what literature and reading really are. Literature exists when it is read, Fish suggests, and its force is an affective force. Furthermore, reading is a temporal process. Formalists assume it is a spatial one as they step back and survey the literary work as if it were an object spread out before them. They may find elegant patterns in the texts they examine and reexamine, but they fail to take into account that the work is quite different to a reader who is turning the pages and being moved, or affected, by lines that appear and disappear as the reader reads.

In a discussion of the effect that a sentence penned by the

seventeenth-century physician Thomas Browne has on a reader reading, Fish pauses to say this about his analysis and also, by extension, about the overall critical strategy he has largely developed: "Whatever is persuasive and illuminating about [it] . . . is the result of my substituting for one question — what does this sentence mean? — another, more operational question — what does this sentence do?" He then quotes a line from John Milton's *Paradise Lost,* a line that refers to Satan and the other fallen angels: "Nor did they not perceive their evil plight." Whereas more traditional critics might say that the "meaning" of the line is "They did perceive their evil plight," Fish relates the uncertain movement of the reader's mind *to* that half-satisfying interpretation. Furthermore, he declares that "the reader's inability to tell whether or not 'they' do perceive and his involuntary question . . . are part of the line's *meaning,* even though they take place in the mind, not on the page" (*Text* 26).

This stress on what pages *do* to minds pervades the writings of most, if not all, reader-response critics. Wolfgang Iser, author of *The Implied Reader* (1974) and *The Act of Reading: A Theory of Aesthetic Response* (1976), finds texts to be full of "gaps," and these gaps, or "blanks," as he sometimes calls them, powerfully affect the reader. The reader is forced to explain them, to connect what the gaps separate, literally to create in his or her mind a poem or novel or play that isn't *in* the text but that the text incites. Stephen Booth, who greatly influenced Fish, equally emphasizes what words, sentences, and passages "do." He stresses in his analyses the "reading experience that results" from a "multiplicity of organizations" in, say, a Shakespeare sonnet (*Essay* ix). Sometimes these organizations don't make complete sense, and sometimes they even seem curiously contradictory. But that is precisely what interests reader-response critics, who, unlike formalists, are at least as interested in fragmentary, inconclusive, and even unfinished texts as in polished, unified works. For it is the reader's struggle to *make sense* of a challenging work that reader-response critics seek to describe.

In *Self-Consuming Artifacts: The Experience of Seventeenth-Century Literature* (1972), Fish reveals his preference for literature that makes readers work at making meaning. He contrasts two kinds of literary presentation. By the phrase "rhetorical presentation," he describes literature that reflects and reinforces opinions that readers already hold; by "dialectical presentation," he refers to works that prod and provoke. A dialectical text, rather than presenting an opinion as if it were truth, challenges readers to discover truths on their own. Such a text may not even have the kind of symmetry that formalist critics seek. Instead of offering a "single, sustained argument," a dialectical text, or self-consuming artifact, may be "so arranged that to enter into the spirit and assumptions of any one of [its] . . . units is implicitly to reject the spirit and assumptions of the unit immediately preceding" (*Artifacts* 9). Such a text needs a reader-response critic to elucidate its workings. Another kind of critic is likely to try to explain why the units are unified and coherent, not why such units are contradicting and "consuming" their predecessors. The reader-response critic proceeds by describing the reader's way of dealing with the sudden twists and turns that character-ize the dialectical text, making the reader return to earlier passages and see them in an entirely new light.

"The value of such a procedure," Fish has written, "is predicated on the idea of meaning as *an event*," not as something "located (presumed to be embedded) *in* the utterance" or "verbal object as a thing in itself" (*Text* 28). By redefining meaning as an event, the reader-response critic once again locates meaning in time: the reader's time. A text exists and signifies while it is being read, and what it signifies or means will de-pend, to no small extent, on *when* it is read. (*Paradise Lost* had some meanings for a seventeenth-century Puritan that it would not have for a twentieth-century atheist.)

With the redefinition of literature as something that only exists meaningfully in the mind of the reader, with the redefinition of the lit-erary work as a catalyst of mental events, comes a concurrent redefini-tion of the reader. No longer is the reader the passive recipient of those ideas that an author has planted in a text. "The reader is *active*," Rosenblatt insists (123). Fish begins "Literature in the Reader" with a similar observation: "If at this moment someone were to ask, 'what are you doing,' you might reply, 'I am reading,' and thereby acknowledge that reading is . . . something *you do*" (*Text* 22). In "How to Recognize a Poem When You See One," he is even more provocative: "Interpret-ers do not decode poems: they make them" (*Text* 327). Iser, in focusing critical interest on the gaps in texts, on what is not expressed, similarly redefines the reader as an active maker. In an essay entitled "Interaction between Text and Reader," he argues that what is missing from a narra-tive causes the reader to fill in the blanks creatively.

Iser's title implies a cooperation between reader and text that is also implied by Rosenblatt's definition of a poem as "what the reader lives through under the guidance of the text." Indeed, Rosenblatt borrowed the term "transactional" to describe the dynamics of the reading pro-cess, which in her view involves interdependent texts and readers interacting. The view that texts and readers make poems together, though, is not shared by *all* interpreters generally thought of as reader-response critics. Steven Mailloux has divided reader-response critics into several categories, one of which he labels "subjective." Subjective critics, like David Bleich (or Norman Holland after his conversion by Bleich), assume what Mailloux calls the "absolute priority of individual selves as creators of texts" (*Conventions* 31). In other words, these critics do not see the reader's response as one "guided" by the text but rather as one motivated by deep-seated, personal, psychological needs. What they find in texts is, in Holland's phrase, their own "identity theme." Holland has argued that as readers we use "the literary work to symbolize and finally to replicate ourselves. We work out through the text our own characteristic patterns of desire" ("UNITY" 816).

Subjective critics, as you may already have guessed, often find themselves confronted with the following question: If all interpretation is a function of private, psychological identity, then why have so many readers interpreted, say, Shakespeare's *Hamlet* in the same way? Different subjective critics have answered the question differently. Holland simply has said that common identity themes exist, such as that involving an oedipal fantasy. Fish, who went through a subjectivist stage, has provided a different answer. In "Interpreting the *Variorum*," he argues that the "stability of interpretation among readers" is a function of shared "interpretive strategies." These strategies, which "exist prior to the act of reading and therefore determine the shape of what is read," are held in common by "interpretive communities" such as the one comprised by American college students reading a novel as a class assignment (*Text* 167, 171).

As I have suggested in the paragraph above, reader-response criticism is not a monolithic school of thought, as is assumed by some detractors who like to talk about the "School of Fish." Several of the critics mentioned thus far have, over time, adopted different versions of reader-response criticism. I have hinted at Holland's growing subjectivism as well as the evolution of Fish's own thought. Fish, having at first viewed meaning as the cooperative production of readers and texts, went on to become a subjectivist, and very nearly a "deconstructor" ready to suggest that all criticism is imaginative creation, fiction about literature, or *metafiction*. In developing the notion of interpretive communities, however, Fish has become more of a social, structuralist, reader-response critic; currently, he is engaged in studying reading communities and their interpretive conventions in order to understand the conditions that give rise to a work's intelligibility.

In spite of the gaps between reader-response critics and even between the assumptions that they have held at various stages of their respective careers, all try to answer similar questions and to use similar strategies to describe the reader's response to a given text. One question these critics are commonly asked has already been discussed: Why do individual readers come up with such similar interpretations if meaning is not embedded *in* the work itself? Other recurring, troubling questions include the following interrelated ones: Just who *is* the reader? (Or, to place the emphasis differently, Just who is *the* reader?) Aren't you reader-response critics just talking about your own idiosyncratic responses when you describe what a line from *Paradise Lost* "does" in and to "the reader's" mind? What about my responses? What if they're different? Will you be willing to say that all responses are equally valid?

Fish defines "the reader" in this way: "*the* reader is the *informed* reader." The informed reader is someone who is "sufficiently experienced as a reader to have internalized the properties of literary discourses, including everything from the most local of devices (figures of speech, etc.) to whole genres." And, of course, the informed reader is in full possession of the "semantic knowledge" (knowledge of idioms, for instance) assumed by the text (*Artifacts* 406).

Other reader-response critics use terms besides "the *informed* reader" to define "*the* reader," and these other terms mean slightly different things. Wayne Booth uses the phrase "the implied reader" to mean the reader "created by the work." (Only "by agreeing to play the role of this created audience," Susan Suleiman explains, "can an actual reader correctly understand and appreciate the work" [8].) Gerard Genette and Gerald Prince prefer to speak of "the narratee, . . . the necessary counterpart of a given narrator, that is, the person or figure who receives a narrative" (Suleiman 13). Like Booth, Iser employs the term "the implied reader," but he also uses "the educated reader" when he refers to what Fish calls the "informed" or "intended" reader. Thus, with different terms, each critic denies the claim that reader-response criticism might lead people to think that there are as many correct interpretations of a work as there are readers to read it.

As Mailloux has shown, reader-response critics share not only questions, answers, concepts, and terms for those concepts but also strategies of reading. Two of the basic "moves," as he calls them, are to show that a work gives readers something to do, and to describe what the reader does by way of response. And there are more complex moves as well. For instance, a reader-response critic might typically (1) cite direct references to reading in the text, in order to justify the focus on reading and show that the inside of the text is continuous with what the reader is doing; (2) show how other nonreading situations in the text nonetheless mirror the situation the reader is in ("Fish shows how in *Paradise Lost* Michael's teaching of Adam in Book XI resembles Milton's teaching of the reader throughout the poem"); and (3) show, therefore, that the reader's response is, or is perfectly analogous to, the topic of the story. For Stephen Booth, *Hamlet* is the tragic story of "an audience that cannot make up its mind." In the view of Roger Easson, Blake's *Jerusalem* "may be read as a poem about the experience of reading *Jerusalem*" (Mailloux, "Learning" 103).

In the pages that follow this introduction, one of the great literary critics of the twentieth century, Wayne C. Booth, poses a series of related questions. Why have so many interpretations of *The Turn of the Screw* been published? Why are they all so different, even contradictory? (Critics don't even agree on whether the ghosts are real or invented; how Miles dies; and whether James's tale is a classic "horror story" or a subtle example of modern psychological fiction.) In addition to asking why *The Turn of the Screw* has proved so controversial, Booth asks even more basic and important questions, such as: "What is the value of writing and reading controversial essays about such a work?" (165). Indeed, what is to be gained by debating about the meaning of *any* text?

To reveal the answers that Booth eventually arrives at would be to spoil the fun of his essay's unfolding argument. Suffice it to say here that in the process of coming to his carefully worked-out conclusions he roughly divides all known interpretations of *The Turn of the Screw* into three broad groups: those readings he calls "straight" (a straight reading views the ghosts as being real, the story as a horror story); those readings he calls "ironic" (according to an ironic reading, the ghosts are the imaginings of a mad governess and the tale is a disguised psychological study); and those readings he calls "mazed" (these are "readings that see the story as itself rejecting any one interpretation" [169]). Booth then proceeds by weighing the positive and negative effects of these three kinds of readings on the *reader*, asking in each case how a friend might be affected or changed — psychologically and/or morally — by being a "straight," "ironic," or "mazed" reader of *The Turn of the Screw*.

Booth states early on that he is writing "ethical criticism," which he classifies as "a version of what is now generally called reader-response criticism." As old as Plato's aesthetic philosophy, ethical criticism is interested not only in how readers respond to the same text in a variety of ways but also in the ethical implications of those various responses. As a practitioner of ethical criticism, Booth consistently — in his own words — invites us "to probe . . . the possible rewards for responding to this story in one way rather than another" (165).

However much he may believe that we, as readers, may and should choose between compelling readings, Booth should not be confused with the kind of subjectivist critic who believes that a text means whatever we make it out to mean. Booth views the author as one who guides the reader's responses — and views readers as agents who are only free within certain limits to make interpretive choices. "Though no one reading can ever triumph over all others," Booth writes, "there are better and worse readings. In short, 'my' readings, like yours, are inherently corrigible, improvable" (176).

As the quotation above amply demonstrates, Booth proves himself to be a reader-oriented critic not only by focusing on a variety of interpretive responses and their affective dimensions but also via his writing style. Throughout his essay, he addresses us directly, dares us to invent readings more preposterous than any that are extant, implores us to see that some readings are more dispensable than others, characterizes himself not as a writer of criticism but as a reader of James, and places his own readings in the contexts of other readings, including the four other readings (and the editor's critical history of the text) published in this volume!

Because of its provocative, reader-involving style, the essay you are about to read is one you will probably find highly unusual: unusual in that it is personal; unusual in that it is sometimes emotionally moving; and unusual, too, insofar as it suggests that what you are doing at this very moment has a value far greater than you may have supposed.

Ross C Murfin

READER-RESPONSE CRITICISM: A SELECTED BIBLIOGRAPHY

Some Introductions to Reader-Response Criticism

Fish, Stanley E. "Literature in the Reader: Affective Stylistics." *New Literary History* 2 (1970): 123–61. Rpt. in *Is There a Text in This Class?* 21–67 and in Primeau 154–79.

Freund, Elizabeth. *The Return of the Reader: Reader-Response Criticism*. London: Methuen, 1987.

Holland, Norman N. "UNITY IDENTITY TEXT SELF." *PMLA* 90 (1975): 813–22.

Holub, Robert C. *Reception Theory: A Critical Introduction*. New York: Methuen, 1984.

Mailloux, Steven. "Learning to Read: Interpretation and Reader-Response Criticism." *Studies in the Literary Imagination* 12 (1979): 93–108.

———. "Reader-Response Criticism?" *Genre* 10 (1977): 413–31.

Rosenblatt, Louise M. "Towards a Transactional Theory of Reading." *Journal of Reading Behavior* 1 (1969): 31–47. Rpt. in Primeau 121–46.

Suleiman, Susan R. "Introduction: Varieties of Audience-Oriented Criticism." Suleiman and Crosman 3–45.

Tompkins, Jane P. "An Introduction to Reader-Response Criticism." Tompkins ix–xxiv.

Reader-Response Criticism in Anthologies and Collections

Garvin, Harry R., ed. *Theories of Reading, Looking, and Listening*. Lewisburg: Bucknell UP, 1981. See the essays by Cain and Rosenblatt.

Leitch, Vincent B. *American Literary Criticism from the Thirties to the Eighties*. New York: Columbia UP, 1988.

Primeau, Ronald, ed. *Influx: Essays on Literary Influence*. Port Washington: Kennikat, 1977. See the essays by Fish, Holland, and Rosenblatt.

Suleiman, Susan R., and Inge Crosman, eds. *The Reader in the Text: Essays on Audience and Interpretation*. Princeton: Princeton UP, 1980. See especially the essays by Culler, Iser, and Todorov.

Tompkins, Jane P., ed. *Reader-Response Criticism: From Formalism to Post-Structuralism*. Baltimore: Johns Hopkins UP, 1980. See especially the essays by Bleich, Fish, Holland, Prince, and Tompkins.

Reader-Response Criticism: Some Major Works

Bleich, David. *Subjective Criticism*. Baltimore: Johns Hopkins UP, 1978.

Booth, Stephen. *An Essay on Shakespeare's Sonnets*. New Haven: Yale UP, 1969.

Eco, Umberto. *The Role of the Reader*. Bloomington: Indiana UP, 1979.

Fish, Stanley Eugene. *Doing What Comes Naturally: Change, Rhetoric, and the Practice of Theory in Literary and Legal Studies*. Durham: Duke UP, 1989.

———. *Is There a Text in This Class? The Authority of Interpretive Communities*. Cambridge: Harvard UP, 1980. In this volume are collected most of Fish's most influential essays, including "Literature in the Reader: Affective Stylistics," "What It's Like to Read *L'Allegro* and *Il Penseroso*," "Interpreting the *Variorum*," "Is There a Text in This Class?" "How to Recognize a Poem When You See One," and "What Makes an Interpretation Acceptable?"

———. *Self-Consuming Artifacts: The Experience of Seventeenth-Century Literature*. Berkeley: U of California P, 1972.

———. *Surprised by Sin: The Reader in "Paradise Lost."* 2nd ed. Berkeley: U of California P, 1971.

Holland, Norman N. *5 Readers Reading*. New Haven: Yale UP, 1975.

Iser, Wolfgang. *The Art of Reading: A Theory of Aesthetic Response*. Baltimore: Johns Hopkins UP, 1978.

———. *The Implied Reader: Patterns of Communication in Prose Fiction from Bunyan to Beckett*. Baltimore: Johns Hopkins UP, 1974.

Jauss, Hans Robert. *Toward an Aesthetic of Reception*. Trans. Timothy Bahti. Intro. Paul de Man. Brighton, Eng.: Harvester, 1982.

Mailloux, Steven. *Interpretive Conventions: The Reader in the Study of American Fiction*. Ithaca: Cornell UP, 1982.

———. *Rhetorical Power*. Ithaca: Cornell UP, 1989.

Messent, Peter. *New Readings of the American Novel: Narrative Theory and Its Application*. New York: Macmillan, 1991.

Prince, Gerald. *Narratology*. New York: Mouton, 1982.

Rabinowitz, Peter. *Before Reading: Narrative Conventions and the Politics of Interpretation*. Ithaca: Cornell UP, 1987.

Radway, Janice A. *Reading the Romance: Women, Patriarchy, and Popular Literature*. Chapel Hill: U of North Carolina P, 1984.

Rosenblatt, Louise M. *The Reader, the Text, the Poem: The Transactional Theory of the Literary Work*. Carbondale, IL: Southern Illinois UP, 1978.

Steig, Michael. *Stories of Reading: Subjectivity and Literary Understanding*. Baltimore: Johns Hopkins UP, 1989.

Exemplary Short Readings of Major Texts

Anderson, Howard. "*Tristram Shandy* and the Reader's Imagination." *PMLA* 86 (1971): 966–73.

Berger, Carole. "The Rake and the Reader in Jane Austen's Novels." *Studies in English Literature, 1500–1900* 15 (1975): 531–44.

Booth, Stephen. "On the Value of *Hamlet*." *Reinterpretations of English Drama: Selected Papers from the English Institute*. Ed. Norman Rabkin. New York: Columbia UP, 1969. 137–76.

Easson, Robert R. "William Blake and His Reader in *Jerusalem*." *Blake's Sublime Allegory*. Ed. Stuart Curran and Joseph A. Wittreich. Madison: U of Wisconsin P, 1973. 309–28.

Holland, Norman N. "*A Portrait* as Rebellion." *A Portrait of the Artist as a Young Man: A Case Study in Contemporary Criticism*. Ed. R. B. Kershner. Boston: Bedford–St. Martin's, 1993. 279–94.

Kirk, Carey H. "*Moby-Dick:* The Challenge of Response." *Papers on Language and Literature* 13 (1977): 383–90.

Leverenz, David. "Mrs. Hawthorne's Headache: Reading *The Scarlet Letter*." *The Scarlet Letter: A Case Study in Contemporary Criticism*. Ed. Ross C Murfin. Boston: Bedford–St. Martin's, 1991. 263–74.

Lowe-Evans, Mary. "Reading with a 'Nicer Eye': Responding to *Frankenstein*." *Mary Shelley, Frankenstein: A Case Study in Contemporary Criticism*. Ed. Johanna M. Smith. Boston: Bedford–St. Martin's, 1992. 215–29.

Rosmarin, Adena. "Darkening the Reader: Reader-Response Criticism and *Heart of Darkness*." *Heart of Darkness: A Case Study in Contemporary Criticism*. Ed. Ross C Murfin. Boston: Bedford–St. Martin's, 1989. 148–69.

Treichler, Paula A. "The Construction of Ambiguity in *The Awakening:* A Linguistic Analysis." *The Awakening: A Case Study in Contemporary Criticism*. Ed. Nancy A. Walker. Boston: Bedford–St. Martin's, 1993. 308–28.

Reader-Response Approaches to
The Turn of the Screw

Booth, Wayne C. *Critical Understanding: The Powers and Limits of Pluralism*. Chicago: U of Chicago P, 1979.

Heller, Terry. *"The Turn of the Screw": Bewildered Vision*. Boston: Twayne, 1989.

Other Work Referred to in
"What Is Reader-Response Criticism?"

Wimsatt, William K., and Monroe C. Beardsley. *The Verbal Icon.* Lexington: U of Kentucky P, 1954. See especially the discussion of
"The Affective Fallacy," with which reader-response critics have so
sharply disagreed.

A READER-RESPONSE PERSPECTIVE

WAYNE C. BOOTH

"He began to read to our hushed little circle":
Are We Blessed or Cursed
by Our Life with *The Turn of the Screw?*

No one who reads Peter Beidler's "Critical History" of *The Turn of
the Screw* (above, 127–51) is likely to call the readers of *The Turn of the
Screw* a "hushed little circle." The circle is not little, and there has been
no hush. Indeed, *The Turn of the Screw* has probably been discussed
more than any other modern story.[1] Some older, longer classics have no
doubt had more pages devoted to them: Homer's great epics, the *Iliad*
and the *Odyssey;* Dante's *Divine Comedy;* Shakespeare's *Hamlet.* And
some longer modern novels may well outdo this story in the number of
printed discussions. But among short works of fiction this one is surely
king. In English alone I have counted, before I got too bored to go on,
more than five hundred titles of books and articles about it, and since it
has been translated and discussed in dozens of other languages the total
must yield more than a lifetime's possible reading. To this one might
add all the unpublished doctoral dissertations and students' essays. And
here we are, in this volume, adding to the total!

---

[1]Stories like this one that are too long to be called short stories but shorter than most
of what we call novels are often called novellas, especially when, as in this case, they cover
an elaborate sequence of events of the kind one finds in novels.

If this sheer quantity seems puzzling, what can we say of the intense contradictions among the readings the critical history reveals? About many great works most readers agree on the basic facts of plot and character and about the responses called for; in discussion, public and private, readers discover that they have felt similar emotions and been led to similar thoughts — in other words, they discover agreement at least about the kind of work they have read. Nobody has ever seriously suggested, for example, that the tragedy *Hamlet* should be responded to as a comedy, or that Hamlet doesn't really die at the end but is just pretending, or that the ghost of Hamlet's father is only Hamlet's crazy invention, or that Hamlet killed his own father.[2] Nobody has ever seriously suggested that the hero of Dickens's *A Tale of Two Cities*, Sidney Carton, should be viewed as really a villain at heart, responsible for all the woes in that book, including the French Revolution itself, or that the events of the novel were all made up by one of the minor characters. Nobody has ever seriously suggested that Jane Austen's *Pride and Prejudice* is a tragedy, or that Elizabeth Bennet, the heroine, really made the whole thing up, as an old maid regretting her spinsterhood. But readers of *The Turn of the Screw* have found themselves unable to agree about the kind of story it is, about the emotional or intellectual responses it calls for, about who does what to whom, or even about who tells which parts of the story. I can think of no other work of art that has stimulated as many contradictory readings.

I want to pursue here the tricky question of what we readers are to make out of all this controversy. It might almost lead us to think that reading such stories and talking about our responses is a pointless, even crazy business — until we remember the variety of "readings" we meet of events in so-called real life. How many interpretations do you think we could find, if we searched hard, for what really happened in the French or American revolutions or the Vietnam War, or for your true motives in some important choice you have made, such as choosing a college or a major?

Still, such disagreement about a story, among readers who all seem to think it is worth reading and discussing, raises many difficult questions. Why do readers, like the five of us you find here, feel compelled

---

[2]Of course there are many playful parodies and transformations of the classics, like Tom Stoppard's turning of *Hamlet* into the story of two minor characters in *Rosencrantz and Guildenstern Are Dead*. But the clever readings that such games offer are quite different from the conflicting readings we consider here. Not only do they not question the "facts" of the originals; they depend on those facts, because readers and spectators cannot fully enjoy the jokes without full knowledge and acceptance of the originals.

to go on reading and re-reading a story the very nature of which we cannot even agree on? Why bother? What is the appeal to us, both of the re-reading and of the debates we engage in? As readers responding to the responses of us "literary critics," how should *you* respond? Should you just give it up as a bad job and go do something more obviously worthwhile? Or should you dig in and read the story again — and again?

Before you decide, you might think a bit about just how much re-reading most critics conduct when they are tempted to write about any literary work. While many of the interpretations Beidler reports seem to me to have been invented without enough attention to the words on the page, most of the authors had read the story many times before feeling comfortable about offering an interpretation. My own experience may be a bit extreme, since this is my third printed discussion, but I think it resembles that of most critics we pay any attention to. Over the years I've read the story many times; I haven't counted but I would guess at least twenty-five. And that's not counting the many times I've re-read puzzling sentences, paragraphs, and whole sections. Last week I read it again, and just today I looked once more at the death of Miles — for the hundred and forty-seventh time! This seemingly irrelevant digression is offered, of course, to convince you that I am the only critic whose incredible care should lead you to accept his views as clinchers!

Of all the challenging questions that such buzzing attention over one small flower raises, it is surprising that so few have asked, "Just what is the value of all this activity for those who engage in it?" What good is it? Does responding to this story, whether we read as we think Henry James would want us to or read looking for interpretations he would never have dreamed of, enhance our lives? This is the main question I am addressing here, but it will lead me to a second, closely related one: What is the value of writing and reading controversial essays about such a work? To read *The Turn of the Screw* is one thing; to write criticism about it, and to read, as you are now doing in this volume, a variety of seemingly conflicting views of what the story is about — that is quite a different thing. And again I ask, What good is it?

In short, I invite you now to probe with me the possible rewards for responding to this story in one way rather than another.

I

As we attempt such thinking, we shall be practicing a kind of literary criticism that for thousands of years was the most popular kind: a version of what is now generally called reader-response criticism. I call my version *ethical criticism:* the discussion of what stories do to the ethos of those who respond to them with full attention (*ethos* is the Greek word for "character"; its meanings include but go beyond what we call personality). Almost all readers took it for granted until quite recently that the most important questions to ask about any story were: How does it ask me to respond, and will that kind of response be good or bad for me? What will this story do to anyone who allows himself (for thousands of years hardly anyone worried about whether female readers might respond differently from males) to get caught up in the events — caught up in the sense of hoping for happiness for some characters and hoping to see other characters punished? Readers who chose to write down their opinions for other readers — "critics" like the five of us in this book — saw their job as in part that of helping others to think about what good or harm a given story or kind of story might yield.

When Plato, writing in *The Republic* almost twenty-five hundred years ago, raised doubts about the possible mis-education resulting from a sympathetic reading of Homer's epics, or when Samuel Johnson, the greatest English critic of the eighteenth century, raised tough questions about the wonderfully comic novel *Tom Jones*, it was as if they thought of their readers as friends whose fate they cared about, asking themselves, Would I want the experience I have had with this story, or the experience that readers are likely to have, to serve other people as a guide to life? or, Do I think of this story as a valuable gift from the author to me and my friends, or do I think of it as some kind of disguised poison? Such readers shared the assumption — one that to me is self-evident but that some modern critics have questioned — that readers are in fact influenced by the stories they read. They also assumed that talking together and writing and reading criticism about our experiences would heighten the good effects of worthwhile stories and weaken the bad effects of potentially harmful ones.[3]

Sometimes such critics seemed to embrace a fairly simple notion of how stories affect us — as if we were likely to imitate any behavior that any story presents, especially if the story asks us to admire that behavior.

---

[3]If this question seems a bit remote from your interests, you might want to think about recent debates over whether a constant diet of violent scenes on television or in the movies is harmful to the young. And if that leads you to want to do further reading and thinking, you might start with an article by Ken Auletta on how moviemakers themselves talk about the potential harm of the violence their "products" exploit ("What Won't They Do," *New Yorker*, May 17, 1993: 45–53).

It is this belief that leads some people to try to ban the publication of certain books or prevent their being on the reading lists in schools and colleges. Like the ancient critics, they rightly assume that readers, and especially young readers, will probably imitate whatever they admire in a story's characters, and the would-be censors conclude — wrongly, in my view — that it would be better for everyone to see or hear only admirable forms of behavior and the purest of language, whether in movies and television or in mental pictures built from books. Such narrowly moral or moralistic criticism could easily ban from our experience large portions of the Bible, many of Chaucer's poems, most of Shakespeare's plays, modern novels like Mark Twain's *The Adventures of Huckleberry Finn* and J. D. Salinger's *The Catcher in the Rye*, and — though perhaps not quite so obviously — *The Turn of the Screw*.[4]

The ethical criticism that is worth practicing avoids that kind of censorship. It does not look for this or that violation of some simple moral code: four-letter words, acts of violence, sexist or racist comments. For the careful ethical critic, everything will depend on the quality of the whole experience that a story offers; every detail, even if it is in itself highly offensive, will be judged in the context of what is seen as that total experience. That many of the heroes of the Torah (Old Testament) commit outrageous sins — Jacob cheating his brother Esau out of his inheritance, the various shenanigans of the young David and other leaders — does not mean that the Bible is a wicked book; to decide whether it is, one must look at the experiences it provides those readers who really pay attention to the context of the various vicious acts. For responsible ethical critics, it is what an author does with a character's actions, and what the reader then does, in turn, that determines the ethical effect.

It will always remain true that some careless readers will tear details out of their context and may thus harm themselves with works that, like the Bible, are written by authors intending nothing but good. The censors are thus right in insisting that stories do change us and can change us harmfully as well as beneficially. Perhaps you can remember a time when, after seeing an exciting movie, you found yourself trying to walk

---

[4]Every year hundreds of works are attacked by purification committees or individuals — "Unfit for young readers!" — and some of the attacks work. You may have experienced in your own schooling the effects of such purges, when your teachers or the school board in your town surrendered to the attackers. I'm not aware that anyone has ever proposed cutting *The Turn of the Screw* from reading lists, but we can be sure that if James had dared make explicit the words that little Miles and Flora were taught by the two villains, it would have been banned by many today, and by all when it first came out.

or talk like your favorite character — or thinking that it would be really cool to have an apartment or car or costume or sexy vocabulary of the kind your hero or heroine displayed. And you may by now have decided that a particular temptation to imitate was a mistake. I have known many self-reproaching smokers who claimed that what they considered a vicious addiction had resulted not from cigarette ads but from observing heroes and heroines in movies lighting up with a sexy flourish or actually sharing — what a thrill! — the same cigarette.

But how can we write or talk about such influencing? How could you warn someone else against a work that had "worked" ill on you, without sounding merely preachy and dogmatic? The task is so difficult that many critics in this century have decided not to attempt it at all. It too often leads to writing that sounds like a simple sermon touting the critic's private morality — as my statement above reveals my strong bias against smoking.

That is only one of the reasons that have led critics to avoid ethical criticism. If the ethical task is to appraise the value of a reading experience (or of listening to musical "stories" or viewing paintings or statues), how do we deal with the troublesome fact — dramatized in extreme form by *The Turn of the Screw* — that different readers experience different responses to the "same" story and argue for seemingly contradictory readings? How can we appraise the experience offered by a story as "good for us" or "bad for us" if there is no single experience — if your response is radically different from mine?

II

Surely the experience of *The Turn of the Screw* by a reader who believes that ghosts are real and who feels personally threatened by characters like Peter Quint and Miss Jessel requires an entirely different appraisal from what we would offer when discussing the response of someone who does not believe in ghosts — one who knows that ghosts do not exist and who feels neither fear nor horror but only curiosity about why James wrote the story in just this way. What is even more troublesome is disagreement among critics about just what standards are to be applied. Two "straight" readers, seeing the ghosts as real and the story as an attempt to "turn the screws" of horror as thrillingly as possible, might flatly disagree with each other about whether the literary experience of thrilling horror is good or bad for "us," or for a given immature reader, or for a former governess now incarcerated in a mental institution.

Because of all this variety, we have to ask our questions as if we were dealing not with one *The Turn of the Screw* but many different ones. Without simplifying too much, we can consider them under the three categories that Beidler's "Critical History" has led us to: straight, ironic, and what I'll call "mazed" — the readings that see the story as itself rejecting any one interpretation.

What is the quality of the experience of the "straight" reader, who assumes that whether or not ghosts actually exist in real life, they can be real at least in ghost stories? Such readers take seriously what is said in the opening section — the part that is sometimes called the frame or prologue; they accept the governess at her own word, and they take literally, as I confess that I do, Douglas's praise of the governess in the opening frame story: "a most charming person . . . the most agreeable woman I've ever known in her position" as governess. She was his sister's governess long ago — she's been herself dead for twenty years — and he's thus had every chance to discover whether she was trustworthy as a governess. His judgment is that "she'd have been worthy of any [position] whatever" (23)[5] — presumably not just as a governess.[6]

Such readers of course find themselves responding to a horrifying story of how two utterly corrupt people return from the dead in the hope of possessing the souls of two helpless little children; of how their innocent and courageous governess, learning of their plans, fights them off, hoping to save the children. For some readers responding in this way, she fails, fails utterly. The ghosts succeed: they do corrupt the children, and despite the governess's best efforts, one of them "possesses" little Miles to the horrifying point of killing him. For some other straight readers, though the governess loses the battle for little Miles's body, she saves his soul from the ultimate human disaster: being possessed by evil.

Readers who see victory for the ghosts naturally see the story as aiming to horrify. What could be more horrifying than the corruption — not just the destruction but the utter possession by evil forces — of two little children who are potentially ideal types of innocence? What could be more horrifying — and many a current movie and television show

---

[5]Page references refer to the text of *The Turn of the Screw* in this volume.
[6]I offered a brief tracing of my then devotedly straight reading in *The Rhetoric of Fiction* (311–16, 369–71). My later reading in *Critical Understanding* (284–301) was still essentially on the governess's side, but it tried to account more fully for the evidence of her increasing approach to psychological breakdown as the battle tensions mount; that reading thus moved somewhat toward the uneasy version of a "mazed" reading that I hint at below.

dramatizes this point — than the portrait of real moral monsters come back from the dead to poison the lives of little "angels"?

While sharing much of this horror, those who see Miles as saved see the story as clearly intending some degree of exultation or sense of triumph: evil is defeated, even though at the cost of Miles's life. At least his soul is saved.

If we ask ethical questions about the offering and acceptance of such a straight gift, whether ending in total disaster or salvation, we face the same comparatively simple problems that would face us if we asked that question about the latest horror movie. The experience itself is conventional, demanding little of us except intense emotional response. We may believe that to be roused to intense emotional response is itself a good thing — especially if it is done by reading words rather than simply surrendering to filmed images and if it happens to people who are otherwise emotional deadheads: Wake up, sluggard, and live for a while with this exciting stuff. Or we may want to say that for some readers — relatively immature or on the brink of emotional breakdown — such stuff is dangerous and ought to be avoided. Or we might want to stress the moral effects of identifying with the governess: the straight reader is invited to be courageous in the face of intense danger and to be a tough, honest defender of decency and justice. Even if her efforts are seen as failing, we will surely want to practice her kind of spunk if we ever find ourselves facing similar wickedness. And if her efforts have in fact saved Miles from possession, we have had a confirmation of just how important it is to face evil head on.

We see, then, that we get no single answer when we ask the question: Was this straight experience of terror and horror worth offering as a gift to our best friend? Or — what is the same thing, really — should your teacher have required you to read it? Since the world of literature is crowded with ghost stories, to have one more is neither especially good nor especially bad. James himself talked of *The Turn of the Screw* as a kind of potboiler, an effort to earn some needed cash by horrifying as many readers as possible. Neither the writing of such a story nor the reading of it matters very much to us one way or another, except as we may be thankful for skillful stories that cure our boredom. No doubt it would be harmful to spend most of our time reading such stuff, but an occasional few hours spent being scared out of our wits can't harm us very much — as those titillated ladies who appear in James's frame make clear: they love the thrill of it (though one suspects that James's way of portraying them reveals his own contempt for simple unalloyed horrifying).

Turning to ironic readings, what is the likely experience of the reader who for one reason or another mistrusts the governess's or Douglas's or the first narrator's account? This reader may or may not believe that Henry James intended us to mistrust one or another of the three, but all or part of what they say happened did not happen as they report it. Such a reader is likely to be absolutely sure that ghosts are not real, and that no ghost ever returned to corrupt an innocent child; that Henry James is himself too sophisticated to believe in ghosts and must have hoped for similarly sophisticated readers; and that James decided to create a story that would no doubt fool some careless readers into overlooking his portrait of a neurotic governess who goes mad and in one way or another destroys an innocent child.

Ironic readers will thus look for every clue that betrays untrustworthiness in the governess's account (or for some, in Douglas's, and for a very small number, the account of the opening narrator, the "I" who says "I remember" on the first page). Such readers usually report considerable pleasure in the ways in which James deliberately misleads the innocent into taking things straight. They also have the fun of becoming shrewd detectives, deciphering increasingly subtle clues that only the cleverest readers can catch. For example, they cite as a deliberate lie the account the governess gives Mrs. Grose of her encounter with Miss Jessel (early in chapter XVI), since it is different from and more detailed than the account she has given earlier. Or they quote her own words about being guilty of "endless obsession" (88), and her admission that she "ached for the proof" (92) that Miles actually did something to get expelled, and that she feels a "thrill of joy at having brought on a proof" (98).

In this reading, the governess's courage will seem entirely deceptive, an obsessive cover-up for her increasingly mad pursuit of imaginary horrors; she herself says, again and again, that the alternative to seeing the ghosts as real is to see herself as "cruel" or "mad" (98).

Like the straight story, this one is also likely to produce horrified responses in readers who engage fully with it; what the governess is seen as doing is awful. The children are victimized, whether we think of the governess as herself totally unsympathetic — a mad tyrant — or, as she is seen in some new interpretations, as herself a sympathetic victim of her own sincere delusions.[7] Straight readers may feel that they have

---

[7]Critics who deal with horror stories too seldom distinguish the radically differing ethical quality of stories that, while horrifying, disgust us, stories that scare us, stories that make us laugh, and — to cut the list short — stories that, like the horror in Shakespeare's *King Lear* and *Macbeth,* both teach us about the nature of evil and also lead us to want to combat it.

reason to fear that the same kind of disaster might strike them or their own children. In the ironic response, by contrast, readers can feel that simple precautions will protect anyone from allowing such a madwoman to succeed: just conduct more careful interviews before you hire your governesses! The master in London is the one who is to blame for not recognizing a madwoman when he sees one. He has consigned his helpless wards to their doom.

The fun of such a reading is likely to be somewhat less innocent than that of the first. Part of the pleasure in it seems to lie in feeling superior to straight readers: You uneducated, superstitious, lazy folks "down there" ought to feel sort of silly not to have caught the subtle clues that we smarties up here have worked out. Critics are like other people: they compete with one another for the badge of Most Perceptive, and the desire to win can tempt them into looking for the most unlikely readings.

On the other hand, if we become convinced that James intended an ironic reading, we can hardly claim that to read the story straight is ethically superior: it would be just plain wrong. Still, I must ask myself, Would I recommend to my best friends that they spend hours and hours working out the "correct" ironic reading of such a story — seeing the governess, say, as a psychopathic killer? I think not. It would not only reinforce my friends' natural temptation to feel superior to other people; it would also confirm any temptation those friends have to feel that women tend to be hysterical and destructive of those they love: "Watch out for women who pretend to be deeply concerned about the moral welfare of their loved ones; and when you read stories told by them, be sure to look behind any masks of virtue they have put on."

According to one view of human nature, however, we could turn that charge around: we should surely praise the ironic story for alerting us to the inherent inclination of every human creature to sin: as some religions suggest, we are "originally sinful." Behind every virtuous-seeming exterior there does indeed lie a heart that was created flawed, "in the beginning," and it is the highest purpose of literature to pull down the facades and expose the viciousness within. A reader who believes that and who possesses sufficient humility might well be led to conclude, reading the ironic story, "I am too much like that destructive governess: I go about the world judging other people's wickedness and ignoring my own. Lord protect me from my own pride. I must change my life, or I will find myself behaving like the governess." This defense does not, however, answer the charge reported by Beidler, a charge that I share, that some of the ironic readings are prompted by sexism (see "Critical History" 138).

But what can we say happens to the "mazed readers" who see the story (as Beidler shows that more and more critics are urging us to do) as a maze with many intentionally deceptive false turns and dead ends? Regardless of what James said he intended, they see the story as ensuring the constant frustration of every interpreter; it leads readers a merry chase through one failed reading after another. If, as a careful reader, you pursue the straight story, with the governess generally trustworthy, you will soon find many signs of her unreliability — the kind I have already cited — and you will see increasing signs of her pathological over-reaction to ambiguous clues. On the other hand, if you pursue the ironic story you will soon be balked by signs that James intends us to see the governess as reliable, the ghosts as absolutely real, and Miles as already in the process of being corrupted — not just the testimony of Douglas to her reliability but a long list of corroborating facts: Miles's expulsion from school before he meets the governess; Miles's strange blowing out of the candle; tiny Flora's ability to row a large boat across the pond; Mrs. Grose's ability to identify Peter Quint from the governess's detailed description of what she has seen; the initially skeptical housekeeper's final assertion that she believes the governess.

For some, the result of such endless revisions of reading responses should be not bitter frustration but a kind of thrill as bafflement yields illumination about the true nature of literature and life: no interpretation of any story, or indeed of any event in real life, can ever be fixed, determinate, counted on to be *the* interpretation; all views are underminable, "deconstructible" — in short, not only should every conclusion be held as temporary, but all controversies must be seen as unresolvable, undecidable, or as some critics put it, "unreadable." The story-as-maze confirms this "sophisticated" — and for some quite exciting — view of life. Miles is both persecuted by ghosts and not persecuted by ghosts; the governess is both mad and not mad; Douglas is both involved in the story as a (disguised) character, and not involved. And so on.

Would I recommend such a "mazed" experience to my best friends? Again the answer must depend on "where my friends are coming from," or "where they are at." If they are already members of that elite club who know that there is only one truth, which is that there is no truth, then I think the story might very well be harmful to them: along with whatever bliss they may initially experience at the sense of liberation from other people's truth is likely to come a complacent sense of cynical superiority. They will feel a bit too comfortable with the "proof," offered by James himself, that they have been right all along: like every other story, *The Turn of the Screw*, if it is read carefully, confirms an anti-truth-truth that only a select band of right-thinking folks have discovered.

On the other hand, I may have friends who are too firmly fixed in certain conventional views of the world — readers who read a story once and know then precisely what to think about it; readers who look at a character, in or out of a story, and quickly decide, whether reading straight or ironically, that he or she belongs to this or that conventional category of good or bad. Such friends could do with some shaking up; things are not what they seem. First readings are almost always inadequate. Every truth proclaimed by any human being is sure to be at best fragmentary, correctable by further truth to be discovered on down the road. *The Turn of the Screw* as maze could well wake up such friends and lead them on to further discovery.

III

Imagine now any teacher — you if you are actually one, your teacher if you are now "here" because of an assignment — trying to decide, on the basis of what I have said so far, whether to require students to read and discuss and write about this story. No teacher can know much in advance about just what kind of response students will have — whether they will most need waking up or settling down, whether they are too much or too little inclined to doubt what anyone says. What is the teacher to do?

Now I could easily offer that teacher a summary of my own reading — one that by now is somewhat different from the ones I printed in 1961 and 1979. It is of course the one reading that is really correct, the one that all readers ought to hold and that would lead to a decisive proclamation about whether your teacher should have recommended *The Turn of the Screw* to you and you should recommend it to your friends.[8] But if I am right in believing that a personal response to the story, and then an honest discussion with others about it, are much more important than being right about any one reading, it will be much

---

[8] I hope, but cannot believe, that my own irony here will never be quoted against me. And I should perhaps add that though I still see James as consciously intending (at least most of the time) a straight story, I am forced to agree now with those who see James-the-imaginer as having been to some degree deflected from his conscious intentions by the intensities of his own encounters with disturbed and superstitious minds. Thus, having changed my mind about it several times over the years, I can hardly agree with those who expect to find the one right final reading.

more valuable to leave you to work out your own response, encouraged as I hope by my turning here to my second large question: What do we think about the value of debating about *The Turn of the Screw*? What can we say about those hundreds of thousands of hours people have spent disputing about it, in print, in classrooms, and in private conversation, not only about the printed version but about the movies and opera based on it?

The question clearly applies sharply to us critics you are meeting in this volume. We are not in any obvious agreement about what the story is or how to discuss it. Even if we got together for prolonged discussion, we would not come out in full agreement about every detail. We know that, and yet we continue to debate about it — knowing full well that such inherently interminable debate is not actually required of us. Even those among us who must publish or perish could easily write about other matters. Why *The Turn of the Screw*? As I've said, few stories have been subjected to anything like this much debate. About most stories that we tell one another, we feel little temptation to spend much time in discussion: they are simply gripping or boring and we leave it at that. What can we say about the value of the time and energy and specific kind of attention that are spent on this story and others like it?

Here we must face the same complication that troubled us in appraising the three contrasting stories themselves: straight, ironic, and mazed. Much will depend on the presuppositions of the reader who engages in debate about James's complex gift. If that reader is already convinced, before reading, that no debate can ever lead to genuine improvement of views, that no views about anything are inherently superior to any other views, then debate about the story is not in itself an activity to value. Why bother? Critical debate in this view can have value only to the degree that it results in persuading us to believe that all ideas are equally questionable.[9] If there will always be counter-evidence for anyone clever enough to locate it, then to persuade readers to have the maze experience in its extremer versions may feel worthwhile, but the time spent on the debate itself will simply be a means to the end of coming to the truth-of-non-truth. On the other hand the reader may have been, in past reading and discussion, unduly eager to land in

---

[9]One well-known critic, who shall be nameless, has sometimes argued that no interpretations are inherently better than others, and that debating about them has only one unquestionable value: it gains jobs and promotions for professors. But I can't believe that he takes himself seriously in such claims, because he often shows a passionate concern to get things right.

certainty, or unwilling to change a reading in the face of hard evidence — Miles's death is obviously sad or horrifying or triumphant, or deliberately puzzling, and so on. For such a reader the experience of having to debate a particular story, the engagement with evidence and counter-evidence, the irresistible temptation to go back and read the story again, can all be in themselves educational: the very process is valuable, regardless of where, at a given stage in the argument, we come out. But that value depends on one strong assumption too often repudiated by the "mazers": though no one reading can ever triumph over all others, there are better and worse readings. In short, "my" readings, like yours, are inherently corrigible, improvable.

As someone who began his mental life expecting to get "the whole thing taped," convinced that sooner or later he could, "in principle," know the truth about just about everything, I would claim that to have been led, by teachers and other critics, to debate just how this or that story ought to be read, just what experience of it ought to be achieved, has been one of life's most precious gifts. Again and again I have found myself, after expressing a firm conclusion in talk or print, simply and embarrassingly proved wrong. I have then had to draw back, re-think, re-read, and try again. Often I have been shocked, or angry, or disoriented. I have then sometimes developed fancy hypotheses in the effort to prove my opponents wrong — only to discover that the hypotheses had nothing to say for themselves except that they were mine. I was wrong again — and again.

Perhaps you will not be surprised to find me concluding, then, that to live in that kind of constantly revising state is not a bad way to live. When are we more fully alive than when grappling with Henry James and then being forced by other readers to go back for another look at his beautiful intricate prose, and then debating further about whether one has re-read those often puzzling words in the best possible — or at least a defensible — way? It's not a bad way to go, not a bad way to go at all. On the contrary I would say that the hours I have spent on this story in the past, and the hours I am spending now, trying to rise to the level of James's kind of mind and of the best of the other minds who have found him worth reading, including yours, my anonymous friends who read me here — these hours have been among the best of my days, or weeks, or years.

Just compare the time we have spent together so far here, you and I, with the time we spent last night watching the latest re-run of the most popular mystery or horror film or the hottest talk show or rock video, or whatever political convention happens to have been on, or the latest sport championship; or the time we spent this morning reading the sports page or the comic strips. While I don't feel any deep regret about the time I spend on activities like that — and I spend time on all of them — I haven't the least doubt about valuing more highly the time I've spent on Henry James and his critics, whether I have agreed with their readings or not. Though some critics have seemed to be merely playing trivial self-promotional games, most have been engaged in the activity Henry James himself most honored: constructing, or in our case re-constructing with his help, a complex, challenging story that becomes, almost miraculously, theirs.

Most of my other valued experiences in life select out from many possible values one or another and play it to the hilt. Sports, sex, food, travel seem to offer shallow pleasures compared with the hours we're spending "here" — here in this curious mental space/nonspace where you as my reader and I as a fellow-reader of Henry James somehow meet. Our experience here is rivaled only by other deep activities: loving, making friends, trying to help others or obtaining help from them — you can no doubt add to this short list. And one wonderful bonus of experiencing stories is the way they can deepen those other deepest experiences. A great part of the fun of seeing a good movie, for example, is arguing about its meanings afterward, with someone whose challenges we respect.

Many of my other valued experiences produce strong emotional responses — "We won the championship!" — but little or no thought. Some other experiences make me think — "Why did Karpov choose just this move at this point in the championship chess match?" — but do not engage my deeper emotions. Some experiences engage me emotionally and also make me think — "How can I outsmart X in this championship match?" — but do not sharpen my sensitivity to and concern for other people's feelings. Responding to Henry James's story, however, and then discussing it with other readers, can "deepen" me in all three dimensions at once. Whether I find myself feeling with the governess or against her, I am, in most though perhaps not all conceivable readings, engaged with the imaginative richness of extraordinary minds and hearts — not just Henry James's but other readers'.

To wrestle with minds and hearts like that, to make my own sense out of one rich piece of the world, that piece itself consisting of characters who themselves think and feel and talk and act in concern for what is good or bad about one another — is not such wrestling the best possible life-instructor as we construct the day-by-day story of our own lives? We all meet many characters daily, some who wish us well and some who will gladly turn the screw another notch in our troubles and pains. Who better than Henry James and his critics can teach us the complex skills we need in "reading" these would-be friends?

Deconstruction
and
The Turn of the Screw

WHAT IS DECONSTRUCTION?

Deconstruction has a reputation for being the most complex and forbidding of contemporary critical approaches to literature, but in fact almost all of us have, at one time, either deconstructed a text or badly wanted to deconstruct one. Sometimes when we hear a lecturer effectively marshal evidence to show that a book means primarily one thing, we long to interrupt and ask what he or she would make of other, conveniently overlooked passages, passages that seem to contradict the lecturer's thesis. Sometimes, after reading a provocative critical article that *almost* convinces us that a familiar work means the opposite of what we assumed it meant, we may wish to make an equally convincing case for our former reading of the text. We may not think that the poem or novel in question better supports our interpretation, but we may recognize that the text can be used to support *both* readings. And sometimes we simply want to make that point: texts can be used to support seemingly irreconcilable positions.

To reach this conclusion is to feel the deconstructive itch. J. Hillis Miller, the preeminent American deconstructor, puts it this way: "Deconstruction is not a dismantling of the structure of a text, but a demonstration that it has already dismantled itself. Its apparently solid ground is no rock but thin air" ("Stevens' Rock" 341). To deconstruct a text isn't to show that all the high old themes aren't there to be found in it. Rather, it is to show that a text — not unlike DNA with its double helix — can have intertwined, opposite "discourses" — strands of narrative, threads of meaning.

Ultimately, of course, deconstruction refers to a larger and more complex enterprise than the practice of demonstrating that a text means contradictory things. The term refers to a way of reading texts practiced by critics who have been influenced by the writings of the French philosopher Jacques Derrida. It is important to gain some understanding of Derrida's project and of the historical backgrounds of his work before reading the deconstruction that follows, let alone attempting to deconstruct a text. But it is important, too, to approach deconstruction with anything but a scholar's sober and almost worshipful respect for knowledge and truth. Deconstruction offers a playful alternative to traditional scholarship, a confidently adversarial alternative, and deserves to be approached in the spirit that animates it.

Derrida, a philosopher of language who coined the term "deconstruction," argues that we tend to think and express our thoughts in terms of opposites. Something is black but not white, masculine and therefore not feminine, a cause rather than an effect, and so forth. These mutually exclusive pairs or dichotomies are too numerous to list but would include beginning/end, conscious/unconscious, presence/absence, speech/writing, and construction/destruction (the last being the opposition that Derrida's word *deconstruction* tries to contain and subvert). If we think hard about these dichotomies, Derrida suggests, we will realize that they are not simply oppositions; they are also hierarchies in miniature. In other words, they contain one term that our culture views as being superior and one term viewed as negative or inferior. Sometimes the superior term seems only subtly superior (*speech, masculine, cause*), whereas sometimes we know immediately which term is culturally preferable (*presence* and *beginning* and *consciousness* are easy choices). But the hierarchy always exists.

Of particular interest to Derrida, perhaps because it involves the language in which all the other dichotomies are expressed, is the hierarchical opposition speech/writing. Derrida argues that the "privileging" of speech, that is, the tendency to regard speech in positive terms and writing in negative terms, cannot be disentangled from the privileging of presence. (Postcards are written by absent friends; we read Plato because he cannot speak from beyond the grave.) Furthermore, according to Derrida, the tendency to privilege both speech and presence is part of the Western tradition of *logocentrism,* the belief that in some ideal beginning were creative *spoken* words, words such as "Let there be light," spoken by an ideal, *present* God. According to logocentric tradition, these words can now only be represented in unoriginal speech or writing (such as the written phrase in quotation marks above). Derrida doesn't seek to reverse the hierarchized opposition between speech and writing, or presence and absence, or early and late, for to do so would be to fall into a trap of perpetuating the same forms of thought and expression that he seeks to deconstruct. Rather, his goal is to erase the boundary between oppositions such as speech and writing, and to do so in such a way as to throw the order and values implied by the opposition into question.

Returning to the theories of Ferdinand de Saussure, who invented the modern science of linguistics, Derrida reminds us that the association of speech with present, obvious, and ideal meaning and writing with absent, merely pictured, and therefore less reliable meaning is suspect, to say the least. As Saussure demonstrated, words are *not* the things they name and, indeed, they are only arbitrarily associated with those things. Neither spoken nor written words have present, positive, identifiable attributes themselves; they have meaning only by virtue of their difference from other words (*red, read, reed*). In a sense, meanings emerge from the gaps or spaces between them. Take *read* as an example. To know whether it is the present or past tense of the verb — whether it rhymes with *red* or *reed* — we need to see it in relation to some other word (for example, *yesterday*).

Because the meanings of words lie in the differences between them and in the differences between them and the things they name, Derrida suggests that all language is constituted by *différance,* a word he has coined that puns on two French words meaning "to differ" and "to defer": words are the deferred presences of the things they "mean," and their meaning is grounded in difference. Derrida, by the way, changes the *e* in the French word *différence* to an *a* in his neologism *différance;* the change, which can be seen in writing but cannot be heard in spoken French, is itself a playful, witty challenge to the notion that writing is inferior or "fallen" speech.

In *De la grammatologie* [*Of Grammatology*] (1967) and *Dissemination* (1972), Derrida begins to redefine writing by deconstructing some old definitions. In *Dissemination,* he traces logocentrism back to Plato,

who in the *Phaedrus* has Socrates condemn writing and who, in all the
great dialogues, powerfully postulates that metaphysical longing for origins and ideals that permeates Western thought. "What Derrida does in
his reading of Plato," Barbara Johnson points out, "is to unfold dimensions of Plato's *text* that work against the grain of (Plato's own) Plato-
nism" (xxiv). Remember: that is what deconstruction does according to
Miller; it shows a text dismantling itself.

In *Of Grammatology,* Derrida turns to the *Confessions* of Jean-
Jacques Rousseau and exposes a grain running against the grain. Rousseau, another great Western idealist and believer in innocent, noble origins, on one hand condemned writing as mere representation, a
corruption of the more natural, childlike, direct, and therefore unde-
vious speech. On the other hand, Rousseau admitted his own tendency
to lose self-presence and blurt out exactly the wrong thing in public. He
confesses that, by writing at a distance from his audience, he often expressed himself better: "If I were present, one would never know what
I was worth," Rousseau admitted (Derrida, *Of Grammatology* 142).
Thus, writing is a *supplement* to speech that is at the same time *necessary*.
Barbara Johnson, sounding like Derrida, puts it this way: "Recourse to
writing . . . is necessary to recapture a presence whose lack has not been
preceded by any fullness" (Derrida, *Dissemination* xii). Thus, Derrida
shows that one strand of Rousseau's discourse made writing seem a secondary, even treacherous supplement, while another made it seem necessary to communication.

Have Derrida's deconstructions of *Confessions* and the *Phaedrus* explained these texts, interpreted them, opened them up and shown us
what they mean? Not in any traditional sense. Derrida would say that
anyone attempting to find a single, correct meaning in a text is simply
imprisoned by that structure of thought that would oppose two readings and declare one to be right and not wrong, correct rather than
incorrect. In fact, any work of literature that we interpret defies the laws
of Western logic, the laws of opposition and noncontradiction. In the
views of poststructuralist critics, texts don't say "A and not B." They say
"A and not-A," as do texts written by literary critics, who are also involved in producing creative writing.

Miller has written that the purpose of deconstruction is to show
"the existence in literature of structures of language which contradict
the law of non-contradiction." Why find the grain that runs against
the grain? To restore what Miller has called "the strangeness of
literature," to reveal the "capacity of each work to surprise the reader,"
to demonstrate that "literature continually exceeds any formula or

theory with which the critic is prepared to encompass it" (Miller, *Fiction* 5).

Although its ultimate aim may be to critique Western idealism and logic, deconstruction began as a response to structuralism and to formalism, another structure-oriented theory of reading. (Deconstruction, which is really only one kind of a poststructuralist criticism, is sometimes referred to as poststructuralist criticism, or even as poststructuralism.)

Structuralism, Robert Scholes tells us, may now be seen as a reaction to modernist alienation and despair (3). Using Saussure's theory as Derrida was to do later, European structuralists attempted to create a *semiology,* or science of signs, that would give humankind at once a scientific and a holistic way of studying the world and its human inhabitants. Roland Barthes, a structuralist who later shifted toward poststructuralism, hoped to recover literary language from the isolation in which it had been studied and to show that the laws that govern it govern all signs, from road signs to articles of clothing. Claude Lévi-Strauss, a structural anthropologist who studied everything from village structure to the structure of myths, found in myths what he called *mythemes,* or building blocks, such as basic plot elements. Recognizing that the same mythemes occur in similar myths from different cultures, he suggested that all myths may be elements of one great myth being written by the collective human mind.

Derrida could not accept the notion that structuralist thought might someday explain the laws governing human signification and thus provide the key to understanding the form and meaning of everything from an African village to a Greek myth to Rousseau's *Confessions.* In his view, the scientific search by structural anthropologists for what unifies humankind amounts to a new version of the old search for the lost ideal, whether that ideal be Plato's bright realm of the Idea or the Paradise of Genesis or Rousseau's unspoiled Nature. As for the structuralist belief that texts have "centers" of meaning, in Derrida's view that derives from the logocentric belief that there is a reading of the text that accords with "the book as seen by God." Jonathan Culler, who thus translates a difficult phrase from Derrida's *L'Écriture et la différence* [*Writing and Difference*] (1967) in his book *Structuralist Poetics* (1975), goes on to explain what Derrida objects to in structuralist literary criticism:

> [When] one speaks of the structure of a literary work, one does so from a certain vantage point: one starts with notions of the mean-

ing or effects of a poem and tries to identify the structures responsible for those effects. Possible configurations or patterns that make
no contribution are rejected as irrelevant. That is to say, an intu-
itive understanding of the poem functions as the "centre" . . . : it
is both a starting point and a limiting principle. (244)

For these reasons, Derrida and his poststructuralist followers reject the
very notion of "linguistic competence" introduced by Noam Chomsky,
a structural linguist. The idea that there is a competent reading "gives a
privileged status to a particular set of rules of reading, . . . granting pre-
eminence to certain conventions and excluding from the realm of language all the truly creative and productive violations of those rules"
(Culler, *Structuralist Poetics* 241).

Poststructuralism calls into question assumptions made about literature by formalist, as well as by structuralist, critics. Formalism, or the
New Criticism as it was once commonly called, assumes a work of literature to be a freestanding, self-contained object, its meanings found in
the complex network of relations that constitute its parts (images,
sounds, rhythms, allusions, and so on). To be sure, deconstruction is
somewhat like formalism in several ways. Both the formalist and the
deconstructor focus on the literary text; neither is likely to interpret a
poem or a novel by relating it to events in the author's life, letters, historical period, or even culture. And formalists, long before
deconstructors, discovered counterpatterns of meaning in the same
text. Formalists find ambiguity and irony, deconstructors find contradiction and undecidability.

Undecidability, as Paul de Man came to define it, is a complex notion easily misunderstood. There is a tendency to assume it refers to
readers who, when forced to decide between two or more equally plausible and conflicting readings motivated by the same text, throw up
their hands and decide that the choice can't be made. But undecidability in fact debunks this whole notion of reading as a decision-making
process carried out on texts by readers. To say we are forced to choose
or decide — or that we are unable to do so — is to locate the problem
of undecidability falsely outside ourselves, and to make it reside within
a text to which we come as an Other. The poststructuralist concept of
undecidability, we might say, deconstructs the either/or type distinction or opposition that structuralists and formalists have made between
reader and text. It entails what de Man calls the "mutual obliteration"
not only of propositions apparently opposed but also of the subject/ob-
ject relation.

Undecidability is thus rather different from ambiguity, as understood by formalists. Formalists believe a complete understanding of a literary work is possible, an understanding in which even the ambiguities will fulfill a definite, meaningful function. Deconstructors confront the apparently limitless possibilities for the production of meaning that develop when the language of the critic enters the language of the text. They cannot accept the formalist view that a work of literary art has organic unity (therefore, structuralists would say, a "center"), if only we could find it. The formalist critic ultimately makes sense of ambiguity; undecidability, by contrast, is never reduced, let alone resolved, by deconstructive reading.

Poststructuralists break with formalists, too, over an issue they have debated with structuralists. The issue involves metaphor and metonymy, two terms for different kinds of rhetorical *tropes,* or figures of speech. *Metonymy* refers to a figure that is chosen to stand for something that it is commonly associated with, or with which it happens to be contiguous or juxtaposed. When said to a waitress, "I'll have the cold plate today" is a metonymic figure of speech for "I'll eat the cold food you're serving today." We refer to the food we want as a plate simply because plates are what food happens to be served on and because everyone understands that by *plate* we mean food. A *metaphor,* on the other hand, is a figure of speech that involves a special, intrinsic, nonarbitrary relationship with what it represents. When you say you are blue, if you believe that there is an intrinsic, timeless likeness between that color and melancholy feeling — a likeness that just doesn't exist between sadness and yellow — then you are using the word *blue* metaphorically.

Although both formalists and structuralists make much of the difference between metaphor and metonymy, Derrida, Miller, and de Man have contended with the distinction deconstructively. They have questioned not only the distinction but also, and perhaps especially, the privilege we grant to metaphor, which we tend to view as the positive and superior figure of speech. De Man, in *Allegories of Reading* (1979), analyzes a passage from Proust's *Swann's Way,* arguing that it is about the nondistinction between metaphor and metonymy — and that it makes its claim metonymically. In *Fiction and Repetition: Seven English Novels* (1982), Miller connects the belief in metaphorical correspondences with other metaphysical beliefs, such as those in origins, endings, transcendence, and underlying truths. Isn't it likely, deconstructors keep implicitly asking, that every metaphor was once a metonym, but that we have simply forgotten what arbitrary juxtaposition or contiguity gave rise to the association that now seems mysteriously special?

The hypothesis that what we call metaphors are really old metonyms may perhaps be made clearer by the following example. We used the word *Watergate* as a metonym to refer to a political scandal that began in the Watergate building complex. Recently, we have used part of the building's name (*gate*) to refer to more recent scandals (*Irangate*). However, already there are people who use and "understand" these terms who are unaware that Watergate is the name of a building. In the future, isn't it possible that *gate,* which began as part of a simple metonym, will seem like the perfect metaphor for scandal — a word that suggests corruption and wrongdoing with a strange and inexplicable rightness?

This is how deconstruction works: by showing that what was prior and privileged in the old hierarchy (for instance, metaphor and speech) can just as easily seem secondary, the deconstructor causes the formerly privileged term to exchange properties with the formerly devalued one. Causes become effects and (d)evolutions become origins, but the result is neither the destruction of the old order or hierarchy nor the construction of a new one. It is, rather, *deconstruction*. In Robert Scholes's words, "If either cause or effect can occupy the position of an origin, then origin is no longer originary; it loses its metaphorical privilege" (88).

Once deconstructed, literal and figurative can exchange properties, so that the prioritizing between them is erased: all words, even dog and cat, are understood to be figures. It's just that we have used some of them so long that we have forgotten how arbitrary and metonymic they are. And, just as literal and figurative can exchange properties, criticism can exchange properties with literature, in the process coming to be seen not merely as a supplement — the second, negative, and inferior term in the binary opposition creative writing/literary criticism — but rather as an equally creative form of work. Would we write if there were not critics — intelligent readers motivated and able to make sense of what is written? Who, then, depends on whom?

"It is not difficult to see the attractions" of deconstructive reading, Jonathan Culler has commented. "Given that there is no ultimate or absolute justification for any system or for the interpretations from it," the critic is free to value "the activity of interpretation itself, . . . rather than any results which might be obtained" (*Structuralist Poetics* 248). Not everyone, however, has so readily seen the attractions of deconstruction. Two eminent critics, M. H. Abrams and Wayne Booth, have observed that a deconstructive reading "is plainly and simply parasitical" on what Abrams calls "the obvious or univocal meaning" (Abrams 457–58). In other words, there would be no deconstructors if critics did not already exist who can see and show central and definite meanings in texts. Miller responded in an essay entitled "The Critic as Host," in which he not only deconstructed the oppositional hierarchy (host/parasite), but also the two terms themselves, showing that each derives from two definitions meaning nearly opposite things. *Host* means "hospitable welcomer" and "military horde." *Parasite* originally had a positive connotation; in Greek, *parasitos* meant "beside the grain" and referred to a friendly guest. Finally, Miller suggests, the words *pasasite* and *host* are inseparable, depending on one another for their meaning in a given work, much as do hosts and parasites, authors and critics, structuralists and poststructuralists.

In the deconstructive reading of *The Turn of the Screw* that follows, Shoshana Felman points out that the story's last chapter contains the word "grasp" in its first and last paragraphs. In the first paragraph, the word is used abstractly to mean "comprehension" or "understanding," whereas in the last it is used concretely to describe the governess's physical "hold" on Miles. As a result of this double word use, James's text is said "to *play* upon the two connotations" of "grasp" and to interrogate the relationship between them.

Entering the story's field of etymological and textual play, Felman reflects on how the quest for understanding — that is, a *mental* "grasp" of things — is a quest for control of meaning and, therefore, power. Pointing out that Cicero used the image of the closed fist and a Latin word that literally meant "a seizing" to describe mental comprehension, she consequently suggests that it is in one sense the governess's mental grasp of what she believes to be reality that proves deadly to the child who dies in her physical grasp.

The act of mental grasping described in the first paragraph of the story's last chapter takes place as the governess is suffering a "fierce split" in her attention. (Just as Miles is answering her question about whether or not he stole her letter, a ghost appears at the window.) Felman uses this fact illustratively to suggest that the quest for meaning, understanding, or clarity of comprehension — a good grasp of what is going on — inevitably involves a (figuratively) violent attempt to triumph over self-division, uncertainty, doubleness. Does not our own act of reading tend to involve the elimination of interpretive possibilities that prove obstacles to clarity? We have been taught to resolve oppositions and contradictions by privileging one meaning or reading and banishing its alternative.

Using the psychoanalytic theory of Jacques Lacan, Felman links the knowledge of which the governess would keep the children unaware — the knowledge she would banish from her own understanding — with the unconscious, which Lacan called "a knowledge one cannot know one knows." Lacan aligns the unconscious with the *signifier* of meaning and consciousness with meaning *signified*, leading Felman to assert that "the act of reading, the attempt to grasp and hold the signified, goes . . . hand in hand with the repression or obliteration of the signifier — a repression the purpose of which is to eliminate meaning's *division*" (197).

Of course, to "see" the "truth" through this kind of process of elimination involves shutting one's eyes to half of the truth and is thus, as Paul de Man has pointed out, a kind of blindness. Intellectual "mastery" of this sort involves the kind of repressive control exercised, according to Felman, in Edmund Wilson's famous reading of the scene in which Flora screws a stick into a piece of wood with a little hole in it. Wilson simply asserts that the "mast" of the little boat is "phallic," thereby concluding that Flora's turn of the screw implies a kind of sexual knowledge. "But it is precisely *not* as an unequivocal *answer* that the text here evokes the phallus," Felman argues, "but on the contrary rather as a *question*, as a figure — itself ambiguous — produced by the enigma of the double meaning of the metaphorical equation: phallus = ship's mast. To say that the mast is in reality a phallus is no more illuminating or unambiguous than to say that the phallus is in reality a mast" (201).

Felman at this point notes the "resemblance" between the words "mast," "master," and "mastery," but rather than coming to the conclusion that there is some important and unambiguous connection among these words and their meanings, she suggests that this "signifying chain" is one in which "the phallus (or the screw, or the mast, or the Master), far from incarnating the unambiguous literal meaning behind things, symbolizes rather the incessant sliding of signification, the very principle of movement and displacement which on the contrary prevents the chain (or the text) from ever stopping at a final, literal, fixed meaning" (202).

Felman is known for essays and books that combine the insights of Lacanian psychoanalytic criticism with deconstruction. The essay that follows is not atypical, making use of Lacan while being deconstructive in its tendency to read the text closely, in its focus on repetitions and oppositions, in its refusal to privilege or hierarchize terms or meanings, and in its liberating interest and suggestive participation in word play (some of which we would miss were it not for Felman's unusual but revealing use of italics). Like other deconstructive critics, Felman would have us see that texts mean "A" at the same time that they mean "not-A," notwithstanding the fact that readers and interpreters who are like James's governess are forever seeking to make them coherent and consistent. Although such interpreters think they have "mastered" the text once they have banished its doubleness — and that split consciousness the text initially engendered — they have in fact murdered the richness, the strangeness, and the evocative ghostliness of the text.

Ross C Murfin

DECONSTRUCTION: A SELECTED BIBLIOGRAPHY

Deconstruction, Poststructuralism, and Structuralism: Introduction, Guides, and Surveys

Arac, Jonathan, Wlad Godzich, and Wallace Martin, eds. *The Yale Critics: Deconstruction in America*. Minneapolis: U of Minnesota P, 1983. See especially the essays by Bové, Godzich, Pease, and Corngold.

Berman, Art. *From the New Criticism to Deconstruction: The Reception of Structuralism and Post-Structuralism*. Urbana: U of Illinois P, 1988.

Butler, Christopher. *Interpretation, Deconstruction, and Ideology: An Introduction to Some Current Issues in Literary Theory*. Oxford: Oxford UP, 1984.

Cain, William E. "Deconstruction in America: The Recent Literary Criticism of J. Hillis Miller." *College English* 41 (1979): 367–82.

Culler, Jonathan. *On Deconstruction: Theory and Criticism After Structuralism*. Ithaca: Cornell UP, 1982.

―――. *Structuralist Poetics: Structuralism, Linguistics, and the Study of Literature*. Ithaca: Cornell UP, 1975. See especially ch. 10.

Esch, Deborah. "Deconstruction." *Redrawing the Boundaries: The Transformation of English and American Literary Studies*. Ed. Stephen Greenblatt and Giles Gunn. New York: MLA, 1992. 374–91.

Gasché, Rodolphe. "Deconstruction as Criticism." *Glyph* 6 (1979): 177–215.

Jay, Gregory. *America the Scrivener: Deconstruction and the Subject of Literary History.* Ithaca: Cornell UP, 1990.

Jefferson, Ann. "Structuralism and Post Structuralism." *Modern Literary Theory: A Comparative Introduction.* Totowa: Barnes, 1982. 84–112.

Leitch, Vincent B. *American Literary Criticism from the Thirties to the Eighties.* New York: Columbia UP, 1988. See especially ch. 10, "Deconstructive Criticism."

———. *Deconstructive Criticism: An Advanced Introduction and Survey.* New York: Columbia UP, 1983.

Lentricchia, Frank. *After the New Criticism.* Chicago: U of Chicago P, 1981.

Melville, Stephen W. *Philosophy Beside Itself: On Deconstruction and Modernism.* Theory and History of Literature 27. Minneapolis: U of Minnesota P, 1986.

Norris, Christopher. *Deconstruction and the Interests of Theory.* Oklahoma Project for Discourse and Theory 4. Norman: U of Oklahoma P, 1989.

———. *Deconstruction: Theory and Practice.* London: Methuen, 1982. Rev. ed. London: Routledge, 1991.

Raval, Suresh. *Metacriticism.* Athens: U of Georgia P, 1981.

Scholes, Robert. *Structuralism in Literature: An Introduction.* New Haven: Yale UP, 1974.

Sturrock, John. *Structuralism and Since.* New York: Oxford UP, 1975.

Selected Works by Jacques Derrida and Paul de Man

de Man, Paul. *Allegories of Reading.* New Haven: Yale UP, 1979. See especially ch. 1, "Semiology and Rhetoric".

———. *Blindness and Insight.* New York: Oxford UP, 1971. Minneapolis: U of Minnesota P, 1983. The 1983 edition contains important essays not included in the original edition.

———. *The Resistance to Theory.* Minneapolis: U of Minnesota P, 1986.

Derrida, Jacques. *Acts of Literature.* Ed. Derek Attridge. New York: Routledge, 1992. Includes a helpful editor's introduction on Derrida and literature.

———. *Dissemination.* 1972. Trans. Barbara Johnson. Chicago: U of Chicago P, 1981. See especially the concise, incisive "Translator's Introduction," which provides a useful point of entry into this work and others by Derrida.

————. *Margins of Philosophy*. Trans. Alan Bass. Chicago: U of Chicago P, 1982.

————. *Of Grammatology*. Trans. Gayatri C. Spivak. Baltimore: Johns Hopkins UP, 1976. Trans. of *De la Grammatologie*. 1967.

————. *The Postcard: From Socrates to Freud and Beyond*. Trans. with intro. Alan Bass. Chicago: U of Chicago P, 1987.

————. *Writing and Difference*. 1967. Trans. Alan Bass. Chicago: U of Chicago P, 1978.

Essays in Deconstruction and Poststructuralism

Barthes, Roland. *S/Z*. Trans. Richard Miller. New York: Hill, 1974. In this influential work, Barthes turns from a structuralist to a poststructuralist approach.

Bloom, Harold, et al., eds. *Deconstruction and Criticism*. New York: Seabury, 1979. Includes essays by Bloom, de Man, Derrida, Miller, and Hartman.

Chase, Cynthia. *Decomposing Figures*. Baltimore: Johns Hopkins UP, 1986.

Harari, Josué, ed. *Textual Strategies: Perspectives in Post-Structuralist Criticism*. Ithaca: Cornell UP, 1979.

Johnson, Barbara. *The Critical Difference: Essays in the Contemporary Rhetoric of Reading*. Baltimore: Johns Hopkins UP, 1980.

————. *A World of Difference*. Baltimore: Johns Hopkins UP, 1987.

Krupnick, Mark, ed. *Displacement: Derrida and After*. Bloomington: Indiana UP, 1987.

Miller, J. Hillis. *Ariadne's Thread: Story Lines*. New Haven: Yale UP, 1992.

————. *The Ethics of Reading: Kant, de Man, Eliot, Trollope, James, and Benjamin*. New York: Columbia UP, 1987.

————. *Fiction and Repetition: Seven English Novels*. Cambridge: Harvard UP, 1982.

————. *Hawthorne and History, Defacing It*. Cambridge: Basil Blackwell, 1991. Contains a bibliography of Miller's work from 1955 to 1990.

————. "Stevens' Rock and Criticism as Cure." *Georgia Review* 30 (1976): 5–31, 330–48.

Ulmer, Gregory L. *Applied Grammatology*. Baltimore: Johns Hopkins UP, 1985.

Other Work Referred to in "What Is Deconstruction?"

Abrams, M. H. "Rationality and the Imagination in Cultural History." *Critical Inquiry* 2 (1976): 447–64.

Poststructuralist Approaches to *The Turn of the Screw*

Brooke-Rose, Christine. "The Squirm of the True: I, An Essay in Non-Methodology; II, A Structural Analysis of Henry James's *The Turn of the Screw*; III, Surface Structure in Narrative." *PTL: A Journal for Descriptive Poetics and Theory of Literature* 1 (1976): 265–94 [Part I]; 1 (1976): 513–46 [Part II]; 2 (1977): 517–62 [Part III].

Felman, Shoshana. "Turning the Screw of Interpretation." *Yale French Studies* 55/56 (1977): 94–207. Rpt. in *Writing and Madness: Literature/Philosophy/Psychoanalysis*. Ithaca: Cornell UP, 1985. 141–247.

Rimmon, Shlomith. *"The Turn of the Screw."* In *The Concept of Ambiguity — the Example of James*. Chicago: U of Chicago P, 1977. 226–66.

A DECONSTRUCTIONIST PERSPECTIVE

SHOSHANA FELMAN

"The grasp with which I recovered him": A Child Is Killed in *The Turn of the Screw*[1]

Insupportable est la mort de l'enfant: elle réalise le plus secret et le plus profond de nos voeux . . .
     Il est remarquable que, jusqu'à ce jour, on se soit plus volontiers arrêté . . . dans la constellation oedipienne, [sur les] fantasmes du meurtre du père, de prise ou de mise en pièces de la mère, laissant pour compte la tentative de meurtre d'Oedipe-enfante dont c'est l'échec qui a assuré et déterminé le destin tragique du héros.[2]

–SERGE LECLAIRE, On tue un enfant

What is the cause of Miles's death? The final paragraph suggests that he is accidentally suffocated by the governess in the strength of her passionate embrace:

The *grasp* with which I *recovered* him might have been that of catching him in his fall. I *caught* him, yes, I *held* him — it may be imagined with what a passion; but at the end of a minute I began to feel what it truly was that I *held*. We were alone with the quiet day, and his little heart, dispossessed, had stopped. (116; unless asterisked, all italics here and below are mine.)

The word "grasp," which commands this closing paragraph, thus appears to account for Miles's death. Interestingly enough, this same word,

---

[1]This essay was originally part VII of a much longer essay, "Turning the Screw of Interpretation" first published in *Yale French Studies* 55/56 (1977): 94–207, and later reprinted in Shoshana Felman, ed., *Literature and Psychoanalysis: The Question of Reading — Otherwise* (Baltimore: Johns Hopkins UP, 1982): 94–207. A slightly different version of the integral essay entitled "Henry James: Madness and the Risks of Practice" has been published, in a different context, in my *Writing and Madness: Literature/Philosophy/Psychoanalysis* (Ithaca: Cornell UP, 1985): 141–247.

[2]"The death of a child is intolerable. It realizes our most secret and profound wish. . . .
     It is remarkable that until recently we seem to have focused in the Oedipus story on fantasies about the murder of the father and the seizure and mutilation of the mother, not paying attention to the attempted murder of the baby Oedipus which assured and made inevitable the tragic destiny of the hero." My translation. *On tue un enfant* was published by Éditions du Seuil in Paris in 1975.

"grasp," also commands the opening paragraph of the last chapter. It is as though the beginning and end of the last chapter were both placed in the grasp of the word "grasp," as though that word had as its role at once to introduce and to bring to a conclusion the story's final act. Here is then the opening sentence of the last chapter:

> My *grasp* of how he received this suffered for a minute from something that I can describe only as a fierce split of my attention — a stroke that at first, as I sprang straight up, reduced me to the mere blind movement of *getting hold of him, drawing him close* and, while I just fell for support against the nearest piece of furniture, instinctively keeping him with his back to the window. (112)

In spite of the apparent symmetry of its two occurrences, however, the word "grasp" does not have the same meaning in both cases: in the opening sentence ("my grasp of how he received this") the word is used in its abstract sense of "comprehension," "understanding"; in the closing sentence ("the grasp with which I recovered him"), it is used in its concrete, physical sense of "clasp," "hold." In repeating the word "grasp" in its two different senses in these two symmetrical, strategic points of the final chapter, James's text seems to play upon the two connotations, to play them off against each other in order to reveal their fundamental interaction and their complicity. The implicit question behind this semantic play which frames the novel's ending thus becomes: What does a "grasp" involve? What is the relation and the interaction between the act of understanding ("my grasp of how he received this") and the act of clasping in one's arms, to the point of suffocating ("the grasp with which I recovered him")? Curiously enough, in a very different context, it is precisely by a similar double image highlighting the interaction between the mental and physical act of grasping that Cicero chooses to reflect upon the very nature of understanding:

> Except for the sage, no one knows anything, and that fact was demonstrated by Zeno by means of a gesture. He held up his hand, its fingers extended. That's representation, *visum*, he said. Then he curled back his fingers a bit. That's assent, *assensus*. Next, he completely closed his hand and made a fist, and declared that that was comprehension, *comprehsio*. That's why he gave it the name *catalepsis* [etymologically, "a seizing"] which had not been used before him. Finally, he brought his left hand toward his right hand and grasped his fist tightly; that, he said, was science, *scientia*, something none but the sage possess. (qtd. in Miller 22)

It is thus the governess's very "science" which seems to kill the child. Just as Cicero illustrates the act of comprehension by the image of a closed fist, James seems to literalize and at the same time ironize the same act by the suffocating gesture of a tightly closed embrace: "Might n't one, to reach his mind, risk the stretch of a stiff arm across his character? . . . The grasp with which I recovered him . . . I caught him, yes, I held him" (108, 116). The comprehension ("grasp," "reach his mind") of the meaning the Other is presumed to know, which constitutes the ultimate aim of any act of reading, is thus conceived as a violent gesture of appropriation, a gesture of domination of the Other. Reading, in other words, establishes itself as a relation not only to knowledge but equally to power; it consists not only of a search for meaning but also of a struggle to control it. Meaning itself thus unavoidably becomes the outcome of an act of violence:

> To do it in *any** way was an *act of violence*, for what did it consist of but the obtrusion of the idea of grossness and guilt on a small helpless creature who had been for me a revelation of the possibilities of beautiful intercourse? . . . I suppose I now *read into our situation a clearness* it could n't have had at the time. (111–12; *James's italics; other italics mine)

But why is violence necessary in order for meaning to appear as "clearness" and as light? What is the obstacle to clearness which the violence of the act of reading must eliminate? What does comprehension ("my grasp of how he received this") suffer from before the physical pressure of its embrace ("the grasp with which I recovered him") ensures its triumph? Let us take another look at the opening lines of the last chapter:

> My grasp of how he received this *suffered* for a minute from something that I can describe only as a *fierce split of my attention* — a stroke that at first, as I sprang straight up, reduced me to the mere blind movement of getting hold of him, drawing him close and, while I just fell for support against the nearest piece of furniture, instinctively keeping him with his back to the window. (112)

Just before this passage, the governess has asked Miles the decisive question of whether he did steal her letter. But her ability to "grasp" the effect of her own question on Miles suffers, as she herself puts it, from a "fierce *split*" of her attention: her attention is divided between Miles and the ghost at the window, between a conscious signifier and the unconscious signifier upon which the latter turns, between a conscious perception and its fantasmatic double, its contradictory extension toward the prohibited unconscious desire which it stirs up. Thus divided, her attention fails to "grasp" the child's reaction. The failure of comprehension therefore springs from the "fierce split" — from the *Spaltung* — of the subject, from the divided state in which meaning seems to hold the subject who is seeking it.[3] But it is precisely this division, this castrating "split," which must be reduced or dominated, denied or overcome, by the violence of a suffocating hold: "something that I can describe only as a fierce split of my attention — a stroke that at first . . . reduced me to the mere blind movement of getting hold of him, drawing him close. . . . yet I believe that no woman so overwhelmed ever in so short a time recovered her command of the *act**" (112–13; *James's italics). James originally wrote "recovered her *grasp* of the act." In the revised New York edition "grasp" is replaced by "command." But what *act* is it of which the governess regains her understanding ("grasp"), that is, her control ("command")?: "It came to me in the very horror of the immediate presence that the act would be, seeing and facing what I saw and faced, to keep the boy himself unaware" (113).

It should be remembered that in this final chapter the entire effort of the governess aims at *reading* the knowledge of the child, and thus at naming truth and meaning. But in this passage, paradoxically enough, the very act of *reading* the child's knowledge turns out to be an act of suppressing, or repressing, part of that knowledge: of "keeping the boy himself *unaware*." As an object of suppression and of repression, the knowledge of the child itself becomes thereby the very emblem of the unconscious; of the unconscious which is always, in a sense, the knowl-

---

[3]Like the ghost, Miles's language (which is responsible for his dismissal from school and is thus related to the missing content of the letter) equally divides the "attention" of the governess and her "grasping" mind, by manifesting a contradiction — a split within language itself — between the statement and the utterance of the child, between the speaker and his speech:

"What then did you do?" . . .
"Well — I said things." . . .
"But to whom did you say them?" . . .
"[To] those I liked."
Those he liked? I seemed to float not into clearness, but into a darker obscure, and within a minute there had come to me out of my very pity the appalling alarm of his being perhaps innocent. . . .
He turned to me again his little beautiful fevered face. "Yes, it was too bad. . . . What I suppose I sometimes said. To write home."

The governess then comments, "I can't name the exquisite pathos of the *contradiction* given to *such a speech by such a speaker*" (114–15). "What the unconscious forces us to examine," writes Lacan, "is the law according to which no utterance can ever be reduced simply to its own statement" (*Écrits* 892).

edge of a child about to die and yet immortal, indestructible; the knowledge of a child dead and yet which one has always yet to kill. "The unconscious," says Jacques Lacan, "is knowledge; but it is a knowledge one cannot know one knows, a knowledge which cannot tolerate knowing it knows"[4] — a knowledge, in other words, which cannot tolerate, and which escapes, in every sense, conscious reflection: "What was prodigious was that at last, by my success, his sense was sealed and his communication stopped: *he knew that he was in presence, but knew not of what*. . . . My eyes went back to the window only to see that the air was clear again. . . . There was nothing there. I felt that the cause was mine and that I should surely get *all* *" (113; *James's italics; other italics mine). The act of reading, the attempt to grasp and hold the signified, goes thus hand in hand with the repression or obliteration of a signifier — a repression the purpose of which is to eliminate meaning's *division*: "The act would be, *seeing* and facing what I *saw* and faced, to keep the boy himself unaware. . . . My eyes went back to the window only to *see* that the air was clear again. . . . There was nothing there" (113). To *see* (and by the same token, to *read*: "to see letters," "to see ghosts") is therefore paradoxically not only to *perceive*, but also *not* to perceive: to actively determine an area as invisible, as excluded from perception, as external by definition to visibility. To see is to draw a limit beyond which vision becomes barred. The rigid closure of the violent embrace implied by the act (by the "grasp") of understanding is linked, indeed, to the violence required to impose a limit beyond which one's eyes must close. For it is not the closing of one's eyes which determines the invisible as its empirical result; it is rather the invisible (the repressed) which predetermines the closing of one's eyes. The necessity of shutting one's eyes actively partakes, indeed, of the very act of seeing, knowing, reading:

> My equilibrium depended on the success of my rigid will, the will *to shut my eyes as tight as possible* to the truth that what I had to deal with was, revoltingly, against nature. I could only get on at all by taking "nature" into my confidence and my account. . . . No attempt, none the less, could well require more tact than just this attempt to supply, one's self, *all** the nature. How could I put even a little of that article into a *suppression of reference* to what had occurred? How on the other hand could I *make a reference* without a *new plunge into the* hideous *obscure*? (108; *James's italics; other italics mine)

[4]1974 Seminar, "Les non-dupes errent" (unpublished).

To grasp: to close one's arms, to stifle. To see: to close one's eyes, to suppress a reference, or else to make a reference and by that very act to take "a new plunge into the hideous obscure," that is, into the invisible. Paradoxically enough, however, it is precisely the imposition of a limit beyond which vision is prohibited which dispels the "split of attention" and at the same time the split of meaning, and which hence makes possible the illusion of total *mastery* over meaning as a whole, as an unimpaired totality[5]: "I seemed to myself for the instant to have *mastered it, to see it all.* . . . My eyes went back to the window only to see that the air was clear again. . . . There was nothing there. I felt that the cause was mine and that I should surely get *all**" (106, 113; *James's italics; other italics mine). The principle of totality being the very principle of a *boundary* and of the repression inherent in it, the text's irony here lies in the suggestion that the illusion of total *mastery*, of "seeing *all*," is in reality a counterpart to the act of "*shutting one's eyes* as tight as possible to the truth.*" Now, to *master*, to become a Master, is inevitably in this text also to become *like the Master*. As the reader will recall, the Master in Harley Street is indeed the incarnation of the very principle of censorship and of the imposition of a limit, as constitutive of authority as such: of the authority of consciousness itself as *mastery*. But his is a mastery which exerts its authority not as an imperative to *know*, but as an imperative *not* to know. To "master," therefore, to understand and "*see it all*," as the governess complacently puts it to herself, is in this text, ironically enough, to occupy the very place of blindness: of the blindness to which the Master voluntarily commits himself at the outset of the story, by ordering the suppression of all information,[6] by prohibiting the governess from informing him of anything at all. Through the governess's

---

[5]Totality as such is both *unique* (since it includes everything, nothing is left outside it) and *univocal* (continuous, coherent, undivided, homogeneous). Thus it is that the governess can say: "'That can have *but one meaning*' . . . to put the thing with some *coherence*" (32). "The principle of coherence," writes E. D. Hirsch, "is precisely the same as the principle of a boundary. Whatever is continuous with the visible part of an iceberg lies inside its boundaries, and whatever lies within these falls under the criterion of continuity. The two concepts are codefining" (54).

[6]This suppression of information is also the function of the masters (the headmasters) of Miles's school, since their letter suppresses all mention of the grounds of the child's dismissal: "I turned it over. 'And these things came round — ?' 'To the *masters*? Oh yes!' he answered very simply. 'But I did n't know they'd tell.' 'The *masters*? They did n't — *they've never told*. That's why I ask you'" (115). The word "master" thus comes to signify, in James's text, at once the principle of authority and the principle of repression — the very principle of the authority to repress: to repress at once mentally and physically, in a psychoanalytical but equally in a political sense (cf. Miles's dismissal from school and, ultimately, his murder).

own action, the quest for mastery will thus repeat itself as a form of blindness: "a stroke that . . . reduced me to the mere *blind* movement of getting hold of him, drawing him close . . . instinctively keeping him with his back to the window. . . . He almost smiled at me in the desolation of his surrender. . . . I was *blind* with *victory* " (112, 114–15). To master, to "see *all*," is thus not only to be blind with victory, but also, and quite literally, to be triumphant *out of* blindness.

The violence of the blind grip through which the governess seizes Miles recalls the image of the quasicompulsive clasping of a sinking boat's helm which the governess evokes so as to metaphorically justify in her own eyes her quest for mastery, her effort to control the situation: "It was in short by just clutching the helm that I avoided total wreck" (106). This metaphor of the boat recurs several times in the text. Marking here the ending of the story, it is also found at the beginning, at the conclusion of the very first chapter: "It was a big ugly . . . house . . . in which I had the fancy of our being almost as lost as a handful of passengers in a great drifting ship. Well, I was strangely at the helm!" (31).

I

The metaphor of the helm serves to bring out the underlying interdependence between meaning and power: to clutch the helm, to steer the ship, is in effect to guide it, to give it a direction and a sense, to control its direction or its sense. Indeed, throughout the story, the governess's very act of reading consists in her imposing meaning, in her imposing sense both as a *directive* and as a *direction* upon the others:

> This was why I had now given to Mrs. Grose's steps *so marked a direction* — a direction making her, when she perceived it, oppose a resistance. . . . "You're *going to the water*, Miss? — you think she's *in** — ?". . . I could only get on at all by taking "nature" into my confidence . . . by treating my monstrous ordeal as *a push in a direction unusual*. . . . "Is she *here**?" Miles panted as he caught with his sealed eyes the *direction* of my words." (95, 108, 116; *James's italics; other italics mine)

In "clutching the helm," in giving direction to the ship she steers, the governess, whose reading alone indeed commands the situation, clutches at power as sense, and at sense as power: she leads us to believe, along with those under her direction, that if her power is meaningful, it is because it is meaning itself which is in power; that it is her sense which commands, and that her command indeed *makes sense.* "It constitutes no little of a character indeed," writes James in the New York Preface [reprinted in this book] to *The Turn of the Screw*, "that she is able to make her particular *credible* statement of such strange matters. She has 'authority,' which is a good deal to have given her" (121). Putting into effect the very title of her function, the "governess" does govern: she does indeed clutch at the helm of the boat with the same kind of violence and forceful determination with which she ultimately grips the body of little Miles. The textual repetition of the metaphor of the boat thus serves to illustrate, through the singular gesture of grasping the rudder bar, the very enterprise of reading as a political project of sense-control, the taking over of the very power implied by meaning.

Curiously enough, the image of the boat recurs in yet another strategic, although apparently unrelated, context in the story: in the incident beside the lake during which the governess comes upon Flora playing (under the influence, thinks the governess, of Miss Jessel) with two pieces of wood out of which Flora is trying to construct a toy boat:

> She had picked up a small flat piece of wood which happened to have in it a *little hole* that had evidently suggested to her the *idea of sticking in another fragment* that might *figure as a mast* and *make the thing a boat.* This second morsel, as I watched her, she was very markedly and intently attempting to *tighten in its place.* . . .
>
> I got hold of Mrs. Grose as soon after this as I could. . . . I still hear myself cry as I fairly threw myself into her arms: "They *know** — it's too monstrous: they know, they know!"
>
> "And what on earth — ?". . .
>
> "Why all that *we** know — and heaven knows what more besides!" (53–54; *James's italics; other italics mine)

This incident is crucial, not only because it constitutes for the governess a decisive proof of the children's knowledge, but also because, implicitly but literally, it evokes an image related to the very title of the story: in attempting to fit the stick into the hole as a mast for her little boat, Flora "tightens it in its place" with a gesture very like that of tightening a screw.

But what precisely does this gesture mean? The screw — or the mast — is evidently, in this incident, at least to the governess's eyes, a phallic symbol, a metaphor connoting sexuality itself. This phallic connotation, the reader will recall, was pointed out and underlined by Edmund

Wilson.[7] Wilson, however, viewed the sexual reference as an *answer*, as the literal, proper meaning which it sufficed to name in order to understand and "see it all," in order to put an end to all textual questions and ambiguities. As an emblem of the sexual act, Flora's boat was for Wilson a simple indication of the literal object — the real organ — desired by the governess without her being able or willing to admit it. But it is precisely *not* as an unequivocal *answer* that the text here evokes the phallus, but on the contrary rather as a *question*, as a figure — itself ambiguous — produced by the enigma of the double meaning of the metaphorical equation: phallus = ship's mast. To say that the mast is in reality a phallus is no more illuminating or unambiguous than to say that the phallus is in reality a mast. The question arises not of what the mast "really is" but of what a phallus — *or* a mast — might be, if they can thus so easily be interchangeable — that is, signify what they are not. What is the meaning of this movement or relay of meaning between the phallus and the mast? And since the mast, which is a figure of the phallus, is also a figure of the *screw*, it seems that the crucial question raised by the text and valorized by its title might be: what is, after all, a *screw* in *The Turn of the Screw*?

Let us take another look at Flora's boat. It is as a phallic symbol that the boat disturbs the governess and convinces her of the perversity of the children: "They *know* — it's too monstrous: they know, they know!" The screw, or the phallic mast, thus constitutes for the governess a key to meaning, a master-signifier: the very key to what the Other knows.

In such a context it is no longer possible to be insensitive to the remarkable phonetic resemblance between the word "mast" and the word "master" which it cannot but bring to mind: indeed, if the mast is a kind of "master," — that is, a dominant element determining both the structure and the movement of a boat — the Master is himself a kind of "mast" which at once determines and supports the structure and the movement of the entire story of *The Turn of the Screw*. As one of the principal elements in a ship, the mast is thus related to the helm which the governess clutches with the same convulsive grasp as that with which she seizes Miles (who is himself a little Master; cf. p. 32: "At this, with one of the quick turns of simple folk, she suddenly flamed up. '*Master* Miles! — *him** an injury?'" (*James's italics).

---

[7]Edmund Wilson was one of the first scholars to offer the suggestion "that the governess who is made to tell the story is a neurotic case of sex repression, and that the ghosts are not real ghosts but hallucinations of the governess" (88).

Now, to suggest that all these metaphorical elements — *Miles* in the governess's arms, the tightly gripped *helm* in the uncanny drifting ship, the little *mast* in Flora's boat, and the *screw* in *The Turn of the Screw* — refer alternately to the phallus *and* to the Master (as well as to one another), is to set up a signifying chain in which the phallus (or the screw, or the mast, or the Master), far from incarnating the unambiguous literal meaning behind things, symbolizes rather the incessant sliding of signification, the very principle of movement and displacement which on the contrary prevents the chain (or the text) from ever stopping at a final, literal, fixed meaning. The phallus, far from being a real object, is in fact a signifier that appears to become a Master — a key to meaning and a key to the knowledge of the Other — only by virtue of its incarnating, like the Master, the very function of the semiotic *bar* — the very principle of imposition of a limit, the principle of censorship and of repression which forever *bars* all access to the signified as such.[8]

> "The question is," said Alice, "whether you *can* make words mean so many different things."
>
> "The question is," said Humpty Dumpty, "which is to be master — that's all." (Carroll 136)

In reaching out both for the master and for the mast, in aspiring to *be*, in fact, herself a master and a mast, in clasping Miles as she would clutch at the ship's helm, the governess becomes, indeed, the *Master* of the ship, the Master of the *meaning* of the story (a master-reader) in two different ways: in clutching the helm, she directs the ship and thus apparently determines and controls its sense, its meaning; but at the same time, in the very gesture of directing, steering, she also masters meaning in the sense that she represses and limits it, striking out its other senses; in manipulating the rudder bar, she also, paradoxically, *bars* the signified. While the governess thus believes herself to be in a position of command and mastery, her grasp of the ship's helm (or of "the little Master" or of the screw she tightens) is in reality the grasp but of a fetish, but of a simulacrum of a signified, like the simulacrum of the

---

[8]Cf. Jacques Lacan, *The Meaning of the Phallus (La signification du phallus)*: "In Freudian thought, the phallus is not a fantasy, if a fantasy is understood to be an imaginary effect. Nor is it as such an object (partial, internal, good, bad, etc.) if the term is used to designate the reality involved in a relationship. It is still less the organ, penis or clitoris, which it symbolizes. It is not without cause that Freud took his reference from the *simulacrum* it was for the ancients. For the phallus is a signifier. . . . It can only play its role under a veil, that is, as itself the sign of the latency which strikes the signifiable as soon as it is raised to the function of a signifier. . . . It then becomes that which . . . bars the signified." My translation is from *Écrits* (690–92).

mast in Flora's toy boat, erected only as a filler, as a stopgap, designed to fill a hole, to close a gap. The screw, however, by the very gesture of its tightening, while seemingly filling the hole, in reality only makes it deeper:

> I was blind with victory, though even then *the very effect that was to have brought him so much nearer* was already that of *added separation*. . . . The grasp with which I recovered him might have been that of catching him in his fall. I caught him, yes, I held him — it may be imagined with what a passion; but at the end of a minute I began to feel *what it truly was that I held*. We were alone with the quiet day, and his little heart, dispossessed, had stopped. (115, 116)

Even though, within this ultimate blind grip of comprehension, the "name" has been "surrendered" and meaning at last *grasped*, the governess's very satisfaction at the successful ending of the reading process is compromised by the radical frustration of a tragic loss: the embrace of meaning turns out to be but the embrace of death; the grasp of the signified turns out to be the grasp but of a corpse. The very enterprise of appropriating meaning is thus revealed to be the strict appropriation of precisely *nothing* — nothing alive, at least: "le démontage impie de la fiction et conséquemment du mécanisme littèraire," writes Mallarmé, "pour étaler la piece principale ou rien . . . le conscient manque chez nous de ce qui là-haut éclate."[9]

Literature, suggests thus Mallarmé, like the letters of *The Turn of the Screw*, contains precisely "nothing"; fiction's mainspring is but "nothing," because consciousness in us is lacking, and cannot account for, "that which bursts." But what, precisely, bursts or splits, if not consciousness itself through the very fact that, possessing *nothing* (as it does in the end of *The Turn of the Screw*), it is dispossessed of its own mastery? What is it that bursts and splits if not consciousness itself to the extent that it remains estranged from that which splits, estranged, in other words, from its own split? When Miles dies, what is once again radically and unredeemably *divided*, is at once the unity of meaning and the unity of its possessor: the governess. The attempt to *master* meaning, which ought to lead to its unification, to the elimination of its contradictions and its "splits," can reach its goal only at the cost, through the infliction of a new wound, of an added split or distance, of an irreversible "separation." The seizure of the signifier creates an unrecoverable

---

[9]"The impious dismantling of fiction and consequently of the literary mechanism as such in an effort to display the principal part or nothing, . . . the conscious lack(s) within us of what, above, bursts out and splits" (Mallarmé 647; my translation).

loss, a fundamental and irreparable castration: the tightened screw, the governed helm, bring about the "supreme surrender of the name" (116), surrender meaning only by cleaving the very power of their holder. Meaning's *possession* is itself ironically transformed into the radical *dispossession* of its possessor. At its final, climactic point, the attempt at grasping meaning and at closing the reading process with a definitive interpretation in effect discovers — and comprehends — only death.

II

The Turn of the Screw could thus be read not only as a remarkable ghost story but also as a no less remarkable detective story: the story of the discovery of a corpse and of a singularly redoubtable crime: the murder of a child. As in all detective stories, the crime is not uncovered until the end. But in contrast to the classical mystery novel plot, this crime is also not committed until the end: paradoxically enough, the process of detection here precedes the committing of the crime. As a *reader*, the governess plays the role of the detective: from the outset she tries to *detect*, by means of logical inferences and decisive "proofs," both the nature of the crime and the identity of the criminal: "It did n't last as *suspense* — it was superseded by horrible *proofs*. . . . I remember . . . my thrill of joy at having brought on a *proof*. . . . I was so determined to have all my *proof* that I flashed into ice to challenge him" (52, 98, 116). Ironically enough, however, not knowing what the crime really consists of, the governess-detective finally ends up committing it herself. This unexpected and uncanny turn given by James's story to the conventions of the mystery novel is also, as it happens, the constitutive narrative peripeteia of one of the best known detective stories of all time, *Oedipus Rex*. In James's text as well as in Sophocles', the self-proclaimed detective ends up discovering that he himself is the author of the crime he is investigating: that the crime is his, that he is, himself, the criminal he seeks. "The interest of crime," writes James, in a discussion of modern mystery dramas, "is in the fact that it compromises the criminal's personal safety. The play is a tragedy, not in virtue of an avenging deity, but in virtue of a preventive system of law; not through the presence of a company of fairies, but through that of an admirable organization of police detectives. Of course, the nearer the criminal and the detective are brought home to the reader, the more lively his " 'sensation.' "[10]

[10]From a review of M. E. Braddon's *Aurora Floyd*, conveniently reprinted in the Norton Critical Edition of *The Turn of the Screw*, p. 98.

The Turn of the Screw appears indeed to have carried this ideal of proximity or "nearness" (of the criminal and the detective to the reader) to its ultimate limits, since the criminal himself is here as close as possible to the detective, and the detective is only a detective in his (her) function as a *reader*. Incarnated in the governess, the detective and the criminal both are but dramatizations of the condition of the reader. Indeed, the governess as at once detective, criminal, and reader is here so intimately "brought home" to the reader that it is henceforth our own search for the mysterious "evil" or the hidden meaning of *The Turn of the Screw* which becomes, in effect, itself nothing other than a repetition of the crime. The reader of *The Turn of the Screw* is also the detective of a crime which in reality is his, and which "returns upon himself." For if it is by the very act of forcing her suspect to confess that the governess ends up committing the crime she is investigating, it is nothing other than the very process of detection which constitutes the crime. The detection process, or reading process, turns out to be, in other words, nothing less than a peculiarly and uncannily effective murder weapon. The story of meaning as such (or of consciousness) thus turns out to be the uncanny story of the crime of its own detection.

Just as, in the end, the detective is revealed to be the criminal, the doctor-therapist, the would-be analyst, herself turns out to be but an analysand. *The Turn of the Screw* in fact deconstructs all these traditional oppositions; the exorcist and the possessed, the doctor and the patient, the sickness and the cure, the symptom and the proposed interpretation of the symptom become here interchangeable, or at the very least, undecidable. Since the governess's "remedy" is itself a symptom, since the patient's "cure" is in effect his murder, nothing could indeed look more like madness than the very self-assurance of the project (of the notion) of therapy itself. There can be no doubt, indeed, that the ship is really drifting, that the governess is in command but of a "drunken boat." Sailing confidently toward shipwreck, the helm that the governess violently "grasps" and "clutches" is indeed the helm of a phantom ship.[11]

WORKS CITED

Carroll, Lewis. *Through the Looking-Glass and What Alice Found There* in *The Complete Illustrated Works of Lewis Carroll*. New York: Avenel, 1982.

[11]Readers who want to read the longer essay from which this piece has been taken are referred to chapter 7 in Felman's *Writing and Madness.*

Felman, Shoshana. "Turning the Screw of Interpretation" (source of the original draft of the excerpt printed here). *Yale French Studies* 55/56 (1977): 94–207 (slightly revised and rpt. as "Madness and the Risks of Practice" in Felman's *Writing and Madness: Literature/Philosophy/Psychoanalysis,* Ithaca: Cornell UP, 1985), 141–247.

Hirsch, E. D. *Validity in Interpretation.* New Haven: Yale UP, 1967.

James, Henry. Review of M. E. Braddon's *Aurora Floyd. The Nation* 1 (November 9, 1865), 593 (rpt. in the Norton edition of *The Turn of the Screw,* 1966, pp. 97–98).

Lacan, Jacques. *Écrits.* Paris: Seuil, 1966.

———. "La signification du phallus" in *Écrits.* Paris: Seuil, 1966.

Mallarmé, Stéphane. *La musique et les lettres* in *Oeuvres complètes.* Paris: Pléiade, 1945.

Miller, J. A. "Théorie de la langue (rudiment)." *Ornicar* No. 1 (January 1975).

Wilson, Edmund. "The Ambiguity of Henry James." *Hound and Horn* 7 (1934): 385–406. Quotations from *The Triple Thinkers,* rev. and enl. ed. New York: Oxford UP, 1948. 88–132.

Psychoanalytic Criticism
and
The Turn of the Screw

WHAT IS PSYCHOANALYTIC CRITICISM?

It seems natural to think about literature in terms of dreams. Like dreams, literary works are fictions, inventions of the mind that, although based on reality, are by definition not literally true. Like a literary work, a dream may have some truth to tell, but, like a literary work, it may need to be interpreted before that truth can be grasped. We can live vicariously through romantic fictions, much as we can through daydreams. Terrifying novels and nightmares affect us in much the same way, plunging us into an atmosphere that continues to cling, even after the last chapter has been read — or the alarm clock has sounded.

The notion that dreams allow such psychic explorations, of course, like the analogy between literary works and dreams, owes a great deal to the thinking of Sigmund Freud, the famous Austrian psychoanalyst who in 1900 published a seminal essay *The Interpretation of Dreams.* But is the reader who feels that Emily Brontë's *Wuthering Heights* is dream-like — who feels that Mary Shelley's *Frankenstein* is nightmarish — necessarily a Freudian literary critic? To some extent the answer has to be yes. We are all Freudians, really, whether or not we have read a single work by Freud. At one time or another, most of us have referred to ego, libido, complexes, unconscious desires, and sexual repression. The premises of Freud's thought have changed the way the Western world thinks about itself. Psychoanalytic criticism has influenced the teachers our teachers studied with, the works of scholarship and criticism they read, and the critical and creative writers *we* read as well.

What Freud did was develop a language that described, a model that explained, a theory that encompassed human psychology. Many of the elements of psychology he sought to describe and explain are present in the literary works of various ages and cultures, from Sophocles' *Oedipus Rex* to Shakespeare's *Hamlet* to works being written in our own day. When the great novel of the twenty-first century is written, many of these same elements of psychology will probably inform its discourse as well. If, by understanding human psychology according to Freud, we can appreciate literature on a new level, then we should acquaint ourselves with his insights.

Freud's theories are either directly or indirectly concerned with the nature of the unconscious mind. Freud didn't invent the notion of the unconscious; others before him had suggested that even the supposedly "sane" human mind was conscious and rational only at times, and even then at possibly only one level. But Freud went further, suggesting that the powers motivating men and women are *mainly* and *normally* unconscious.

Freud, then, powerfully developed an old idea: that the human mind is essentially dual in nature. He called the predominantly passional, irrational, unknown, and unconscious part of the psyche the *id,* or "it." The *ego,* or "I," was his term for the predominantly rational, logical, orderly, conscious part. Another aspect of the psyche, which he called the *superego,* is really a projection of the ego. The superego almost seems to be outside of the self, making moral judgments, telling us to make sacrifices for good causes even though self-sacrifice may not be quite logical or rational. And, in a sense, the superego *is* "outside," since much of what it tells us to do or think we have learned from our parents, our schools, or our religious institutions.

What the ego and superego tell us *not* to do or think is repressed, forced into the unconscious mind. One of Freud's most important contributions to the study of the psyche, the theory of repression, goes something like this: much of what lies in the unconscious mind has been put there by consciousness, which acts as a censor, driving underground unconscious or conscious thoughts or instincts that it deems unacceptable. Censored materials often involve infantile sexual desires, Freud postulated. Repressed to an unconscious state, they emerge only in disguised forms: in dreams, in language (so-called Freudian slips), in creative activity that may produce art (including literature), and in neurotic behavior.

According to Freud, all of us have repressed wishes and fears; we all have dreams in which repressed feelings and memories emerge disguised, and thus we are all potential candidates for dream analysis. One of the unconscious desires most commonly repressed is the childhood wish to displace the parent of our own sex and take his or her place in the affections of the parent of the opposite sex. This desire really involves a number of different but related wishes and fears. (A boy — and it should be remarked in passing that Freud here concerns himself mainly with the male — may fear that his father will castrate him, and he may wish that his mother would return to nursing him.) Freud referred to the whole complex of feelings by the word "oedipal," naming the complex after the Greek tragic hero Oedipus, who unwittingly killed his father and married his mother.

Why are oedipal wishes and fears repressed by the conscious side of the mind? And what happens to them after they have been censored? As Roy P. Basler puts it in *Sex, Symbolism, and Psychology in Literature* (1975), "from the beginning of recorded history such wishes have been restrained by the most powerful religious and social taboos, and as a result have come to be regarded as 'unnatural,'" even though "Freud found that such wishes are more or less characteristic of normal human development":

> In dreams, particularly, Freud found ample evidence that such wishes persisted. . . . Hence he conceived that natural urges, when identified as "wrong," may be repressed but not obliterated. . . . In the unconscious, these urges take on symbolic garb, regarded as nonsense by the waking mind that does not recognize their significance. (14)

Freud's belief in the significance of dreams, of course, was no more original than his belief that there is an unconscious side to the psyche. Again, it was the extent to which he developed a theory of how dreams work — and the extent to which that theory helped him, by analogy, to understand far more than just dreams — that made him unusual, important, and influential beyond the perimeters of medical schools and psychiatrists' offices.

The psychoanalytic approach to literature not only rests on the theories of Freud; it may even be said to have *begun* with Freud, who was interested in writers, especially those who relied heavily on symbols. Such writers regularly cloak or mystify ideas in figures that make sense only when interpreted, much as the unconscious mind of a neurotic disguises secret thoughts in dream stories or bizarre actions that need to be interpreted by an analyst. Freud's interest in literary artists led him to make some unfortunate generalizations about creativity; for example, in the twenty-third lecture in *Introductory Lectures on Psycho-Analysis* (1922), he defined the artist as "one urged on by instinctive needs that are too clamorous" (314). But it also led him to write creative literary criticism of his own, including an influential essay on "The Relation of a Poet to Daydreaming" (1908) and "The Uncanny" (1919), a provocative psychoanalytic reading of E. T. A. Hoffmann's supernatural tale "The Sandman."

Freud's application of psychoanalytic theory to literature quickly caught on. In 1909, only a year after Freud had published "The Relation of a Poet to Daydreaming," the psychoanalyst Otto Rank published *The Myth of the Birth of the Hero*. In that work, Rank subscribes to the notion that the artist turns a powerful, secret wish into a literary fantasy, and he uses Freud's notion about the "oedipal" complex to explain why the popular stories of so many heroes in literature are so similar. A year after Rank had published his psychoanalytic account of heroic texts, Ernest Jones, Freud's student and eventual biographer, turned his attention to a tragic text: Shakespeare's *Hamlet*. In an essay first published in the *American Journal of Psychology*, Jones, like Rank, makes use of the oedipal concept: he suggests that Hamlet is a victim of strong feelings toward his mother, the queen.

Between 1909 and 1949 numerous other critics decided that psychological and psychoanalytic theory could assist in the understanding of literature. I. A. Richards, Kenneth Burke, and Edmund Wilson were among the most influential to become interested in the new approach. Not all of the early critics were committed to the approach; neither were all of them Freudians. Some followed Alfred Adler, who believed that writers wrote out of inferiority complexes, and others applied the ideas of Carl Gustav Jung, who had broken with Freud over Freud's emphasis on sex and who had developed a theory of the *collective* unconscious. According to Jungian theory, a great work of literature is not a disguised expression of its author's personal, repressed wishes; rather, it is a manifestation of desires once held by the whole human race but now repressed because of the advent of civilization.

It is important to point out that among those who relied on Freud's models were a number of critics who were poets and novelists as well.

Conrad Aiken wrote a Freudian study of American literature, and poets such as Robert Graves and W. H. Auden applied Freudian insights when writing critical prose. William Faulkner, Henry James, James Joyce, D. H. Lawrence, Marcel Proust, and Toni Morrison are only a few of the novelists who have either written criticism influenced by Freud or who have written novels that conceive of character, conflict, and creative writing itself in Freudian terms. The poet H. D. (Hilda Doolittle) was actually a patient of Freud's and provided an account of her analysis in her book *Tribute to Freud*. By giving Freudian theory credibility among students of literature that only they could bestow, such writers helped to endow earlier psychoanalytic criticism with a largely Freudian orientation that has only begun to be challenged in the last two decades.

The willingness, even eagerness, of writers to use Freudian models in producing literature and criticism of their own consummated a relationship that, to Freud and other pioneering psychoanalytic theorists, had seemed fated from the beginning; after all, therapy involves the close analysis of language. René Wellek and Austin Warren included "psychological" criticism as one of the five "extrinsic" approaches to literature described in their influential book, *Theory of Literature* (1942). Psychological criticism, they suggest, typically attempts to do at least one of the following: provide a psychological study of an individual writer; explore the nature of the creative process; generalize about "types and laws present within works of literature"; or theorize about the psychological "effects of literature upon its readers" (81). Entire books on psychoanalytic criticism began to appear, such as Frederick J. Hoffman's *Freudianism and the Literary Mind* (1945).

Probably because of Freud's characterization of the creative mind as "clamorous" if not ill, psychoanalytic criticism written before 1950 tended to psychoanalyze the individual author. Poems were read as fantasies that allowed authors to indulge repressed wishes, to protect themselves from deep-seated anxieties, or both. A perfect example of author analysis would be Marie Bonaparte's 1933 study of Edgar Allan Poe. Bonaparte found Poe to be so fixated on his mother that his repressed longing emerges in his stories in images such as the white spot on a black cat's breast, said to represent mother's milk.

A later generation of psychoanalytic critics often paused to analyze the characters in novels and plays before proceeding to their authors. But not for long, since characters, both evil and good, tended to be seen by these critics as the author's potential selves or projections of various repressed aspects of his or her psyche. For instance, in *A Psychoanalytic*

Study of the Double in Literature (1970), Robert Rogers begins with the view that human beings are double or multiple in nature. Using this assumption, along with the psychoanalytic concept of "dissociation" (best known by its result, the dual or multiple personality), Rogers concludes that writers reveal instinctual or repressed selves in their books, often without realizing that they have done so.

In the view of critics attempting to arrive at more psychological insights into an author than biographical materials can provide, a work of literature is a fantasy or a dream — or at least so analogous to daydream or dream that Freudian analysis can help explain the nature of the mind that produced it. The author's purpose in writing is to gratify secretly some forbidden wish, in particular an infantile wish or desire that has been repressed into the unconscious mind. To discover what the wish is, the psychoanalytic critic employs many of the terms and procedures developed by Freud to analyze dreams.

The literal surface of a work is sometimes spoken of as its "manifest content" and treated as a "manifest dream" or "dream story" would be treated by a Freudian analyst. Just as the analyst tries to figure out the "dream thought" behind the dream story — that is, the latent or hidden content of the manifest dream — so the psychoanalytic literary critic tries to expose the latent, underlying content of a work. Freud used the words *condensation* and *displacement* to explain two of the mental processes whereby the mind disguises its wishes and fears in dream stories. In condensation several thoughts or persons may be condensed into a single manifestation or image in a dream story; in displacement, an anxiety, a wish, or a person may be displaced onto the image of another, with which or whom it is loosely connected through a string of associations that only an analyst can untangle. Psychoanalytic critics treat metaphors as if they were dream condensations; they treat metonyms — figures of speech based on extremely loose, arbitrary associations — as if they were dream displacements. Thus figurative literary language in general is treated as something that evolves as the writer's conscious mind resists what the unconscious tells it to picture or describe. A symbol is, in Daniel Weiss's words, "a meaningful concealment of truth as the truth promises to emerge as some frightening or forbidden idea" (20).

In a 1970 article entitled "The 'Unconscious' of Literature," Norman Holland, a literary critic trained in psychoanalysis, succinctly sums up the attitudes held by critics who would psychoanalyze authors, but without quite saying that it is the *author* that is being analyzed by the psychoanalytic critic. "When one looks at a poem psychoanalytically," he writes, "one considers it as though it were a dream or as though some ideal patient [were speaking] from the couch in iambic pentameter." One "looks for the general level or levels of fantasy associated with the language. By level I mean the familiar stages of childhood development — oral [when desires for nourishment and infantile sexual desires overlap], anal [when infants receive their primary pleasure from defecation], urethral [when urinary functions are the locus of sexual pleasure], phallic [when the penis or, in girls, some penis substitute is of primary interest], oedipal." Holland continues by analyzing not Robert Frost but Frost's poem "Mending Wall" as a specifically oral fantasy that is not unique to its author. "Mending Wall" is "about breaking down the wall which marks the separated or individuated self so as to return to a state of closeness to some Other" — including and perhaps essentially the nursing mother ("Unconscious" 136, 139).

While not denying the idea that the unconscious plays a role in creativity, psychoanalytic critics such as Holland began to focus more on the ways in which authors create works that appeal to *our* repressed wishes and fantasies. Consequently, they shifted their focus away from the psyche of the author and toward the psychology of the reader and the text. Holland's theories, which have concerned themselves more with the reader than with the text, have helped to establish another school of critical theory: reader-response criticism. Elizabeth Wright explains Holland's brand of modern psychoanalytic criticism in this way: "What draws us as readers to a text is the secret expression of what we desire to hear, much as we protest we do not. The disguise must be good enough to fool the censor into thinking that the text is respectable, but bad enough to allow the unconscious to glimpse the unrespectable" (117).

Holland is one of dozens of critics who have revised Freud significantly in the process of revitalizing psychoanalytic criticism. Another such critic is R. D. Laing, whose controversial and often poetical writings about personality, repression, masks, and the double or "schizoid" self have (re)blurred the boundary between creative writing and psychoanalytic discourse. Yet another is D. W. Winnicott, an "object relations" theorist who has had a significant impact on literary criticism. Critics influenced by Winnicott and his school have questioned the tendency to see reader/text as an either/or construct; instead, they have seen reader and text (or audience and play) in terms of a *relationship* taking place in what Winnicott calls a "transitional" or "potential space" — space in which binary terms like real and illusory, objective and subjective, have little or no meaning.

Psychoanalytic theorists influenced by Winnicott see the transitional or potential reader/text (or audience/play) space as being *like* the space entered into by psychoanalyst and patient. More important, they also see it as being similar to the space between mother and infant: a space characterized by trust in which categorizing terms such as *knowing* and *feeling* mix and merge and have little meaning apart from one another.

Whereas Freud saw the mother-son relationship in terms of the son and his repressed oedipal complex (and saw the analyst-patient relationship in terms of the patient and the repressed "truth" that the analyst could scientifically extract), object-relations analysts see both relationships as *dyadic* — that is, as being dynamic in both directions. Consequently, they don't depersonalize analysis or their analyses. It is hardly surprising, therefore, that contemporary literary critics who apply object-relations theory to the texts they discuss don't depersonalize critics or categorize their interpretations as "truthful," at least, not in any objective or scientific sense. In the view of such critics, interpretations are made of language — itself a transitional object — and are themselves the mediating terms or transitional objects of a relationship.

Like critics of the Winnicottian School, the French structuralist theorist Jacques Lacan focuses on language and language-related issues. He treats the unconscious *as* a language and, consequently, views the dream not as Freud did (that is, as a form and symptom of repression) but rather as a form of discourse. Thus we may study dreams psychoanalytically in order to learn about literature, even as we may study literature in order to learn more about the unconscious. In Lacan's seminar on Poe's "The Purloined Letter," a pattern of repetition like that used by psychoanalysts in their analyses is used to arrive at a reading of the story. According to Wright, "the new psychoanalytic structural approach to literature" employs "analogies from psychoanalysis . . . to explain the workings of the text as distinct from the workings of a particular author's, character's, or even reader's mind" (125).

Lacan, however, did far more than extend Freud's theory of dreams, literature, and the interpretation of both. More significantly, he took Freud's whole theory of psyche and gender and added to it a crucial third term — that of language. In the process, he both used and significantly developed Freud's ideas about the oedipal stage and complex.

Lacan points out that the pre-oedipal stage, in which the child at first does not even recognize its independence from its mother, is also a pre*verbal* stage, one in which the child communicates without the medium of language, or — if we insist on calling the child's communications a language — in a language that can only be called *literal*. ("Coos," certainly, cannot be said to be figurative or symbolic.) Then, while still in the pre-oedipal stage, the child enters the *mirror* stage.

During the mirror period, the child comes to view itself and its mother, later other people as well, *as* independent selves. This is the stage in which the child is first able to fear the aggressions of another, to desire what is recognizably beyond the self (initially the mother), and, finally, to want to compete with another for the same, desired object. This is also the stage at which the child first becomes able to feel sympathy with another being who is being hurt by a third, to cry when another cries. All of these developments, of course, involve projecting beyond the self and, by extension, constructing one's own self (or "ego" or "I") as others view one — that is, as *another*. Such constructions, according to Lacan, are just that: constructs, products, artifacts — fictions of coherence that in fact hide what Lacan calls the "absence" or "lack" of being.

The mirror stage, which Lacan also refers to as the *imaginary* stage, is fairly quickly succeeded by the oedipal stage. As in Freud, this stage begins when the child, having come to view itself as self and the father and mother as separate selves, perceives gender and gender differences between its parents and between itself and one of its parents. For boys, gender awareness involves another, more powerful recognition, for the recognition of the father's phallus as the mark of his difference from the mother involves, at the same time, the recognition that his older and more powerful father is also his rival. That, in turn, leads to the understanding that what once seemed wholly his and even indistinguishable from himself is in fact someone else's: something properly desired only at a distance and in the form of socially acceptable *substitutes*.

The fact that the oedipal stage roughly coincides with the entry of the child into language is extremely important for Lacan. For the linguistic order is essentially a figurative or "Symbolic order"; words are not the things they stand for but are, rather, stand-ins or substitutes for those things. Hence boys, who in the most critical period of their development have had to submit to what Lacan calls the "Law of the Father" — a law that prohibits direct desire for and communicative intimacy with what has been the boy's whole world — enter more easily into the realm of language and the Symbolic order than do girls, who have never really had to renounce that which once seemed continuous with the self: the mother. The gap that has been opened up for boys, which includes the gap between signs and what they substitute — the gap marked by the phallus and encoded with the boy's sense of his maleness — has not opened up for girls, or has not opened up in the same way, to the same degree.

For Lacan, the father need not be present to trigger the oedipal stage; nor does his phallus have to be seen to catalyze the boy's (easier) transition into the Symbolic order. Rather, Lacan argues, a child's recognition of its gender is intricately tied up with a growing recognition of the system of names and naming, part of the larger system of substitutions we call language. A child has little doubt about who its mother is, but who is its father, and how would one know? The father's claim rests on the mother's *word* that he is in fact the father; the father's relationship to the child is thus established through language and a system of marriage and kinship — names — that in turn is basic to rules of everything from property to law. The name of the father (*nom du père*, which in French sounds like *non du père*) involves, in a sense, nothing of the father — nothing, that is, except his word or name.

Lacan's development of Freud has had several important results. First, his sexist-seeming association of maleness with the Symbolic order, together with his claim that women cannot therefore enter easily into the order, has prompted feminists not to reject his theory out of hand but, rather, to look more closely at the relation between language and gender, language and women's inequality. Some feminists have gone so far as to suggest that the social and political relationships between male and female will not be fundamentally altered until language itself has been radically changed. (That change might begin dialectically, with the development of some kind of "feminine language" grounded in the presymbolic, literal-to-imaginary, communication between mother and child.)

Second, Lacan's theory has proved of interest to deconstructors and other poststructuralists, in part because it holds that the ego (which in Freud's view is as necessary as it is natural) is a product or construct. The ego-artifact, produced during the mirror stage, *seems* at once unified, consistent, and organized around a determinate center. But the unified self, or ego, is a fiction, according to Lacan. The yoking together of fragments and destructively dissimilar elements takes its psychic toll, and it is the job of the Lacanian psychoanalyst to "deconstruct," as it were, the ego, to show its continuities to be contradictions as well.

The author of the psychoanalytic essay that follows, Stanley Renner, is one of the latest in a long line of critics who have assumed that the "true" and "richer" reading of *The Turn of the Screw* is one that views the text not as a ghost story but, rather, as a "dramatization of a woman's psychosexual problem and the damage it does to the children in her charge" (223). One thing that makes Renner's approach new and different is the fact that it seeks to answer a question previous psychoanalytic critics have by and large avoided: If we are to take the "ghosts" of the story as the projections of a mentally skewed governess, then why does James see to it that the governess's description of the male ghost is identified by an astonished Mrs. Grose as Peter Quint, a deceased former valet?

Having posed the question, Renner sets it aside for awhile, taking a close look at the character of the governess and showing that her "background, inexperience, vulnerability, anxiety and fear, and susceptibility to romantic emotions" all make her a candidate for what James's contemporaries would have called "sexual hysteria" in general and, more specifically, a "hysterical fit." The governess, in Renner's view, experiences just such a fit when the erotically charged, attractive male figure she at first thinks she sees suddenly becomes a very different sort of figure, a frightening male with a pale, long face, small but penetrating eyes, thin lips, and curly red hair. This transformation of an erotically attractive image of man into a decidedly repulsive one is, according to Renner, driven by a "fear of male sexuality" that would have gone hand in hand with the erotic longings of a nineteenth-century parson's daughter.

James, Renner shows, would have been familiar with the term "sexual hysteria"; indeed, it seems likely that he knew Breuer and Freud's *Studien über Hysterie*. Furthermore, as Oscar Cargill has shown, James's own sister, Alice, had been said to be a sexual hysteric. But James was drawing and commenting upon more than his sister, more than Freudian theory, and more than sexual hysteria in *The Turn of the Screw*. He was also, as Renner demonstrates, exploring "the physiognomics of fictional characterization" — that is, the *stereotypical* nature of the way in which Victorian minds would have hallucinated about the sexual male, and the stereotypical way in which Victorian writers (whose works at once influenced and reflected the influences of contemporary thinking) represented "evil, which in Victorian times tended to mean sexual evil." (The pale, red-haired, sharp-eyed physiognomy of Quint as envisioned by the governess, Renner argues, resembles any number of "bad men" in late eighteenth- and nineteenth-century Victorian and continental novels.)

Renner's approach to *The Turn of the Screw* is typical of Freudian psychoanalytic criticism insofar as it grounds literary images and even plots in psychic fantasies and their inhibition or repression — in this case the governess's sexual longings and simultaneous attempts to bury those longings at great psychic cost to herself and her charges. But Renner, unlike Freud and early psychoanalytic critics influenced by Freud, does not attempt to psychoanalyze the author by reading the text as if it were James's unintentionally revealing dream. Rather, he views James as a highly deliberative framer of words who understood human nature along lines suggested by Freud and who, therefore, fashioned the characters in his fiction accordingly.

If that were all Renner did, his psychoanalytic approach would be of interest, although less than contemporary. But Renner goes further by adding a *cultural* dimension to our understanding of psychology and of the psychological dimensions of texts. The hallucination that a person experiences when undergoing an attack of something like hysteria, Renner argues, is not just some private imagining; rather, it is historically determined — that is, a representation of a cultural stereotype. (If such a hallucination takes place in an influential work of fiction, it is a reinforcement, as well as a representation, of a cultural stereotype.) To put this another way: cultures, as well as individuals, have fantasies and fears — fantasies and fears that they "write" through novelists such as Dickens and Thackeray and, of course, Henry James.

Ross C Murfin

PSYCHOANALYTIC CRITICISM: A SELECTED BIBLIOGRAPHY

Some Short Introductions to Psychological and Psychoanalytic Criticism

Holland, Norman. "The 'Unconscious' of Literature." *Contemporary Criticism*. Ed. Norman Bradbury and David Palmer. Stratford-upon-Avon Series 12. New York: St. Martin's, 1970. 131–54.

Natoli, Joseph, and Frederik L. Rusch, comps. *Psychocriticism: An Annotated Bibliography*. Westport: Greenwood, 1984.

Scott, Wilbur. *Five Approaches to Literary Criticism*. London: Collier-Macmillan, 1962. See the essays by Burke and Gorer as well as Scott's introduction to the section "The Psychological Approach: Literature in the Light of Psychological Theory."

Wellek, René, and Austin Warren. *Theory of Literature*. New York:

Harcourt, 1942. See the chapter "Literature and Psychology" in pt. 3, "The Extrinsic Approach to the Study of Literature."

Wright, Elizabeth. "Modern Psychoanalytic Criticism." *Modern Literary Theory: A Comparative Introduction*. Ed. Ann Jefferson and David Robey. Totowa: Barnes, 1982. 113–33.

Freud, Lacan, and Their Influence

Basler, Roy P. *Sex, Symbolism, and Psychology in Literature*. New York: Octagon, 1975. See especially 13–19.

Clément, Catherine. *The Lives and Legends of Jacques Lacan*. Trans. Arthur Goldhammer. New York: Columbia UP, 1983.

Freud, Sigmund. *Introductory Lectures on Psycho-Analysis*. Trans. Joan Riviere. London: Allen, 1922.

Gallop, Jane. *Reading Lacan*. Ithaca: Cornell UP, 1985.

Hoffman, Frederick J. *Freudianism and the Literary Mind*. Baton Rouge: Louisiana State UP, 1945.

Hogan, Patrick Colm, and Lalita Pandit, eds. *Lacan and Criticism: Essays and Dialogue on Language, Structure, and the Unconscious*. Athens: U of Georgia P, 1990.

Kazin, Alfred. "Freud and His Consequences." *Contemporaries*. Boston: Little, 1962. 351–93.

Lacan, Jacques. *Écrits: A Selection*. Trans. Alan Sheridan. New York: Norton, 1977.

———. *Feminine Sexuality: Lacan and the école freudienne*. Ed. Juliet Mitchell and Jacqueline Rose. Trans. Rose. New York: Norton, 1982.

———. *The Four Fundamental Concepts of Psychoanalysis*. Trans. Alan Sheridan. London: Penguin, 1980.

Macey, David. *Lacan in Contexts*. New York: Verso, 1988.

Meisel, Perry, ed. *Freud: A Collection of Critical Essays*. Englewood Cliffs: Prentice, 1981.

Muller, John P., and William J. Richardson. *Lacan and Language: A Reader's Guide to "Écrits."* New York: International UP, 1982.

Porter, Laurence M. *"The Interpretation of Dreams": Freud's Theories Revisited*. Twayne's Masterwork Studies Series. Boston: G. K. Hall, 1986.

Reppen, Joseph, and Maurice Charney. *The Psychoanalytic Study of Literature*. Hillsdale: Analytic, 1985.

Schneiderman, Stuart. *Jacques Lacan: The Death of an Intellectual Hero*. Cambridge: Harvard UP, 1983.

————. *Returning to Freud: Clinical Psychoanalysis in the School of Lacan*. New Haven: Yale UP, 1980.

Selden, Raman. *A Reader's Guide to Contemporary Literary Theory*. 2nd ed. Lexington: U of Kentucky P, 1989. See "Jacques Lacan: Language and the Unconscious."

Sullivan, Ellie Ragland. *Jacques Lacan and the Philosophy of Psychoanalysis*. Champaign: U of Illinois P, 1986.

Sullivan, Ellie Ragland, and Mark Bracher, eds. *Lacan and the Subject of Language*. New York: Routledge, 1991.

Trilling, Lionel. "Art and Neurosis." *The Liberal Imagination*. New York: Scribner's, 1950. 160–80.

Wilden, Anthony. "Lacan and the Discourse of the Other." In Lacan, *Speech and Language in Psychoanalysis*. Trans. Wilden. Baltimore: Johns Hopkins UP, 1981. (Published as *The Language of the Self* in 1968.) 159–311.

Psychoanalysis, Feminism, and Literature

Chodorow, Nancy. *The Reproduction of Mothering: Psychoanalysis and the Sociology of Gender*. Berkeley: U of California P, 1978.

Gallop, Jane. *The Daughter's Seduction: Feminism and Psychoanalysis*. Ithaca: Cornell UP, 1982.

Garner, Shirley Nelson, Claire Kahane, and Madelon Sprengnether. *The (M)other Tongue: Essays in Feminist Psychoanalytic Interpretation*. Ithaca: Cornell UP, 1985.

Irigaray, Luce. *This Sex Which Is Not One*. Trans. Catherine Porter. Ithaca: Cornell UP, 1985.

————. *The Speculum of the Other Woman*. Trans. Gillian C. Gill. Ithaca: Cornell UP, 1985.

Jacobus, Mary. "Is There a Woman in This Text?" *New Literary History* 14 (1982): 117–41.

Kristeva, Julia. *The Kristeva Reader*. Ed. Toril Moi. New York: Columbia UP, 1986. See especially the selection from *Revolution in Poetic Language*, 89–136.

Mitchell, Juliet. *Psychoanalysis and Feminism*. New York: Random House, 1974.

Mitchell, Juliet, and Jacqueline Rose, "Introduction I" and "Introduction II." Lacan, *Feminine Sexuality: Jacques Lacan and the école freudienne*. New York: Norton, 1985. 1–26, 27–57.

Sprengnether, Madelon. *The Spectral Mother: Freud, Feminism, and Psychoanalysis*. Ithaca: Cornell UP, 1990.

Psychological and Psychoanalytic Studies of Literature

Bettelheim, Bruno. *The Uses of Enchantment: The Meaning and Importance of Fairy Tales.* New York: Knopf, 1976. Although this book is about fairy tales instead of literary works written for publication, it offers model Freudian readings of well-known stories.

Crews, Frederick C. *Out of My System: Psychoanalysis, Ideology, and Critical Method.* New York: Oxford UP, 1975.

———. *Relations of Literary Study.* New York: MLA, 1967. See the chapter "Literature and Psychology."

Diehl, Joanne Feit. "Re-Reading *The Letter:* Hawthorne, the Fetish, and the (Family) Romance." *Nathaniel Hawthorne, The Scarlet Letter.* Ed. Ross C Murfin. Case Studies in Contemporary Criticism Series. Ed. Ross C Murfin. Boston: Bedford–St. Martin's, 1991. 235–51.

Hallman, Ralph. *Psychology of Literature: A Study of Alienation and Tragedy.* New York: Philosophical Library, 1961.

Hartman, Geoffrey, ed. *Psychoanalysis and the Question of the Text.* Baltimore: Johns Hopkins UP, 1978. See especially the essays by Hartman, Johnson, Nelson, and Schwartz.

Hertz, Neil. *The End of the Line: Essays on Psychoanalysis and the Sublime.* New York: Columbia UP, 1985.

Holland, Norman N. *Dynamics of Literary Response.* New York: Oxford UP, 1968.

———. *Poems in Persons: An Introduction to the Psychoanalysis of Literature.* New York: Norton, 1973.

Kris, Ernest. *Psychoanalytic Explorations in Art.* New York: International, 1952.

Lucas, F. L. *Literature and Psychology.* London: Cassell, 1951.

Natoli, Joseph, ed. *Psychological Perspectives on Literature: Freudian Dissidents and Non-Freudians: A Casebook.* Hamden: Archon Books–Shoe String, 1984.

Phillips, William, ed. *Art and Psychoanalysis.* New York: Columbia UP, 1977.

Rogers, Robert. *A Psychoanalytic Study of the Double in Literature.* Detroit: Wayne State UP, 1970.

Skura, Meredith. *The Literary Use of the Psychoanalytic Process.* New Haven: Yale UP, 1981.

Strelka, Joseph P. *Literary Criticism and Psychology.* University Park: Pennsylvania State UP, 1976. See especially the essays by Lerner and Peckham.

Weiss, Daniel. *The Critic Agonistes: Psychology, Myth, and the Art of Fiction*. Ed. Eric Solomon and Stephen Arkin. Seattle: U of Washington P, 1985.

Lacanian Psychoanalytic Studies of Literature

Collings, David. "The Monster and the Imaginary Mother: A Lacanian Reading of *Frankenstein*." *Mary Shelley, Frankenstein*. Ed. Johanna M. Smith. Case Studies in Contemporary Criticism Series. Ed. Ross C Murfin. Boston: Bedford–St. Martin's, 1992. 245–58.

Davis, Robert Con, ed. *The Fictional Father: Lacanian Readings of the Text*. Amherst: U of Massachusetts P, 1981.

———. "Lacan and Narration." *Modern Language Notes* 5 (1983): 843–1063.

Felman, Shoshana, ed. *Literature and Psychoanalysis: The Question of Reading: Otherwise*. Baltimore: Johns Hopkins UP, 1982.

———, ed. *Jacques Lacan and the Adventure of Insight: Psychoanalysis in Contemporary Culture*. Cambridge: Harvard UP, 1987.

Froula, Christine. "When Eve Reads Milton: Undoing the Canonical Economy." *Canons*. Ed. Robert von Hallberg. Chicago: U of Chicago P, 1984. 149–75.

Homans, Margaret. *Bearing the Word: Language and Female Experience in Nineteenth-Century Women's Writing*. Chicago: U of Chicago P, 1986.

Muller, John P., and William J. Richardson, eds. *The Purloined Poe: Lacan, Derrida, and Psychoanalytic Reading*. Baltimore: Johns Hopkins UP, 1988. Includes Lacan's seminar on Poe's "The Purloined Letter."

Psychoanalytic Approaches to James and *The Turn of the Screw*

Cranfill, Thomas Mabry, and Robert Lanier Clark, Jr. *An Anatomy of "The Turn of the Screw."* Austin: U of Texas P, 1965.

Edel, Leon. "The Little Boys." In *Henry James: The Treacherous Years, 1895–1901*. London: Hart-Davis, 1969. 191–203.

Goddard, Harold C. "A Pre-Freudian Reading of *The Turn of the Screw*." *Nineteenth-Century Fiction* 12 (1957): 1–36.

Halttunen, Karen. " 'Through the Cracked and Fragmented Self': William James and *The Turn of the Screw*." *American Quarterly* 40 (1988): 472–90.

Katan, M., M.D. "A Causerie on Henry James's *The Turn of the Screw*." *The Psychoanalytic Study of the Child* 17 (1962): 473–93.

Lydenberg, John. "The Governess Turns the Screws." *Nineteenth-Century Fiction* 12 (1957): 37–58.

Spilka, Mark. "Turning the Freudian Screw: How Not to Do It." *Literature and Psychology* 13 (1963): 105–11.

Wilson, Edmund. "The Ambiguity of Henry James." *Hound and Horn* 7 (1934): 385–406. Rpt. in *The Triple Thinkers,* rev. and enl. ed. New York: Oxford UP, 1948. 88–132.

A PSYCHOANALYTIC PERSPECTIVE

STANLEY RENNER

"Red hair, very red, close-curling": Sexual Hysteria, Physiognomical Bogeymen, and the "Ghosts" in *The Turn of the Screw*

For readers and critics for whom the true — and clearly the richer — story of James's *The Turn of the Screw* is its dramatization of a woman's psychosexual problem and the damage it does to the children in her charge, the immovable stumbling block has always been the governess's detailed description of Peter Quint, a man dead and buried whom she has never seen. If James does not mean for readers to take Quint (and subsequently Miss Jessel) as a bona fide ghost, so the argument runs, why does he arrange things so that the only way to account for her description of him is that she has seen a supernatural manifestation? As Peter Beidler has shown in his "critical history" of the story earlier in this volume, efforts thus far to circumvent this obstacle have not settled the issue. In this essay I want to show that the story provides its own eminently logical, quite unsupernatural, indeed, deeply naturalistic, accounting for the manifestations the governess describes. The logic of this line of development has escaped observation, I believe, because it derives from idea structures that have since faded from general awareness: the symptomatology of female sexual hysteria and the supposed behavioral significance of human physiognomy. What the governess sees on her first encounter with the famous "ghosts" of Bly, the experience that sets in motion the story's central line of development, is thus not the ghost of a dead man she has never seen but the projection of her own sexual hysteria in the form of stereotypes deeply embedded in the mind of the culture. The story's spectral figures, colored by the governess's sexual fear and disgust, symbolize the adult sexuality just beginning to "possess" Miles and Flora as they hover on the brink of puberty. Frantically trying to block the emergence of their sexuality, the governess does damage to their natural development that, in the case of the male child, proves fatal.

The first appearance of an apparition in the story and the governess's state of mind on that occasion are, of course, crucial to understanding the ghosts and their place in James's design. As the story itself asserts, "the fact to be in possession of" is that the governess is a parson's daughter leaving the shelter of home for the first time, coming up to London in "trepidation," and encountering a young gentleman presented in the story as a girl's romantic dream, from whom she accepts employment (25). As the Jamesian narrator of the prologue deduces, and Douglas, who knew the governess and tells her story, does not deny, she "succumbed" to the "seduction exercised by the splendid young man" (27). Thus James pointedly calls attention to a group of characterizing details about the governess — her sheltered religious background, inexperience, vulnerability, anxiety and fear, and susceptibility to romantic emotions — that establish her as a virtual Victorian cliché of sexual ambivalence. With her almost classic conflict between idealistic innocence and naive romantic impulses she is the virginal ingénue encountering sexual danger in the form of a "handsome," "bold" young gentleman bachelor with "charming ways with women," enjoying a life of pleasurable self-indulgence (25). This emphasis on the governess's susceptibility to romantic emotions is an important feature of the buildup to the first apparition.

With this preparation the reader comes to the governess's first encounter with the apparitions that harrow her throughout the story: she sees a frightening male ghost that she later describes so particularly that Mrs. Grose, in astonishment and consternation, identifies it as Peter Quint, deceased former valet of the children's uncle and guardian, who, with the last governess, also deceased, had previously shared the charge of the children. When, however, the episode is read closely in the light of the turn-of-the-century understanding of sexual hysteria, it unfolds as a remarkably astute dramatization of an actual hysterical attack.

Although she suppresses the erotic component of her impulses, it is clear that the governess is indulging in romantic fantasies of her dashing young gentleman employer as she enjoys an evening stroll, the children "tucked away" in bed: how "charming" it would be, she fancies, if "some one would appear there at the turn of a path and would stand before me and smile and approve" (37). And then she does see him. Whatever the psychic validity of the phenomenon James presents in this scene, it is clear that the governess is able to conjure up in her fantasy such a powerful impression that she feels she is actually seeing someone not present. And what she sees, at least at first, is her gentleman employer's "handsome face" reflecting the "kind light" of approval with which she has hoped he will notice her. With "the sense that [her] imagination had . . . turned real," she declares unequivocally, "he did stand there!" (37).

But then as she views this figure from her own imagination she experiences an indescribable "bewilderment of vision": the figure now before her, she explains, "was not the person I had precipitately supposed" (38). Readers have customarily accepted the governess's own explanation for what happens to her vision: that her first impression was mistaken and that the figure that ultimately stands before her has been there all along. But the fact is that she was not mistaken; her identification of the handsome gentleman is too positive, too emphatic to have been a mistake. What has actually happened is that the attractive male figure she first imagines is transformed in her own mind into the frightening male figure she subsequently projects. That the transformation is brought about by fear — specifically fear of male sexuality — is the clear implication of the terms in which the governess explains the "shock" to her sensibility caused by the figure that ultimately met her eyes: "an unknown man in a lonely place is a permitted object of fear to a young woman privately bred" (37, 38).

James's technical knowledge of sexual hysteria has been well established, both his almost certain familiarity with Breuer and Freud's *Studien über Hysterie* and his "personal acquaintance" with an actual case of hysteria in "the illness of his sister [Alice] and with the delusions and fantasies of that illness" (Cargill 247). Thus it should not be surprising that in *The Turn of the Screw* he could portray an accurate, virtually textbook case of sexual hysteria. The most convenient source for the understanding of sexual hysteria at the time of *The Turn of the Screw* is Havelock Ellis, who provides, in "Auto-Erotism," an exhaustive survey of contemporary opinion on the subject. James could not have known Ellis's discussion, which was not published until 1901, but he would have gotten his information from the same sources. I make no claims, by the way, for the validity of turn-of-the-century assumptions about sexual hysteria, which are presently being challenged. My point is only how faithfully James reproduces these assumptions in his characterization of the governess.

Briefly summarized, sexual hysteria, as it was understood in the milieu of *The Turn of the Screw*, is a psychosexual disorder mainly afflicting women, particularly women with "fine qualities of mind and character." It is caused by a profound conflict between their natural sexual impulses and the repression of sexuality required by society and exaggerated by Victorian idealism — a conflict in the hysterical, Havelock Ellis explains, "between their ideas of right and the bent of their inclinations" (220). The classic symptom of hysteria is thus "'a paradoxical sexual instinct' . . . by which, for instance, sexual frigidity is combined with intense sexual preoccupations"(213). The resulting conflict can be of such intensity as to precipitate some kind of "nervous explosion" (231). "Pitres and others," Ellis notes, "refer to the frequently painful nature of sexual hallucinations in the hysterical" (217). In some cases "nausea and vomiting" or an "actual hysterical fit" may occur (223, 225).

Today the term "sexual hysteria" is familiar, but less so is its substance, the actual syndrome designated by the name. Thus, even though the term has been applied to the governess (Huntley 229), no one has shown how exactly she fits the profile of a typical sexual hysteric. It would be hard to imagine a more classic manifestation of its symptomatology than James's governess. Her "superiority of character" (Ellis 220) revealed in her sense of responsibility for the children is unquestionable. She exhibits, in classic form, the conflict between sexual impulse and inhibition found by clinicians of the time at the root of the disorder, suffering from "sexual needs . . . and in large measure, indeed, . . . precisely through the struggle with them, through the effort to thrust sexuality aside" (Ellis 224). A "fluttered anxious girl out of a Hampshire vicarage," the governess is clearly in a state of extreme tension of the kind most likely to trigger an attack of hysteria. And she fits the profile of the typical female hysteric in several ways: she is a "single woman . . . whose sexual needs are unsatisfied"; she appears to be "attractive to men"; she leads the kind of "small, smothered life" conducive to hysteria; and she is extremely suggestible (218, 229). Indeed, in typifying the hysterical situation Ellis mentions the case of a governess much like that of James's protagonist: "in one case," he writes, "a governess, whose training has been severely upright, is, in spite of herself and without any encouragement, led to experience for the father of the children under her care an affection which she refuses to acknowledge even to herself" (221).[1] James's governess, according to all the evidence in *The Turn of the Screw*, is the product of a training "severely upright," and she feels, "without any encouragement," an attraction to the paternal figure (if not the father) of the household in which she is employed, which she regards as only the desire to please an employer and merit his approval.

Not only does James's governess fit the classic profile of the female sexual hysteric, she also experiences the "hysterical fit" observed by turn-of-the-century clinicians. That her first hallucination precipitates a "nervous explosion" of some intensity is clear from her own account. Like that of the classic hysteric, her "mental activity . . . is split up, and only a part of it is conscious" (Ellis 220). Her initial fantasy of her handsome employer is conscious, but his transformation into a figure embodying her fear of sexuality is generated by deep-rooted unconscious inhibitions. The effect — "the shock I had suffered," as she describes it — is a manifestation of the kind of "shock to the sexual emotions" that, according to Freud, could "scarcely fail sometimes to produce such a result" (231). "Something is introduced into psychic life which refuses to merge in the general flow of consciousness" (222), and that something is the governess's unacknowledged sexual attraction to the charming gentleman: it does not fit with her idealized romantic and spiritualized notions about love. The resulting "collision," as she herself terms the experience, between her conscious ideals and her unconscious impulses triggers in her emotions a profound disturbance. "Driven" by her "agitation," as she confesses, and only half conscious, she "must, in circling about the place, have walked three miles" (39–40). As the hysterical shock involves shame and disgust and often "cannot even be talked about" (Ellis 222), so the governess, upon encountering Mrs. Grose, "somehow measured the importance of what I had seen by my thus finding myself hesitate to mention it" (40).

If the figure the governess "sees" is an example of the "frequently painful nature of sexual hallucinations in the hysterical" (Ellis 217), a manifestation of her deep fear of sexuality engendered when her unacknowledged sexual impulses intrude themselves into her idealized romantic fantasy of her employer — when, to put it another way, the relationship she fantasizes begins to take its natural course toward a sexual consummation — the logical question to be addressed is "What form would such a hallucination take?" Obviously, it would be a male figure,

---

[1] Ellis is most likely alluding to "The Case of Miss Lucy R.," included in *Studien über Hysterie,* the case that Oscar Cargill convincingly links to *The Turn of the Screw* (156).

and it would be sexually threatening. The figure the governess sees is male, and the "fear" she feels is like that stirred in "a young woman privately bred" by "an unknown man in a lonely place." Assuming, then, this generalized embodiment of a threatening sexual male figure, if the governess were to imagine the apparition in human form, what particular features might it be expected to have? The answer is that there existed in the culture a widely recognized stereotype of the predatory sexual male, a set of typical features and characteristics that such a figure would be presupposed to manifest. Logically enough, it is this figure that the governess describes in *The Turn of the Screw*.

I

Europe in the nineteenth century was much intrigued by the theory that there exists in human nature a determinative relationship between physiognomical features and character. In a recent book Graeme Tytler documents "the universality of physiognomy in nineteenth-century Europe" and in particular the immense influence of the physiognomical speculations of Johann Caspar Lavater, an eighteenth-century Swiss clergyman, whose *Physiognomische Fragmente* in four volumes was certainly, Tytler says, known about by "most nineteenth-century men of letters" (316). Widely popularized in newspapers and periodicals, physiognomical theory exercised a significant influence on the novel during the period from the early 1770s to about the 1880s as the pseudo-scientific spuriousness of its conclusions came to be increasingly recognized. There is no evidence that James knew Lavater's work firsthand. But there is evidence beyond the elaborate physiognomical portrait the governess describes in *The Turn of the Screw* that he knew something of the subject, as when in his description of Caspar Goodwood in *The Portrait of a Lady* he mentions "blue eyes of a remarkable fixedness . . . and a jaw of the somewhat angular mould which is supposed to bespeak resolution" (47). And it is certain that James would have been well versed secondhand in the physiognomics of fictional characterization: the roster of writers named by Tytler as most influenced by physiognomy — Fielding, Dickens, the Brontës, Thackeray, Balzac, Flaubert, George Sand — reads like a gallery of novelists most familiar to James.

To demonstrate the physiognomical stereotypicality of the fearful male figure the governess hallucinates, whose actual unreality James may be implying in her remark that "'he's like nobody,'" it will be useful to reproduce her description at length:

"He has no hat. . . . He has red hair, very red, close-curling, and a pale face, long in shape, with straight good features and little rather queer whiskers that are as red as his hair. His eyebrows are somehow darker; they look particularly arched and as if they might move a good deal. His eyes are sharp, strange — awfully; but I only know clearly that they're rather small and very fixed. His mouth's wide, and his lips are thin, and except for his little whiskers he's quite clean-shaven. He gives me a sort of sense of looking like an actor. . . . He's tall, active, erect, . . . but never — no, never! — a gentleman. . . ."

[Mrs. Grose] visibly tried to hold herself. "But he *is* handsome?"

I saw the way to help her. "Remarkably!"

"And dressed — ?"

"In somebody's clothes. They're smart, but they're not his own."

She broke into a breathless affirmative groan. "They're the master's!" (46–47)

Certain details of this description can be traced to more general assumptions than those of physiognomical theory. The figure is remarkably handsome, and "the handsome man," according to general prejudice, particularly in men, "is likely to be a cad." Quite ready "for his own immediate profit . . . to defy the conventions that other men subscribe to," the cad "may dress and adorn himself in what is commonly condemned as bad taste" as "a crude and external manifestation of his disregard of the conventions of masculine behaviour." Thus he has no scruples against "taking advantage of the susceptibility which women exhibit in the presence of good-looking men." Usually with "neat and symmetrical features" and "attractive to many women," the cad is hampered neither by "a bad reputation nor bad manners . . . : his aim is not love or even philandering, but amour" (Brophy 85–86). Presumably, the fearful male figure the governess hallucinates, with his "straight good features," his somehow not quite suitable clothes, his "secret disorders, vices more than suspected," and his success with women — "He did what he wished," Mrs. Grose says, "with them all" (46, 51, 57) — emanates from some such stereotype.

Beyond conveying this general aura of sexual danger, however, the governess's description of the threatening male specter she conjures up turns out to be a detailed physiognomical portrait, the most telling feature of which is its "red hair, very red, close-curling." "Most nineteenth-century novelists," Tytler observes, "are concerned, like their predecessors, almost entirely with the color of the hair" (213).

While red hair, according to Lavater, is said to characterize "a person supremely good or supremely evil" (Tytler 215), the consensus has always favored the latter view, a prejudice that can be traced as far back as the Bible. Indeed, there is a close connection, not at all surprising in view of Lavater's clerical vocation, between physiognomical stereotypes and biblical personifications of evil. In the Old Testament the association of red hair with evil would have been reinforced by the story of Esau, who yielded to fleshly appetite, sold his God-given birthright for a mess of pottage, and spawned the lineage repudiated by Jehovah. More telling against red hair was the suspicion that Judas must have been a redhead (Cooper 75). Still more relevant to the governess's hallucinations in *The Turn of the Screw* is the knowledge that in ancient lore it was held that Satan materialized in the form of a red-haired male. It would not be surprising if a parson's daughter, hysterically projecting an image of her sexual fear and revulsion, were to envision a figure embodying features of this long-standing assumption about the human form assumed by the Tempter himself.

Indeed, the correspondence is striking. The threatening male figure she projects has "*very* red hair" (emphasis added). In *The Devil in Legend and Literature* Maximilian Rudwin observes that "the Devil's beard as well as his hair is usually of a flaming red color" (48). The figure she sees is associated with "vices more than suspected" (*Turn* 51); among other things, to be sure, "Satan is famed as the greatest gambler ever known upon or under the earth" (Rudwin 143). And other details of her portrait whose place in the design of the story has remained obscure are at least traceable to lore about Satan. The odious figure gave the governess "a sort of sense of looking like an actor." "The Devil is likewise regarded as the inventor of the drama," Rudwin reports; "indeed, the actors were regarded by the Catholic Church in the Middle Ages, and even for many centuries afterwards, as servants of Satan" (259). Finally, the penchant of the governess's projected figure to wear the clothes of a gentleman in order to be taken for what he decidedly is not is very much a part of his Satanic aura:

> The Devil . . . has on clothes which any gentleman might wear. . . . It has been his greatest ambition to be a gentleman, in outer appearance at least; and to his credit it must be said that he has so well succeeded in his efforts to resemble a gentleman that it is now very difficult to tell the two apart. (Rudwin 50)

Thus, in projecting in human form the embodiment of her deep, puritanical fear of evil, which in Victorian times tended to mean sexual evil, the governess envisions an attractive male figure, one to whom she would instinctively respond — a figure projected in the form of the Tempter himself, as that form was imprinted in the mind of the culture of which she is representative. But her projection draws also on stereotypes established in the physiognomical lore of the preceding centuries. The importance of Lavater in the considerable influence of physiognomical theories on the nineteenth century, and particularly on important novelists, has been mentioned. But there were many other practitioners in the field, and in their writings, as well as in those of novelists influenced by physiognomical lore, can be found most of the details of the apparition the governess projects. This is a precarious business at best: the spuriousness of the science assures that one can find almost as many different readings of the same features and expressions as there are physiognomists. But there is pretty solid agreement supporting Lavater's suspicion of red hair. The mind of Chaucer's Miller, for example, with a beard red "as any sowe or fox," runs to "synne and harlotries." Swift equips Gulliver with the prevailing prejudice against red hair. In describing the Yahoos — "cunning, malicious, treacherous and revengeful" as well as "cowardly . . . insolent, abject, and cruel" — Gulliver observes "that the *Red-Haired* of both Sexes are more libidinous and mischievous than the rest" and finds it curious that the female Yahoo with a lecherous eye for him did not have "Hair . . . of a Red Colour, (which might have been some Excuse for an Appetite a little irregular)" (232–33). Among physiognomists, Joseph Simms, after acknowledging that "many cases might be cited in which red-haired persons have been very amiable," finds nevertheless that this color, "if curliness is added [Quint's hair is "very red, close-curling"], indicates a . . . disposition to ardent love," and if it is very coarse "is a sign of propensities much too animal" (402). Paolo Mantegazza agrees that "red hair, although rare, is disliked by nearly all because it is an almost monstrous type" (62). Although, as Tytler points out, physiognomical (as well as phrenological) explanations for human behavior had lost credibility for perceptive people by the end of the nineteenth century, their assumptions remained in some minds so ingrained as to be almost taken for granted. Thus in *Ann Veronica* (1914), as Ann and her fellow suffragettes are arraigned after their raid on the House of Commons, H. G. Wells describes "a disagreeable young man, with red hair and a loose mouth, seated at the reporter's table . . . sketching her" (252).

If, by general agreement, red hair is a sign of lechery, other features of the male sex villain the governess projects can also be found with threatening significance in physiognomical lore. The figure's eyes, for example, — "sharp, strange — awfully; . . . rather small and very fixed" — which give the governess "such a bold hard stare" (46, 41), have a strong sexual significance. According to Simms, "there is a close connection between the eyes and the sexual organs" (229). To the authoritative Lavater, "small, and deep sunken eyes, [are] bold in opposition; not discouraged, intriguing, and active in wickedness" (3:179). The significance of the figure's eyebrows — "particularly arched and as if they might move a great deal" — is also explained by physiognomy: the arch by Mantegazza, who finds that the proud and impudent "have arched eyebrows which are often raised" (180), the movement by Lavater, who explains that "the motion of the eyebrows contains numerous expressions, especially of ignoble passions; pride, anger and contempt: the supercilious man . . . despises, and is despicable" (3:183). The wide mouth and thin lips of the governess's figure fit Mantegazza's observation that "no face recalls the expression of cruelty so much as a wanton one," and "the expression of cruelty is almost exclusively concentrated round the mouth; . . . The mouth is closed, the corners are drawn back as far as possible, . . . The eye is clear, widely opened, and fixed upon the victim" (178). Even the "habit of going about bareheaded" (the governess's figure "has no hat" [23]) attracts physiognomical attention (Tytler 294). Indeed, the essence of the governess's projected figure, embodying her hysterical but unconscious sexual horror, is very like what Lavater says one would see if he or she were to imagine a wicked, lecherous man:

> Rude, savage, ruffianly, danger-contemning, strength. It is a crime to him to have committed small mischief; his stroke, like his aspect, is death. He does not oppress, he destroys. To him murder is enjoyment, and the pangs of others a pleasure. The form of his bones denotes his strength, his eye a thirst of blood, his eyebrow habitual cruelty, his mouth deriding contempt, his nose grim craft, his hair and beard choleric power. (3:249–50)

II

Not only is it reasonably certain that James knew about physiognomical theories and the use of such devices by novelists familiar to him, then, but he also creates in his governess a character who fits the profile of the typical sexual hysteric, who has a hysterical hallucination, and whose mind projects her sexual fear in a form that draws on the very religious and physiognomical stereotypes with which such a mind as hers would logically be furnished. It remains to show some striking prototypes of the governess's physiognomically stereotypical redheaded sex villain in popular novels of the era.

A link to one such prototype exists in *The Turn of the Screw* itself: the governess is reading *Amelia* just before her third hallucination of the figure identified as Quint (65). *Amelia* contains a similar figure, Robinson, who has Quint's long pale face, red hair (actually "a red Beard"), and clothes that call a kind of disreputable attention to themselves.[2] Although Robinson is not, to the reader's knowledge, sexually villainous, his life resembles Quint's, at least the latter's reputation for "strange passages and perils, secret disorders, vices more than suspected" (51). Robinson is a gambler, cheat, thief, and criminal conspirator. The governess, not having finished the novel, would not know of his repentance in the end and thus could be expected to regard him with emotions that might contribute to her fearful hallucinations. Even more terrifying, however, in this novel with its undercurrent of sexual danger and ruin are its interpolated histories of young women betrayed by their naive indulgence in the pleasurable sensations excited by the attentions of attractive men: Miss Mathews, seduced by a soldier under false promises of marriage, and Mrs. Bennet, seduced by a nobleman after quaffing only "Half a Pint of Small Punch," which had been drugged. The latter's case would have been especially terrible to the governess, for Mrs. Bennet was the naive, sheltered daughter of a clergyman and got into trouble precisely by entertaining romantic fantasies of an attractive man: she intended only to "indulge [her] Vanity and Interest at once, without being guilty of the least Injury" (295). The warnings of both these wretched fallen women must surely have terrified the governess. Miss Mathews offers her fate as a warning to every woman "to deal with Mankind with Care and Caution . . . and never to confide too much in the Honesty of a Man, nor in her own Strength, where she has so much at Stake; let her remember she walks on a Precipice, and the bottomless Pit is to receive her, if she slips; nay, if she makes but one false Step" (53). Mrs. Bennet warns "that the Woman who gives up the least Outwork of her Virtue, doth, in that very Moment, betray the Citadel" (295). Indulging in romantic fantasies of her dashing gentleman employer, the governess, had she read thus far into *Amelia*, might indeed suddenly discover herself on the way to ruin, the outworks of her virtue undermined by her own susceptibility to an attractive male. Small won-

---

[2]May L. Ryburn has called attention to the resemblance between Fielding's Robinson and the figure the governess describes. Ryburn observes quite logically that this parallel "would seem to lay the ghosts to rest forever, except as they existed in the governess's mind" (237).

der, in such a case, that the gentleman of her fantasy should metamorphose into a villainous projection of sexual fear.

Although my primary focus here is on Quint, I might mention that, just as the governess does not need (and indeed does not have) any knowledge of Peter Quint to accomplish the transformation, so her complementary projection of the female counterpart of her sexual fear does not require knowledge of Miss Jessel and her shame: it is, in an important sense, the governess herself, the awful projection of herself ruined by the sexual evil toward which her own sexual impulses are urging her. Paul N. Siegel is another critic who views the female figure the governess sees, a genteel woman ruined by indulging her sexual impulses, as a fearful projection of the governess herself and also of the adult sexual female Flora will become. Siegel discusses James's subtle dramatization of the governess's psychosexual ambivalence: she is horrified at Miss Jessel's sexuality and its consequences and terrified of her own susceptibility to sexual feeling, of which she is subconsciously aware; but she is also fascinated and excited, because of her powerful attraction to her employer, by identifying herself with Miss Jessel and her indulgence of sexual desires. Although he does not pursue its consequences, Siegel also senses James's implication that Miss Jessel in some way prefigures in the governess's mind a Flora grown up and hardened by sexual experience (36). The story's most telling hint of this is in the episode of the girl's second excursion to the lake. With the awful vision of Miss Jessel burning in her mind, the governess sees that Flora's "incomparable childish beauty had suddenly failed, had quite vanished. . . . She was hideously hard; she had turned common and almost ugly." Flora's indignant response to her accusations seems to the governess like "that of a vulgarly pert little girl in the street" (99).

Tytler's demonstration of the physiognomical awareness reflected in *Amelia* is corroborated by Fielding's mention of the term "physiognomist" in the novel (47) as well as by the physiognomical description of the villainous Robinson. But Robinson is not a sexual villain. The projection of the governess's fear is even more in the lineage of numerous redhaired male villains rendered, like her projected figure, in detailed physiognomical portraits in some of the best-known novels of the era. One such character, who appeared just before the governess's ordeal at Bly, is Fagin, the consummate villain of Dickens's *Oliver Twist*. Fagin insinuated his way into the consciousness of thousands of readers every month from February 1837 to April 1839. Beyond the "quantity of matted red hair" that obscured his "villainous-looking and repulsive face," there is scant description of Fagin with physiognomical import, although he is "lynx-eyed," has a "pale lip," and is seen on one occasion "raising his eyebrows" (294, 87, 325). But he is certainly "hideously" villainous, personifying an evil power capable of entrapping a tender, angelic child in a hideous morass of evil, and the typifying description of him as "like some loathsome reptile, engendered in the slime and darkness through which he moved: crawling forth by night, in search of some rich offal for a meal" (128, 135), might conceivably have contributed to the governess's vision of Quint. Today, a time deeply troubled by the specter of child sexual abuse, it might even be suspected that Fagin's lasciviousness extends beyond the jewels and coins he hoards to the children he manipulates so greedily and that his possession of the pure, innocent Oliver might involve designs such as those the governess fears Quint has on Miles. If the governess had indeed read *Oliver Twist*, Fagin's embodiment of all that would have been lawless and vile to someone with her proper upbringing, together with his particular penchant for seducing children into lives of evil, could hardly have failed to color her projection of her fears.

Later Dickens would elaborate with fuller physiognomical detail and more pointed sexual innuendo on this character type in the figure of Uriah Heep, with his slimy designs on the saintly Agnes in *David Copperfield*. Although Heep, like Fagin, is anything but handsome, "this red-bearded animal," "this detestable Rufus," has the hair color, pale face, wide mouth, and piercing eyes of the figure the governess projects in *The Turn of the Screw*. Heep's face is "pale" and "cadaverous," "his mouth [is] widened" like a gargoyle's, and his eyes, "sleepless . . . like two red suns," were a "shadowless red" and "looked as if they had scorched their lashes off" (362).

An older, aristocratic version of the same character type is Lord Steyne, the sharkish nobleman who undoes Becky Sharp in Thackeray's *Vanity Fair*. Steyne's description captures the grotesquerie, as well as several details, of the portrait of Heep. His "shining bald head . . . was fringed with red hair. He had thick bushy eyebrows, with little twinkling bloodshot eyes. . . . His jaw was underhung, and when he laughed, two white buck-teeth protruded themselves and glistened savagely in the midst of the grin" (366).

In *Daniel Deronda*, Henleigh Mallinger Grandcourt, like the governess's figure, is handsome, and, as Gwendolyn Harleth discovers, trails, like Quint, a past of secret disorders and vices, like gambling and keeping a mistress, more than suspected. Grandcourt is "decidedly handsome," has "a mere fringe of reddish-blond hair," a complexion of "a faded fairness resembling that of an actress," and "long narrow grey eyes" that "looked at Gwendolyn persistently with a slightly exploring gaze" (79, 80).

This list of prototypes for the figure the governess describes could be extended considerably — even, it has been argued, into the realm of real life. It is deliciously pertinent to note, at this point, that in view of his "reddish, untamed beard," descriptions of him as "an ugly fellow" with a "pasty" face, "red nose," "rusty red beard," and "little slatey-blue eyes," his reputation as a "dangerous seducer of women," and his own self-perception that "there clung about him a 'faint but unmistakable flavor of brimstone,'" the figure upon whom Peter Quint is based has been decisively identified by E. A. Sheppard: "He is George Bernard Shaw" (61–62).

To be sure, the governess, whose ordeal takes place in the 1840s, could not have known the redheaded sexual villains Heep, Steyne, and Grandcourt, although she might have known Fagin. My point is, rather, that James, writing in 1897, surely did know them and that in creating the figure she describes he drew the same *type* of character, one whose lineage in literary history, James is careful to imply, she would have been familiar with. The only book she is shown reading in *The Turn of the Screw* is *Amelia*, but through her remarks about her reading at Bly James implies that, free from the strict censorship of the vicarage, utterly on her own, and with a good deal of time on her hands, the governess fell with avidity on the "roomful of old books at Bly" — books of a kind that had come into her "sequestered home" only "to the extent of a distinctly deprecated reknown" — the very category of books that could not fail to whet "the unavowed curiosity of [her] youth." No catalog of the library at Bly has survived, but one category of its holdings was "last-century fiction" (64, 65) — fiction, that is, full of the ordeals of virginal ingénues pursued by sexual villains. At the time of her first manifestation of hysterical symptoms when she projects the red-headed sex fiend, she has already been some weeks at Bly. If she is, as is likely, immersed in eighteenth-century fiction full of Gothic terror — fiction, as Tytler demonstrates, steeped in physiognomical lore — the figure she describes is exactly what might be expected.

There can be no doubt that James *could* have done what I have proposed. His own upbringing as a boy in a proper household, "surrounded by admonishing governesses, a permissive father, an often stern ambiguous mother" (Edel 22), would have provided, in general outlines, a prototype for the situation as well as the atmosphere at Bly.

(Indeed, there is good reason to suspect, in view of James's own well-known sexual problem [8][3] and Douglas's pointed hints to the Jamesian narrator of the opening frame that when "he looked at me, . . . he saw what he spoke of" [22], that it is his own story James tells in *The Turn of the Screw*.) In his familiarity with the work of his brother William, coupled with his knowledge of sexual hysteria, its supposed causes, and its manifestations, James certainly possessed the requisite psychological acumen to dramatize the psychology of sexual fear in a maternal figure and its effect on the children in her charge. And, given his artistic seriousness and penchant for subtlety, as well as the persistent undercurrent of sexual preoccupation in his work, despite his prim distaste for the explicit airing of sexual matters, what I have suggested is, I believe, precisely what he *would* do with the story. Indeed, the demonstrable extent to which the governess represents a classic case of sexual hysteria and the fact that the figure she projects is a classic example of physiognomical cliché, deliberately elaborated for ironic effect, serve to indicate James's intentions in *The Turn of the Screw*. It is not a ghost story but a psychological drama about the disastrous effects of Victorian sexual attitudes on the development of children.[4]

In light of the foregoing, a belated, perhaps ironic sympathy is due poor Edmund Wilson for his ordeal over *The Turn of the Screw*: he was on the right track but could never get over the obstacle of the ghosts. Wilson was right: the problem *is* with the troubled sexuality of the governess, who, the story pointedly emphasizes, was greatly attracted to the gentleman who employed her but was also, in an exaggerated but quintessentially Victorian way, deeply fearful of and hostile toward sexuality. As she indulges her romantic feelings toward her attractive employer, she senses subconsciously that by thus relaxing her sexual defenses even so innocuously she has set foot on the path to ruin. At that point, the attractive male projection of her pleasurable sensations changes to the terrifying male projection of her fear. The figure she projects emerges from her own subconscious imprinting by religious and cultural stereotypes of the villainously libidinous male, with numerous precedents in the literature of the period, colored, conceivably, by some awareness of the views of Lavater himself, who had established a reputation throughout Europe as a preacher as well as a physiognomist (Tytler

---

[3]See also Edel, especially in Preface (xi–xii) and the index under "James, Henry: Psychosexual problems."

[4]A conclusion also reached by Jane Nardin, who asserts that *The Turn of the Screw* "is neither about evil metaphysically conceived, nor about madness clinically conceived, but rather [about] a particular social milieu and the way it affects people living in it" (142).

24). Thus awakened, the governess's hysterical fear of sexuality is super-added to her sense of her duty as governess of two children approaching puberty. Not really mad, merely deeply Victorian in the grip of a powerful cultural ideal, she takes upon herself the role of angel in the house — guardian of idealized, spiritualized love and sexual purity. Along the same line she is, as James seems to have realized, a manifestation of the Great Governess of the era, representing maternal control over the sexual mores of the household and thus of the culture at large.

Through the figures the governess projects — one representing her fear and revulsion at male sexuality, the other her fear and disgust at female reciprocation of male lust (she realizes with a spasm of ambivalence that what went on between Quint and Jessel "must have been also what *she* [Miss Jessel] wished!" [57]) — James contrives to objectify her sexual state of mind. But the main line of development in the story is the effect such a deep aversion to sexual phenomena has on the development of children. But how does one dramatize in fiction such psychological effects? James's solution to the problem is masterful. The "ghosts," which work well enough on the literal level (where many learned critics have enjoyed them), become, on the figurative level, a means of objectifying the psychology of both the governess and the children and also the psychological meaning and consequences of her behavior toward them: they represent both her fear and her revulsion at the children's natural sexual development. For, of course, the sexual male and female figures so fearfully on the governess's mind *are* possessing Miles and Flora: they are merely the adult sexual beings the children will become when the sexuality latent in childhood emerges through adolescence and establishes itself in adulthood. This possession, however, is not evil; it is merely natural. The many elaborate explications of the evil in *The Turn of the Screw* notwithstanding, the only evil the story presents is that Quint and Jessel were sexually active. The powerful aura of evil that pervades the story emanates from the psyche of the governess, who, after all, tells the story: it is her hysterical aversion to sexuality, heightened for satirical effect by James's subtle irony.

In her compulsion to keep the children from being possessed with this evil, then, the governess is actually blocking their normal sexual development. Naturally, when she looks so anxiously at Miles and Flora, children entering puberty, she sees signs of their sexual maturation — the adult male with an attraction to young and pretty women in Miles and the adult female with a reciprocal attraction to handsome young men in Flora. In trying to suppress all manifestations of their natural sexual development she inflicts grievous damage on their psyches. With apt oedipal implications, James allows Flora to escape to the protection of the father figure; but the male child, trapped in the psychosexual undertow of the mother-son relationship, is destroyed.

So James does not arrange things so that the only way to account for the governess's description of the apparition Mrs. Grose identifies as Peter Quint is that she has seen a supernatural manifestation: he contrives it so that she describes a hysterical projection of her own sexual aversion coupled with a powerful sense of duty to keep the children in her charge free of sexual taint. But a question yet remains. If the red-headed sexual male does, as I have demonstrated, well up hysterically in the governess's mind from physiognomical stereotypes, how does it happen that this figure so closely resembles the real person Peter Quint? The answer is not, certainly, that James believed in physiognomical science and meant to represent through Quint an actual living embodiment of the theory. For, as he was undoubtedly aware, the physiognomical stereotype, as well as the evil ascribed to Quint and Jessel, was a purely subjective phenomenon, an attitude of mind. In an atmosphere of increasing rationality, Tytler explains, there emerged, as the nineteenth century wore on, a "subtler treatment of physiognomy" which tended to treat it "as a problematic sign of the observer's own moral character" (319). Thus in *The Turn of the Screw* the governess's physiognomical imprinting, like her sense of sexual evil, is part of her characterization as an upright and idealistic person, but one with problematically unhealthy attitudes toward sexuality. I suspect rather that James made it appear that the governess describes a real person dead and buried because he felt it imperative that the story appear to be a ghost story. Such dissembling would help explain the notorious ambiguity of his various comments on the story. With the example fresh on his mind of the storm of opprobrium that had fallen upon Thomas Hardy when he ventured to criticize Victorian sexual sanctities — showing, for example, through Tess that a sexual lapse did not really commit a girl to hopeless depravity and through Jude that the spiritual-love ideal could turn marriage into a torment for people with normal sexual desires — James knew that he could not say openly what he wanted to say in *The Turn of the Screw*. What he wanted to say was that the angel in the house might really be an angel of psychic destruction, votary of an ideal moving through society from house to house doing mortal damage to human sexual development and especially, since male sexuality has always seemed more irrepressible than female, to the sexual development of boys like Miles, whose death, of course, is not actual but symbolic of the permanent harm done to the very core — the "heart" — of his sexual being. Thus James produced *The Turn of the Screw*, a ghost story that would materialize interestingly on the figurative level as one of the most remarkable psychological dramas in literature.

For that, ultimately, is the story of *The Turn of the Screw* — a more significant story, I maintain, than either a ghost story or a parable of some amorphous good and evil. If that is still debatable, the assertion that the psychological drama is more humanly relevant both to James's time and to our own is surely not. At least a story about the damage done to the sexual development of children by Victorian sexual fear and disgust would satisfy James's own requirement that the art of fiction must achieve an imitation of life.

WORKS CITED

Brophy, John. *The Human Face*. London: Harrap, 1945.

Cargill, Oscar. "*The Turn of the Screw* and Alice James." *PMLA* 78 (1963): 238–49.

Cooper, Wendy. *Hair, Sex, Society, Symbolism*. New York: Stein, 1971.

Dickens, Charles. *David Copperfield*. New York: Washington Square, 1958.

———. *Oliver Twist*. New York: Holt, 1962.

Edel, Leon. *Henry James: A Life*. New York: Harper, 1985.

Eliot, George. *Daniel Deronda*. New York: Harper, 1961.

Ellis, Havelock. "Auto-Erotism." *Studies in the Psychology of Sex*. 2 vols. New York: Random, 1936. 1, pt. 1: 163–283.

Fielding, Henry. *Amelia*. Middletown: Wesleyan UP, 1983.

Huntley, H. Robert. "James's *The Turn of the Screw*: Its 'Fine Machinery.'" *American Imago* 34 (1977): 224–37.

James, Henry. *The Portrait of a Lady*. Norton Critical Edition. Ed. Robert D. Bamberg. New York: Norton, 1975.

Lavater, J. C. *Essays on Physiognomy; for the Promotion of Knowledge and the Love of Mankind*. Trans. Thomas Holcroft. 3 vols. London: Robinson, 1789.

Mantegazza, Paolo. *Physiognomy and Expression*. New York: Scribner's, 1914.

Nardin, Jane. "*The Turn of the Screw*: The Victorian Background." *Mosaic* 12 (1978): 131–42.

Rudwin, Maximilian. *The Devil in Legend and Literature*. Chicago and London: Open Court, 1931.

Ryburn, May L. "*The Turn of the Screw* and *Amelia*: A Source for Quint?" *Studies in Short Fiction* 16 (1979): 235–37.

Sheppard, E[lizabeth]. A. *Henry James and "The Turn of the Screw."* Auckland: Auckland UP, 1974.

Siegel, Paul N. "'Miss Jessel': Mirror Image of the Governess." *Literature and Psychology* 18 (1968): 30–38.

Simms, Joseph. *Physiognomy Illustrated; or Nature's Revelation of Character*. New York: Murray, 1889.

Swift, Jonathan. *Gulliver's Travels*. Norton Critical Edition. Ed. Robert A. Greenberg. New York: Norton, 1961.

Thackeray, William Makepeace. *Vanity Fair*. Riverside Edition. Boston: Houghton, 1963.

Tytler, Graeme. *Physiognomy in the European Novel: Faces and Fortunes*. Princeton: Princeton UP, 1982.

Wells, H. G. *Ann Veronica*. New York: Smith, 1932.

Feminist Criticism
and
The Turn of the Screw

WHAT IS FEMINIST CRITICISM?

Feminist criticism comes in many forms, and feminist critics have a variety of goals. Some are interested in rediscovering the works of women writers overlooked by a masculine-dominated culture. Others have revisited books by male authors and reviewed them from a woman's point of view to understand how they both reflect and shape the attitudes that have held women back.

Since the early 1970s three strains of feminist criticism have emerged, strains that can be categorized as French, American, and British. These categories should not be allowed to obscure either the global implications of the women's movement or the fact that interests and ideas have been shared by feminists from France, Great Britain, and the United States. British and American feminists have examined similar problems while writing about many of the same writers and works, and American feminists have recently become more receptive to French theories about femininity and writing. Historically speaking, however, French, American, and British feminists have examined similar problems from somewhat different perspectives.

French feminists have tended to focus their attention on language, analyzing the ways in which meaning is produced. They have concluded

242

that language as we commonly think of it is a decidedly male realm. Drawing on the ideas of the psychoanalytic philosopher Jacques Lacan, French feminists remind us that language is a realm of public discourse. A child enters the linguistic realm just as it comes to grasp its separateness from its mother, just about the time that boys identify with their father, the family representative of culture. The language learned reflects a binary logic that opposes such terms as active/passive, masculine/feminine, sun/moon, father/mother, head/heart, son/daughter, intelligent/sensitive, brother/sister, form/matter, phallus/vagina, reason/emotion. Because this logic tends to group with masculinity such qualities as light, thought, and activity, French feminists have said that the structure of language is phallocentric: it privileges the phallus and, more generally, masculinity by associating them with things and values more appreciated by the (masculine-dominated) culture. Moreover, French feminists believe, "masculine desire dominates speech and posits woman as an idealized fantasy-fulfillment for the incurable emotional lack caused by separation from the mother" (Jones 83).

In the view of French feminists, language is associated with separation from the mother. Its distinctions represent the world from the male point of view, and it systematically forces women to choose: either they can imagine and represent themselves as men imagine and represent them (in which case they may speak, but will speak as men) or they can choose "silence," becoming in the process "the invisible and unheard sex" (Jones 83).

But some influential French feminists have argued that language only *seems* to give women such a narrow range of choices. There is another possibility, namely that women can develop a *feminine* language. In various ways, early French feminists such as Annie Leclerc, Xavière Gauthier, and Marguerite Duras have suggested that there is something that may be called *l'écriture féminine:* women's writing. Recently, Julia Kristeva has said that feminine language is "semiotic," not "symbolic." Rather than rigidly opposing and ranking elements of reality, rather than symbolizing one thing but not another in terms of a third, feminine language is rhythmic and unifying. If from the male perspective it seems fluid to the point of being chaotic, that is a fault of the male perspective.

According to Kristeva, feminine language is derived from the preoedipal period of fusion between mother and child. Associated with the maternal, feminine language is not only a threat to culture, which is patriarchal, but also a medium through which women may be creative in new ways. But Kristeva has paired her central, liberating claim — that truly feminist innovation in all fields requires an understanding of the relation between maternity and feminine creation — with a warning. A feminist language that refuses to participate in "masculine" discourse, that places its future entirely in a feminine, semiotic discourse, risks being politically marginalized by men. That is to say, it risks being relegated to the outskirts (pun intended) of what is considered socially and politically significant.

Kristeva, who associates feminine writing with the female body, is joined in her views by other leading French feminists. Hélène Cixous, for instance, also posits an essential connection between the woman's body, whose sexual pleasure has been repressed and denied expression, and women's writing. "Write your self. Your body must be heard," Cixous urges; once they learn to write their bodies, women will not only realize their sexuality but enter history and move toward a future based on a "feminine" economy of giving rather than the "masculine" economy of hoarding (Cixous 250). For Luce Irigaray, women's sexual pleasure (*jouissance*) cannot be expressed by the dominant, ordered, "logical," masculine language. She explores the connection between women's sexuality and women's language through the following analogy: as women's *jouissance* is more multiple than men's unitary, phallic pleasure ("woman has sex organs just about everywhere"), so "feminine" language is more diffusive than its "masculine" counterpart. ("That is undoubtedly the reason . . . her language . . . goes off in all directions and . . . he is unable to discern the coherence," Irigaray writes [101–03].)

Cixous's and Irigaray's emphasis on feminine writing as an expression of the female body has drawn criticism from other French feminists. Many argue that an emphasis on the body either reduces "the feminine" to a biological essence or elevates it in a way that shifts the valuation of masculine and feminine but retains the binary categories. For Christine Fauré, Irigaray's celebration of women's difference fails to address the issue of masculine dominance, and a Marxist-feminist, Catherine Clément, has warned that "poetic" descriptions of what constitutes the feminine will not challenge that dominance in the realm of production. The boys will still make the toys, and decide who gets to use them. In her effort to redefine women as political rather than as sexual beings, Monique Wittig has called for the abolition of sexual categories that Cixous and Irigaray retain and revalue as they celebrate women's writing.

American feminist critics have shared with French critics both an interest in and a cautious distrust of the concept of feminine writing.

Annette Kolodny, for instance, has worried that the "richness and variety of women's writing" will be missed if we see in it only its "feminine mode" or "style" ("Some Notes" 78). And yet Kolodny herself proceeds, in the same essay, to point out that women *have* had their own style, which includes reflexive constructions ("she found herself crying") and particular, recurring themes (clothing and self-fashioning are two that Kolodny mentions; other American feminists have focused on madness, disease, and the demonic).

Interested as they have become in the "French" subject of feminine style, American feminist critics began by analyzing literary texts rather than philosophizing abstractly about language. Many reviewed the great works by male writers, embarking on a revisionist rereading of literary tradition. These critics examined the portrayals of women characters, exposing the patriarchal ideology implicit in such works and showing how clearly this tradition of systematic masculine dominance is inscribed in our literary tradition. Kate Millett, Carolyn Heilbrun, and Judith Fetterley, among many others, created this model for American feminist criticism, a model that Elaine Showalter came to call "the feminist critique" of "male-constructed literary history" ("Poetics" 25).

Meanwhile another group of critics including Sandra Gilbert, Susan Gubar, Patricia Meyer Spacks, and Showalter herself created a somewhat different model. Whereas feminists writing "feminist critique" have analyzed works by men, practitioners of what Showalter used to refer to as "gynocriticism" have studied the writings of those women who, against all odds, produced what she calls "a literature of their own." In *The Female Imagination* (1975), Spacks examines the female literary tradition to find out how great women writers across the ages have felt, perceived themselves, and imagined reality. Gilbert and Gubar, in *The Madwoman in the Attic* (1979), concern themselves with well-known women writers of the nineteenth century, but they too find that general concerns, images, and themes recur, because the authors that they treat wrote "in a culture whose fundamental definitions of literary authority are both overtly and covertly patriarchal" (45).

If one of the purposes of gynocriticism is to (re)study well-known women authors, another is to rediscover women's history and culture, particularly women's communities that have nurtured female creativity. Still another related purpose is to discover neglected or forgotten women writers and thus to forge an alternative literary tradition, a canon that better represents the female perspective by better representing the literary works that have been written by women. Showalter, in *A Literature of Their Own* (1977), admirably began to fulfill this purpose, providing a remarkably comprehensive overview of women's writing through three of its phases. She defines these as the "Feminine, Feminist, and Female" phases, phases during which women first imitated a masculine tradition (1840–80), then protested against its standards and values (1880–1920), and finally advocated their own autonomous, female perspective (1920 to the present).

With the recovery of a body of women's texts, attention has returned to a question raised in 1978 by Lillian Robinson: Doesn't American feminist criticism need to formulate a theory of its own practice? Won't reliance on theoretical assumptions, categories, and strategies developed by men and associated with nonfeminist schools of thought prevent feminism from being accepted as equivalent to these other critical discourses? Not all American feminists believe that a special or unifying theory of feminist practice is urgently needed; Showalter's historical approach to women's culture allows a feminist critic to use theories based on nonfeminist disciplines. Kolodny has advocated a "playful pluralism" that encompasses a variety of critical schools and methods. But Jane Marcus and others have responded that if feminists adopt too wide a range of approaches, they may relax the tensions between feminists and the educational establishment necessary for political activism.

The question of whether feminism weakens or fortifies itself by emphasizing its separateness — and by developing unity through separateness — is one of several areas of debate within American feminism. Another area of disagreement touched on earlier, between feminists who stress universal feminine attributes (the feminine imagination, feminine writing) and those who focus on the political conditions experienced by certain groups of women at certain times in history, parallels a larger distinction between American feminist critics and their British counterparts.

While it has been customary to refer to an Anglo-American tradition of feminist criticism, British feminists tend to distinguish themselves from what they see as an American overemphasis on texts linking women across boundaries and decades and an underemphasis on popular art and culture. They regard their own critical practice as more political than that of American feminists, whom they have often faulted for being uninterested in historical detail. They would join such American critics as Myra Jehlen to suggest that a continuing preoccupation with women writers might create the danger of placing women's texts out-side the history that conditions them.

In the view of British feminists, the American opposition to male stereotypes that denigrate women has often led to counterstereotypes of feminine virtue that ignore real differences of race, class, and culture among women. In addition, they argue that American celebrations of individual heroines falsely suggest that powerful individuals may be im-mune to repressive conditions and may even imply that *any* individual can go through life unconditioned by the culture and ideology in which she or he lives.

Similarly, the American endeavor to recover women's history — for example, by emphasizing that women developed their own strategies to gain power within their sphere — is seen by British feminists like Judith Newton and Deborah Rosenfelt as an endeavor that "mystifies" male oppression, disguising it as something that has created for women a spe-cial world of opportunities. More important from the British stand-point, the universalizing and "essentializing" tendencies in both Amer-ican practice and French theory disguise women's oppression by highlighting sexual difference, suggesting that a dominant system is im-pervious to political change. By contrast, British feminist theory empha-sizes an engagement with historical process in order to promote social change.

In the essay that follows, Priscilla Walton's focus is on *The Turn of the Screw* as a story by a male novelist whose narrator is a young woman whose *narrative,* in turn, is re-related by a man named Douglas and another, nameless narrator. More generally, she is interested in the way women have been characterized in patriarchal narratives and in feminine subjectivity — that is, the position from which women speak.

Using historical facts and psychoanalytic theory, Walton shows why a writer like James would have felt the need to "objectify," "legitimate," and "validate" the vision and words of a young governess by creating a frame story involving men telling tales around a fire. She also shows how that process serves to *in*validate everything the governess sees and relates. For Walton, *The Turn of the Screw* is a work in which James sought "to write from a feminine perspective and still retain the author-ity of his maleness, . . . concomitantly draw[ing] upon the governess's feminine lack of authority" to produce "the complexity of his text" (254).

Victorian women, Walton reminds us, were spoken to; they were not speakers. They were not generally thought of as thinking, feeling subjects *with* desires but, rather, as the objects *of* male desire. If they did come to be viewed as having desires of their own (Walton, using the psychoanalytic theory of Jacques Lacan, refers to desire as the "marker of subjectivity" [257]), then they were thought of as lunatics or whores, for desire was associated with sexuality, whereas sane and legitimate women were not sexual beings.

As a governess, Walton points out, James's narrator occupied a particularly problematic and questionable place in Victorian culture: "In that governesses served as mother substitutes, they performed the role of the 'pure' woman; however, since they were single women, they also posed a threat to the structure of the home" (257). James's governess is a particularly threatening figure in that she is a speaker, a narrator, as well. She must "perform as a speaking subject in her narrative, and, since the subject is constructed through desire, she must exhibit desire in order to assume this position" (258).

Walton pays particular attention to the subtle, sexual innuendoes that permeate Douglas's remarks about the governess. As a result of the prologue in which these suggestive remarks are made, the governess's story is shown to be "trivialized" from the start. The governess "is at a disadvantage when she assumes the 'I' and the 'eye' of the narrative," Walton argues; "her delegitimization is one of the factors contributing to the confusion over her credibility as a narrator" (260).

In developing her argument, Walton discusses the "male gaze," which "serves as a marker of sexuality and control" insofar as it allows a person to be a "spectator" and not a "spectacle" (260, 262). She focuses on the governess's fantasy that she is the object of her master's gaze, as well as on her tragic, subsequent construction of a "fictive male gaze" of her own.

In its final pages, Walton's essay is about Mrs. Grose and Miss Jessel, who respectively figure the proper and the improper, the maternal and the "fallen," images of women between which the governess-narrator is painfully torn. It is also about the character of Flora, whose three adult women models are the mother (Mrs. Grose), the whore (Miss Jessel), and a governess who "cannot offer [her] a model different from those offered by Miss Jessel or Mrs. Grose because she has not yet forged such a place for herself" (264).

Walton's essay combines those forms of feminism that have been generally categorized as French, American, and British. Making use of the writings of Luce Irigaray, Walton shows an interest in issues of patriarchy and language that is characteristic of French feminism. At the same time, her concern with the way in which women have been represented by male authors is typical of American feminist inquiry. Finally, her focus on the governess as a representative of class as well as gender and her sense that gender, class, and "power imbalance" (footnote 7) played an important role in the "production of *The Turn of the Screw*" (254) reflect the concern of much British feminism.

Ross C Murfin

FEMINIST CRITICISM: A SELECTED BIBLIOGRAPHY

French Feminist Theories

Beauvoir, Simone de. *The Second Sex.* 1953. Trans. and ed. H. M. Parshley. New York: Bantam, 1961.

Cixous, Hélène. "The Laugh of the Medusa." Trans. Keith Cohen and Paula Cohen. *Signs* 1 (1976): 875–94.

Cixous, Hélène, and Catherine Clément. *The Newly Born Woman.* Trans. Betsy Wing. Minneapolis: U of Minnesota P, 1986.

French Feminist Theory. Special issue, *Signs* 7.1 (1981).

Irigaray, Luce. *This Sex Which Is Not One.* Trans. Catherine Porter. Ithaca: Cornell UP, 1985.

Jones, Ann Rosalind. "Inscribing Femininity: French Theories of the Feminine." *Making a Difference: Feminist Literary Criticism.* Ed. Gayle Greene and Coppélia Kahn. London: Methuen, 1985. 80–112.

Kristeva, Julia. *Desire in Language: A Semiotic Approach to Literature and Art.* Ed. Leon S. Roudiez. Trans. Thomas Gora, Alice Jardine, and Roudiez. New York: Columbia UP, 1980.

Marks, Elaine, and Isabelle de Courtivron, eds. *New French Feminisms: An Anthology.* Amherst: U of Massachusetts P, 1980.

Moi, Toril, ed. *French Feminist Thought: A Reader.* Oxford: Basil Blackwell, 1987.

British and American Feminist Theories

Belsey, Catherine, and Jane Moore, eds. *The Feminist Reader: Essays in Gender and the Politics of Literary Criticism.* New York: Basil Blackwell, 1989.

Benhabib, Seyla, and Drucilla Cornell, eds. *Feminism as Critique: On the Politics of Gender.* Minneapolis: U of Minnesota P, 1987.

Collins, Patricia Hill. *Black Feminist Thought: Knowledge, Consciousness, and the Politics of Empowerment.* Boston: Unwin Hyman, 1990.

de Lauretis, Teresa, ed. *Feminist Studies/Critical Studies*. Bloomington: Indiana UP, 1986.

Feminist Readings: French Texts/American Contexts. Special issue,
Yale French Studies 62 (1982). Essays by Jardine and Spivak.

Fuss, Diana. *Essentially Speaking: Feminism, Nature and Difference*.
New York: Routledge, 1989.

Herndl, Diana Price, and Robyn Warhol, eds. *Feminisms: An Anthology of Literary Theory and Criticism*. New Brunswick: Rutgers UP,
1991.

hooks, bell. *Ain't I a Woman?: Black Women and Feminism*. Boston:
South End, 1981.

Keohane, Nannerl O., Michelle Z. Rosaldo, and Barbara C. Gelpi,
eds. *Feminist Theory: A Critique of Ideology*. Chicago: U of Chicago P, 1982.

Kolodny, Annette. "Dancing Through the Minefield: Some Observations on the Theory, Practice, and Politics of a Feminist Literary
Criticism." Showalter, *New Feminist Criticism* 144–67.

———. "Some Notes on Defining a 'Feminist Literary Criticism.'"
Critical Inquiry 2 (1975). 78

The Lesbian Issue. Special issue, *Signs* 9 (Summer 1984).

Malson, Micheline, et al., eds. *Feminist Theory in Practice and Process*.
Chicago: U of Chicago P, 1986.

Rich, Adrienne. *On Lies, Secrets, and Silence: Selected Prose, 1966–1979*.
New York: Norton, 1979.

Showalter, Elaine. "Toward a Feminist Poetics." Showalter, *New Feminist Criticism* 125–43.

———, ed. *The New Feminist Criticism: Essays on Women, Literature,
and Theory*. New York: Pantheon, 1985.

The Feminist Critique

Fetterley, Judith. *The Resisting Reader: A Feminist Approach to American Fiction*. Bloomington: Indiana UP, 1978.

Greer, Germaine. *The Female Eunuch*. New York: McGraw, 1971.

Millett, Kate. *Sexual Politics*. Garden City: Doubleday, 1970.

Robinson, Lillian S. *Sex, Class, and Culture*. 1978. New York:
Methuen, 1986.

Wittig, Monique. *Les Guérillères*. Trans. David Le Vay. 1969. New
York: Avon, 1973.

Woolf, Virginia. *A Room of One's Own*. New York: Harcourt, 1929.

Women's Writing and Creativity

Abel, Elizabeth, ed. *Writing and Sexual Difference*. Chicago: U of Chicago P, 1982.

Abel, Elizabeth, Marianne Hirsch, and Elizabeth Langland, eds. *The Voyage In: Fictions of Female Development*. Hanover: UP of New England, 1983.

Auerbach, Nina. *Communities of Women: An Idea in Fiction*. Cambridge: Harvard UP, 1978.

Christian, Barbara. *Black Feminist Criticism: Perspectives on Black Women Writers*. New York: Pergamon, 1985.

Gilbert, Sandra M., and Susan Gubar. *The Madwoman in the Attic: The Woman Writer and the Nineteenth-Century Literary Imagination*. New Haven: Yale UP, 1979.

Jacobus, Mary, ed. *Women Writing and Writing about Women*. New York: Barnes, 1979.

Miller, Nancy K., ed. *The Poetics of Gender*. New York: Columbia UP, 1986.

Newton, Judith Lowder. *Women, Power and Subversion: Social Strategies in British Fiction, 1778–1860*. Athens: U of Georgia P, 1981.

Poovey, Mary. *The Proper Lady and the Woman Writer: Ideology as Style in the Works of Mary Wollstonecraft, Mary Shelley, and Jane Austen*. Chicago: U of Chicago P, 1984.

Showalter, Elaine. *A Literature of Their Own: British Women Novelists from Brontë to Lessing*. Princeton: Princeton UP, 1977.

Marxist and Class Analysis

Barrett, Michèle. *Women's Oppression Today: Problems in Marxist Feminist Analysis*. London: Verso, 1980.

Delphy, Christine. *Close to Home: A Materialist Analysis of Women's Oppression*. Trans. and ed. Diana Leonard. Amherst: U of Massachusetts P, 1984.

Hartsock, Nancy C. M. *Money, Sex, and Power: Toward a Feminist Historical Materialism*. Boston: Northeastern UP, 1985.

Kaplan, Cora. *Sea Changes: Culture and Feminism*. London: Verso, 1986.

Mitchell, Juliet. *Woman's Estate*. New York: Pantheon, 1971.

Newton, Judith, and Deborah Rosenfelt, eds. *Feminist Criticism and Social Change: Sex, Class and Race in Literature and Culture*. New York: Methuen, 1985.

Sargent, Lydia, ed. *Women and Revolution: A Discussion of the*

Unhappy Marriage of Marxism and Feminism. Montreal: Black Rose, 1981.

Women's History/Women's Studies

Bridenthal, Renate, and Claudia Koonz, eds. *Becoming Visible: Women in European History.* Boston: Houghton, 1977.

Farnham, Christie, ed. *The Impact of Feminist Research in the Academy.* Bloomington: Indiana UP, 1987.

Kelly, Joan. *Women, History and Theory.* Chicago: U of Chicago P, 1984.

McConnell-Ginet, Sally, et al., eds. *Woman and Language in Literature and Society.* New York: Praeger, 1980.

Mitchell, Juliet, and Ann Oakley, eds. *The Rights and Wrongs of Women.* London: Penguin, 1976.

Newton, Judith L., et al., eds. *Sex and Class in Women's History.* London: Routledge, 1983.

Riley, Denise. *"Am I That Name?": Feminism and the Category of "Women" in History.* Minneapolis: U of Minnesota P, 1988.

Rowbotham, Sheila. *Woman's Consciousness, Man's World.* Harmondsworth: Penguin, 1973.

Schipper, Mineke, ed. *Unheard Words: Women and Literature in Africa, the Arab World, Asia, the Caribbean, and Latin America.* London: Allison, 1985.

Scott, Joan Wallach. *Gender and the Politics of History.* New York: Columbia UP, 1988.

Smith-Rosenberg, Carroll. *Disorderly Conduct: Visions of Gender in Victorian America.* New York: Knopf, 1985.

Feminism and Other Critical Approaches

Armstrong, Nancy, ed. *Literature as Women's History I.* A special issue of *Genre* 19–20 (1986–87).

Benstock, Shari. *Textualizing the Feminine: On the Limits of Genre.* Norman: U of Oklahoma P, 1991.

Diamond, Irene, and Lee Quinby, eds. *Feminism and Foucault: Reflections on Resistance.* Boston: Northeastern UP, 1988.

Elliot, Patricia. *From Mastery to Analysis: Theories of Gender in Psychoanalytic Criticism.* Ithaca: Cornell UP, 1990.

Feminist Studies 14 (1988). Special issue on feminism and deconstruction.

Gallop, Jane. *The Daughter's Seduction: Feminism and Psychoanalysis.* Ithaca: Cornell UP, 1982.

Keller, Evelyn Fox. *Reflections on Gender and Science.* New Haven: Yale UP, 1985.

Meese, Elizabeth, and Alice Parker, eds. *The Difference Within: Feminism and Critical Theory.* Amsterdam/Philadelphia: John Benjamins, 1989.

Penley, Constance, ed. *Feminism and Film Theory.* New York: Routledge, 1988.

Feminist Approaches to James and *The Turn of the Screw*

Cohen, Paula Marantz. "Freud's *Dora* and James's *Turn of the Screw:* Two Treatments of the Female 'Case.'" *Criticism* 28 (1986): 73–87.

Klingenberg, Patricia N. "The Feminine 'I': Silvia Ocampo's Fantasies of the Subject." *Romance Language Annual* 6 (1989): 488–94.

Moon, Heath. "More Royalist Than the King: The Governess, the Telegraphist, and Mrs. Gracedew." *Criticism* 24 (1982): 16–35.

Walton, Priscilla L. *The Disruption of the Feminine in Henry James.* Toronto: U of Toronto P, 1992. 3–12.

A FEMINIST PERSPECTIVE

PRISCILLA L. WALTON

"What then on earth was I?": Feminine Subjectivity and *The Turn of the Screw*

The Turn of the Screw has been called the "small problem child" of James's fiction (Seltzer 66). For at least half a century, the diametrically opposed readings to which the story gives rise have led to a critical debate over whether it should be interpreted as a ghost story or as a case study of madness. I would like to look at *The Turn of the Screw* from a different perspective. Since the confusion the story generates arises from the reliability or the unreliability of James's female narrator, I will argue that *The Turn of the Screw* serves as an exemplar of the problematic nature of feminine representation (the way a woman is characterized in a story) and feminine subjectivity (the position from which she speaks). Indeed, the difficulties a Victorian woman encounters when she attempts to speak are highlighted in the production of *The Turn of the Screw*, which does not comprise a female writer's attempt to express herself, but rather a male writer's effort to cross-dress and write from her vantage point.

Because Henry James rarely employs a first-person narrative voice in his fiction, and even points out the weaknesses of first-person narration in his Preface to *The Ambassadors* (320–22), his mode of presentation in *The Turn of the Screw* is noteworthy. Perhaps it is coincidental that James prefers an "I" narration in this particular story, but his adoption of a female voice invites critical speculation on power imbalances. The conflict between the "I" of the primary narrator and the "I" of the writer, in *The Turn of the Screw*, draws attention to the ways in which James is able to write from a feminine perspective and still retain the authority of his maleness, while he concomitantly draws upon the governess's feminine lack of authority for the complexity of his text. As female authors' frequent adoption of male pseudonyms suggests, a story bearing the signature of a man has commanded more respect, historically, than a story bearing the signature of a woman; hence, when James dons the "I" of the first-person narrator of *The Turn of the Screw*, his voice carries with it more authority than would that of a female writer engaged in the same activity. As a male writer writing in a female voice, then, James utilizes the gender power imbalance by taking it upon himself to represent femininity, at the same time that he distances himself from femininity through his masculine signature. This situation is exacerbated by the means through which he obtained the source of his story.

I

In the Preface (quoted in part on pp. 117–24) to the New York Edition of *The Turn of the Screw*, James locates the "origin" of the novella in a story he heard while visiting at a country house. James's male host related to James a tale he had been told by a woman. James writes: "The story would have been thrilling could she but have found herself in better possession of it" (118). Consequently, the feminine teller (whom James did not hear tell the story) is constructed as an inferior narrator through James's reflections. Nonetheless, although "on the surface there was n't much" (118) to her story, that story provides James with an opportunity to supply her text with the depth he believes it lacks.

As the superior author, James is able to contribute the writerly touches that will turn the unnamed woman's story into his own "master"/piece.

The ways in which the unnamed female source is delegitimized in James's Preface are mirrored in the ways in which James's female protagonist is delegitimized in *The Turn of the Screw*. Just as James "eyed" and assessed the potential of the feminine tale that he later transformed into his literary text, so his unnamed narrator and Douglas "eye" and assess the governess and her tale before they relate her narrative. The female narratives are doubly buried, thus, first by James as the more adept teller of the unnamed woman's story, and later by Douglas and the narrator within the tale itself. This situation works to shape readers' responses to the governess, since she is distanced from her readers and, when she is finally allowed to speak, her "I" has become less commanding than either her author's "I" or the "I" of her tellers. As a result, *The Turn of the Screw* effectively dramatizes the disenfranchisement of feminine subjectivity.

Before proceeding, it is important to note the ways in which the feminine "I" functions in mimicry of the masculine "I." Because patriarchy does not accord a woman a position from which to speak, when she does assume a subject position — or performs as the "I" of the discourse — the "I" she adopts is displaced and deferred (Grosz 72). Since woman lacks man's subjective authority, her "I" serves as a shadow of his "I," or becomes a transformed "you" in relation to him.[1] We see this process at play in the production of *The Turn of the Screw*, which suggests that femininity is a mere masquerade of male subjectivity, in that male writers are shown to be more capable of performing as women (or telling women's stories) than women. This pattern reflects the position of women within patriarchy wherein they are "objectified," or turned into objects whose purpose is to support the male subject.

In psychoanalytic theory, subjectivity is defined by the space accorded to the "I" of discourse, or the position of the speaker in relation to the audience. This speaker/audience paradigm is apt, for in patriarchy women have performed as receivers rather than as speakers.[2]

---

[1]Luce Irigaray also argues this point when she contends that femininity is a form of masquerade: "I think the masquerade has to be understood as what women do in order to recuperate some element of desire, to participate in man's desire, but at the price of renouncing their own. In the masquerade, they submit to the dominant economy of desire in an attempt to remain 'on the market' in spite of everything. But they are there as objects for sexual enjoyment, not as those who enjoy" (133–34).

[2]For more information on Lacan's theories and their use in feminist practice, see Elizabeth Grosz's *Jacques Lacan: A Feminist Introduction,* Elizabeth Wright's *Psychoanalytic Criticism: Theory in Practice,* and Chris Weedon's *Feminist Practice & Poststructuralist Theory* (43–73).

Patriarchal subjectivity, as is evident in Jacques Lacan's work, depends upon the construction of a female audience for the affirmation of the male subject.[3] In other words, the creation of an audience is necessary to the position of the speaker, for a speaker is not a speaker unless he is speaking *to* someone (I use the male pronoun deliberately here). The desire for the object of one's attentions is a process that is integral to the constitution of the subject; desire *for* the Other affirms a sense of the subject's difference *from* the Other. This difference establishes the subject's status as "subject" through comparison with the "object." In patriarchy, woman — as the ultimate Other — is posited as the object of the male gaze; she is cast as the (passive) object that is watched rather than as the (active) subject who watches. The act of gazing, therefore, signals the assumption of a subject position.

Patriarchy bars woman both from subjectivity and the desire that is indicative of it. Defined as "lack" (devoid of the Phallus), a woman is denied her own sexuality when she is placed in a passive object position. Should she exhibit desire, and hence exhibit signs of subjectivity, she is derided, quelled, and dismissed. Any indication of desire on her part signals her attempt to perform as a subject of discourse, and this is a position that the patriarchal order cannot afford her, for it requires her objectification in order to affirm the subjectivity of the male.

The production and the construction of *The Turn of the Screw* highlight the problems inherent in a woman's assumption of subjectivity. James's narrative begins with a prologue in which the reader is introduced to a group of country-house guests seated around a fire, telling and listening to ghost stories. The prologue is "written" by an unnamed narrator and "read" by one of the guests, Douglas, who starts to tell a story told to him by a governess he knew as a youth. Rather than the teller, therefore, the governess, whose story comprises the bulk of *The Turn of the Screw*, is initially objectified as a character in Douglas's story.

It is unusual that readers encounter the governess's story by way of a prologue, for prologues rarely accompany a fictional work of the

---

[3]Lacan posits subjectivity in relation to the female object in *The Four Fundamental Concepts of Psycho-Analysis:* "What the voyeur is looking for and finds is merely a shadow, a shadow behind the curtain. There he will phantasize any magic of presence, the most graceful of girls, for example, even if on the other side there is only a hairy athlete" (182). He goes on to discuss the gaze in a gender-specific context: "The spectacle of the world, in this sense, appears to us as all-seeing. This is the phantasy to be found in the Platonic perspective of an absolute being to whom is transferred the quality of being all-seen. At the very level of the phenomenal experience of contemplation, this all-seeing aspect is to be found in the satisfaction of a woman who knows that she is being looked at, on condition that one does not show her that one knows that she knows" (75).

Victorian period. As a result, the presence of the prologue gives rise to questions as to why it is necessary, questions that I would suggest relate to the subject position the governess will assume in her story.[4] Ostensibly, the two narrators work to contextualize and explain the governess's narrative, which Douglas will shortly present; they legitimize the story that is to come. And the reasons why the story requires legitimization can be found in the contradictory significations of a governess's position in Victorian households. That is, the governess requires male validation because her employment as governess places her character in question (where it remains, since readers continue to disagree over her "reliability").

The problems that governesses generate in Victorian discourse arise from the problematic nature of single women and their sexuality, a sexuality which, because it connotes desire, serves as a marker of subjectivity. Governesses were single women employed to act as mother substitutes. Frequently lower class, or at least lower than the class of their employers, governesses were a source of controversy. In Victorian culture, women inhabited three generalized spaces: the mother, the whore, and the lunatic. As legitimate mother figures, women could not be sexual beings, for "respectable" women were posited as pure and asexual. Those women who displayed sexual inclinations were constructed as either whores or lunatics, a signal of the unacceptability of feminine sexuality. In that governesses served as mother substitutes, they performed the role of the "pure" woman; however, since they were single women, they also posed a threat to the structure of the home. As Mary Poovey discusses in relation to *Jane Eyre*, governesses were caught in a sexual double bind:

> That representations of the governess in the 1840s brought to her contemporaries' minds not just the middle-class ideal she was meant to reproduce, but the sexualized and often working-class women against whom she was expected to defend, reveals the mid-Victorian fear that the governess could not protect middle-class values because she could not be trusted to regulate her own sexuality. The lunatic's sexuality might have been . . . contained . . . but the prostitute's sexual aggression was undisguised; to introduce either such sexuality or such aggression into the middle-class home would have been tantamount to fomenting revolution. (131)

Poovey's argument demonstrates the ways in which the Victorian signification of "governess" slipped between mother, whore, and lunatic.

---

[4]This reading of the prologue is drawn, in part, from my *Disruption of the Feminine in Henry James;* the argument here, however, is quite different.

This in itself would necessitate the character reference which Douglas, as the governess's supporter, supplies for her in the prologue. To complicate matters further, the governess will perform as a speaking subject in her narrative, and, since the subject is constructed through desire, she must exhibit desire in order to assume this position. The narrator and Douglas, therefore, are trying to establish the governess's credentials as a good and "reputable" (read credible) woman, who is not a desiring subject; but her position as subject of her own narrative draws attention to the desire they attempt to downplay.

Although Douglas tries to dismiss the sexual connotations of the governess's position, he draws attention to her sexual attractions by admitting to his own infatuation with her. Douglas introduces the governess with the observation: " 'She was the most agreeable woman I 've ever known in her position; she 'd have been worthy of any whatever' " (23). Clearly, his audience picks up on the sexual implications of his statement, for Douglas goes on to add: " 'Oh yes; don't grin: I liked her extremely and am glad to this day to think she liked me too' " (23). Douglas's infatuation with the governess leads the fireside group to speculate on his relationship with her:

> "Well, if I don't know who she was in love with I know who *he* was."
> "She was ten years older," said her husband.
> "*Raison de plus* — at that age! But it's rather nice, his long reticence." . . .
> "The outbreak," I returned, "will make a tremendous occasion of Thursday night"; and every one so agreed with me that in the light of it we lost all attention for everything else. (24)

Yet Douglas's attraction to the governess works not to his disadvantage but to hers. If he is in love with the governess, then he is not a "reliable" judge of her character, an inference that would invalidate the character reference he provides for her.

Once Douglas has opened the discussion by highlighting the governess's appeal for him, her own potential as sexual being becomes the focus of discussion. The narrator suggests: " 'She was in love,' " to which Douglas responds, " 'You *are* acute. Yes, she was in love. That is she *had* been. That came out — she could n't tell her story without its coming out. I saw it, and she saw I saw it; but neither of us spoke of it' " (23). What was absent from Douglas's conversation with the governess (literally, here, the gap that was created by the governess's unspoken love interest) is filled when Douglas relates that conversation to the fireside group, and the mention of the governess's desire works to diminish her credibility.

Further, when Douglas characterizes the governess for his audience, he emphasizes her inexperience and sexual susceptibility. He describes her as "a fluttered anxious girl out of a Hampshire vicarage" (25) applying for her first position. According to Douglas, the governess was impressed with her prospective employer, who "was handsome and bold and pleasant, off-hand and gay and kind. He struck her, inevitably, as gallant and splendid" (25). Moreover, "she figured him as rich, but as fearfully extravagant — saw him all in a glow of high fashion, of good looks, of expensive habits, of charming ways with women" (25). The governess's predilection for the master is clear, and again, the attention of the fireside group focuses on the sexual connotations of Douglas's narrative:

> "The moral of which was of course the seduction exercised by the splendid young man. She succumbed to it."
> He [Douglas] got up and, as he had done the night before, went to the fire, gave a stir to a log with his foot, then stood a moment with his back to us. "She saw him only twice."
> "Yes, but that's just the beauty of her passion."
> A little to my surprise, on this, Douglas turned round to me. "It *was* the beauty of it." (27)

Douglas attempts to establish the governess's love as pure and beautiful (hence, asexual), but his listeners receive a different impression, as their responses to Douglas's story indicate. Similarly, the way in which the governess is characterized by Douglas — young, inexperienced, nervous — renders her suspect and undermines the authority of her narrative. In addition, the prologue also works, on a different level, to characterize femininity, for the governess is not the only female figure who appears in the opening pages of the story.

Interestingly, as Douglas is about to read the governess's story, the group around the fire becomes smaller:

> The departing ladies who had said they would stay did n't, of course, thank heaven, stay: they departed, in consequence of arrangements made, in a rage of curiosity, as they professed, produced by the touches with which he had already worked us up. But that only made his little final auditory more compact and select, kept it, round the hearth, subject to a common thrill. (25)

Although the departure of the "ladies" here appears to be of little consequence, it works to establish traditional views of women as superfluous — changeable, flighty — best dispensed with so as to provide the group left, presumably largely male, with a "common thrill." The structure of the audience, therefore, resembles a peep show, and that which will be peeped at are the governess's secrets. As the object of speculation, as well as the object of the predominantly male audience's gaze, the governess's assumption of subject status, apparent in the "I" of her narrative, is undercut even before she begins to speak.

The governess's story, which Douglas begins to read from her first-person narrative, has been structurally trivialized as a result of the prologue. Hence, when the shift from the unnamed narrator's "I" to the governess's "I" occurs, her "I" commands less authority than her male counterpart's. In effect, as the story has demonstrated through the introductory prologue and the departure of the female guests, the governess is at a disadvantage when she assumes the "I" and the "eye" of the narrative; her delegitimization is one of the factors contributing to the confusion over her credibility as a narrator. If readers interpret the tale as a story of possession, they will accept the governess as a suitable mother-substitute figure who is necessarily asexual; if readers interpret the tale as a story of madness, the governess's sexuality will serve as evidence of her insanity. The governess's viability as a narrator thus depends upon the repression of her sexuality,[5] at the same time that her desire is necessary to her performance as a subject.

II

The male gaze of the fireside group, which has worked to color readers' reception of the governess, resurfaces in the story she relates. While walking in the grounds of Bly, the governess herself constructs a fictive male gaze. Although this construction indicates the governess's own desire for objectification (a situation not unusual in patriarchy, for patriarchy conditions women to welcome their own commodification[6]), it also serves as an indication of the governess's desire for a male companion, presumably, in this passage, the master in Harley Street:

> One of the thoughts that, as I don't in the least shrink now from noting, used to be with me in these wanderings was that it would be as charming as a charming story suddenly to meet some one.

[5]Although he argues to a different purpose, Edmund Wilson was one of the first critics to name the unnamable — the governess's repressed sexuality — which led him to perceive her as deranged (see Wilson's article "The Ambiguity of Henry James").

[6]For further examples of women's conditioned desire for objectification, see Naomi Wolf's *The Beauty Myth*.

> Some one would appear there at the turn of a path and would stand before me and smile and approve. I did n't ask more than that — I only asked that he should *know;* and the only way to be sure he knew would be to see it, and the kind light of it, in his handsome face. That was exactly present to me — by which I mean the face was — when, on the first of these occasions, at the end of a long June day, I stopped short on emerging from one of the plantations and coming into view of the house. (37)

The governess does not encounter the master, but rather a male figure atop a tower; this man "only peeps" (46), yet his peeping signals his effort to subvert the governess's subject status by constructing her as the object of his gaze. The appearance of the male apparition, however, also underscores the sexual subtext of the governess's thought, and thereby affirms the governess's sexuality and her subjectivity. The man, whom readers later learn is Peter Quint, is standing at the top of one of a pair of phallic towers that "were probably architectural absurdities, redeemed in a measure indeed by not being wholly disengaged nor of a height too pretentious, dating, in their gingerbread antiquity, from a romantic revival that was already a respectable past" (38). Quint's figure, "very erect, as it struck me" (39), highlights the sexual implications of the governess's sighting, and emphasizes her possession of a potentially dangerous sexuality.

The gazes constructed in the narrative are problematic, in keeping with the governess's assumption of a subject position. Initially, the governess fantasizes herself as the object of the gaze of the master in Harley Street. Quint assumes the master's place when he "peeps" at her, and re-constructs her as the object of his gaze, a situation that is exemplified in her next meeting with him:

> He was the same — he was the same, and seen, this time, as he had been seen before, from the waist up, the window, though the dining-room was on the ground floor, not going down to the terrace on which he stood. His face was close to the glass, yet the effect of this better view was, strangely, just to show me how intense the former had been. He remained but a few seconds — long enough to convince me he also saw and recognized; but it was as if I had been looking at him for years and had known him always. Something, however, happened this time that had not happened before; his stare into my face, through the glass and across the room, was as deep and hard as then, but it quitted me for a moment during which I could still watch it, see it fix successively several other things. (43)

Although initially Quint is posited as the gazer in this scene, the gaze shifts when the governess usurps his position.[7] She becomes the gazer when she steps outside, takes Quint's place, and peers through the window herself. This is a significant moment in the story, since the gaze serves as a marker of sexuality and control.

As film theorists have argued, when a woman "sees" clearly, her transformation from spectacle (object) into spectator (subject) is highlighted.[8] Hence, when the governess (who is posited as the object of Quint's gaze twice) appropriates Quint's gaze, her action serves to indicate her intention to appropriate his place. The governess is in the process of assuming a position of (male) authority, and the difficulties of her endeavor are figured when her view is impeded. The governess tries to master the gaze by looking through the window as Quint has done, but her gaze is arrested by Mrs. Grose — a representation of maternal respectability. Symbolically, the patriarchally inscribed mother role must be overcome in order for the governess to perform as a subject.

The female models with which the governess is faced at Bly signal the traditional spaces inhabited by women. The governess is confronted with the responsible mother figure in Mrs. Grose, the housekeeper, and the sexually fraught whore figure in Miss Jessel, the previous governess. Not surprisingly, it is Mrs. Grose, the "proper" feminine character, who alerts the governess to the dangers inherent in rejecting a patriarchally inscribed role, which she dramatizes through telling the story of Miss Jessel. In response to the governess's query about her predecessor ("'What was the lady who was here before?'"), Mrs. Grose explains:

> "The last governess? She was also young and pretty — almost as young and almost as pretty, Miss, even as you."

[7]It is not insignificant that the male whose gaze the governess seeks to appropriate is of a lower class, but it is not surprising. The class difference between the governess and Quint mitigates (but does not erase) the power imbalance that results from their gender difference.

[8]Mary Ann Doane stresses the importance of the female gaze in relation to cinematic representation: "The woman with glasses signifies simultaneously intellectuality and undesirability; but the moment she removes her glasses . . . she is transformed into spectacle, the very picture of desire. Now, it must be remembered that the cliché is a heavily loaded moment of signification, a social knot of meaning. It is characterized by an effect of ease and naturalness. Yet the cliché has a binding power so strong that it indicates a precise moment of ideological danger or threat — in this case, the woman's appropriation of the gaze. Glasses worn by a woman in the cinema do not signify a deficiency in seeing but an active looking, or even simply the fact of seeing as opposed to being seen. The intellectual woman looks and analyzes, and in usurping the gaze she poses a threat to an entire system of representation" (27). Doane's contention highlights the significance of the governess's assumption of the male gaze in *The Turn of the Screw*.

"Ah then I hope her youth and her beauty helped her. . . . Was she careful — particular?"

Mrs. Grose appeared to try to be conscientious. "About some things — yes."

"But not about all?"

Again she considered. "Well, Miss — she's gone. I won't tell tales." (34)

Miss Jessel, whose story is (not) told, constitutes a portrait of a woman fallen. Mrs. Grose confirms that Miss Jessel "*was* infamous" (56) and had dealings with the valet, Quint: " 'He did what he wished. . . . With them all' " (57). Mrs. Grose adds of Miss Jessel, " 'Poor woman — she paid for it!' " (57). Miss Jessel's acquiescence to Quint has wrought her downfall, but it is not acquiescence that "threatens" the governess, it is usurpation — she is performing as a subject, a position traditionally allotted to men.

III

The difficulties involved in the governess's effort to create a space for herself outside of patriarchal boundaries are metaphorically represented in her struggle for the children. While she believes she is engaged in a battle with the ghosts for the children's souls, she is also, symbolically, involved in overcoming patriarchal definitions of womanhood. Rejecting the ineffectual role played by Mrs. Grose, the respectable matron character, the governess attempts to define herself against the sexualized whore figure, Miss Jessel, as she tries to supplant the male-authority figure, Peter Quint. Neither of these roles can help her in her struggle for a subject position, however, as is made clear when the governess cannot replace Miss Jessel for Flora, or Quint for Miles. The governess does not want to assume Miss Jessel's place, and resists the negative connotations of feminine sexuality represented in the previous governess's characterization; but her attempt to perform like Quint is also doomed to failure, since she is not male and cannot usurp his position. She must perform as a *feminine* subject, but she has no model of feminine subjectivity to follow.

Flora becomes the battleground on which the story's three female characters struggle, since Flora, as the girl child, is being schooled into femininity. In one important passage, the governess sees Miss Jessel while she is supervising Flora. As the governess watches Miss Jessel, and thus assumes the position of the gazer, Flora indulges in what Edmund Wilson has flagged as sexual behavior [Ambiguity 173]: "She had

picked up a small flat piece of wood which happened to have in it a little
hole that had evidently suggested to her the idea of sticking in another
fragment that might figure as a mast and make the thing a boat" (54).
Flora's endeavor, here, is significant, for it signals both the need for
feminine subjectivity as well as the patriarchal fear of feminine sexuality.
Since Flora is unable to express her budding desire in anything other
than male terms — her (masculine) effort to penetrate a piece of wood
with a stick — the importance of the governess's project is
foregrounded because the governess is attempting to open a space that
would allow for the formulation and articulation of a positive feminine
sexuality. But, that Flora is exhibiting desire, a desire that is denied to
Victorian women, also points to the dangers that desiring female role
models pose to girls growing into patriarchally defined womanhood,
which has no place for constructive feminine sexuality. Neither of
Flora's female teachers can help her, for Miss Jessel, who has succumbed
to her desire, has become a whore figure, and the present governess,
who displays desire as a subject, is a sexualized but patriarchally undefin-
able figure at this point. While Flora would not think in these terms, the
confusion the two governesses engender in her is apparent in her sexually transgressive behavior.

Later in the story Flora escapes to the lake, and all of the female
characters meet in one scene. The governess confronts Miss Jessel in an
attempt to vanquish her, and, symbolically, to signify her rejection of
the whore role Miss Jessel represents. In so doing, she is attempting to
create a place for herself that departs from the asexual mother role
played by Mrs. Grose and the sexual whore role played by Miss Jessel.
The repercussions of the slippage in gender roles are dramatized when
Flora — who combines the traits of both traditional feminine character-
izations — shifts her status from innocent child to experienced woman.
The governess perceives Flora as "a vulgarly pert little girl in the street"
(99) whose "incomparable childish beauty had suddenly failed, had
quite vanished. I've said it already — she was literally, she was hideously
hard; she had turned common and almost ugly" (99). The governess
cannot offer Flora a model different from those offered by Miss Jessel or
Mrs. Grose because she has not yet forged such a place for herself; as a
result, Flora rejects the governess and returns to the safety of the roles
she knows. Flora cries to Mrs. Grose: " 'Take me away, take me away —
oh take me away from *her!* ' "(100), and reverts to a child-innocent status that is less fraught with gender-bending tension. The matronly Mrs.
Grose provides Flora with a "safe" if limited role model, which the gov-

erness, who has refused to conform to patriarchal definitions of womanhood, cannot offer her.

Because the governess cannot reassume the position of the mother,
Flora casts her in the only other feminine position with which she has
become familiar — she associates the governess with the sexualized
whore figure. Flora complains of the governess to Mrs. Grose, and
while Mrs. Grose does (not) repeat what Flora has told her, she indicates, through her omission, Flora's assessment of the governess:

> "I've *heard* — !"
> "Heard?"
> "From that child — horrors! There!" she sighed with tragic re-
> lief. "On my honour, Miss, she says things — !" . . .
> "She's so horrible?"
> I saw my colleague scarce knew how to put it. "Really shock-
> ing."
> "And about me?"
> "About you, Miss — since you must have it. It's beyond every-
> thing, for a young lady; and I can't think wherever she must have
> picked up — "
> "The appalling language she applies to me? I can then!" (104)

The governess's inability to offer Flora a role model leads to Flora's
indictment of her as a whore figure. Steering between the good mother
role and the whore role, the governess's own place in the narrative is
indeterminate. Although her sexuality situates her in the whore space,
the governess refuses to repress her desire and continues to perform as
a subject. This effort leads to her battle of wills with Quint, as the male
subject, for possession of Miles.

Left alone with Miles, after Mrs. Grose takes Flora from Bly, the
governess tries to extract a confession from him as to the reason he was
expelled from school. During the confession scene, Quint again peers in
the window: "Peter Quint had come into view like a sentinel before a
prison. The next thing I saw was that, from outside, he had reached the
window, and then I knew that, close to the glass and glaring in through
it, he offered once more to the room his white face of damnation"
(112). The governess, in effect, seeks to wrest the gaze from Quint, just
as she attempts to wrest Miles from him. As she confronts Miles, she is
aware of the gaze from the window:

> For there again, against the glass, as if to blight his confession and
> stay his answer, was the hideous author of our woe — the white

face of damnation. I felt a sick swim at the drop of my victory and
all the return of my battle, so that the wildness of my veritable
leap only served as a great betrayal. I saw him, from the midst of
my act, meet it with a divination, and on the perception that even
now he only guessed, and that the window was still to his own
eyes free, I let the impulse flame up to convert the climax of his
dismay into the very proof of his liberation. "No more, no more,
no more!" I shrieked to my visitant as I tried to press him against
me. (115–16)

The governess does displace Quint, since Miles had "jerked straight
round, stared, glared again, and seen but the quiet day" (116), and has
succeeded in mastering the gaze. But her mastery cannot be positive for
her since she cannot assume Quint's place. She does not yet understand
that her subjectivity must be established and cannot be appropriated;
feminine subjectivity involves more than a mimicry of male subjectivity.
Her victory over Quint, therefore, is only a Pyrrhic victory that leads to
the death of Miles: "We were alone with the quiet day, and his little
heart, dispossessed, had stopped" (116). When Miles's heart stops, so
does the paternal lineage at Bly, for the governess's ineffectual attempt
to usurp Quint's position results in the death of the male heir. This
conclusion, then, embodies the male anxiety that ensues from a
woman's refusal to play her patriarchally inscribed role. But, as the text
acknowledges male fears of eradication at the hands of powerful
women, it also draws attention to the need for feminine subjectivity.

The governess struggles to open a space for herself in patriarchal
discourse, a discourse that cannot afford her a place. Without an example of feminine subjectivity after which to model herself, the governess
attempts to disassociate herself from the whore position in which her
sexuality would necessarily locate her, and opts to masquerade as a male
subject. She does not recognize that her femininity impedes her from
performing as a man. Whether James intended to write a tale that de-
picted the difficulties inherent in a woman's assumption of a subject
position, or to produce a story that demonstrated the threat engendered
by such an assumption, his story effectively draws attention to the patriarchal boundaries that work to confine women's sexuality and subjectivity. Miles's death foregrounds the ways in which feminine insurgence
jeopardizes the status quo. And the governess, who has attempted to
appropriate a place not accorded to her within the triptych of patriarchal
feminine constructions — mother, whore, lunatic — is forced back
within patriarchal confines. Should the reader accept the ghosts as
"real," then the governess can serve as a mother figure like Mrs. Grose.

Should the reader reject this interpretation, there is only one conventional explanation that would account for the governess's behavior, as the critical controversy that surrounds the story suggests. Indeed, if Mrs. Grose is the "good mother," and Miss Jessel, the "whore," then the governess occupies the only feminine role left open to her when critics label her "mad" and position her within the feminine triptych as the "lunatic."

WORKS CITED

Doane, Mary Ann. *Femme Fatales: Feminism, Film Theory, Psychoanalysis.* New York: Routledge, 1991.

Grosz, Elizabeth. *Jacques Lacan: A Feminist Introduction.* London: Routledge, 1990.

Irigaray, Luce. *This Sex Which Is Not One.* Trans. Catherine Porter. Ithaca: Cornell UP, 1985.

James, Henry. Preface to *The Ambassadors. The Art of the Novel.* Ed. R. P. Blackmur. New York: Scribner's, 1962. 307–26.

Lacan, Jacques. *The Four Fundamental Concepts of Psycho-Analysis.* Ed. Jacques-Alain Miller. Trans. Alan Sheridan. New York: Norton, 1981.

Poovey, Mary. *Uneven Developments: The Ideological Work of Gender in Mid-Victorian England.* Chicago: U of Chicago P, 1988.

Seltzer, Mark. *Henry James and the Art of Power.* Ithaca: Cornell UP, 1984.

Walton, Priscilla L. *The Disruption of the Feminine in Henry James.* Toronto: U of Toronto P, 1992.

Weedon, Chris. *Feminist Practice & Poststructuralist Theory.* New York: Basil Blackwell, 1987.

Wilson, Edmund. "The Ambiguity of Henry James." *Hound and Horn* 7 (1938): 385–406. Rpt. in *The Triple Thinkers*, rev. and enl. ed. New York: Oxford UP, 1948. 88–132.

Wolf, Naomi. *The Beauty Myth.* Toronto: Random, 1990.

Wright, Elizabeth. *Psychoanalytic Criticism: Theory in Practice.* London: Routledge, 1984.

Marxist Criticism

and

The Turn of the Screw

WHAT IS MARXIST CRITICISM?

To the question "What is Marxist criticism?" it may be tempting to respond with another question: "What does it matter?" In light of the rapid and largely unanticipated demise of Soviet-style communism in the former USSR and throughout Eastern Europe, it is understandable to suppose that Marxist literary analysis would disappear too, quickly becoming an anachronism in a world enamored with full market capitalism.

In fact, however, there is no reason why Marxist criticism should weaken, let alone disappear. It is, after all, a phenomenon distinct from Soviet and Eastern European communism, having had its beginnings nearly eighty years before the Bolshevik revolution and having thrived, since the 1940s, mainly in the West — not as a form of communist propaganda but rather as a form of critique, a discourse for interrogating *all* societies and their texts in terms of certain specific issues. Those issues — including race, class, and the attitudes shared within a given culture — are as much with us as ever, not only in contemporary Russia but also in the United States.

The argument could even be made that Marxist criticism has been strengthened by the collapse of Soviet-style communism. There was a time, after all, when few self-respecting Anglo-American journals would use Marxist terms or models, however illuminating, to analyze Western issues or problems. It smacked of sleeping with the enemy. With the collapse of the Kremlin, however, old taboos began to give way. Even the staid *Wall Street Journal* now seems comfortable using phrases like "worker alienation" to discuss the problems plaguing the American business world.

The assumption that Marxist criticism will die on the vine of a moribund political system rests in part on another mistaken assumption, namely, that Marxist literary analysis is practiced only by people who would like to see society transformed into a Marxist-communist state, one created through land reform, the redistribution of wealth, a tightly and centrally managed economy, the abolition of institutionalized religion, and so on. In fact, it has never been necessary to be a communist political revolutionary to be classified as a Marxist literary critic. (Many of the critics discussed in this introduction actually *fled* communist societies to live in the West.) Nor is it necessary to like only those literary works with a radical social vision or to dislike books that represent or even reinforce a middle-class, capitalist world-view. It is necessary, however, to adopt what most students of literature would consider a radical definition of the purpose and function of literary criticism.

More traditional forms of criticism, according to the Marxist critic Pierre Macherey, "set . . . out to deliver the text from its own silences by coaxing it into giving up its true, latent, or hidden meaning." Inevitably, however, non-Marxist criticism "intrude[s] its own discourse between the reader and the text" (qtd. in Bennett 107). Marxist critics, by contrast, do not attempt to discover hidden meanings in texts. Or, if they do, they do so only after seeing the text, first and foremost, as a material product to be understood in broadly historical terms. That is to say, a literary work is first viewed as a product *of* work (and hence of the realm of production and consumption we call economics). Second, it may be looked upon as a work that *does* identifiable work of its own. At one level, that work is usually to enforce and reinforce the prevailing ideology, that is, the network of conventions, values, and opinions to which the majority of people uncritically subscribe.

This does not mean that Marxist critics merely describe the obvious. Quite the contrary: the relationship that the Marxist critic Terry Eagleton outlines in *Criticism and Ideology* (1978) among the soaring cost of books in the nineteenth century, the growth of lending libraries, the practice of publishing "three-decker" novels (so that three borrowers could be reading the same book at the same time), and the changing *content* of those novels is highly complex in its own way. But the complexity Eagleton finds is not that of the deeply buried meaning of the text. Rather, it is that of the complex web of social and economic relationships that were prerequisite to the work's production. Marxist criticism does not seek to be, in Eagleton's words, "a passage from text to reader." Indeed, "its task is to show the text as it cannot know itself, to manifest those conditions of its making (inscribed in its very letter) about which it is necessarily silent" (43).

As everyone knows, Marxism began with Karl Marx, the nineteenth-century German philosopher best known for writing *Das Kapital,* the seminal work of the communist movement. What everyone doesn't know is that Marx was also the first Marxist literary critic (much as Sigmund Freud, who psychoanalyzed E. T. A. Hoffman's supernatural tale "The Sandman," was the first Freudian literary critic). During the 1830s Marx wrote critical essays on writers such as Goethe and Shakespeare (whose tragic vision of Elizabethan disintegration he praised).

The fact that Marxist literary criticism began with Marx himself is hardly surprising, given Marx's education and early interests. Trained in the classics at the University of Bonn, Marx wrote literary imitations, his own poetry, a failed novel, and a fragment of a tragic drama (*Oulanem*) before turning to contemplative and political philosophy. Even after he met Friedrich Engels in 1843 and began collaborating on works such as *The German Ideology* and *The Communist Manifesto,* Marx maintained a keen interest in literary writers and their works. He and Engels argued about the poetry of Heinrich Heine, admired Hermann Freiligrath (a poet critical of the German aristocracy), and faulted the playwright Ferdinand Lassalle for writing about a reactionary knight in the Peasants' War rather than about more progressive aspects of German history.

As these examples suggest, Marx and Engels would not — indeed, could not — think of aesthetic matters as being distinct and independent from such things as politics, economics, and history. Not surprisingly, they viewed the alienation of the worker in industrialized, capitalist societies as having grave consequences for the arts. How can people mechanically stamping out things that bear no mark of their producer's individuality (people thereby "reified," turned into things themselves) be expected to recognize, produce, or even consume things of beauty? And if there is no one to consume something, there will soon be no one to produce it, especially in an age in which production (even of something like literature) has come to mean *mass* (and therefore profitable) production.

In *The German Ideology* (1846), Marx and Engels expressed their sense of the relationship between the arts, politics, and basic economic reality in terms of a general social theory. Economics, they argued, provides the "base" or "infrastructure" of society, but from that base emerges a "superstructure" consisting of law, politics, philosophy, religion, and art.

Marx later admitted that the relationship between base and superstructure may be indirect and fluid: every change in economics may not be reflected by an immediate change in ethics or literature. In *The Eighteenth Brumaire of Louis Bonaparte* (1852), he came up with the word *homology* to describe the sometimes unbalanced, often delayed, and almost always loose correspondence between base and superstructure. And later in that same decade, while working on an introduction to his *Political Economy,* Marx further relaxed the base-superstructure relationship. Writing on the excellence of ancient Greek art (versus the primitive nature of ancient Greek economics), he conceded that a gap sometimes opens up between base and superstructure — between economic forms and those produced by the creative mind.

Nonetheless, *at* base the old formula was maintained. Economics remained basic and the connection between economics and superstructural elements of society was reaffirmed. Central to Marxism and Marxist literary criticism was and is the following "materialist" insight: consciousness, without which such things as art cannot be produced, is not the source of social forms and economic conditions. It is, rather, their most important product.

Marx and Engels, drawing upon the philosopher G. W. F. Hegel's theories about the dialectical synthesis of ideas out of theses and antitheses, believed that a revolutionary class war (pitting the capitalist class against a proletarian, antithetical class) would lead eventually to the synthesis of a new social and economic order. Placing their faith not in the idealist Hegelian dialectic but, rather, in what they called "dialectical materialism," they looked for a secular and material salvation of humanity — one in, not beyond, history — via revolution and not via divine intervention. And they believed that the communist society eventually established would be one capable of producing new forms of consciousness and belief and therefore, ultimately, great art.

The revolution anticipated by Marx and Engels did not occur in their century, let alone lifetime. When it finally did take place, it didn't happen in places where Marx and Engels had thought it might be successful: the United States, Great Britain, and Germany. It happened, rather, in 1917 Russia, a country long ruled by despotic czars but also enlightened by the works of powerful novelists and playwrights, including Chekhov, Pushkin, Tolstoy, and Dostoyevsky.

Perhaps because of its significant literary tradition, Russia produced revolutionaries like Nikolai Lenin, who shared not only Marx's interest in literature but also his belief in literature's ultimate importance. But it was not without some hesitation that Lenin endorsed the significance of texts written during the reign of the czars. Well before 1917 he had questioned what the relationship should be between a society undergoing a revolution and the great old literature of its bourgeois past.

Lenin attempted to answer that question in a series of essays on Tolstoy that he wrote between 1908 and 1911. Tolstoy — the author of *War and Peace* and *Anna Karenina* — was an important nineteenth-century Russian writer whose views did not accord with all of those of young Marxist revolutionaries. Continuing interest in a writer like Tolstoy may be justified, Lenin reasoned, given the primitive and unenlightened economic order of the society that produced him. Since superstructure usually lags behind base (and is therefore usually *more* primitive), the attitudes of a Tolstoy were relatively progressive when viewed in light of the monarchical and precapitalist society out of which they arose.

Moreover, Lenin also reasoned, the writings of the great Russian realists would *have* to suffice, at least in the short run. Lenin looked forward, in essays like "Party Organization and Party Literature," to the day in which new artistic forms would be produced by progressive writers with revolutionary political views and agendas. But he also knew that a great proletarian literature was unlikely to evolve until a thoroughly literate proletariat had been produced by the educational system.

Lenin was hardly the only revolutionary leader involved in setting up the new Soviet state who took a strong interest in literary matters. In 1924 Leon Trotsky published a book called *Literature and Revolution*, which is still acknowledged as a classic of Marxist literary criticism.

Trotsky worried about the direction in which Marxist aesthetic theory seemed to be going. He responded skeptically to groups like Proletkult, which opposed tolerance toward pre- and non-revolutionary writers, and which called for the establishment of a new, proletarian culture. Trotsky warned of the danger of cultural sterility and risked unpopularity by pointing out that there is no necessary connection between the quality of a literary work and the quality of its author's politics.

In 1927 Trotsky lost a power struggle with Josef Stalin, a man who believed, among other things, that writers should be "engineers" of "human souls." After Trotsky's expulsion from the Soviet Union, views held by groups like Proletkult and the Left Front of Art (LEF), and by theorists such as Nikolai Bukharin and A. A. Zhdanov, became more prevalent. Speaking at the First Congress of the Union of Soviet Writers in 1934, the Soviet author Maxim Gorky called for writing that would "make labor the principal hero of our books." It was at the same writers' congress that "socialist realism," an art form glorifying workers and the revolutionary State, was made Communist party policy and the official literary form of the USSR.

Of those critics active in the USSR after the expulsion of Trotsky and the unfortunate triumph of Stalin, two critics stand out. One, Mikhail Bakhtin, was a Russian, later a Soviet, critic who spent much of his life in a kind of internal exile. Many of his essays were written in the 1930s and not published in the West or translated until the late 1960s. His work comes out of an engagement with the Marxist intellectual tradition as well as out of an indirect, even hidden, resistance to the Soviet government. It has been important to Marxist critics writing in the West because his theories provide a means to decode submerged social critique, especially in early modern texts. He viewed language — especially literary texts — in terms of discourses and dialogues. Within a novel written in a society in flux, for instance, the narrative may include an official, legitimate discourse, plus another infiltrated by challenging comments and even retorts. In a 1929 book on Dostoyevsky and a 1940 study titled *Rabelais and His World,* Bakhtin examined what he calls "polyphonic" novels, each characterized by a multiplicity of voices or discourses. In Dostoyevsky the independent status of a given character is marked by the difference of his or her language from that of the narrator. (The narrator's voice, too, can in fact be a dialogue.) In works by Rabelais, Bakhtin finds that the (profane) language of the carnival and of other popular festivals plays against and parodies the more official discourses, that is, of the king, church, or even socially powerful intellectuals. Bakhtin influenced modern cultural criticism by showing, in a sense, that the conflict between "high" and "low" culture takes place not only between classic and popular texts but also between the "dialogic" voices that exist within many books — whether "high" or "low."

The other subtle Marxist critic who managed to survive Stalin's dictatorship and his repressive policies was Georg Lukács. A Hungarian who had begun his career as an "idealist" critic, Lukács had converted to Marxism in 1919; renounced his earlier, Hegelian work shortly thereafter; visited Moscow in 1930–31; and finally emigrated to the USSR in 1933, just one year before the First Congress of the Union of Soviet Writers met. Lukács was far less narrow in his views than the most strident Stalinist Soviet critics of the 1930s and 1940s. He disliked much socialist realism and appreciated prerevolutionary, realistic novels that broadly reflected cultural "totalities" — and were populated with characters representing human "types" of the author's place and time. (Lukács was particularly fond of the historical canvasses painted by the early nineteenth-century novelist Sir Walter Scott.) But like his more rigid and censorious contemporaries, he drew the line at accepting non-revolutionary, modernist works like James Joyce's *Ulysses*. He con-demned movements like Expressionism and Symbolism, preferring works with "content" over more decadent, experimental works charac-terized mainly by "form."

With Lukács its most liberal and tolerant critic from the early 1930s until well into the 1960s, the Soviet literary scene degenerated to the point that the works of great writers like Franz Kafka were no longer read, either because they were viewed as decadent, formal experiments or because they "engineered souls" in "nonprogressive" directions. Of-ficially sanctioned works were generally ones in which artistry lagged far behind the politics (no matter how bad the politics were).

Fortunately for the Marxist critical movement, politically radical critics *outside* the Soviet Union were free of its narrow, constricting pol-icies and, consequently, able fruitfully to develop the thinking of Marx, Engels, and Trotsky. It was these non-Soviet Marxists who kept Marxist critical theory alive and useful in discussing all *kinds* of literature, written across the entire historical spectrum.

Perhaps because Lukács was the best of the Soviet communists writ-ing Marxist criticism in the 1930s and 1940s, non-Soviet Marxists tended to develop their ideas by publicly opposing those of Lukács. German dramatist and critic Bertolt Brecht countered Lukács by ar-guing that art ought to be viewed as a field of production, not as a container of "content." Brecht also criticized Lukács for his attempt to enshrine realism at the expense not only of other "isms" but also of poetry and drama, both of which had been largely ignored by Lukács.

Even more outspoken was Brecht's critical champion Walter Benjamin, a German Marxist who, in the 1930s, attacked those conven-tional and traditional literary forms conveying a stultifying "aura" of culture. Benjamin praised Dadaism and, more important, new forms of art ushered in by the age of mechanical reproduction. Those forms — including radio and film — offered hope, he felt, for liberation from capitalist culture, for they were too new to be part of its stultifyingly ritualistic traditions.

But of all the anti-Lukácsians outside the USSR who made a contribution to the development of Marxist literary criticism, the most important was probably Théodor Adorno. Leader since the early 1950s of the Frankfurt school of Marxist criticism, Adorno attacked Lukács for his dogmatic rejection of nonrealist modern literature and for his belief in the primacy of content over form. Art does not equal science, Adorno insisted. He went on to argue for art's autonomy from empirical forms of knowledge, and to suggest that the interior monologues of modernist works (by Beckett and Proust) reflect the fact of modern alienation in a way that Marxist criticism ought to find compelling.

In addition to turning against Lukács and his overly constrictive canon, Marxists outside the Soviet Union were able to take advantage of insights generated by non-Marxist critical theories being developed in post–World War II Europe. One of the movements that came to be of interest to non-Soviet Marxists was structuralism, a scientific approach to the study of humankind whose proponents believed that all elements of culture, including literature, could be understood as parts of a system of signs. Using modern linguistics as a model, structuralists like Claude Lévi-Strauss broke the myths of various cultures down into "mythemes" in an attempt to show that there are structural correspondences or homologies between the mythical elements produced by various human communities across time.

Of the European structuralist Marxists, one of the most influential was Lucien Goldmann, a Rumanian critic living in Paris. Goldmann combined structuralist principles with Marx's base-superstructure model in order to show how economics determines the mental structures of social groups, which are reflected in literary texts. Goldmann rejected the idea of individual human genius, choosing to see works, instead, as the "collective" products of "trans-individual" mental structures. In early studies, such as *The Hidden God* (1955), he related seventeenth-century French texts (such as Racine's *Phèdre*) to the ideology of Jansenism. In later works, he applied Marx's base-superstructure model even more strictly, describing a relationship between economic conditions and texts unmediated by an intervening, collective consciousness.

In spite of his rigidity and perhaps because of his affinities with structuralism, Goldmann came to be seen in the 1960s as the proponent of a kind of watered-down, "humanist" Marxism. He was certainly viewed that way by the French Marxist Louis Althusser, a disciple not of Lévi-Strauss and structuralism but rather of the psychoanalytic theorist Jacques Lacan and of the Italian communist Antonio Gramsci, famous for his writings about ideology and "hegemony." (Gramsci used the latter word to refer to the pervasive, weblike system of assumptions and values that shapes the way things look, what they mean, and therefore what reality *is* for the majority of people within a culture.)

Like Gramsci, Althusser viewed literary works primarily in terms of their relationship to ideology, the function of which, he argued, is to (re)produce the existing relations of production in a given society. Dave Laing, in *The Marxist Theory of Art* (1978), has attempted to explain this particular insight of Althusser's by saying that ideologies, through the "ensemble of habits, moralities, and opinions" that can be found in any literary text, "ensure that the work-force (and those responsible for re-producing them in the family, school, etc.) are maintained in their position of subordination to the dominant class" (91). This is not to say that Althusser thought of the masses as a brainless multitude following only the dictates of the prevailing ideology: Althusser followed Gramsci in suggesting that even working-class people have some freedom to struggle against ideology and to change history. Nor is it to say that Althusser saw ideology as being a coherent, consistent force. In fact, he saw it as being riven with contradictions that works of literature sometimes expose and even widen. Thus Althusser followed Marx and Gramsci in believing that although literature must be seen in *relation* to ideology, it — like all social forms — has some degree of autonomy.

Althusser's followers included Pierre Macherey, who in *A Theory of Literary Production* (1966) developed Althusser's concept of the relationship between literature and ideology. A realistic novelist, he argued, attempts to produce a unified, coherent text, but instead ends up producing a work containing lapses, omissions, gaps. This happens because within ideology there are subjects that cannot be covered, things that cannot be said, contradictory views that aren't recognized as contradictory. (The critic's challenge, in this case, is to supply what the text cannot say, thereby making sense of gaps and contradictions.)

But there is another reason why gaps open up and contradictions become evident in texts. Works don't just reflect ideology (which Goldmann had referred to as "myth" and which Macherey refers to as a system of "illusory social beliefs"); they are also "fictions," works of art, *products* of ideology that have what Goldmann would call a "world-view" to offer. What kind of product, Macherey implicitly asks, is identical to the thing that produced it? It is hardly surprising, then, that Balzac's fiction shows French peasants in two different lights, only one of which is critical and judgmental, only one of which is baldly ideological. Writing approvingly on Macherey and Macherey's mentor Althusser in *Marxism and Literary Criticism* (1976), Terry Eagleton says: "It is by giving ideology a determinate form, fixing it within certain fictional limits, that art is able to distance itself from [ideology], thus revealing . . . [its] limits" (19).

A follower of Althusser, Macherey is sometimes referred to as a "post-Althusserian Marxist." Eagleton, too, is often described that way, as is his American contemporary, Fredric Jameson. Jameson and Eagleton, as well as being post-Althusserians, are also among the few Anglo-American critics who have closely followed and significantly developed Marxist thought.

Before them, Marxist interpretation in English was limited to the work of a handful of critics: Christopher Caudwell, Christopher Hill, Arnold Kettle, E. P. Thompson, and Raymond Williams. Of these, Williams was perhaps least Marxist in orientation: he felt that Marxist critics, ironically, tended too much to isolate economics from culture; that they overlooked the individualism of people, opting instead to see them as "masses"; and that even more ironically, they had become an elitist group. But if the least Marxist of the British Marxists, Williams was also by far the most influential. Preferring to talk about "culture" instead of ideology, Williams argued in works such as *Culture and Society 1780–1950* (1958) that culture is "lived experience" and, as such, an interconnected set of social properties, each and all grounded in and influencing history.

Terry Eagleton's *Criticism and Ideology* (1978) is in many ways a response to the work of Williams. Responding to Williams's statement, in *Culture and Society,* that "there are in fact no masses; there are only ways of seeing people as masses" (289), Eagleton writes: "That men and women really are now unique individuals was Williams's (unexceptionable) insistence; but it was a proposition bought at the expense of perceiving the fact that they must mass and fight to achieve their full individual humanity. One has only to adapt Williams's statement to 'There are in fact no classes; there are only ways of seeing people as classes' to expose its theoretical paucity" (*Criticism* 29).

Eagleton goes on, in *Criticism and Ideology,* to propose an elaborate theory about how history — in the form of "general," "authorial," and "aesthetic" ideology — enters texts, which in turn may revivify, open up, or critique those same ideologies, thereby setting in motion a process that may alter history. He shows how texts by Jane Austen, Matthew Arnold, Charles Dickens, George Eliot, Joseph Conrad, and T. S. Eliot deal with and transmute conflicts at the heart of the general and authorial ideologies behind them: conflicts between morality and individualism, individualism and social organicism and utilitarianism.

As all this emphasis on ideology and conflict suggests, a modern British Marxist like Eagleton, even while acknowledging the work of a British Marxist predecessor like Williams, is more nearly developing the ideas of continental Marxists like Althusser and Macherey. That holds, as well, for modern American Marxists like Fredric Jameson. For although he makes occasional, sympathetic references to the works of Williams, Thompson, and Hill, Jameson makes far more *use* of Lukács, Adorno, and Althusser as well as non-Marxist structuralist, psychoanalytic, and poststructuralist critics.

In the first of several influential works, *Marxism and Form* (1971), Jameson takes up the question of form and content, arguing that the former is "but the working out" of the latter "in the realm of superstructure" (329). (In making such a statement Jameson opposes not only the tenets of Russian Formalists, for whom content had merely been the fleshing out of form, but also those of so-called vulgar Marxists, who tended to define form as mere ornamentation or window-dressing.) In his later work *The Political Unconscious* (1981), Jameson uses what in *Marxism and Form* he had called "dialectical criticism" to synthesize out of structuralism and poststructuralism, Freud and Lacan, Althusser and Adorno, a set of complex arguments that can only be summarized reductively.

The fractured state of societies and the isolated condition of individuals, he argues, may be seen as indications that there originally existed an unfallen state of something that may be called "primitive communism." History — which records the subsequent divisions and alienations — limits awareness of its own contradictions and of that lost, Better State, via ideologies and their manifestation in texts, whose strategies essentially contain and repress desire, especially revolutionary desire, into the collective unconscious. (In Conrad's *Lord Jim*, Jameson shows, the knowledge that governing classes don't *deserve* their power is contained and repressed by an ending that metaphysically blames Nature for the tragedy and that melodramatically blames wicked Gentleman Brown.)

As demonstrated by Jameson in analyses like the one mentioned above, textual strategies of containment and concealment may be discovered by the critic, but only by the critic practicing dialectical criticism, that is to say, a criticism aware, among other things, of its *own* status as ideology. All thought, Jameson concludes, is ideological; only through ideological thought that knows itself as such can ideologies be seen through and eventually transcended.

Bruce Robbins begins the essay that follows by reminding us that "the many varieties of Marxist criticism have two things in common. First they put texts into historical context. [Then] they try to change that context — to have an effect on history" (283). To place *The Turn of the Screw* in its historical context, Robbins looks at the story in relation to the history of English governesses and house servants.

Focusing on the relationship between the narrating governess and two ghosts — ghosts whose very ghostliness keeps us from thinking about them as real people, as house servants who led real lives and had real histories — Robbins suggests that James attempted to "resist" the kind of "historical interpretation" that would bring to bear a "knowledge of social groups and ideologies" (285). The ghosts, he suggests, are among the means James used to effect that resistance. "How can a critic talk about ideology," Robbins asks, "when the major characters are not social beings, but supernatural ones?" (285).

The fact that the governess's lower-class associates are ghosts is not surprising, Robbins's subsequent analysis of Douglas's narrative reveals, in that working-class people were *like* ghosts to their social superiors, who neither needed nor wanted to deal with them as real people and who usually only thought about them when the noises of their work drifted up from downstairs. Ironically, the same attitude toward the lower classes that made the death of the former governess a mere "awkwardness" for the master is replicated in the attitude of the governess-narrator toward her social inferiors, for although governesses were not free to associate with their masters, they also thought of themselves (and were thought of as being) several notches above house servants in the Victorian social hierarchy.

Focusing on passages and scenes in the story, Robbins goes on to show that what individuals were willing to say to one another, what they saw when they looked at one another, what they knew about themselves, and what they were willing to *admit* they knew about themselves were all functions of class and class consciousness. James's governess, for instance, will not allow herself to see the analogy between her own situation and the tragic story of Miss Jessel and Peter Quint, because to do so she would have to see that her own love for the master "is a sort of inverted parallel" (288) to Miss Jessel's love for a man of even lower social station.

Having shown, in the early pages of his essay, how James sought to resist historical readings of his story, Robbins turns his attentions to a consideration of the ways in which *The Turn of the Screw* "questions the society it describes more searchingly than [the governess] does" (291). To do so, he places a great deal of interpretive weight on a conversation between the governess and Miles, who seems to be able to see through the unfairness of the society that surrounds him because of the fact that he has been raised by servants in "bizarre isolation." "Without interference from the upper classes," Robbins contends, "the children have become little democrats, unable to see the sin in transgressing those class divisions that the adult world takes for granted" (293). Through the children, whom Robbins views as "innocent" in a "challenging sense," James — and perhaps even the governess — can see "what [the children] see," namely, "the absurdity of believing that 'the others' [i.e., members of the servant class] don't 'count' " (293).

Robbins proceeds by engaging in a fruitful discussion of the story's ending, which he places in the context of the romance tradition as understood by Fredric Jameson. And he ends his essay by bringing it full circle, by helping us see that it has that second feature all Marxist readings have in common, namely, the attempt to change the historical context in which we read, to have an actual *effect* on history. What he doesn't discuss is a less obvious feature his analysis has in common with other Marxist analyses — the tendency both to show that the text reinforces the prevailing ideology and, at the same time, to reveal those gaps that occasionally allow the author to show, and us to see, the tragic contradictions implicit in such an ideology.

Ross C Murfin

MARXIST CRITICISM: A SELECTED BIBLIOGRAPHY

Marx, Engels, Lenin, and Trotsky

Engels, Friedrich. *The Condition of the Working Class in England*. Ed. and trans. W. O. Henderson and W. H. Chaloner. Stanford: Stanford UP, 1968.

Lenin, V. I. *On Literature and Art*. Moscow: Progress, 1967.

Marx, Karl. *Selected Writings*. Ed. David McLellan. Oxford: Oxford UP, 1977.

Trotsky, Leon. *Literature and Revolution*. New York: Russell, 1967.

General Introductions to and Reflections on Marxist Criticism

Bennett, Tony. *Formalism and Marxism*. London: Methuen, 1979.

Demetz, Peter. *Marx, Engels, and the Poets*. Chicago: U of Chicago P, 1967.

Eagleton, Terry. *Literary Theory: An Introduction*. Minneapolis: U of Minnesota P, 1983. See chapter on Marxism.

————. *Marxism and Literary Criticism*. Berkeley: U of California P, 1976.

Elster, Jon. *An Introduction to Karl Marx*. Cambridge: Cambridge UP, 1985.

————. *Nuts and Bolts for the Social Sciences*. Cambridge: Cambridge UP, 1989.

Fokkema, D. W., and Elrud Kunne-Ibsch. *Theories of Literature in the Twentieth Century: Structuralism, Marxism, Aesthetics of Reception, Semiotics*. New York: St. Martin's, 1977. See ch. 4, "Marxist Theories of Literature."

Frow, John. *Marxism and Literary History*. Cambridge: Harvard UP, 1986.

Jefferson, Ann, and David Robey. *Modern Literary Theory: A Critical Introduction*. Totowa: Barnes, 1982. See the essay "Marxist Literary Theories," by David Forgacs.

Laing, Dave. *The Marxist Theory of Art*. Brighton, Eng.: Harvester, 1978.

Selden, Raman. *A Readers' Guide to Contemporary Literary Theory*. Lexington: U of Kentucky P, 1985. See ch. 2, "Marxist Theories."

Slaughter, Cliff. *Marxism, Ideology and Literature*. Atlantic Highlands: Humanities, 1980.

Some Classic Marxist Studies and Statements

Adorno, Théodor. *Prisms: Cultural Criticism and Society*. Trans. Samuel Weber and Sherry Weber. Cambridge: MIT P, 1982.

Althusser, Louis. *For Marx*. Trans. Ben Brewster. New York: Pantheon, 1969.

Althusser, Louis, and Etienne Balibar. *Reading Capital*. Trans. Ben Brewster. New York: Pantheon, 1971.

Bakhtin, Mikhail. *The Dialogic Imagination: Four Essays*. Ed. Michael Holquist. Trans. Caryl Emerson. Austin: U of Texas P, 1981.

———. *Rabelais and His World*. Trans. Hélène Iswolsky. Cambridge: MIT P, 1968.

Benjamin, Walter. *Illuminations*. Ed. with introd. by Hannah Arendt. Trans. H. Zohn. New York: Harcourt, 1968.

Caudwell, Christopher. *Illusion and Reality*. 1935. New York: Russell, 1955.

———. *Studies in a Dying Culture*. London: Lawrence, 1938.

Goldmann, Lucien. *The Hidden God*. New York: Humanities, 1964.

———. *Towards a Sociology of the Novel*. London: Tavistock, 1975.

Gramsci, Antonio. *Selections from the Prison Notebooks*. Ed. Quintin Hoare and Geoffrey Nowell Smith. New York: International UP, 1971.

Kettle, Arnold. *An Introduction to the English Novel*. New York: Harper, 1960.

Lukács, Georg. *The Historical Novel*. Trans. H. Mitchell and S. Mitchell. Boston: Beacon, 1963.

———. *Studies in European Realism*. New York: Grosset, 1964.

———. *The Theory of the Novel*. Cambridge: MIT P, 1971.

Marcuse, Herbert. *One-Dimensional Man*. Boston: Beacon, 1964.

Thompson, E. P. *The Making of the English Working Class*. New York: Pantheon, 1964.

———. *William Morris: Romantic to Revolutionary*. New York: Pantheon, 1977.

Williams, Raymond. *Culture and Society 1780–1950*. New York: Harper, 1958.

———. *The Long Revolution*. New York: Columbia UP, 1961.

———. *Marxism and Literature*. Oxford: Oxford UP, 1977.

Wilson, Edmund. *To the Finland Station*. Garden City: Doubleday, 1953.

Studies by and of Post-Althusserian Marxists

Dowling, William C. *Jameson, Althusser, Marx: An Introduction to "The Political Unconscious."* Ithaca: Cornell UP, 1984.

Eagleton, Terry. *Criticism and Ideology: A Study in Marxist Literary Theory*. London: Verso, 1978.

———. *Exiles and Émigrés*. New York: Schocken, 1970.

Jameson, Fredric. *Marxism and Form: Twentieth-Century Dialectical Theories of Literature*. Princeton: Princeton UP, 1971.

———. *The Political Unconscious: Narrative as a Socially Symbolic Act.* Ithaca: Cornell UP, 1981.

Macherey, Pierre. *A Theory of Literary Production*. Trans. G. Wall. London: Routledge, 1978.

Marxist Approaches to *The Turn of the Screw*

Fussell, Edwin. "The Ontology of *The Turn of the Screw*." *Journal of Modern Literature* 8 (1980): 118–28.

McMaster, Graham. "Henry James and India: A Historical Reading of *The Turn of the Screw*." *Clio* 18 (1988): 23–40.

Robbins, Bruce. "Shooting off James's Blanks: Theory, Politics, and *The Turn of the Screw*." *Henry James Review* 5 (1984): 192–99.

A MARXIST PERSPECTIVE

BRUCE ROBBINS

"They don't much count, do they?": The Unfinished History of *The Turn of the Screw*

The many varieties of Marxist criticism have two things in common. First, they put texts into historical context. But unlike certain other styles of historical criticism, they also do something else. They try to change that context — to have an effect on history.

The number of possible contexts into which any text could be placed may not be infinite, but it is certainly large. Setting out to interpret *The Turn of the Screw* historically, one might look for example at the England of the 1890s, in which Henry James was writing, or at the America of the 1840s and 1850s, in which he was growing up, or again at the America of the 1990s, in which we read him now. And within each of these periods, we might examine the story in its relation to very different histories. There is the history (or *her*story, as some feminists have begun to say) of women, which might urge us to see the governess, in a somewhat heroic light, as making a challenging entry into a wider world of employment. Or, on the contrary, we might see her as a male fantasy of the *femme fatale*. There is the history of education, which might encourage us to ask different questions, say, about the governess's desire to "possess" her pupils or about how serious the offense would have to be for a child like Miles to get expelled from boarding school. More obviously, there is the history of class; the unique discomforts of being a governess, who belongs neither with the masters far above her nor, quite, with the servants immediately below her, are inexplicable without it. The meaning of Quint's being "too free" (50) with the other servants is similarly inexplicable without the history of sexuality. The history of childhood might divert our attention from the controversy about the reality of the ghosts and focus it instead on taboos against speaking to children about topics like sex and death, taboos that from a child's point of view turn sex and death into ghostly half-realities. Perhaps James's story asks what it might mean for anyone, whether ghost or not, to "corrupt" children. The ghost-story genre has its own (literary) history. And then there is the social history of the literary marketplace, where ghost stories "sell" better than more "serious" fiction.

Marxist criticism can and does talk about any and all of these contexts. But for Marxist critics — and it is their politics I am talking about, not the far more diverse politics of the authors they analyze — the decision to say more about one and less about another in any given interpretation, and about what to look for within it, depends on a premise that Marx expressed in his famous "Theses on Feuerbach": "The philosophers have only *interpreted* the world differently, the point is, to *change* it" (Marx 199). The second and perhaps definitive assumption that Marxist criticism makes, in other words, is that history is unfinished, and that, however modestly, our interpretations should and will help push it in one direction or another, slow it down or speed it up.

I

In interpreting *The Turn of the Screw*, it may help to know that, since the beginnings of the English novel in the eighteenth century, the point of view of fictional servants and governesses has often been closely associated with those energies that have been pushing hardest to change the world. From Samuel Richardson's *Pamela* (1740) to Charlotte Brontë's *Jane Eyre* (1847) — which James's governess clearly has in mind when she alludes to "an unmentionable relative kept in unsuspected confinement" (39) — the servant or governess who is in love with a master far above her in wealth and rank, yet who somehow manages to marry him in the end, has carried with her the aspirations of generations of women and men who are discontented with the limited possibilities offered them by their society. Through such figures, the novel has refashioned the folktale of Cinderella into sophisticated allegories of collective upward mobility in which all those who did not own mansions like Bly could imaginatively participate.

What does all this imply about *The Turn of the Screw?* Like Pamela and Jane Eyre, James's governess does most of the narrating of her text, thus forcing us to identify, at least provisionally, with her perspective and her hopes. And like the other protagonists, she too is clearly in love with her distant master. Yet her version of the Cinderella story is frustrated, truncated, unfinished. She doesn't get the guy; indeed, she never even sees him again. In her own eyes, as she admits, she is trying her best to win his love by heroically protecting his niece and nephew from the ghosts. But heroic or not, she manages only to alienate Flora and to kill Miles — an outcome that doesn't become more pleasant to contemplate if one judges, as many readers do, that the ghosts are her own inventions or hallucinations. What happens, then, to the aspirations that the reader invests in her? Has James written a sort of counterargument to the Cinderella narrative, the darker allegory of a society in which hopes of upward mobility have come to seem misguided, doomed to failure, and horribly destructive?

Even if we agree to consider *The Turn of the Screw* as a class allegory, this is clearly not the whole truth about it. For one thing, the story has little to say about the governess's relations with the master. It has a great deal to say, on the other hand, about her relations with the ghosts. And odd as this may seem, it is her relations with the ghosts that lead us to the very heart of the story's reflections on social hierarchy and its refashioning of social allegory.

In the Preface to the 1908 edition of *The Turn of the Screw* (117–124 in this book), James states his intention not to specify the evil of the ghosts, but to leave it to the imagination of the reader. "I cast my lot with pure romance," he says (122). "There is not only from beginning to end of the matter not an inch of expatiation, but my values are positively all blanks" (123). James clearly resists historical interpretation, which would fill in these blanks with knowledge of social groups and ideologies, and he uses the ghosts in his resistance. How can a critic talk about ideology when the major characters are not social beings, but supernatural ones? On the other hand, whether or not the ghosts are real, they are definitely and unmistakably the ghosts *of a former servant* and *a former governess.* There is some doubt about what they *are,* but there is no doubt at all about what they *were*. And if one looks at the text with class in mind, one sees that *The Turn of the Screw* is systematic, indeed almost obsessive, in its confusion of ghosts and servants. Both categories are impalpable, alien, and threatening — at least, to their masters. Both seem (to their masters) to fill the house with unexplained noises, mysteries, signs of some other, unimaginable life. When the governess describes "the faint sense I had had, the first night, of . . . something undefinably astir in the house" (65), she sounds as if, instead of setting the mood for a ghost story, she were unconsciously describing a house where people live who don't count as people, people who are not supposed to be "present" in the full sense, who are there only for the convenience of the "real" inhabitants.

After all, it is intriguing how much the ghosts have in common, looked at from above, with servants who are *not* ghosts, who are very much alive. In Douglas's narrative at the opening of the story, we are given a paraphrase of the master's account of Miss Jessel, while interviewing the governess for her job: "She had done for them quite beautifully — she was a most respectable person — till her death, the great awkwardness of which had, precisely, left no alternative but the school for little Miles" (26). Think about the syntax of this sentence — "the great awkwardness of which" — and the choice of the word "awkwardness." Not only is there no expression of sympathy or other comment on the death, as one might have expected, but the speaker does not even consider the death important enough to bring the sentence to a close, thereby leaving a decent interval before returning to his business. Instead, the sentence rushes immediately on to another subordinate clause. (Significantly, the death itself is in a subordinate clause; dying doesn't even rate an independent clause of its own.) The sentence hastens on to the word "awkwardness," which of course refers exclusively and ostentatiously to the effect of the death on the master's arrangements, its *inconvenience* for *him*. Douglas's listeners do not miss the casual brutality of this; they ask whether the governess's position brought with it "necessary danger to life" (27). In a sense, this is just James's point: from the perspective of the master — though not, it seems, from the perspective of Douglas or his listeners — a governess's life doesn't matter. For him and his kind, Miss Jessel never *was* real. She was already a sort of ghost.

Douglas's narrative hammers this home: "There were, further, a cook, a housemaid, a dairywoman, an old pony, an old groom and an old gardener, all likewise thoroughly respectable" (26). The point is made, of course, with the pony. Cooks, ponies, and gardeners are equal, leveled out as items on a list of Bly's possessions; none of these servants counts more than an animal. Servants, like ghosts, are something less than human beings.

This idea must be suggested in *Douglas's* narrative, however, because the governess herself, in spite of her own in-between class position, shares much of the same hierarchical attitude as her master. If her master turns his subordinates into ghosts, so too in a sense does the governess. Consider the scene in which the governess gets the story of Quint and Jessel out of Mrs. Grose, the housekeeper: " 'Come, there was something between them,' " the governess insists. Mrs. Grose replies,

> "There was everything."
> "In spite of the difference — ?"
> "Oh of their rank, their condition" — she brought it woefully out. "*She* was a lady."
> I turned it over; I again saw. "Yes — she was a lady."
> "And he so dreadfully below," said Mrs. Grose.
> I felt that I doubtless need n't press too hard, in such company, on the place of a servant in the scale; but there was nothing to prevent an acceptance of my companion's own measure of my predecessor's abasement. (57)

The governess cannot agree openly with Mrs. Grose that Quint was "so dreadfully below" Miss Jessel without seeming to imply, impolitely, that Mrs. Grose is "dreadfully below" herself. When the social station of the person you are addressing is at stake, there are severe limits on what can be said. But everything the governess says about the ghosts is subject to such limits. And so is everything she hears. For if there are things that the governess cannot say to Mrs. Grose because of the class difference between them, the story invites us to see that there are also things Mrs. Grose will not be able to say to the governess, and for the same reason. Mrs. Grose's supposed belief in the reality of the ghosts (though she never actually sees them) is the only support the governess has when she fears that she herself may be "cruel" or "mad" (98). But could an inferior like Mrs. Grose ever tell her superior, "in supreme authority" at Bly (26), that she *was* cruel or mad? Aren't the housekeeper's "plunges of submission" (96) to the governess's view of things exactly that, moments of "submission" to the governess's authority?

Power and hierarchy interrupt what can be said, forcing communication into "obscure and roundabout allusions" (30). They even determine what can be *seen*. Arriving at the great house of Bly from a poor country parsonage, the governess notes that she has never before had the luxury of seeing her entire body, for she has never had access to such large mirrors: "the long glasses in which, for the first time, I could see myself from head to foot" (28). Even self-knowledge seems to depend, for James, on one's place and power in the social hierarchy. The hierarchical microcosm that James displays in *The Turn of the Screw* is therefore full of socially produced gaps, lapses, ambiguities. And it is in these spaces of necessary obscurity that the ghosts emerge and operate. To the extent that the story is about the ghosts, it is not merely (as everyone knows) about ambiguity; it is also about the *social production* of ambiguity.

Another reason for turning our attention to the ghosts after considering the governess's love for the master is that the forbidden love between Peter Quint and Miss Jessel (the fact that we are told his first name but not hers is another reminder of their class difference) is a sort of inverted parallel to it. The former governess, like the present governess, has allowed her erotic desires to stray across class lines; the only difference is that the object of Miss Jessel's feelings is someone below her on the social scale (Quint) rather than someone above her (the master in Harley Street). One might imagine, therefore, that the governess would recognize in the story of those tragic lovers something of her own longings. Of course she does not. On the contrary, their class transgression immediately brands them in her eyes as *evil* spirits rather than *good* spirits, which Henry James showed some interest in. (In James's notebook entry of January 22, 1888, for example, the ghost desires to "interpose, redeem, protect" [*Notebooks* 9].) Indeed, it seems at times as if the fact that Quint and Jessel appear to her as ghosts is less important and even less horrifying to the governess than the social violation they committed while they were alive.

Consider for example the conversation with Mrs. Grose in which the governess describes her first sighting of Quint. The man she saw on the tower was not a gentleman, the governess says. Mrs. Grose responds in an incomplete sentence: "But if he is n't a gentleman — " As so often, the governess fills in the blank herself: "What *is* he? He's a horror" (45). In order to be a horror, it appears, there is no need of supernatural props or special effects, no need to be a ghost at all. It is enough to occupy a gentleman's place, or to wear his clothes, without being a gentleman. Here the governess as much as admits that in her mind, supernatural evil cannot be readily distinguished from the "unnaturalness" of servants stepping out of their designated place.

The story's willingness to consider the ghosts less as supernatural

phenomena than as social phenomena, and more particularly as a servant and a governess who refuse to be bound by their station, can also
be deduced from the circumstances in which the ghosts are made to
appear. Each makes a carefully staged entry "below" the governess on
the staircase. In a society which routinely referred to class difference in
terms of "upstairs" (the domain of the masters) and "downstairs" (the
domain of the servants), these staircase scenes are heavily charged with
the symbolism of hierarchy. "I knew that there was a figure on the
stair. . . . The apparition had reached the landing halfway up and was
therefore on the spot nearest the window, where, at sight of me, it
stopped short and fixed me exactly as it had fixed me from the tower
and from the garden." Then "I saw the figure disappear; . . . I definitely
saw it turn, as I might have seen the low wretch to which it had once
belonged turn on receipt of an order, and pass . . . straight down the
staircase and into the darkness" (66). The adjective "low" makes a connection between their physical positions, higher and lower on the staircase, and their moral or class positions. Quint has been trying to rise,
but the governess sends him back down where he belongs. It seems
clear that, in class terms, this is a tiny allegory of frustrated upward mobility. And as we shall see, there is some reason to ask whether it might
not be a moral allegory as well.

The next sighting is also on the staircase:

> Looking down it from the top I once recognised the presence of a
> woman seated on one of the lower steps with her back presented
> to me, her body half-bowed and her head, in an attitude of woe,
> in her hands. I had been there but an instant, however, when she
> vanished without looking round at me. . . . I wondered whether,
> if instead of being above I had been below, I should have had the
> same nerve for going up that I had lately shown Quint. (68)

Here the ghost is not rising. Sitting on "one of the lower steps" and
with a body "half-bowed," she suggests on the contrary someone who
has descended. All of this would correspond to how the governess sees
her predecessor's social transgression: Miss Jessel has "lowered" herself
by falling in love with a servant. Even more interesting, though, is the
final speculation: the governess's willingness to imagine *herself*, like Miss
Jessel, "below" rather than "above" and seeking the "nerve for going up."

The comparison of herself to Miss Jessel is fragmentary but telling.
And it becomes stronger and more visible in the scene where the governess decides not to run away from Bly. Having "made up my mind to
cynical flight," she says,

I remember sinking down at the foot of the staircase — suddenly
collapsing there on the lowest step and then, with a revulsion, recalling that it was exactly where, more than a month before, in
the darkness of night and just so bowed with evil things, I had
seen the spectre of the most horrible of women. At this I was able
to straighten myself; I went the rest of the way up; I made, in my
turmoil, for the schoolroom, where there were objects belonging
to me that I should have to take. (84–85)

There she finds herself again in "the presence" of Miss Jessel's ghost:

Seated at my own table in the clear noonday light I saw a person
whom, without my previous experience, I should have taken at
the first blush for some housemaid who might have stayed at
home to look after the place and who, availing herself of rare relief
from observation and of the schoolroom table and my pens, ink
and paper, had applied herself to the considerable effort of a letter
to her sweetheart. (85)

If the governess at first places herself in the exact spot where she has
seen Miss Jessel, she then sees Miss Jessel sitting at her own official spot,
"at my own table." Some force — perhaps her unconscious, perhaps
only James's text — is evidently pushing her to ask what points of simi-
larity there might be between her and the ghost. As if offering a slightly
displaced answer to this question, the governess then imagines a servant
who is borrowing her writing materials. The governess's eagerness to
insist on how different she herself is from such a servant, to insist on her
own superiority, is odd, given that this servant is a figment of her imagination. (Thanks to her "previous experience," she implies, she has instantly recognized that this is *not* a servant, but Miss Jessel.) But her
sense of superiority is nonetheless manifest: the phrase "considerable
effort" reminds us that writing letters may be difficult for maids, but it
is easy for governesses. This is the same mockery of the uneducated servants that we can hear in the phrase "perturbation of scullions" (50), a
phrase that "scullions" — that is, those lowest of kitchen servants who
wash the dishes — could not be expected to pronounce with assurance.
But if the governess is making such a considerable effort to distance
herself, it is clearly because she is finding it difficult not to *recognize*
herself in Miss Jessel and her situation. Why does she imagine a "sweetheart" as the recipient of the letter? Much of the story has come to focus
on the question of whether she herself can now communicate with the
master: a man she has been forbidden to write to and is forbidden to

think of as a possible sweetheart, just as the maid is forbidden to have a sweetheart.

After this unconscious alignment with her made-up maid, the governess experiences an extraordinary moment of self-questioning, a moment of moral leveling. Her assumption of moral superiority to Miss Jessel, her "vile predecessor," this "most horrible of women," suddenly slips: "she had looked at me long enough to appear to say that her right to sit at my table was as good as mine to sit at hers. While these instants lasted indeed I had the extraordinary chill of a feeling that it was I who was the intruder" (85). This identification of her interests with the lovelorn, tragic Miss Jessel becomes still more intense in the last scene of confrontation between them. At the lake, the governess notices Miss Jessel's ghost not with horror but with a "thrill of joy": "She was there, so I was justified; she was there, so I was neither cruel nor mad." Thus she sends the other governess "an inarticulate message of gratitude" (98).

II

Further than this gratitude the governess does not seem to go. Yet there is reason to think that Henry James has pushed his story further — that *The Turn of the Screw* questions the society it describes more searchingly than its protagonist does. The evidence in favor of this claim comes not from the governess but from the children. Miles has been accused, remember, of excessive intimacy with a "base menial." In his final, fatal confrontation with the governess, when the subject of his expulsion from school is at last brought up, it is this theme of intimacy with servants that James dramatically returns to: "We continued silent while the maid was with us — as silent, it whimsically occurred to me, as some young couple who, on their wedding-journey, at the inn, feel shy in the presence of the waiter. He turned round only when the waiter had left us. 'Well — so we're alone!'" (109).

This is the end of the eleventh weekly installment in the original *Collier's Weekly* serialization of the story. The next and last installment begins by opening up the ironies of Miles's statement: the various senses in which they are not, after all, "alone." In my interpretation, the brief conversation that follows is the very heart of the story:

> "Oh more or less." I imagine my smile was pale. "Not absolutely. We should n't like that!" I went on.
> "No — I suppose we should n't. Of course we've the others."
> "We've the others — we've indeed the others," I concurred.

"Yet even though we have them," he returned, still with his hands in his pockets and planted there in front of me, "they don't much count, do they?"

I made the best of it, but I felt wan. "It depends on what you call 'much'!" (109).

On one level, of course, Miles and the governess are simply trying to fill up an uncomfortable silence, and that purpose can be served by words that are not especially meaningful. But the subject of "the others" is in fact quite meaningful for them. Who are these "others"? If Miles is not admitting here to the existence of the ghosts, as seems unlikely in light of what follows, then he can only be talking about the servants. And when he says that they "don't much count, do they?" he is not giving his *own* opinion; rather, he is provocatively questioning the *governess's* opinion. We have seen multiple proofs that to her, indeed, the servants "don't much count." And we have also seen evidence that to him they *do* count to a rather extraordinary if also understandable degree. An orphan whose guardian is absent and indifferent, Miles has spent months "perpetually together" (60) with a servant, and he has lived through that servant's death — an event, along with Miss Jessel's death, that might well explain a great deal of mysterious behavior on the part of the children. He has been reprimanded for this unbecoming friendship by Mrs. Grose — "*she* liked to see young gentlemen not forget their station" (60) — and he has snapped back at her with a response that the governess takes as a sign of his corruption. Miles's answer, we are told, is "bad": bad because it rudely reminds Mrs. Grose that she too is a "base menial," no doubt, but also bad, we may surmise, in a larger or more ideological sense: as an expression of Miles's rejection of class hierarchy. This is after all just what we might expect him to be learning in those instructive months when, "quite as if Quint were his tutor" (60), he was "perpetually together" with a servant who was engaged in a forbidden relation with a woman above him in rank. Perhaps — this we cannot know for sure — it is even the message contained in those things he said at school that caused him to be thrown out, things we recall he said only to those he liked. In Victorian England, to assert that "the others" do "count" might well have been enough to earn expulsion from a respectable school.

Aside from Peter Quint and Mrs. Grose, the only one of the other servants who is named in *The Turn of the Screw* is "Luke," the servant who was supposed to mail the governess's letter to the master. It seems significant that Miles's last request (116) is to speak to him. Even if it is only to protect the secret of who took the letter — and we don't know that this is in fact his motive — it is clear that Luke does "count" for Miles. In short, Miles is well placed to wonder how it happens that Luke and the other servants "don't much count" for the governess, or for the society she uncomfortably represents. Miles has refused to play along with the willful blindness of his class that consigns the servants to willed, organized invisibility — that makes them all ghostly. He is not "corrupted" by the ghosts, in other words, but is still more charming and extraordinary than he at first seems to be.

One virtue of this interpretation is that it preserves and indeed deepens the charming innocence of the children. Interpretations that judge the ghosts and the children to be joined with each other in the pursuit of evil are obliged to conclude that the children are secretly corrupted, an idea that many readers will find hard to take. The alternative I propose is to take them as innocent in a real if also a challenging sense. Thanks to their bizarre isolation, raised by servants alone, without interference from the upper classes, the children have become little democrats, unable to see the sin in transgressing those class divisions that the adult world takes for granted. What they do see, therefore, as the governess cannot, is the absurdity of believing that "the others" don't "count."

III

If this reading has its virtues, it also has at least one major problem: it makes Miles's death into a tragedy that is even worse, if possible, than one might otherwise feel. The governess does precisely what she accuses the servant-ghosts of wanting to do. We have no evidence of her assertion that the ghosts want to "possess" the children. We have a great deal of evidence, on the other hand, of her own desire to possess them. She who, *as* an upper servant, possesses almost nothing else but her responsibility to the children — little time of her own, no love, and hardly any life — comes back to "the chance of possessing" the children (91) with fierce repetitiveness: "'They're not mine — they're not ours. They're his and they're hers!'" (74). The ending is of course the most painful: "'What does he matter now, my own? — what will he *ever* matter? I have you,' I launched at the beast, 'but he has lost you for ever!'" Her desire for possession is fulfilled in Miles's death: "his little heart, dispossessed, had stopped" (116). And what is sacrificed by the governess's misplaced protective zeal, in this view, is not the boy's life alone, but also the extraordinary beauty of the alternative social vision he embodied — a vision of social equality to which she is utterly blind.

Or is she? There is no question that *The Turn of the Screw* ends in a moment of loss and desolation. Whether we imagine that the governess has frightened Miles to death or embraced him to the point of suffocation, the scaring and the caring leave us with a bitter image of democratic innocence slain, ironically, not by the absolute might of the governing class but by the relative weakness of its indoctrinated underlings, the "governessing" class. Yet this view of the ending does not neatly resolve all the meanings the story has so energetically unleashed. Some of them spill over, and for a criticism which insists that history is unfinished, these excess meanings may well be crucial. A few pages before the end, the governess notices something new in the servants. Or rather, she makes an unprecedented connection between the servants and her own concerns: "For the first time, I could see in the aspect of others a confused reflexion of the crisis" (106). Significantly, the servants take on or take over, as she sees them now, just that word that James was to use in the Preface for his own "values" in writing the ghost story, and for the ghosts themselves: "The maids and the men looked blank" (106). Blankness, which had seemed to mark an avoidance of history, both on the part of James and on the part of the governess, now appears as the mark of historical "crisis," a sign rich in suppressed or at any rate unexpressed inner feelings. This is the "perturbation of scullions" that the governess could not see before. She can see more of it now. She has perhaps made some progress.

The governess may not learn all of her lesson, but James puts it there to be learned, if only by the discerning reader. In the New York Preface, as I said, James in effect calls *The Turn of the Screw* a romance, a genre in which the malignity of the ghosts can remain blank, motiveless, unspecified. But if this choice of genre protects some secrets, it gives away others. In particular, it hints at the secret identity of *the* "others," the villains or enemies — that is, their identity with the protagonist. In *The Political Unconscious* Fredric Jameson describes romance as a

> symbolic answer to the perplexing question of how my enemy can be thought of as being *evil* (that is, as other than myself and marked by some absolute difference), when what is responsible for his being so characterized is simply the *identity* of his own conduct with mine, the which — challenges, points of honor, tests of strength — he reflects as in a mirror image. Romance "solves" this conceptual dilemma by producing a new narrative. . . . The hostile knight, in armor, exudes that insolence which marks a fundamental refusal of recognition and stamps him as the bearer of the cate-

gory of evil, up to the moment in which, defeated and unmasked, he asks for mercy and *tells his name* . . . at which point . . . he becomes one knight among others and loses all his sinister unfamiliarity. (Jameson 118–19; emphases in original)

There is of course no moment in *The Turn of the Screw* when "the antagonist *ceases* to be a villain" (119), as Jameson says, when the mask of otherness is lifted and evil evaporates from the world. But to judge from the critical controversy surrounding this text, much of it might be said to build toward just such a missing scene. The sightings of the ghosts, along with scenes I have not discussed, all suggest that in some sense the ghosts are mirror images, duplications, reenactments of the governess and her situation. These connections between governess and ghosts have been assembled as evidence, mainly by the antighost party, in order to undermine the governess's narrative credibility. Yet in the light of Jameson's description of romance, these parallels could also be interpreted in another way. They could be seen as continual, unanswered beckonings to a recognition that, like the unmasking of the "villain" in medieval romance, would convert these threatening aliens into mere versions of herself.

Here we must remember that, for the governess, the collapse of class otherness is erotically charged with pleasure as well as negatively charged with threat. What the governess herself desires is, as we set out by saying, nothing but the erotic transgression of class. Her love for the master, which is reaffirmed in the narrative frame at the start of the story, requires that at some future point she herself will repeat the ghosts' transgression and indulge a love prohibited by the social hierarchy. Of course, the text does not actually follow her romance script. But its unrealized happy end — victory over the ghosts and union with the master — is present in a sense from the outset.

Recall how far the text goes not only to show that evil is defined in class terms but also to remind us that the governess herself is, after all, nothing but an upper servant. The crowning example, perhaps, is her cross-examination of Mrs. Grose concerning Miles and his intimacy with Quint. Again she puts words in Mrs. Grose's mouth:

> "If Quint — on your remonstrance at the time you speak of — was a base menial, one of the things Miles said to you, I find myself guessing, was that you were another." Again her admission was so adequate that I continued: "And you forgave him that?"
>
> "Would n't *you?*"
>
> "Oh yes!" And we exchanged there, in the stillness, a sound of the oddest amusement. (61)

What is both odd and amusing here is the double meaning. Mrs. Grose's "Would n't *you?*" could of course be taken as meaning simply, "Wouldn't you forgive him if he said something equally outrageous to you, knowing what a wonderful child he is?" But it can also be taken to mean, "Wouldn't you forgive him for saying that *you* are a base menial — since you are just as much a menial as I am?" Mrs. Grose's "Would n't *you?*" suggests to the governess, in a style approaching that of stage comedy, what so many critics of *The Turn of the Screw* have suggested in a more scholarly mode: her resemblance to the servant-ghosts. From this resemblance we can deduce the fragility of an "evil" that depends for its existence on nothing more than the illusion of otherness. In this sense it can be maintained that *The Turn of the Screw* projects an unrealized "happy ending": the return of Bly to the classless Edenic state in which the governess first found it, the ghostlike evaporation from her world of the "evil" that she added to it. These happy events would result from her recognition of what so many voices are trying to tell her: her identity with "the others."

And what of critics, who like the governess are teachers of the young? The Marxist critic who constructs this implicit sequel to the story is not simply trying (like the governess) to soften the cruel knowledge of social reality. Rather, the critic is trying to learn from the governess's pupils how to change social reality, trying to edge history in the direction that James's children have pointed out to us. The point of this piece of criticism is to help ensure that children in the future will know that the others *do* count.

WORKS CITED

James, Henry. *The Notebooks of Henry James.* Ed. F. O. Matthiessen and Kenneth B. Murdock. New York: Oxford UP, 1947.

Jameson, Fredric. *The Political Unconscious.* Ithaca: Cornell UP, 1947.

Marx, Karl. "Theses on Feuerbach" in Karl Marx and Friedrich Engels, *The German Ideology.* Ed. R. Pascal. New York: International, 1947.

Glossary of Critical
and Theoretical Terms

Most terms have been glossed parenthetically where they first appear in the text. Mainly, the glossary lists terms that are too complex to define in a phrase or a sentence or two. A few of the terms listed are discussed at greater length elsewhere (feminist criticism, for instance); these terms are defined succinctly and a page reference to the longer discussion is provided.

AFFECTIVE FALLACY First used by William K. Wimsatt and Monroe C. Beardsley to refer to what they regarded as the erroneous practice of interpreting texts according to the psychological responses of readers. "The Affective Fallacy," they wrote in a 1946 essay later republished in *The Verbal Icon* (1954), "is a confusion between the poem and its *results* (what it *is* and what it *does*). . . . It begins by trying to derive the standards of criticism from the psychological effects of a poem and ends in impressionism and relativism." The affective fallacy, like the intentional fallacy (confusing the meaning of a work with the author's expressly intended meaning), was one of the main tenets of the New Criticism, or formalism. The affective fallacy has recently been contested by reader-response critics, who have deliberately dedicated their efforts to describing the way individual readers and "interpretive communities" go about "making sense" of texts.

See also: Authorial Intention, Formalism, Reader-Response Criticism.

AUTHORIAL INTENTION Defined narrowly, an author's intention in writing a work, as expressed in letters, diaries, interviews, and conversations. Defined more broadly, "intentionality" involves unexpressed motivations, designs, and purposes, some of which may have remained unconscious.

The debate over whether critics should try to discern an author's intentions (conscious or otherwise) is an old one. William K. Wimsatt and Monroe

C. Beardsley, in an essay first published in the 1940s, coined the term "intentional fallacy" to refer to the practice of basing interpretations on the expressed or implied intentions of authors, a practice they judged to be erroneous. As proponents of the New Criticism, or formalism, they argued that a work of literature is an object in itself and should be studied as such. They believed that it is sometimes helpful to learn what an author intended, but the critic's real purpose is to show what is actually in the text, not what an author intended to put there.

See also: Affective Fallacy, Formalism.

BASE *See* Marxist Criticism.

BINARY OPPOSITIONS *See* Oppositions.

BLANKS *See* Gaps.

CANON Since the fourth century, used to refer to those books of the Bible that the Christian church accepts as being Holy Scripture. The term has come to be applied more generally to those literary works given special status, or "privileged," by a culture. Works we tend to think of as "classics" or the "Great Books" produced by Western culture — texts that are found in every anthology of American, British, and world literature — would be among those that constitute the canon.

Recently, Marxist, feminist, minority, and Third World critics have argued that, for political reasons, many excellent works never enter the canon. Canonized works, they claim, are those that reflect — and respect — the culture's dominant ideology and/or perform some socially acceptable or even necessary form of "cultural work." Attempts have been made to broaden or redefine the canon by discovering valuable texts, or versions of texts, that were repressed or ignored for political reasons. These have been published both in traditional and in nontraditional anthologies. The most outspoken critics of the canon, especially radical critics practicing cultural criticism, have called into question the whole concept of canon or "canonicity." Privileging no form of artistic expression that reflects and revises the culture, these critics treat cartoons, comics, and soap operas with the same cogency and respect they accord novels, poems, and plays.

See also: Cultural Criticism, Feminist Criticism, Ideology, Marxist Criticism.

CONFLICTS, CONTRADICTIONS *See* Gaps.

CULTURAL CRITICISM A critical approach that is sometimes referred to as "cultural studies" or "cultural critique." Practitioners of cultural criticism oppose "high" definitions of culture and take seriously popular cultural forms. Grounded in a variety of continental European influences, cultural criticism nonetheless gained institutional force in England, in 1964, with the founding of the Centre for Contemporary Cultural Studies at Birmingham University. Broadly interdisciplinary in its scope and approach, cultural criticism views the text as the locus and catalyst of a complex network of political and economic discourses. Cultural critics share with Marxist critics an interest in the ideological contexts of cultural forms.

DECONSTRUCTION A poststructuralist approach to literature that is strongly influenced by the writings of the French philosopher Jacques Derrida.

Deconstruction, partly in response to structuralism and formalism, posits the undecidability of meaning for all texts. In fact, as the deconstructionist critic J. Hillis Miller points out, "deconstruction is not a dismantling of the structure of a text but a demonstration that it has already dismantled itself." See "What Is Deconstruction?" pp. 179–89.

DIALECTIC Originally developed by Greek philosophers, mainly Socrates and Plato, as a form and method of logical argumentation; the term later came to denote a philosophical notion of evolution. The German philosopher G. W. F. Hegel described dialectic as a process whereby a thesis, when countered by an antithesis, leads to the synthesis of a new idea. Karl Marx and Friedrich Engels, adapting Hegel's idealist theory, used the phrase "dialectical materialism" to discuss the way in which a revolutionary class war might lead to the synthesis of a new social economic order. The American Marxist critic Fredric Jameson has coined the phrase "dialectical criticism" to refer to a Marxist critical approach that synthesizes structuralist and poststructuralist methodologies.

See also: Marxist Criticism, Structuralism, Poststructuralism.

DIALOGIC *See* Discourse.

DISCOURSE Used specifically, can refer to (1) spoken or written discussion of a subject or area of knowledge; (2) the words in, or text of, a narrative as opposed to its story line; or (3) a "strand" within a given narrative that argues a certain point or defends a given value system.

More generally, "discourse" refers to the language in which a subject or area of knowledge is discussed or a certain kind of business is transacted. Human knowledge is collected and structured in discourses. Theology and medicine are defined by their discourses, as are politics, sexuality, and literary criticism.

A society is generally made up of a number of different discourses or "discourse communities," one or more of which may be dominant or serve the dominant ideology. Each discourse has its own vocabulary, concepts, and rules, knowledge of which constitutes power. The psychoanalyst and psychoanalytic critic Jacques Lacan has treated the unconscious as a form of discourse, the patterns of which are repeated in literature. Cultural critics, following Mikhail Bakhtin, use the word "dialogic" to discuss the dialogue *between* discourses that takes place within language or, more specifically, a literary text.

See also: Cultural Criticism, Ideology, Narrative, Psychoanalytic Criticism.

FEMINIST CRITICISM An aspect of the feminist movement whose primary goals include critiquing masculine-dominated language and literature by showing how they reflect a masculine ideology; writing the history of unknown or undervalued women writers, thereby earning them their rightful place in the literary canon; and helping create a climate in which women's creativity may be fully realized and appreciated. See "What Is Feminist Criticism?" pp. 242–49.

FIGURE *See* Metaphor, Metonymy, Symbol.

FORMALISM Also referred to as the New Criticism, formalism reached its height during the 1940s and 1950s, but it is still practiced today. Formalists treat a work of literary art as if it were a self-contained, self-referential object. Rather than basing their interpretations of a text on the reader's response, the author's stated intentions, or parallels between the text and historical contexts (such as the author's life), formalists concentrate on the relationships *within* the text that give it its own distinctive character or form. Special attention is paid to repetition, particularly of images or symbols, but also of sound effects and rhythms in poetry.

Because of the importance placed on close analysis and the stress on the text as a carefully crafted, orderly object containing observable formal patterns, formalism has often been seen as an attack on Romanticism and impressionism, particularly impressionistic criticism. It has sometimes even been called an "objective" approach to literature. Formalists are more likely than certain other critics to believe and say that the meaning of a text can be known objectively. For instance, reader-response critics see meaning as a function either of each reader's experience or of the norms that govern a particular "interpretive community," and deconstructors argue that texts mean opposite things at the same time.

Formalism was originally based on essays written during the 1920s and 1930s by T. S. Eliot, I. A. Richards, and William Empson. It was significantly developed later by a group of American poets and critics, including R. P. Blackmur, Cleanth Brooks, John Crowe Ransom, Allen Tate, Robert Penn Warren, and William K. Wimsatt. Although we associate formalism with certain principles and terms (such as the "Affective Fallacy" and the "Intentional Fallacy" as defined by Wimsatt and Monroe C. Beardsley), formalists were trying to make a cultural statement rather than establish a critical dogma. Generally Southern, religious, and culturally conservative, they advocated the inherent value of literary works (particularly of literary works regarded as beautiful art objects) because they were sick of the growing ugliness of modern life and contemporary events. Some recent theorists even suggest that the rising popularity of formalism after World War II was a feature of American isolationism, the formalist tendency to isolate literature from biography and history being a manifestation of the American fatigue with wider involvements.

See also: Affective Fallacy, Authorial Intention, Deconstruction, Reader-Response Criticism, Symbol.

GAPS When used by reader-response critics familiar with the theories of Wolfgang Iser, refers to "blanks" in texts that must be filled in by readers. A gap may be said to exist whenever and wherever a reader perceives something to be missing between words, sentences, paragraphs, stanzas, or chapters. Readers respond to gaps actively and creatively, explaining apparent inconsistencies in point of view, accounting for jumps in chronology, speculatively supplying information missing from plots, and resolving problems or issues left ambiguous or "indeterminate" in the text.

Reader-response critics sometimes speak as if a gap actually exists in a text; a gap is, of course, to some extent a product of readers' perceptions. Different readers may find gaps in different texts, and different gaps in the same text. Furthermore, they may fill these gaps in different ways, which is why, a reader-response critic might argue, works are interpreted in different ways.

Although the concept of the gap has been used mainly by reader-response critics, it has also been used by critics taking other theoretical approaches. Practitioners of deconstruction might use "gap" when speaking of the radical contradictoriness of a text. Marxists have used the term to speak of everything from the gap that opens up between economic base and cultural superstructure to the two kinds of conflicts or contradictions to be found in literary texts. The first of these, they would argue, results from the fact that texts reflect ideology, within which certain subjects cannot be covered, things that cannot be said, contradictory views that cannot be recognized as contradictory. The second kind of conflict, contradiction, or gap within a text results from the fact that works don't just reflect ideology: they are also fictions that, consciously or unconsciously, distance themselves from the same ideology.

See also: Deconstruction, Ideology, Marxist Criticism, Reader-Response Criticism.

GENRE   A French word referring to a kind or type of literature. Individual works within a genre may exhibit a distinctive form, be governed by certain conventions, and/or represent characteristic subjects. Tragedy, epic, and romance are all genres.

Perhaps inevitably, the term "genre" is used loosely. Lyric poetry is a genre, but so are characteristic *types* of the lyric, such as the sonnet, the ode, and the elegy. Fiction is a genre, as are detective fiction and science fiction. The list of genres grows constantly as critics establish new lines of connection between individual works and discern new categories of works with common characteristics. Moreover, some writers form hybrid genres by combining the characteristics of several in a single work.

Knowledge of genres helps critics to understand and explain what is conventional and unconventional, borrowed and original, in a work.

HEGEMONY   Given intellectual currency by the Italian communist Antonio Gramsci, the word (a translation of *egemonia*) refers to the pervasive system of assumptions, meanings, and values — the web of ideologies, in other words — that shapes the way things look, what they mean, and therefore what reality *is* for the majority of people within a given culture.

See also: Ideology, Marxist Criticism.

IDEOLOGY   A set of beliefs underlying the customs, habits, and/or practices common to a given social group. To members of that group, the beliefs seem obviously true, natural, and even universally applicable. They may seem just as obviously arbitrary, idiosyncratic, and even false to outsiders or members of another group who adhere to another ideology. Within a society, several ideologies may coexist, or one or more may be dominant.

Ideologies may be forcefully imposed or willingly subscribed to. Their component beliefs may be held consciously or unconsciously. In either case, they come to form what Johanna M. Smith has called "the unexamined ground of our experience." Ideology governs our perceptions, judgments, and prejudices — our sense of what is acceptable, normal, and deviant. Ideology may cause a revolution; it may also allow discrimination and even exploitation.

Ideologies are of special interest to sociologically oriented critics of literature because of the way in which authors reflect or resist prevailing views in their texts. Some Marxist critics have argued that literary texts reflect and reproduce the ideologies that produced them; most, however, have shown how ideologies are riven with contradictions that works of literature manage to expose and widen. Still other Marxists have focused on the way in which texts themselves are characterized by gaps, conflicts, and contradictions between their ideological and anti-ideological functions.

Feminist critics have addressed the question of ideology by seeking to expose (and thereby call into question) the patriarchal ideology mirrored or inscribed in works written by men — even men who have sought to counter sexism and break down sexual stereotypes. New historicists have been interested in demonstrating the ideological underpinnings not only of literary representations but also of our interpretations of them. Fredric Jameson, an American Marxist critic, argues that all thought is ideological, but that ideological thought that knows itself as such stands the chance of seeing through and transcending ideology.

See also: Cultural Criticism, Feminist Criticism, Marxist Criticism, New Historicism.

IMAGINARY ORDER One of the three essential orders of the psychoanalytic field (see Real and Symbolic Order), it is most closely associated with the senses (sight, sound, touch, taste, and smell). The infant, who by comparison to other animals is born premature and thus is wholly dependent on others for a prolonged period, enters the Imaginary order when it begins to experience a unity of body parts and motor control that is empowering. This usually occurs between six and eighteen months, and is called by Lacan the "mirror stage" or "mirror phase," in which the child anticipates mastery of its body. It does so by identifying with the *image* of wholeness (that is, seeing its own image in the mirror, experiencing its mother as a whole body, and so on). This sense of oneness, and also difference from others (especially the mother or primary caretaker), is established through an image or a vision of harmony that is both a mirroring and a "mirage of maturation" or false sense of individuality and independence. The Imaginary is a metaphor for unity, is related to the visual order, and is always part of human subjectivity. Because the subject is fundamentally separate from others and also internally divided (conscious/unconscious), the apparent coherence of the Imaginary, its fullness and grandiosity, is always false, a *mis*recognition that the ego (or "me") tries to deny by imagining itself as coherent and empowered. The Imaginary operates in conjunction with the Real and Symbolic and is not a "stage" of development equivalent to Freud's "pre-oedipal stage," nor is it pre-linguistic.

See also: Psychoanalytic Criticism, Real, Symbolic Order.

IMPLIED READER A phrase used by some reader-response critics in place of the phrase "the reader." Whereas "the reader" could refer to any idiosyncratic individual who happens to have read or to be reading the text, "the implied reader" is *the* reader intended, even created, by the text. Other reader-response critics seeking to describe this more generally conceived reader have spoken of the "informed reader" or the "narratee," who is "the necessary counterpart of a given narrator."

See Reader-Response Criticism.

INTENTIONAL FALLACY *See* Authorial Intention.

INTENTIONALITY *See* Authorial Intention.

INTERTEXTUALITY The condition of interconnectedness among texts. Every author has been influenced by others, and every work contains explicit and implicit references to other works. Writers may consciously or unconsciously echo a predecessor or precursor; they may also consciously or unconsciously disguise their indebtedness, making intertextual relationships difficult for the critic to trace.

Reacting against the formalist tendency to view each work as a freestanding object, some poststructuralist critics suggested that the meaning of a work only emerges intertextually, that is, within the context provided by other works. But there has been a reaction, too, against this type of intertextual criticism. Some new historicist critics suggest that literary history is itself too narrow a context and that works should be interpreted in light of a larger set of cultural contexts.

There is, however, a broader definition of intertextuality, one that refers to the relationship between works of literature and a wide range of narratives and discourses that we don't usually consider literary. Thus defined, intertextuality could be used by a new historicist to refer to the significant interconnectedness between a literary text and nonliterary discussions of or discourses about contemporary culture. Or it could be used by a poststructuralist to suggest that a work can only be recognized and read within a vast field of signs and tropes that is *like* a text and that makes any single text self-contradictory and "undecidable."

See also: Discourse, Formalism, Narrative, New Historicism, Poststructuralism, Trope.

MARXIST CRITICISM An approach that treats literary texts as material products, describing them in broadly historical terms. In Marxist criticism, the text is viewed in terms of its production and consumption, as a product *of* work that does identifiable cultural work of its own. Following Karl Marx, the founder of communism, Marxist critics have used the terms "base" to refer to economic reality and "superstructure" to refer to the corresponding or "homologous" infrastructure consisting of politics, law, philosophy, religion, and the arts. Also following Marx, they have used the word "ideology" to refer to that set of cultural beliefs that literary works at once reproduce, resist, and revise. See "What Is Marxist Criticism?" pp. 268–80.

METAPHOR The representation of one thing by another related or similar thing. The image (or activity or concept) used to represent or "figure" something else is known as the "vehicle" of the metaphor; the thing represented is called the "tenor." In other words, the vehicle is what we substitute for the tenor. The relationship between vehicle and tenor can provide much additional meaning. Thus, instead of saying, "Last night I read a book," we might say, "Last night I plowed through a book." "Plowed through" (or the activity of plowing) is the vehicle of our metaphor; "read" (or the act of reading) is the tenor, the thing being figured. The increment in meaning through metaphor is fairly obvious. Our audience knows not only *that* we read but also *how* we read, because to read a book in the way that a plow rips through earth is surely to read in a relentless, unreflective way. Note that in the sentence above, a new metaphor — "rips through" — has been used to explain an old one. This serves (which is a metaphor) as an example of just how thick (another metaphor) language is with metaphors!

Metaphor is a kind of "trope" (literally, a "turning," that is, a figure of speech that alters or "turns" the meaning of a word or phrase). Other tropes include allegory, conceit, metonymy, personification, simile, symbol, and synecdoche. Traditionally, metaphor and symbol have been viewed as the principal tropes; minor tropes have been categorized as *types* of these two major ones. Similes, for instance, are usually defined as simple metaphors that usually employ "like" or "as" and state the tenor outright, as in "My love is like a red, red rose." Synecdoche involves a vehicle that is a *part* of the tenor, as in "I see a sail" meaning "I see a boat." Metonymy is viewed as a metaphor involving two terms commonly if arbitrarily associated with (but not fundamentally or intrinsically related to) each other. Recently, however, deconstructors such as Paul de Man and J. Hillis Miller have questioned the "privilege" granted to metaphor and the metaphor/metonymy distinction or "opposition." They have suggested that all metaphors are really metonyms and that all figuration is arbitrary.

See also: Deconstruction, Metonymy, Oppositions, Symbol.

METONYMY The representation of one thing by another that is commonly and often physically associated with it. To refer to a writer's handwriting as his or her "hand" is to use a metonymic "figure" or "trope." The image or thing used to represent something else is known as the "vehicle" of the metonym; the thing represented is called the "tenor."

Like other tropes (such as metaphor), metonymy involves the replacement of one word or phrase by another. Liquor may be referred to as "the bottle," a monarch as "the crown." Narrowly defined, the vehicle of a metonym is arbitrarily, not intrinsically, associated with the tenor. In other words, the bottle just happens to be what liquor is stored in and poured from in our culture. The hand may be involved in the production of handwriting, but so are the brain and the pen. There is no special, intrinsic likeness between a crown and a monarch; it's just that crowns traditionally sit on monarchs' heads and not on the heads of university professors. More broadly, "metonym" and "metonymy" have been used by recent critics to refer to a wide range of figures and tropes. Deconstructors have questioned the distinction between metaphor and metonymy.

See also: Deconstruction, Metaphor, Trope.

NARRATIVE A story or a telling of a story, or an account of a situation or of events. A novel and a biography of a novelist are both narratives, as are Freud's case histories.

Some critics use the word "narrative" even more generally; Brook Thomas, a new historicist, has critiqued "narratives of human history that neglect the role human labor has played."

NEW CRITICISM *See* Formalism.

NEW HISTORICISM One of the most recent developments in contemporary critical theory, its practitioners share certain convictions, the major ones being that literary critics need to develop a high degree of historical consciousness and that literature should not be viewed apart from other human creations, artistic or otherwise.

See also: Authorial Intention, Deconstruction, Formalism, Ideology, Poststructuralism, Psychoanalytic Criticism.

OPPOSITIONS A concept highly relevant to linguistics, since linguists maintain that words (such as "black" and "death") have meaning not in themselves, but in relation to other words ("white" and "life"). Jacques Derrida, a poststructuralist philosopher of language, has suggested that in the West we think in terms of these "binary oppositions" or dichotomies, which on examination turn out to be evaluative hierarchies. In other words, each opposition — beginning/end, presence/absence, or consciousness/unconsciousness — contains one term that our culture views as superior and one term that we view as negative or inferior.

Derrida has "deconstructed" a number of these binary oppositions, including two — speech/writing and signifier/signified — that he believes to be central to linguistics in particular and Western culture in general. He has concurrently critiqued the "law" of noncontradiction, which is fundamental to Western logic. He and other deconstructors have argued that a text can contain opposed strands of discourse and, therefore, mean opposite things: reason *and* passion, life *and* death, hope *and* despair, black *and* white. Traditionally, criticism has involved choosing between opposed or contradictory meanings and arguing that one is present in the text and the other absent.

French feminists have adopted the ideas of Derrida and other deconstructors, showing not only that we think in terms of such binary oppositions as male/female, reason/emotion, and active/passive, but that we also associate reason and activity with masculinity and emotion and passivity with femininity. Because of this, they have concluded that language is "phallocentric," or masculine-dominated.

See also: Deconstruction, Discourse, Feminist Criticism, Poststructuralism.

PHALLUS The symbolic value of the penis that organizes libidinal development and which Freud saw as a stage in the process of human subjectivity. Lacan viewed the Phallus as the representative of a fraudulent power (male over female) whose "law" is a principle of psychic division (conscious/unconscious) and sexual difference (masculine/feminine). The Symbolic order (see Symbolic) is ruled by the Phallus, which of itself has no inherent meaning *apart from* the power and meaning given to it by individual cultures and societies, and represented by the name of the father as lawgiver and namer.

POSTSTRUCTURALISM The general attempt to contest and subvert structuralism initiated by deconstructors and certain other critics associated with psychoanalytic, Marxist, and feminist theory. Structuralists, using linguistics as a model and employing semiotic (sign) theory, posit the possibility of knowing a text systematically and revealing the "grammar" behind its form and meaning. Poststructuralists argue against the possibility of such knowledge and description. They counter that texts can be shown to contradict not only structuralist accounts of them but also themselves. In making their adversarial claims, they rely on close readings of texts and on the work of theorists such as Jacques Derrida and Jacques Lacan.

Poststructuralists have suggested that structuralism rests on distinctions between "signifier" and "signified" (signs and the things they point toward), "self" and "language" (or "text"), texts and other texts, and text and world that are overly simplistic, if not patently inaccurate. Poststructuralists have shown how all signifieds are also signifiers, and they have treated texts as "intertexts." They have viewed the world as if it *were* a text (we desire a certain car because it *symbolizes* achievement) and the self as the subject, as well as the user, of language; for example, we may shape and speak through language, but it also shapes and speaks through us.

See also: Deconstruction, Feminist Criticism, Intertextuality, Psychoanalytic Criticism, Semiotics, Structuralism.

PSYCHOANALYTIC CRITICISM Grounded in the psychoanalytic theories of Sigmund Freud, it is one of the oldest critical methodologies still in use. Freud's view that works of literature, like dreams, express secret, unconscious desires led to criticism and interpreted literary works as manifestations of the authors' neuroses. More recently, psychoanalytic critics have come to see literary works as skillfully crafted artifacts that may appeal to *our* neuroses by tapping into our repressed wishes and fantasies. Other forms of psychological criticism that diverge from Freud, although they ultimately derive from his insights, include those based on the theories of Carl Jung and Jacques Lacan. See "What Is Psychoanalytic Criticism?" pp. 207–18.

READER-RESPONSE CRITICISM An approach to literature that, as its name implies, considers the way readers respond to texts, as they read. Stanley Fish describes the method by saying that it substitutes for one question, "What does this sentence mean?" a more operational question, "What does this sentence do?" Reader-response criticism shares with deconstruction a strong textual orientation and a reluctance to define a single meaning for a work. Along with psychoanalytic criticism, it shares an interest in the dynamics of mental response to textual cues. See "What Is Reader-Response Criticism?" pp. 152–59.

REAL One of the three orders of subjectivity (see Imaginary and Symbolic), the Real is the intractable and substantial world that resists and exceeds interpretation. The Real cannot be imagined, symbolized, or known directly. It constantly eludes our efforts to name it (death, gravity, the physicality of objects are examples of the Real), and thus challenges both the Imaginary and the Symbolic orders. The Real is fundamentally "Other," the mark of the divide between conscious and unconscious, and is signaled in language by gaps, slips, speechlessness, and the sense of the uncanny. The Real is not what we call "reality." It is the stumbling block of the Imaginary (which thinks it can "imagine" anything, including the Real) and of the Symbolic, which tries to bring the Real under its laws (the Real exposes the "phallacy" of the Law of the Phallus). The Real is frightening; we try to tame it with laws and language and call it "reality."

See also: Imaginary Order, Psychoanalytic Criticism, Symbolic Order.

SEMIOLOGY, SEMIOTIC *See* Semiotics.

SEMIOTICS The study of signs and sign systems and the way meaning is derived from them. Structuralist anthropologists, psychoanalysts, and literary critics developed semiotics during the decades following 1950, but much of the pioneering work had been done at the turn of the century by the founder of modern linguistics, Ferdinand de Saussure, and the American philosopher Charles Sanders Peirce.

Semiotics is based on several important distinctions, including the distinction between "signifier" and "signified" (the sign and what it points toward) and the distinction between "langue" and "parole." *Langue* (French for "tongue," as in "native tongue," meaning language) refers to the entire system within which individual utterances or usages of language have meaning; *parole* (French for "word") refers to the particular utterances or usages. A principal tenet of semiotics is that signs, like words, are not significant in themselves, but instead have meaning only in relation to other signs and the entire system of signs, or langue.

The affinity between semiotics and structuralist literary criticism derives from this emphasis placed on langue, or system. Structuralist critics, after all, were reacting against formalists and their procedure of focusing on individual words as if meanings didn't depend on anything external to the text.

Poststructuralists have used semiotics but questioned some of its underlying assumptions, including the opposition between signifier and signified. The feminist poststructuralist Julia Kristeva, for instance, has used the word "semiotic" to describe feminine language, a highly figurative, fluid form of discourse that she sets in opposition to rigid, symbolic masculine language.

See also: Deconstruction, Feminist Criticism, Formalism, Poststructuralism, Oppositions, Structuralism, Symbol.

SIMILE *See* Metaphor.

SOCIOHISTORICAL CRITICISM *See* New Historicism.

STRUCTURALISM A science of humankind whose proponents attempted to show that all elements of human culture, including literature, may be understood as parts of a system of signs. Structuralism, according to Robert Scholes, was a reaction to " 'modernist' alienation and despair."

Using Ferdinand de Saussure's linguistic theory, European structuralists such as Roman Jakobson, Claude Lévi-Strauss, and Roland Barthes (before his shift toward poststructuralism) attempted to develop a "semiology" or "semiotics" (science of signs). Barthes, among others, sought to recover literature and even language from the isolation in which they had been studied and to show that the laws that govern them govern all signs, from road signs to articles of clothing.

Particularly useful to structuralists were two of Saussure's concepts: the idea of "phoneme" in language and the idea that phonemes exist in two kinds of relationships: "synchronic" and "diachronic." A phoneme is the smallest consistently significant unit in language; thus, both "a" and "an" are phonemes, but "n" is not. A diachronic relationship is that which a phoneme has with those that have preceded it in time and those that will follow it. These "horizontal" relationships produce what we might call discourse or narrative and what Saussure called "parole." The synchronic relationship is the "vertical" one that a word has in a given instant with the entire system of language ("langue") in which it may generate meaning. "An" means what it means in English because those of us who speak the language are using it in the same way at a given time.

Following Saussure, Lévi-Strauss studied hundreds of myths, breaking them into their smallest meaningful units, which he called "mythemes." Removing each from its diachronic relations with other mythemes in a single myth (such as the myth of Oedipus and his mother), he vertically aligned those mythemes that he found to be homologous (structurally correspondent). He then studied the relationships within as well as between vertically aligned columns, in an attempt to understand scientifically, through ratios and proportions, those thoughts and processes that humankind has shared, both at one particular time and across time. One could say, then, that structuralists followed Saussure in preferring to think about the overriding langue or language of myth, in which each mytheme and mytheme-constituted myth fits meaningfully, rather than about isolated individual paroles or narratives. Structuralists followed Saussure's lead in believing what the poststructuralist Jacques Derrida later decided he could not subscribe to — that sign systems must be understood in terms of binary oppositions. In analyzing myths and texts to find basic structures, structuralists tended to find that opposite terms modulate until they are finally resolved or reconciled by some intermediary third term. Thus, a structuralist reading of *Paradise Lost* would show that the war between God and the bad angels becomes a rift between God and sinful, fallen man, the rift then being healed by the Son of God, the mediating third term.

See also: Deconstruction, Discourse, Narrative, Poststructuralism, Semiotics.

SUPERSTRUCTURE *See* Marxist Criticism.

SYMBOL A thing, image, or action that, although it is of interest in its own right, stands for or suggests something larger and more complex — often an idea or a range of interrelated ideas, attitudes, and practices.

Within a given culture, some things are understood to be symbols: the flag of the United States is an obvious example. More subtle cultural symbols might be the river as a symbol of time and the journey as a symbol of life and its manifold experiences.

Instead of appropriating symbols generally used and understood within their culture, writers often create symbols by setting up, in their works, a complex but identifiable web of associations. As a result, one object, image, or action suggests others, and often, ultimately, a range of ideas.

A symbol may thus be defined as a metaphor in which the "vehicle," the thing, image, or action used to represent something else, represents many related things (or "tenors") or is broadly suggestive. The urn in Keats's "Ode on a Grecian Urn" suggests many interrelated concepts, including art, truth, beauty, and timelessness.

Symbols have been of particular interest to formalists, who study how meanings emerge from the complex, patterned relationships between images in a work, and psychoanalytic critics, who are interested in how individual authors and the larger culture both disguise and reveal unconscious fears and desires through symbols. Recently, French feminists have also focused on the symbolic. They have suggested that, as wide-ranging as it seems, symbolic language is ultimately rigid and restrictive. They favor semiotic language and writing, which, they contend, is at once more rhythmic, unifying, and feminine.

See also: Feminist Criticism, Metaphor, Psychoanalytic Criticism, Trope.

SYMBOLIC ORDER One of the three orders of subjectivity (see Imaginary Order and Real), it is the realm of law, language, and society; it is the repository of generally held cultural beliefs. Its symbolic system is language, whose agent is the father or lawgiver, the one who has the power of naming. The human subject is commanded into this preestablished order by language (a process that begins long before a child can speak) and must submit to its orders of communication (grammar, syntax, and so on). Entrance into the Symbolic order determines subjectivity according to a primary law of referentiality that takes the male sign (phallus, see Phallus) as its ordering principle. Lacan states that both sexes submit to the Law of the Phallus (the law of order, language, and differentiation) but their individual relation to the law determines whether they see themselves as — and are seen by others to be — either "masculine" or "feminine." The Symbolic institutes repression (of the Imaginary), thus creating the unconscious, which itself is structured like the language of the symbolic. The unconscious, a timeless realm, cannot be known directly, but it can be understood by a kind of translation that takes place in language — psychoanalysis is the "talking cure." The Symbolic is not a "stage" of development (as is Freud's "oedipal stage") nor is it set in place once and for all in human life. We constantly negotiate its threshold (in sleep, in drunkenness) and can "fall out" of it altogether in psychosis.

See also: Psychoanalytic Criticism, Imaginary Order, Real.

SYNECDOCHE *See* Metaphor, Metonymy.

TENOR *See* Metaphor, Metonymy, Symbol.

TROPE A figure, as in "figure of speech." Literally a "turning," that is, a turning or twisting of a word or phrase to make it mean something else. Principal tropes include metaphor, metonymy, simile, personification, and synecdoche.

See also: Metaphor, Metonymy.

VEHICLE *See* Metaphor, Metonymy, Symbol.

About the Contributors

THE VOLUME EDITOR

Peter G. Beidler is the Lucy G. Moses Distinguished Professor of English at Lehigh University. He has published widely on Chaucer, Native American literature, and American literature. His most recent scholarly book is *Ghosts, Demons, and Henry James: "The Turn of the Screw" at the Turn of the Century* (1989). He taught as a Fulbright professor in China in 1987–88. In 1983 he was named National Professor of the Year by the Council for Advancement and Support of Education.

THE CRITICS

Wayne C. Booth is the Professor of English and Ideas and Methods Emeritus at the University of Chicago. His many books include several classics of literary theory and criticism, among them *The Rhetoric of Fiction* (1961, revised edition 1983), *The Rhetoric of Irony* (1974), and *The Company We Keep: An Ethics of Fiction* (1988). A distinguished teacher, he has published *The Vocation of Teacher* (1988). His most recent book is *The Art of Growing Older* (1992), an anthology of poems and meditations with extended commentary.

Shoshana Felman is the Thomas E. Donnelley Professor of French and Comparative Literature at Yale University. She is the author of

The Literary Speech Act: Don Juan with Austin, or Seduction in Two Languages (1984), *Writing and Madness: Literature/Philosophy/Psychoanalysis* (1985), *Jacques Lacan and the Adventure of Insight: Psychoanalysis in Contemporary Culture* (1987), and *Testimony: Crises of Witnessing in Literature, Psychoanalysis and History* (1992).

Stanley Renner is professor of English at Illinois State University. He has published books and articles on Joseph Conrad, D. H. Lawrence, T. S. Eliot, and others as well as on James.

Bruce Robbins is professor of English and comparative literature at Rutgers University. He is the author of *The Servant's Hand: English Fiction from Below* (1986) and *Secular Vocations: Intellectuals, Professionalism, Culture* (1993). He is the editor of *Intellectuals: Aesthetics, Politics, Academics* (1990) and *The Phantom Sphere* (1993). He co-edits the journal *Social Text*.

Priscilla L. Walton is assistant professor of English at Carleton University in Canada. She is the author of *The Disruption of the Feminine in Henry James* (1992).

THE SERIES EDITOR

Ross C Murfin, general editor of *Case Studies in Contemporary Criticism*, is dean of the College of Arts and Sciences and professor of English at the University of Miami. He has taught at Yale University and the University of Virginia and has published scholarly studies of Joseph Conrad, Thomas Hardy, Nathaniel Hawthorne, and D. H. Lawrence.

(continued from p. iv)

"'Red hair, very red, close-curling': Sexual Hysteria, Physiognomical Bogeymen, and the 'Ghosts' in *The Turn of the Screw*" by Stanley Renner was originally published in *Nineteenth-Century Literature* 43 (1988). Reprinted, revised, with permission of the editors of that journal.